CAPITAL, LABOR, AND STATE

CAPITAL, LABOR, AND STATE

The Battle for American Labor Markets from the Civil War to the New Deal

DAVID BRIAN ROBERTSON

ROWMAN & LITTLEFIELD PUBLISHERS, INC.
Lanham • Boulder • New York • Oxford

ROWMAN & LITTLEFIELD PUBLISHERS, INC.

Published in the United States of America
by Rowman & Littlefield Publishers, Inc.
4720 Boston Way, Lanham, Maryland 20706
http://www.rowmanlittlefield.com

12 Hid's Copse Road
Cumnor Hill, Oxford OX2 9JJ, England

British Library Cataloging in Publication Information Available

Library of Congress Cataloging-in-Publication Data

Robertson, David Brian, 1951–
    Capital, labor, and state : the battle for American labor markets from the Civil War to
the New Deal / David Brian Robertson
    p. cm.
    Includes bibliographical references and index.
    ISBN 0-8476-9728-2 (cloth : alk. paper)—ISBN 0-8476-9729-0 (pbk. : alk. paper)
    1. Labor unions—Government policy—United States—History. 2. Labor unions—United
States—Political activity—History. 3. Labor policy—United States—History. 4.
Capitalism—United States—History. 5. Industrial relations—United States—History. 6.
AFL-CIO—History. 7. Comparative industrial relations. I. Title: American labor markets
from the Civil War to the New Deal. II. Title.

HD6508.R616   2000
331.8'0973'09034—dc21
                                                                    99-087953

Printed in the United States of America

♾™ The paper used in this publication meets the minimum requirements of
American National Standard for Information Sciences—Permanence of Paper for
Printed Library Materials, ANSI/NISO Z39.48-1992.

Dedicated to Cathie Robertson

CONTENTS

FIGURES AND TABLES

PREFACE

The central question of this book is why the United States has governed its labor markets in a way that is so distinctively tilted toward employers, while comparable nations moved further and faster to limit employers' choices in the workplace. The answer turns on whether American labor market policy always has been so exceptional, and if not, when, how, and why it became exceptional.

STUDYING AMERICAN POLICY
DEVELOPMENT SYSTEMATICALLY

To find answers to these questions, I extensively analyzed public and private documents and existing histories of labor market policy. I focused on the period from 1865 to the early New Deal because the foundations of contemporary labor market policy developed in these years, and because American labor market policy clearly became exceptional after the turn of the century.

As a social scientist, I also used conceptual tools to ensure that this historical analysis would be as systematic, inclusive, and impartial as it was thorough and detailed. Many excellent historical studies describe specific work relationships and the origins of specific programs. Some studies examine the development of a specific type of labor market policy during a particular period. None of these existing studies address the central questions of this book in a systematic and inclusive way.

To answer these central questions, I employed three analytical tools. First, I developed and applied a conceptual map of labor market policy to identify all of the programs that had to be included to answer the questions systematically. Second, I analyzed the policy strategies that shaped the support and opposition to all these programs. Third, I detailed the effects of government institutions on these strategies and subsequent policy outcomes.

A Conceptual Map of Labor Market Policy

Because labor market policy is a pattern of separate programs, one must start with a comprehensive conceptual map of different types of labor market programs. Chapter 1 uses four types of labor market policy to identify thoroughly the labor market programs that emerged on the public agenda between the mid-nineteenth century and the 1930s. Any thorough account of American labor market policy development must relate these programs to one another through the strategies of labor, business, reformers, and others with a stake in the programs. Later chapters show how these programs evolved, how they related to the larger battle between workers and employers, and how they related to other elements of labor market policy. This task required detailed analysis of the formation, adoption, and implementation of a large number of distinct labor market programs.

This conceptual map helps ensure a more thorough and impartial answer to the book's central question in three ways. First, the map makes it certain that all the important labor market initiatives of the period are taken into account. Without beginning with a conceptual map, one can overestimate the importance of some programs, ignore the importance of others, and misunderstand the significance of still others. It is very tempting to study programs that sparked sensational conflict when they were enacted, or that continue to have a demonstrable impact on workers today. But there were many public programs that generated little visibility beyond the relatively small number of people with a stake in them, and there were many programs that were presumed to be much more important when they were enacted than they were subsequently. By starting with a conceptual map of programs to study, an analyst must take seriously the agendas that contemporary employers, labor leaders, and policy experts considered important. The analyst must try to explain how these policy proponents and opponents understood the advantages of proposed programs in terms of their ongoing, broader battles for control of the labor market. For example, it would be easy to dismiss the eight-hour laws and labor statistics bureaus supported by American trade unions in the late 1800s as undeserving of extensive analysis. In the end, these programs accomplished little for the trade unionists who passionately advocated them. But a prior conception of labor market policy compels the analyst to take these programs seriously and investigate why trade unionists thought these programs could lay the cornerstone for increased worker power in the market place. Such a conceptual map is especially important for drawing attention to policy choices that were *not* made and to policy opportunities foregone.

Second, a conceptual map is essential for identifying when American exceptionalism became marked and permanent. A focus on a single program or policy type, rather than on the overall mix of labor market effort, can result in a misspec-ification of the timing of American policy divergence. Recent books on Ameri-can trade union policy, for example, suggest that American policy conservatism was rooted by the early 1890s when court decisions constrained trade union power and the Knights of Labor failed to offer an inclusive and political vehicle for the Amer-ican trade union movement. The emphasis on court decisions naturally follows from a narrow focus on trade union law as interpreted by court cases of the 1880s and early 1890s. From a broader policy perspective, though, the American Feder-ation of Labor (AFL) developed a plausible policy agenda in the early 1900s for establishing inclusive labor protections under union auspices. Its strategy was not so different from that of union leadership in Germany and Britain at the time. In 1901, moreover, there was reasonable evidence that the federal government would respond favorably to this agenda. The subsequent defeat of this agenda marks the essential turning point of both American policy and trade union strategy.

Third, a conceptual map is necessary for revealing the political relationship among disparate labor market programs. When business and labor chose to invest resources in achieving some kinds of programs rather than others, they did so expecting higher returns from such programs. The AFL's support was especially essential for labor market programs in the early twentieth century, and it is impossible to understand policy outcomes in the period without under-standing how each related to the others in the AFL's policy agenda.

Policy Strategy

While a conceptual map is essential for understanding *what* labor market policy was, it is necessary to understand policy strategy to appreciate *how* and *why* labor market policy developed so uniquely in the United States. Policy strategy is defined as the set of purposes, expectations, assumptions, and other premises that policymakers communicate when they deliberate specific propos-als for engaging government in labor markets. By pursuing one strategy over others for using government to solve labor market problems, policymakers moved public policy down a distinct evolutionary path.

Starting with a map of the programs that required explanation, I examined congressional hearings and debates; bureaucratic reports; publications of busi-ness, labor, and reform organizations; unpublished archives; and other sources of information about the labor market policy strategies of businessmen, reformers, politicians, and participants in policymaking. Often, different publications (notably the AFL's *American Federationist* and the National Association of Man-ufacturers' *American Industries*) provided different partisan perspectives on a spe-cific proposal. Occasionally, these partisan sources tacitly debated labor market governance with each other. As I studied these documents, I asked several questions about the strategies evident in these policy discussions. How did policy advocates and opponents define labor market problems? How did they conceive the relationship between specific policy proposals and their larger goals for the labor market? Why was a policy proposal advanced at a particular time rather than earlier or later? How did the proposal fit with other programs, with political experience, and with assumptions about future implementation and policy developments? How did policymakers adjust elements of the proposed program in anticipation of (or response to) institutional obstacles or political opposition?

This analysis of policy strategy helped make my research more thorough and systematic in three ways. First, the focus on policy strategy required that I lay aside my preconceptions as much as possible and understand the policy agenda from the participants' points of view. A careful reading of the documents shows that the basic ideas about work, joblessness, working conditions, and trade unions that influenced policy were changing rapidly in these years. Ideas about the appropriate role of government, the consequences of government action, and the way government could serve group interests also changed rapidly as new problems emerged and the lessons of experience accumulated. Reconstructing the reasons that participants put forward for specific policy changes helped me supercede analytical biases, especially hindsight, as I reconstructed the logic of support and opposition for individual programs.

Second, the focus on policy strategy made it possible to understand more accurately and completely the reasons why American labor market policy developed so uniquely in this period. The individuals who advocated or opposed specific programs understood that broader forces such as culture, ideology, institutions, economic circumstances, and group power were constraining the policy agenda and creating new policy opportunities. These broad forces affect policymaking when key policymakers perceive and integrate them into their assumptions, preferences, and calculations about specific policy proposals. Policy strategy, then, provides indispensable evidence of the way policymakers themselves understood the policy effect of broad social, economic, and political forces. Put another way, participants' strategies reveal the way specific policy outcomes result from the way individual calculation reacts to compelling economic and political imperatives. By studying the strategy behind a carefully selected group of programs, and then comparing these strategies across programs, one can systematically understand the larger social, economic, and political causes of policy development.

Third, policy strategy inevitably emphasizes the politics of policymaking. Politics involves contests over the control of government for some purpose, to advance some interest. Public policy, defined as a pattern of government action, must then be understood in the broad sense as the reason for politics (holding an elected office per se is only an ultimate goal for a fraction of policymakers, and those motivated by election must account for the effect of their policy positions on their election prospects). Understood this way, policy strategy aims to increase advantage and power through the use of government programs. Policymakers support or oppose specific programs because of their political interests. Shrewd legislators, elected executives, interest group leaders, and policy reformers always have understood this logic. Individual policymakers championed or fought against specific labor market programs because they anticipated that these would provide them with measurable labor market advantages, electoral rewards, legal and bureaucratic benefits, or leverage in future policy battles. Policy strategies, in short, reveal the fundamental political dynamics of the relationship between capital, labor, and the state.

The strategies of organized labor, business, and reformers were intensely political in this sense. Labor leaders sought to enlarge trade union power so that unions could determine the terms of employment. These union leaders preferred to set the terms of employment on their own terms, without interference from government. Union leaders turned to government when they believed that government could help them achieve their goals without sacrificing their autonomy. AFL leaders advocated specific programs that enlarged union power, and they unnecessarily opposed programs that undermined that power. The AFL supported regulation, labor statistics, and public employment offices when they believed that trade unionists themselves would implement these programs for labor's benefit. Business also judged labor market policy proposals in terms of their effects on employer prerogatives. Business opposed programs that reduced managerial prerogatives, but supported programs such as workers' compensation that made labor costs more stable and predictable. Employers of different sizes, in different market sectors, and in different regions sometimes had different stakes in specific proposals and took conflicting political positions on them. Academic policy reformers also pursued political goals in this broad sense. Reformers, for example, supported the creation of commissions in which "public" members like themselves would arbitrate labor market conflicts; not surprisingly, the proposed commissions ensured that experts like themselves would staff and hold the balance of power in determining policy outcomes.

Political Institutions and Policy Strategy

To understand policy strategy, in turn, it is essential to understand how political institutions shape the purposes, expectations, assumptions, and other premises of those who seek and make public policy. Political institutions include legislatures; elected executives; bureaucracies; courts in the national, state, and local governments; and the political parties and interest groups that organize conflict over elections and public policy. Political institutions have a more immediate and direct effect on policy strategy than other factors. These institutions make some policy options impossible, others unlikely, and still others politically possible and attractive. Employers, labor leaders, and reformers had to tailor their policy plans to the political institutions that formulate, adopt, implement, and adjudicate disputes about public programs. Policymakers modified their labor market strategies as they accumulated knowledge about ways that political institutions dealt with their agendas.

I asked several questions about the way political institutions affect the policy strategies of labor and business leaders, policy reformers, and public officials. First, how did political institutions limit the policy agenda? Did these institutions rule out some policy options? Most notably, did the lack of accepted authority make it impossible for a particular institution or level of government to address a specific problem or implement a particular program? What effect did that incapacity have on labor market policy strategies?

Within the constraints of accepted authority, how difficult was it for an interest to get government to do what it wanted government to do? Did public policy offer a feasible and reliable way for unions, employers, or others to gain labor market advantage? If one invested heavily in winning a policy battle, could one rely on government to implement the program as expected? The more difficult it is to win a policy victory, or the more unreliable the result of a policy victory, the less likely it is that an interest will seek a policy solution to a problem, and the more likely it will abandon public policy as a weapon for achieving its goals.

Did political institutions encourage or discourage cooperation among employers, among workers, and between employers and workers? Did political institutions make it relatively easy for interests to cooperate in pursuit of identical or related objectives? The more that political institutions discourage strategies of cooperation, the more they encourage strategies of conflict and confrontation.

THE PLAN OF THE BOOK

Chapter 1 more fully explains the conceptual map of labor market policy and identifies the programs that must be included in a systematic analysis of the development of American labor market policy between the Civil War and 1900. Chapter 1 also explains more fully how American policymaking institutions affected policy strategy in this period.

Chapters 2 and 3 trace the development of American labor leaders' policy strategy from the 1860s to 1900. In these years, unionists frequently invested substantial effort to win government help and protection. Labor leaders became increasingly frustrated by public policy, though, as their experiences proved that

American government was an unreliable ally. By 1900, the leaders of the AFL made the expansion of "union shops" central to their strategy for strengthening their labor market position. In this approach, unions would militantly unionize the industrial economy in direct confrontation with employers.

Chapter 4 shows how political structure gave employers unusually strong motives and unusually effective means to defend their prerogatives against this union shop strategy. As interstate rivalry, anti-trust laws, and the spread of competition across state lines made it impossible for employers to secure industry-wide price and production agreements, larger employers responded with mergers. The giant corporations that emerged from the turn of the century merger movement did not need to cooperate with labor, and generally kept unions out of industrial plants. Because they could not make enforceable, marketwide agreements on prices and production, smaller employers had no more need of unions than did the large corporations. Militant union shop tactics threatened their production, supplies, and sales. Many smaller manufacturers, then, joined in an aggressive "open shop" counterattack against the union shop strategy at the turn of the century. In the following years, these employers used the courts and American federalism skillfully to limit the effect of labor reform on employers' prerogatives.

Chapter 5 shows how the employer "open shop" counterattack narrowed and skewed the strategies of trade unions, reformers, and politicians from 1900 to the New Deal. Defeats of American miners and the machinists muted their influence in the American Federation of Labor. The conservative influence of the skilled crafts strengthened because the open shop did much less damage to the building trades and other crafts. As employers became increasingly dominant in American labor markets, reformers became increasingly attracted to labor market reforms that made employers responsible for worker protection. These uniquely American solutions for worker protection strengthened employers' dominance of American labor markets. Politicians adapted electoral strategies to this developing chain of events by temporizing on labor proposals that challenged employer prerogatives.

Chapters 6, 7, 8, and 9 systematically demonstrate the way that these policy strategies resulted in American labor market policy that gave employers exceptional autonomy by the New Deal. Chapter 6 shows that, though governments enacted numerous hour, wage, and child labor regulations, neither comprehensive nor incremental policy tactics could successfully establish universal labor protections, even for children. The AFL rejected general protections for male workers because such laws could not be relied upon and because they threatened to undermine the union shop strategy. Chapter 7 shows how the open shop drive and institutional fragmentation defeated the AFL's protracted policy campaign for the unrestricted right to use strikes, boycotts, and other economic weapons. Uniquely American policy features—the extensive use of court injunctions and the existence of a law banning combinations restraining trade—became powerful checks on the AFL's strategy of self-reliance.

Chapter 8 shows that progressive reformers' efforts to engage government in a more active role in managing labor markets foundered when unions or employers failed to take an interest in new labor market institutions that they could not control. As a result, American public employment offices and vocational education affected American labor markets only at the margins. Work insurance, examined in Chapter 9, most clearly illustrates how the narrowed AFL policy strategy abandoned the protection of many workers to private employers. Unions and employers supported workers' compensation laws because work injury insurance created a more reliable system than civil lawsuits. Progressive reformers pressed for health insurance as the "next logical step" for work insurance in the United States. Unions and employers had much less stake in sickness insurance, however, and opposed it. When unemployment insurance emerged on the national agenda in the Depression, the most successful plans proposed by reformers gave employers exceptional proprietorship of the program.

Finally, chapter 10 shows how American labor market policy remained exceptional and became a model for other nations in the late twentieth century. The New Deal constituted the most formidable challenge to employer prerogatives in the nation's history, and its policy cramped employers to an unprecedented extent. New Deal policymakers, though, inherited a legacy of institutions, habits, and commitments that boxed in their strategies and limited their ability to constrain employers' managerial freedoms. Those initiatives that restricted employers in the 1930s had eroded seriously by the late 1940s. Today, American employers continue to enjoy exceptional autonomy in labor markets. Since, the international economic stagnation of the 1970s, American labor market policy has been discussed as a potential model for nations seeking to increase economic growth. American political institutions make this model difficult to import, however. Even if it were easy to import, American labor market policy has had questionable consequences for economic growth, individual economic security, and fairness.

ACKNOWLEDGMENTS

I've benefited enormously from the support and advice of many friends as this project developed. I especially thank Neil Mitchell, Cathie Jo Martin, Charles Noble, Colin Gordon, and Michael Goldfield for extensive and thoughtful comments on the argument. Linda Kowalcky, Kenny Thomas, Gary Marks, Daniel Ernst, Eileen McDonagh, Jonathan Rees, Robert Asher, William Graebner, Sanford Jacoby, Alfred Diamant, Dennis Judd, Vernon Blackburn, Judson MacLaury, and John Martin also helped me with their special insights and information. I am indebted to three anonymous reviewers, including one for *Studies in American Political Development,* whose lucid comments helped me strengthen this argument enormously. Dennis Judd, Don Critchlow, Carol Kohfeld, Don Phares, and Terry Jones went above and beyond the call of duty in supporting this project and me. Fenton Martin deserves mention for locating and sending me a very obscure Indiana law. At the University of Missouri–St. Louis, many graduate students who have been subjected to drafts of this work have made it better; of these, Tyler Fitch, Yu-Yuan Kuan, Carroll Thomas, Maureen Gilbride, Thomas Boehm, and Lisa Panczer provided especially helpful data, sources, and wonderful suggestions on elements and iterations of this argument. Other students that deserve thanks include Alexis Andres, Shellagh Carper, Nancy Langley, Mette Lingaard, Ted Powers, Megan Slack, Jeanne Theis, Andy Theising, Dana Hullinger, Elaine Hays, David Fistein, Arlene Vogelsang, E. G. Phillips, and Claude Louishomme. The award-winning departmental staff, Jan Frantzen, Lana Vierdag, and Linda Miller, were characteristically patient, efficient, and supportive. At Rowman & Littlefield, Steve Wrinn, Mary Carpenter, Lynn Gemmell, and Luann Reed-Siegel made this book much better. I appreciate their care, help, and professionalism very much.

A portion of this book appeared as "Voluntarism against the Open Shop: Labor and Business Strategies in the Battle for American Labor Markets," *Studies in American Political Development* 13 (Spring 1999): 146–85. Earlier versions were presented at the International Conference on Socioeconomics in 1997 and at the George Meany Center in 1996; the late Stuart Kaufman was a great help in supporting the presentation of this paper before an audience of labor historians. I appreciate the help provided by the U.S. Library of Congress, the U.S. National Archives, the Hagley Museum and Library, the George Meany Center, the Illinois State Historical Library, the Western Historical Manuscripts collection of the University of Missouri, the University of Wisconsin, and Georgetown University. Library staff at the University of Missouri–St. Louis, Washington University, and St. Louis Universities were extraordinarily helpful. At the UM–St. Louis library, Mary Doran, Frances Piesbergen, Mary Zettwoch, Lucinda Williams, Sandy Snell, and Linda d'Avingon provided exceptional help in locating arcane documents and making them accessible.

The Public Policy Research Centers at the University of Missouri–St. Louis, the Research Board of the University of Missouri, and the Hagley Museum and Library provided valuable support for portions of this research. Even with all this help, I want readers to be assured that any remaining errors or ambiguities are completely my responsibility.

Bryan Robertson showed remarkable tolerance during the writing of this book; watching his unlimited potential unfold has been inspirational. More than anyone else, Cathie Robertson made this book possible. It couldn't have happened without her proofreading, comments, and suggestions over the many years of its development. Most important, she offered support, patience, comfort, and words of encouragement for the project from conception to completion—a task that would have discouraged a less caring and decisive soul. No one could ask for a more loyal, supportive, and caring companion, friend, and soul mate. At long last, I can dedicate this completed book to her.

ACRONYMS AND ABBREVIATIONS

AABA	American Anti-Boycott Association
AALL	American Association for Labor Legislation
AFL	American Federation of Labor
CES	Committee on Economic Security
CMIU	Cigar Makers' International Union
CWAWU	Carriage, Wagon, and Automobile Workers' Union
FLSA	Fair Labor Standards Act of 1938
FOTLU	Federation of Organized Trades and Labor Unions
GAO	Government Accounting Office
GPO	Government Printing Office
IAM	International Association of Machinists
ICC	Interstate Commerce Commission
IMA	Illinois Manufacturers' Association
ITU	International Typographical Union
IWW	Industrial Workers of the World
LIS	Luxembourg Income Study
NAM	National Association of Manufacturers
NCF	National Civic Federation
NCID	National Council for Industrial Defense
NCL	National Consumers' League
NCLC	National Child Labor Committee
NIRA	National Industrial Recovery Act
NLRA	National Labor Relations Act
NLRB	National Labor Relations Board
NLU	National Labor Union
NMTA	National Metal Trades Association
NSPIE	National Society for the Promotion of Industrial Education
OECD	Organization for Economic Cooperation and Development
RFC	Reconstruction Finance Corporation

SFIO	Section Française de l'Internationale Ouvrière [French Socialist party]
TERA	Temporary Emergency Relief Administration [New York]
TUC	Trades Union Congress [British]
UAW	United Auto Workers
UMWA	United Mine Workers of America

1

AMERICAN LABOR MARKET POLICY, STRATEGY, AND POLITICAL INSTITUTIONS

To understand the origins of American labor market policy, one must have tools for analyzing the *content* of that policy, the *strategies* that informed that content, and the political *institutions* that made these strategies seem reasonable. This chapter begins by furnishing a conceptual map of the content of American labor market policy from the Civil War to the New Deal. The map identifies each important proposal to regulate and manage American labor markets, to compensate workers, and to govern trade unions. This policy map reveals that American labor market governance did not differ significantly from that in comparable nations until the turn of the century. Like other nations, the United States protected employers' freedom in the nineteenth century. When other nations began to set substantial boundaries on employers' labor market prerogatives after 1900, however, the United States pursued a distinct path that protected American employers' freedom to an exceptional degree.

The chapter next explains the importance of understanding the policy strategies that shaped these programs and proposals. Labor leaders, employers, reformers, and policymakers distinctively shaped American labor market governance by changing over time the way they defined policy problems, conceived of public solutions, and set their priorities for government action. Trade union leaders and employers had the greatest stake in using public policy to increase their labor market power. During this period, American trade union leaders narrowed their policy demands, depending instead on direct confrontations with employers to expand their influence over the terms of employment. While labor leaders in Great Britain, Germany, and other nations were drawn reluctantly into independent labor politics and universal government protections of labor in these years, labor leaders in the United States pursued a confrontational and increasingly restricted strategy aimed at increasing the advantages of crafts workers. American employers responded to labor's confrontational strategy with

1

unusually vehement opposition. Natural conflict between employers and workers developed in the United States into a wide-ranging battle for labor market control. Employers mobilized to maintain union-free shops and beat back policy proposals that challenged their right to manage. Some supplied a kind of shadow labor market policy consisting of corporate welfare programs, self-regulation, company unions, and personnel management. As it became clear in the 1920s that American employers had largely been successful in defending their labor market prerogatives, influential reformers adapted to this political reality by designing uniquely "American" labor market policy agenda that largely conceded employer control of labor markets.

Finally the chapter shows how American political institutions powerfully altered the battle for American labor markets by encouraging the exceptional self-reliance of American labor and the exceptional anti-labor antagonism of American employers. American political institutions made it very difficult to introduce measures limiting employer prerogatives. Even when such measures emerged on the agenda, political institutions made it difficult to enact or implement them. Additionally, these institutions made it difficult for workers to organize union movements or working-class political parties strong enough to attempt to overcome these inherent institutional obstacles.

CONCEPTUAL MAP OF AMERICAN
LABOR MARKET POLICY

How did the United States govern its labor markets between the Civil War and the Great Depression? Did it govern its labor markets differently than other nations? In these years, American policymakers seriously weighed many proposals for regulating, managing, and organizing these markets. In some form, many of these proposals developed into enduring laws, public programs, and public organizations. Individual laws, programs, and organizations did not result from a deliberate overall plan, however. For the most part, policymakers formulated, adopted, and implemented these proposals separately, with little or no explicit connection to one another. In this respect, American policymakers were no different from their counterparts abroad. Governments in industrializing nations became engaged in labor markets small step by small step. Most of these steps aimed to answer specific interest demands; crises; bursts of public indignation; and unexpected economic, social, and political events. Most came from expedient compromises among contentious policy advocates, and did not reflect rational planning. Once established, most individual programs developed separately from one another. Although each nation used similar policy tools to govern labor markets, each mixed these instruments in different ways.

Because no nation developed labor market policy over the course of these decades according to a deliberate, overarching plan, there is no easy way to determine whether or not the United States governed its labor markets in a different way than other nations. To establish systematically whether or not the United States pursued a different path in governing labor markets, one must compare individual laws, programs, and institutions across nations. A simple conceptual map of labor market policy is essential for this comparison. Such a map specifies different types of labor market policy to identify comprehensively all the important public labor market initiatives of the period. Important initiatives are those that had or aimed to have a substantial and sustained effect on the relationship of employers and workers. Any effort to identify a labor market policy pattern must be able to relate the pattern to each of these initiatives. A conceptual map also ensures that the timing of the divergence of American labor market policy is identified accurately.

The conceptual map distinguishes four different types (or areas) of government intervention in labor markets. First, governments regulate labor markets, prohibiting some labor market behaviors or outcomes. Second, they promulgate rules for trade union activity and collective bargaining. Third, governments attempt actively to steer and direct labor market outcomes. Fourth, they compensate workers for circumstances that cause lost income, such as work injuries or involuntary joblessness.

These different types of labor market policy require public officials to serve different roles. Regulation primarily requires that public officials act as police. Trade union law places them in the role of diplomats, arbiters, and power brokers. Active labor market policy requires that they act as microeconomic managers, adjusting supply and demand in specific situations. Work insurance requires that they assess claims for public compensation. Though these roles differ, each of them potentially places public officials squarely in the middle of conflicts between employers and employees. In that sense, each activity is intensely political. Whether intended or not, these can profoundly affect the balance of power between workers and employers.

An initial conceptual map traced the development of labor market policy across nations from the nineteenth century to the Depression, identifying trends in regulation, active management, trade union, and work insurance policy. Special attention was given to Great Britain, Germany, France, Canada, and Australia as nations most comparable to the United States and most closely monitored by American policymakers. Governments first entered labor markets as regulators to police child labor, dangerous working conditions, and other specific problems. Following Great Britain's lead, the industrializing nations and American states had established laws by the 1870s requiring the public inspection of factory conditions.[1] When workers demanded shorter hours, governments began to enact legislation aimed at limiting the workday and workweek.[2] Governments next began to regulate wages. In 1896 the government of Victoria, Australia, set minimum wages for unorganized workers in low-wage industries. By the turn of the century, other Australian states and Great Britain followed this example. These regulations initially covered only the most vulnerable workers, such as women and children, or workers in dangerous industries such as mining and rail transport. In the first decades of the twentieth century, most nations had extended wage and hour regulation to a large part of the workforce. By doing so, these nations substantially limited employers' labor market prerogatives.

While governments extended labor regulation, trade unions were insisting on the freedom to organize workers and to strike, boycott, and picket employers. The United States had acknowledged the legality of trade union agreements before the Civil War,[3] but from the 1870s to 1900, new laws and judicial rulings restricted American unions' freedom of action. Restrictions on collective working-class activity were common in industrializing countries at this time. Nations began to relax some of these constraints on union activity by the early 1900s. Many nations created arbitration and conciliation mechanisms that involved government in labor conflicts more extensively. Arbitration became a central part of labor's strategy for increasing its labor market power in Australia, providing protection against wage cutting in economic slumps.[4] When World War I caused severe labor shortages, the industrialized nations supervised the unprecedented unionization of their industries. By the 1920s, trade unions generally had gained substantial freedom of action at the expense of employers' managerial prerogatives (though union strength ebbed in the 1920s).

As regulation spread and unions gained power, governments tried to manipulate labor markets more actively to address widespread industrial problems such as mass unemployment. Massachusetts established a bureau of labor to gather information on the workforce, wages, prices, and specific employment problems. Other governments instituted similar labor statistics bureaus. These new agencies influenced the labor market policy agenda thereafter. Special commissions, permanent congressional committees, and new government agencies, notably the U.S. Department of Labor, monitored labor markets and initiated public efforts to manipulate them. Immigration controls and crafts licensing limited access to jobs. Governments initiated public works programs and public employment offices to mitigate involuntary joblessness[5] and refashioned apprenticeship and vocational education for the changing labor market. By the 1920s, governments in many industrializing nations played a substantial role in manipulating labor supply and demand.

Work insurance initially developed because nineteenth-century laws made compensation for work injuries slow, complex, and uncertain and left both workers and employers dissatisfied. Workers' compensation laws replaced the patchwork of individual court awards with predictable schedules of compensation for industrial injuries. Work injury insurance constituted the initial social insurance program of the modern welfare state.[6] Other work insurance programs followed. Great Britain initiated the first national unemployment insurance program in 1911.

The preceding description of the general development of labor market policy provides the background for a more thorough conceptual map of American programs and proposals for labor market regulation, management, insurance, and trade union policy from 1865 to 1932. This conceptual map is shown in table 1.1, which lists the programs and proposals in this period that contemporaries viewed as important, according to public records of contemporary deliberations. The list includes new bureaus, standing committees, and temporary investigating commissions with broad authority. It excludes specific court decisions and commissions set up to investigate specific situations, such as strikes.[7] A systematic account of American labor market policy must account for all these programs and proposals.[8]

Table 1.1:   The American Labor Market Policy Agenda, 1865–1932

1. Regulation

State laws establishing eight hours as the legal workday (1867*)
State child labor restrictions with enforcement (1867*)
U.S. laws establishing eight-hour days on federal government work
    (1867, 1892, 1912)
State laws restricting working hours for children, with enforcement (1867*)
State laws establishing eight-hour days on state government works (1868*)
State laws restricting working hours for women (1874*)
Enforceable state factory inspection laws (1879*)
State laws regulating private employment agencies (1885*)
State laws establishing eight-hour days for street railways, railroads,
    and mines (1886*)
U.S. law establishing eight-hour days for postal workers and public
    printer (1888)
State laws setting wages on public works at "prevailing" levels (1892*)
U.S. Hours of Service Act (for railroads, 1907)
U.S. Seamen's Act (1915)
U.S. eight-hour law for railroads (Adamson Act, 1916)
Proposed state laws universally restricting the workday to eight hours (1914*)
Proposed U.S. law to restrict the workday to eight hours in the steel
    industry (1912)
New York State Factory Investigating Commission (1911)
State minimum wage laws for women (1912*)

Table 1.1 Continued

U.S. child labor law (Keating–Owen Act, 1916)
U.S. child labor tax (1918)
U.S. constitutional amendment banning child labor (1923)
U.S. regulation of prison-made goods (Hawes–Cooper Act, 1929)
U.S. prevailing wage law (Davis–Bacon Act, 1931)
Proposed U.S. law to restrict the workweek to thirty hours (Black thirty-hour bill, 1932)

2. Trade Unions and Collective Bargaining Policy

State laws protecting unions from the common law doctrine of
    conspiracy (1873*)
State laws protecting workers' collective employment action (1869*)
State laws providing for mediation and conciliation of labor disputes (1886*)
Federal law providing for the incorporation of trade unions (1886)
State legal protection of union labels and symbols (1887*)
State arbitration boards (1887*)
State laws providing for the incorporation of trade unions (1888*)
Federal railroad arbitration process (1888)
U.S. Pullman Strike Commission (1894)
Federal railroad mediation (Erdman Act, 1898)
State and federal court expansion of injunctive power (late nineteenth century)
Proposed U.S. law restricting application of conspiracy and injunctions
    to labor (1900)
Labor provisions of U.S. anti-trust law (Clayton Act, 1914)
U.S. Railway Labor Act (1926)
U.S. labor injunction limitations (Norris–La Guardia Act, 1932)

3. Labor Market Management

U.S. House Committee on Labor (1867)
U.S. Senate Committee on Labor (1870)
State Labor Statistics Bureaus (1869*)
U.S. Chinese Exclusion Act (1882, 1892)
U.S. Senate Committee on the Relations between Capital and Labor (1883)
U.S. Alien Control Labor (Foran) Act (1885)
U.S. Bureau of Labor (1886)
State laws licensing specific crafts (late nineteenth century)
State Public Employment Offices (1890*)
U.S. Bureau of Immigration (1891)
U.S. Industrial Commission (1898*1902)
State laws for advance planning of public works (1917*)
U.S. Department of Commerce and Labor (1903)
State laws supporting industrial education (1906*)
U.S. Division of Information in Bureau of Immigration (1907)

Table 1.1 Continued

State industrial commissions (1911*)
U.S. Department of Labor (1912–1913)
U.S. Commission on Industrial Relations (1914)
World War I labor market programs (1917–1918)
U.S. literacy test for immigrants (1917)
U.S. Vocational Education (Smith–Hughes) Act (1917)
U.S. immigration restriction (1921, 1924)
U.S. Woman's Bureau (1920)
U.S. Federal Employment Stabilization Board (1930)
State work relief programs (1931*)
U.S. Emergency Relief and Construction Act (1932)
U.S. Employment Service (1933)

4. Work Insurance

State Laws Limiting Employer's Liability Defenses (1887*)
State Workers' Compensation Laws (1902, 1911*)
Federal Workman's Compensation Act (1908)
State proposals for public health insurance (1917*)
State unemployment insurance laws (1932*)

(date*) indicates the date of the initial state program; other states initiated similar programs in the same year or in later years.

Tables 1.1, 1.2, and 1.3, and figure 2.1 draw from a chronological list of state, federal, and selected foreign labor market programs from the mid-1860s to 1933. This list provided a systematic inventory of policy development used for the narrative analysis in later chapters. The chronology integrated key election results, strikes, and other political and economic events with important programs and proposals for labor market regulation, management, work insurance, and trade union policy. This list pinpointed key turning points in the ebb and flow of the battle for American labor markets, and revealed how labor market issues that seemed superficially unrelated were in fact part of a larger labor market battle.

AMERICAN LABOR MARKET POLICY EXCEPTIONALISM

American labor market policy may initially appear to have been exceptional from the beginning.[9] The development of public labor market initiatives presented in table 1.2, however, offers systematic and comparative evidence that American labor market policy was *un*exceptional as late as the 1890s. Sometime after the turn of the century, American labor market policy came to differ substantially from that of any comparable nation.

At the close of the nineteenth century, no nation's labor market policy substantially limited employers' prerogatives to hire; fire; and control wages, hours, and working conditions. In this sense, American labor market policy did not differ essentially from that of other industrializing nations. It is true that Great Britain had more advanced factory legislation than the United States, that Australia and New Zealand had instituted minimum wage laws, and that Germany had established social insurance. It also is true that apprenticeship withered in the United States and that enforcement of laws was uneven and frequently lax. But table 1.2 shows that the United States also had initiated trailblazing labor market programs before other countries and that by no means did every other major industrial nation enact major labor market programs before the United States. The table lists American states as a separate category because the states did most of the governing of American labor markets until the New Deal. By 1900, seven U.S. states enacted laws establishing the eight-hour day as the legal working day. These laws stimulated intense opposition and support (see chapter 2). Though these statutes ultimately had little practical effect, no other country had even attempted to enact such general hours laws by 1900.[10] A Massachusetts enforceable factory act preceded effective national factory inspection in Sweden and Denmark (1889), France (1892), South Australia (1894), Queensland and New South Wales, Australia (1896), and Ontario (1897) and Quebec (1894), Canada.[11]

The United States also led the world in establishing labor statistics bureaus and state public employment offices. Massachusetts created the world's first labor statistics bureau, and the U.S. Bureau of Labor was the first national labor statistics bureau.[12] In 1890, Ohio preceded any nation in the world by authorizing establishment of five public employment offices. By 1899, six states (including New York) also had created public employment offices,[13] while among national governments only New Zealand had similar offices. American immigration restrictions also tended to precede those in Canada and Australia.[14] The states that enacted these laws included a substantial part of the industrial workforce (table 1.3). The United States enacted federal laws restricting immigration before Canada and Australia enacted similar restrictions.

American courts had tolerated unions earlier than other nations, and the United States did not overtly repress unions in the way Germany had done in the late nineteenth century. In the 1880s, and in international comparison, New York and Pennsylvania were relatively progressive in respecting workers'

Table 1.2: Dates When Governments Initiated the Use of Labor Market Instruments

	U.S. State	U.S. National	Great Britain	France	Germany
1. Regulation					
Eight-Hour Workday Law	1867 (Ill.)	1938	none	1919	1918
Factory Inspectors	1877 (Mass.)	1970	1833	1874	1878
Minimum Wage	1912 (Mass.)	1938	1909	1950	none
2. Labor Market Management					
Labor Statistics Bureau	1869 (Mass.)	1885	1893	1891	1902
Public Labor Exchanges	1890 (Ohio)	1933	1909	1911	1914
3. Governing Trade Unions					
Mediation and Conciliation	1886 (Mass./N.Y.)	1888* 1913	1896	1854	1890
4. Work Insurance					
Workers' Compensation	1911 (10 states)	none	1897	1898	1884
Unemployment Insurance	1932 (Wis.)	1935	1911	1914	1927

* Common carriers (railroads) only.

Sources: Eight-Hour Laws: John R. Commons and John B. Andrews, *The Principles of Labor Legislation* (New York: Harper and Brothers., 1916), 229; Gary Cross, *Worktime and Industrialization: An International History* (Philadelphia: Temple University Press, 1988), 162, 165. *Factory Inspectors* (a law authorizing the appointment of designated factory inspectors made factory legislation "enforceable"): William Franklin Willoughby, *State Activities in Relation to Labor in the United States* (Baltimore: Johns Hopkins University Press, 1901), 34–35; George M. Price, *Administration of Labor Laws and Factory Inspection in Certain European Countries,* U.S. Bureau of Labor Statistics Bulletin 142 (Washington, D.C.: Government Printing Office, 1914), 9–10, 37, 110, 179. *Minimum Wages:* Commons and Andrews, *The Principles of Labor Legislation,* 174–90; G. Starr, *Minimum Wage Fixing* (Geneva: International Labour Office, 1981). *Labor Statistics Bureaus:* U.S. Bureau of Labor," *Bureaus of Labor in the United States,* Bulletin 54 (Washington, D.C.: GPO, 1904), 993; U.S. Industrial Commission, *Report of the Industrial Commission on the Condition of Foreign Legislation upon Matters Affecting General Labor,* vol. 16 (Washington, D.C.: GPO, 1901), 224–25; George W. W. Hanger, "Bureaus of Statistics of Labor in Foreign Countries, *Bulletin of the Bureau of Labor* 54 (September 1904), 1023. *Public Labor Exchanges:* U.S. Department of Labor, Bureau of Employment Security, "The Public Employment System in the United States, 1933–1953," *Employment Security Review* 20 (June 1953): 4. *Mediation/Arbitration:* Commons and Andrews, *Principles of Labor Legislation,* 128–31. *Work Insurance:* Harry Weiss, "Employers' Liability and Workmen's Compensation," in *History of Labor in the United States,* John R. Commons, et al., 564–77; Peter Flora and Jens Alber, "Modernization, Democratization, and the Development of Welfare States in Western Europe," in *The Development of Welfare States in Europe and America,* ed. Peter Flora and Arnold J. Heidenheimer (New Brunswick, N.J.: Transaction Books, 1981), 59.

right to organize.[15] Arbitration programs were established at about the same time in Great Britain, Germany, and the United States. The United States was not even very different from other nations in bringing workers' compensation, the initial social insurance program in many nations, to the public agenda. Otto von Bismarck's Germany inaugurated workers' compensation programs in 1884. By the turn of the century Austria (in 1887), Great Britain (in 1897), and France (in 1898) had followed Germany's example.[16] New York reformers had introduced similar legislation in that state's legislature a year after Great Britain enacted its initial law.

America's previously unexceptional labor market policy began to diverge fundamentally from other countries in the early twentieth century. Other nations departed permanently from the norm of labor market laissez-faire, while the United States did not. Great Britain, Germany, and other industrializing nations began to knit labor regulations, work insurance, employment services, and trade union laws into a fabric of universal and effective worker protections that imposed substantial constraints on employers' labor market prerogatives. This emerging policy changed the basic relationship of capital, labor, and the state from one in which employers enjoyed unhindered freedom into one in which the state compromised employer freedom to ensure a floor of worker protections.

Superficially, American governments after 1900 enacted many programs that resembled those abroad. The U.S. Department of Labor established a presumptive beachhead for a more active federal role in labor markets. Federal support for vocational education and federal labor market management during World War I seemed to fortify the national role. Federal laws enacted in the 1910s regulated employment in the shipping and railroad industries and banned

Table 1.3:   Employment in States with Selected Labor Market Programs, 1899

	Number of States	Percent of U.S. Employment in These States
Bureaus of Labor Statistics	27	92.1%
Factory Inspectors	11	70.4
Public Employment Offices*	4	33.5

*Excludes two states providing for mail order services.

Sources: References for table 1.2, above; Donald B. Dodd, *Historical Statistics of the States of the United States: Two Centuries of the Census, 1790–1990* (Westport, Conn.: Greenwood Press, 1993), passim; U.S. Bureau of Labor, *Bureaus of Labor in the United States,* Bulletin 54 (Washington, D.C.: GPO, 1904): 993; U.S. Department of Labor, Bureau of Employment Security, "The Public Employment System in the United States, 1933–1953," *Employment Security Review 20* (June 1953): 4; William Franklin Willoughby, *State Activities in Relation to Labor in the United States* (Baltimore: Johns Hopkins University Press, 1901), 34–35.

child labor. Unions believed that the Clayton Act (1914) protected their powers. Many states established stricter regulation of women's and children's work in the Progressive Era, and enforcement improved. Some American states set minimum wages for women and children.[17] By the end of 1922, thirty states had set a legal maximum workday of eight hours for children under the age of sixteen, and by 1930 forty-one states had established legal maximum working hours for women.[18] On the eve of the Depression, thirty-three states had created public employment offices. Forty-one states enacted workers' compensation laws between 1911 and 1920. Wisconsin enacted the first American unemployment insurance program in 1932.[19]

Despite these initiatives, American labor market policy did not constitute a fabric of worker protections that substantially limited employers' managerial prerogatives. By 1932 the United States gave employers unusual latitude in the labor market, even compared to Great Britain, which intervened in labor markets less actively than many continental European nations. American labor market policy had limited reach and was severely fragmented and uneven. In effect, the United States in the first one-third of the century implemented labor market regulation, management, and trade union and work insurance policies in a way that buttressed, rather than compromised, employers' freedom of action. Events in the 1920s and early 1930s reinforced differences that had been established in the Progressive Era.

Labor market regulation in the United States remained an exceptional patchwork of limited protections, uneven laws, and poor enforcement while other nations established a floor of universal work standards. British courts increasingly restricted employers' dismissal rights, for example, but American judges generally refused to interfere with employers' discretion to fire employees at will;[20] the United States still provides less protection against arbitrary dismissal than any other industrialized nation.[21] By the early 1920s, an international eight-hour movement resulted in enforceable legal limits on the workday in most nations, but not in the United States (or Great Britain).[22] American court decisions struck down state and national efforts to set minimum wages, limit child labor, and regulate private employment offices, though such regulations were common abroad. State laws concerning lawsuits for workplace injury generally were less favorable to workers than British laws.[23]

American law allowed employers to evade unions freely, resulting in the confinement of the unions' freedom of economic action; other countries did more to help trade unions gain and hold labor market power. The British Trades Disputes Act (1906) put both unions and employers' associations beyond the reach of judicial rulings against conspiracy, restraint of trade, and abridgment of contract judgments.[24] In comparison, the Clayton Act of 1914 had little practical effect on American protection of employers' legal rights to battle unions. In contrast to British courts, American jurists protected employer freedom from trade unions, often overturning legislative protections for unions.[25] British judges had pioneered the notion that courts could utilize injunctions to stop unions from striking, boycotting, or picketing employers, but made little use of them. American courts, though, "saw the possibilities of the injunction and bettered the instruction." American courts had already used injunctions to put down the extensive railroad strikes of 1886 and decisively defeat the 1894 American Railway Union strike against the Pullman Palace Sleeping Car Company.[26] These relatively limited uses of the labor injunction were expanded widely after the turn of the century, and employers routinely sought injunctions to hamper effective union action.[27]

American governments implemented active management programs that, except for World War I, affected labor markets only marginally. American labor statistics bureaus retreated to technical issues and eschewed a broader role as a source of labor market policy ideas. Virtually all major industrialized nations governed labor markets vigorously through nationalized public employment services during World War I. Unlike other nations, the United States virtually abandoned its wartime employment office network after the war. In many states, the public employment offices languished, and by the early 1930s these offices had far less of a role in American labor markets than comparable offices abroad (table 1.4). The vocational education program did not link school to the labor market as closely as similar efforts in Europe.[28] Apprenticeship atrophied to an unusual extent in the United States.[29]

The United States especially lagged behind Europe in providing compensation for workers in the early twentieth century. Though workers' compensation reached the New York State agenda in 1898, not until 1911 had a single American state enacted a workers' compensation law that withstood a legal challenge. Most American states enacted work injury compensation laws after 1911, but in the aggregate these laws left an unusual amount of discretion to employers. British workers' compensation covered virtually the entire labor force by the 1930s. Only thirteen American states, however, even required employers to take out work injury insurance. Many states exempted industries in highly competitive markets (such as logging in Maine) from mandatory coverage. Large numbers of industrial workers depended on the "antiquated" process of employers' liability suits.[30] The national government never enacted a workers' compensation law.[31] American states never enacted a health insurance law in the Progressive Era, when reformers pressed it as the next logical step in the worker protection agenda. When Wisconsin enacted the first American unemployment insurance program in 1932, that program took care to protect employers' interests through the device of experience rating (see chapter 9).

Table 1.4: Labor Market Penetration of Public Employment Offices in Selected Nations prior to the Depression

Country	Labor Force (thousands)	Placements (thousands)	Percent (Column 2/1)	Number of Offices
Great Britain	20,212 (1926)	1,083 (1926)	5.4%	1062
Germany	31,139 (1921)	5,200 (1921)	16.7	361
France	21,524 (1929)	1,468 (1929)	6.8	n.a.
Japan	27,743 (1927)*	2,365 (1927)	8.5	n.a.
United States	49,885 (1930)	1,346 (1930)	2.7	180

*Estimated by the author from 1920 and 1930 data.

Sources: Labor force figures are estimates based on Peter Flora, *State, Economy and Society in Western Europe, 1815–1975: A Data Handbook*, 2 vols. (St. James Press, 1983), 1: 502, 516, 524; U.S. Bureau of Labor Statistics, *Historical Statistics of the United States: Colonial Times to 1970* (Washington, D.C.: GPO, 1975), 135; and Ryoshin Minami, *The Economic Development of Japan: A Quantitative Study* (New York: St. Martin's, 1986); Employment office figures from Paul H. Douglas and Aaron Director, *The Problem of Unemployment* (New York: Macmillan, 1931), 289–316, 336.

American employers reinforced their hold on labor markets in this period by creating, in effect, a "shadow" labor market policy that they fully controlled. Ford Motor Company and other large corporations acted unilaterally to improve wages, hours, and working conditions, for example. Several firms created "company" unions to temper and channel worker militancy and to prevent independent unions from making inroads among employees. Many firms instituted personnel departments, training programs, and other types of programs that established the active management of internal labor markets. General Electric Company and other large firms established a model of corporate welfare and work insurance programs for employees. Though these private initiatives never touched a majority of American workers, this "shadow" private labor market policy had two important effects on the development of American labor market policy. First, it gave business leaders a justification for public policies that would protect their power in labor markets. Second, these initiatives furnished policymakers with an ostensibly workable model of labor market policy that employers fully controlled.

POLICY STRATEGY AND AMERICAN LABOR MARKET POLICY EXCEPTIONALISM

To understand why American labor market policy diverged so markedly from that of comparable nations, it is necessary to examine the policy strategies of labor leaders, employers, and other participants in the policymaking process. Policy strategy is the set of purposes, expectations, assumptions, and other premises that policymakers communicate when they deliberate specific proposals for engaging government in labor markets. American policymakers moved American labor market policy down a singular evolutionary path by pursuing policy strategies that were unlike those used abroad.

These policy strategies, rather than being part of a deliberate plan, incidentally connected the laws, programs, organizations, and proposals described in table 1.1. The strategies of labor and employers are evident in the publications, convention proceedings, public policy statements, and archival records of the American Federation of Labor (AFL), the National Association of Manufacturers, the U.S. Chamber of Commerce, and other organizations that policymakers accepted as the voice of these interests. While these organizations did not fully represent the American working class or American employers, policymakers and the organizations themselves had a mutual interest in accepting them as legitimate intermediaries of organized labor and employers, and as proximate representatives for the aggregate interests of these groups. Their official views on public policy had substantial impact on policy agenda. Moreover, these organizations had extensive experience in shaping the policy process by the early 1900s. As a result, the strategies of the leaders of these organizations largely served as the strategy of labor and business in the American policy process of the early twentieth century. The strategies of other participants, including partisan legislators, labor reformers, political executives, and administrators, are taken from the public records of the policy process: legislative debates, hearings, documents and reports, executive statements, and archival sources.

The strategies evident in these policy discussions help reveal why American labor market policy developed in such a unique way. Of particular importance are the expected advantages and disadvantages of a particular proposal for the labor market power of employers, unions, and reformers. The ways that policy adversaries, especially labor and business, defined labor market problems and the relationship between these problems and their stated goals are crucial for understanding policy development. Also crucial are the reasons that advocates pressed for a proposal at a particular time, why they believed that some alternatives were politically feasible and others were not, and why they behaved in a way that gave a higher priority to one proposal than to others. Analyzing the ways that advocates related a proposal to their larger agenda; their political experience; likely political opposition and obstacles; and irresistible social, economic, and political imperatives force aside modern preconceptions and permit an understanding of the policy agenda from the participants' own ever evolving point of view. Individual proposals are both freestanding projects and parts of an ongoing process of strategic adjustment in pursuit of labor market power.

Employers and labor leaders who opposed each other a century ago viewed government primarily as an instrument that could protect, promote, or undermine their power in labor markets. Public policy had only instrumental value to unions and employers, becoming attractive only when direct methods of labor market confrontation failed. The AFL, the National Association of Manufacturers, the Chamber of Commerce, legislators, presidents, governors, and prominent reformers championed or fought against individual labor market programs because they anticipated that specific programs would provide them with measurable labor market advantages, electoral rewards, legal and bureaucratic benefits, or leverage in future policy battles.

Labor leaders initially advocated an ambitious agenda for broad government support of trade union power, but they began to narrow their agenda substantially in the late nineteenth century. After the Civil War, unions placed great strategic importance on eight-hour laws, union incorporation, and public offices staffed by unionists. AFL leaders supported regulation, labor statistics, and public employment offices when they believed that reliable trade unionists themselves would implement these programs for labor's benefit. At the end of the nineteenth century, however, AFL leaders no longer presumed that government would intervene on labor's behalf. American labor leaders had endured constant frustration in their efforts to enlist government help in battles with employers. Instead, the AFL articulated a vision of a union shop economy in which unions fully organized the industrial economy and set the terms of employment. By pursuing a strategy for unilateral control of labor markets through union shops, labor leaders gradually came to oppose government programs on behalf of male workers on the theory that such government help would make union membership less attractive to these workers and thus hurt unions. The AFL's opposition to such programs gradually caused it to remove itself from the American policy agenda until the Depression.

Employers were interested in public policy when it threatened their labor market prerogatives to hire, fire, and set the conditions of employment. These prerogatives were threatened by strict and inclusive labor regulations; by laws that encouraged strikes, picketing, and boycotts; and by programs that aided organized labor. Until the turn of the century, American employers fought these measures on an ad hoc basis. Often individual employers turned to courts to defeat such intrusions. After the turn of the century, though, business as a political interest became more organized and visible. The National Association of Manufacturers (NAM) redefined itself as an association opposed to the AFL's policy agenda. At the same time, a vast merger movement created large corporations in many mass production industries. These corporations enjoyed substantial power to resist unions and objectionable public policy proposals.

The opposition of the small manufacturers and the large corporations diminished labor's policy influence. Employers did not win every policy battle, but they won the war for unparalleled autonomy to manage their labor forces as they saw fit.

Policy reformers and politicians adjusted to the reality of labor's strategic retreat and employers' strategic policy success by acquiescing to employers' labor market autonomy. Influential reformers wrote uniquely American proposals for labor market policy, tailored to "American conditions" that would garner business support or at least split employer opposition. The culmination of this approach was the "American plan" for unemployment insurance that gave employers a substantial degree of proprietorship over the program.

AMERICAN POLITICAL INSTITUTIONS AND LABOR MARKET POLICY STRATEGIES

American labor market policy protected employers' prerogatives because American political institutions made alternative strategies unworkable. Political institutions directly and powerfully affected the way that employers, labor leaders, and labor market reformers thought about government as a solution to their labor market problems. Constitutions, laws, and "working rules"[32] determine the government's authority to address a labor market problem; the way that legislatures, elected executives, bureaucracies, and courts make public policy; and the rules by which political parties and interest groups pursue their goals. These given institutional arrangements make some policy options impossible, others unlikely, and still others politically feasible and relatively attractive. If policymaking is complex and arduous, or if the end result is unreliable, policy becomes a less feasible route to achieving broader labor market goals. Even when two societies have very comparable economic situations and cultural values, differences in their political institutions can result in different approaches to public policy.[33]

In three ways, American political institutions worked against labor market strategies that limited employer prerogatives. First, these institutions restricted the policy agenda, making it nearly impossible for American government even to consider seriously some restrictions on employers. Second, even when a proposal got on the agenda, these institutions made it difficult to enact laws that limited employer prerogatives and made those laws that were enacted difficult to implement. Third, these institutions discouraged the cooperation among employers, labor, and government that elsewhere facilitated the expansion of government influence in labor markets.

How American Political Institutions Narrowed the Policy Agenda

American political institutions made it difficult legally to limit employer prerogatives. The federal government exercised little authority over employers while the United States industrialized. Though the states had much more authority to regulate employers, interstate economic competition ensured that it would be politically unfeasible for even the most progressive states to intrude on employers excessively.

As interpreted until 1937, the U.S. Constitution prohibited the federal government from interfering in markets, including labor markets, within state boundaries. The federal government had authority only to supervise commerce across state lines. Between the Civil War and the New Deal, then, national policy could reach only a fraction of American employment. Federal power extended to indisputable instances of interstate commerce (such as railroads); the federally governed District of Columbia; and programs affecting federal government employees, federal contractors, and veterans. Until the 1930s, the limited labor market jurisdiction of the federal government made it impractical to advocate inclusive federal labor protections in peacetime. Reformers and unions advocated "model" worker protection laws for the fragments of the labor market that the federal government controlled, such as the District of Columbia. These model laws, however, could not provide a foundation for a national labor market policy.

While the United States industrialized, state governments had jurisdiction over most American workplaces. The constitution, though, denied state officials' authority to protect their employers from business competitors in other states. This form of federalism—competitive American federalism[34]—was unique. It created strong disincentives for states to implement labor laws that would impose high costs on in-state industries.[35] American states could not protect these industries from competitors out of state. If state labor regulations raised employers' payroll costs, the state could not compensate the employer by taxing goods imported from states without such regulations.[36] State officials, then, felt powerful pressures to resist proposals to intrude on employer autonomy; American political adversaries routinely charge their opponents with policies that diminish the prosperity of their jurisdiction.[37] State officials had strong reasons to compete with other states to keep legal burdens on employers to a minimum, or even to reduce regulations in a "race to the bottom."[38] Competitive American federalism strengthened the "privileged position" of business in the American policymaking process.[39]

Policymakers constantly invoked interstate economic competition in policy debates from at least the 1850s into the New Deal years.[40] Complaints about the effect of labor laws on state businesses helped to defeat or eviscerate factory laws,[41] eight-hour laws, [42] convict labor regulation,[43] laws requiring one days' rest in seven,[44] child labor laws,[45] minimum wage laws,[46] workers' compensation laws,[47] and compulsory health insurance laws.[48] The United States Industrial Commission in 1902 indicated that competition among manufacturers in different states constituted a greater obstacle to the limitation of working hours than foreign competition. "[A] single State with advanced labor legislation can not protect itself against the cheap labor and long workday of another State," concluded the commission in its Final Report.[49] Even when it struck down the federal child labor law, the U.S. Supreme Court explicitly conceded that interstate competition created disincentives for public intrusions on employer prerogatives.[50]

The wide disparity among states' wealth and resources greatly intensified this economic competition. An immense economic gap separated the relatively affluent northeastern and midwestern states from the relatively poor southern states. Massachusetts was as industrialized as any region in the world, while many southern states had little industrial development and a large pool of unskilled workers. While estimated per capita wealth of the United States was $1,165 in 1900, the South's per capita wealth was only $509 (a figure that includes railroads, mines, and other properties owned by outside interests). The first income tax in the 1910s revealed that the South, with just over a quarter of the nation's population, had only 11 percent of the nation's taxable income. Southern leaders used interstate competition to turn this gap to their advantage, advertising their economic conditions to attract northern investment and jobs. In 1904, the president of the Georgia Industrial Association urged manufacturers that "If things don't work out right in New England, come down where conditions are better! Try Georgia! Georgia has fine undeveloped water powers, good native labor, plenty of cotton, and the latch string is hanging out to cotton manufacturers especially."[51] This "latch string" included wages much lower than those in the older industrial areas. In 1909, when the average annual wage for manufacturing workers in the United States was $518, southern workers earned $452.[52] Few child labor laws (and little enforcement of those few laws) inhibited employers from hiring even less expensive child labor for textile mills, glass factories, and other enterprises.

How did any labor laws come into effect if interstate economic competition was so powerful a force? It was not unusual for some employers to support specific labor policy proposals as a result of economic competition. Some employers, such as North Carolina textile makers or West Virginia coal operators, were eager to race to the bottom; other employers, such as New England textile interests or Ohio mine operators, supported the creation of a floor under labor standards to prevent such competition. Second, in states with extensive industry, such as Massachusetts, New York, Ohio, and Illinois, industrialization created a large bloc of voters who supported laws restricting employers. These states pioneered many kinds of labor legislation because officials recognized the electoral gains that could result from responding to this constituency. But even in these states, legislators always were cautioned that innovative labor legislation threatened business, jobs, and taxes in the state. A manufacturer critical of Massachusetts' Progressive Era social policies complained about the erosion of its textile industry to the southeastern states. He acidly observed that "[f]or the last generation, Massachusetts has allowed itself to become the social laboratory in which all kinds of freak legislation has been tried out for the benefit of the rest of the country."[53]

How the Separation of Powers Diminished the Value of Policy Solutions

Even when labor market proposals got on the public agenda, it was difficult to enact programs and, if enacted, to implement them reliably. The U.S. and state constitutions thrust the policymaking branches of government into tacit rivalry for power, creating the most fragmented and inert policymaking process of any large capitalist democracy. The separation of powers made American state and national governments less capable of making a credible commitment to labor protection than governments in any other industrial nation. These difficulties made it costly and potentially futile for labor to try to use government against employers.

At the national level and in every industrialized state, any labor market law required the approval of two co-equal houses of the legislature and at least the tacit approval of the elected executive (president or governor). A proposal could win superficial endorsement from legislative leaders, but disappear before reaching a vote. Opponents could effectively bury a proposal by steering it to hostile committees or saddling it with fatal conditions, loopholes, or rules. The elongated policy process could consume months during which opponents could mobilize and economic circumstances become unfavorable. To ensure that a proposal would become law, interests learned that they needed to invest substantial time and tenacious effort to monitor legislative progress, preparing to return session after session to secure legislation they desired. The high cost of securing legislation worked against trade unions. Employers usually had a natural advantage in resources, and also had a natural tactical advantage in defending against proposed changes in the status quo.

Competitive American federalism increased these policy costs still further. Without national jurisdiction over worker protection, employers, workers, and reformers could only overcome the obstacle of interstate economic competition by campaigning for labor market laws that were uniform in every state. The campaigns for uniform laws, however, required tremendous resources as reformers lobbied in dozens of state capitals. Their arduous state-by-state campaigns to win reforms exhausted the limited resources of reform proponents.[54] These uniform laws had to be designed to convince leaders in each state that they would not be placed at a short-term competitive disadvantage with other states that lagged behind in policy adoption. Given the diversity of endowments and level of industrialization among the American states a century ago, this task of legislative design was daunting.

Moreover, because the policy process separated implementation from legislation, public executives and courts could render a program meaningless even if it survived the legislative gauntlet. American public executives often could undermine such a program by implementing it ineffectively or selectively. Legislatures sometimes invited such distorted implementation with imprecise and vague legislative language.

Judges exercised ample independent power to reinterpret statutes and to enjoin challengers to employer prerogatives. When the number of economic conflicts on court dockets multiplied after the Civil War, courts struck down many state laws that interfered with employers. At the same time, the federal courts interpreted the Fifth and Fourteenth Amendments to the constitution—provisions that prohibited government from taking property without "due process"—as protecting business from government interference. As the legal definition of property broadened to include an employer's business, courts sometimes used the due process clause to prohibit unions from using strikes, boycotts, and pickets to damage business. These limitations on federal and state power created a "no man's land" in which neither federal nor state law could reach employer prerogatives.

Political scientists and historians have paid special attention to the ways in which the courts caused American trade unions to narrow their policy strategy and depend more heavily on impediments and interest strategies. Victoria Hattam, for example, argues that English courts did not subvert Parliamentary labor laws as American courts undermined American labor laws, and thus did not foreclose the possibility of legislative successes for trade unions. Hattam concludes that "State institutions had shaped [American] trade union strategy . . . both through what it precluded and through what it allowed. The power of the courts in the sphere of industrial relations provided few rewards for political action, while simultaneously fostering a more legalistic, contract-oriented system of collective bargaining."[55] William Forbath argues that in this period "Courts shaped labor's strategic calculus," causing American unions to relinquish a broad-gauged political strategy based on a labor or socialist party.[56] As this chapter and the following chapters argue, the courts were not the sole source of labor's distrust of government. Federalism, implementation problems, and the employer counterattack were at least as important as the courts in determining the AFL's strategic withdrawal from broad-based policy solutions.[57]

Labor market programs that survived this process and were implemented faithfully tended to represent interests shared virtually unanimously—or the interests of a determined faction demanding benefits to which virtually everyone else was largely indifferent. Small programs and limited protections could survive the process if they provided narrow benefits without sparking intense opposition; in this way, states created licensing programs for specific occupations, for example. Only widespread popular support, favorable circumstances, and effective leadership could help overcome employer opposition to laws that threatened business. The number of labor market laws enacted in this period testifies to the fact that these conditions often were met. When both employers and unions supported government efforts, as in the case of vocational education and workers' compensation, the potential veto points in the system gave way to economic consensus. But these conditions were not met uniformly, or met in every state. When the conditions were not met across the states, the lack of universal action acted as a drag on incremental policy development much more than was true for national laws abroad.

Arguments about the importance of protecting women in the labor market provided a persuasive counterargument to labor market laissez-faire in the Progressive Era, when public regulation of working conditions for females expanded. While male legislators and judges resisted universal laws that protected workers of both genders, these policymakers yielded to claims that law could protect children from exploitation and that women required special protection as mothers, potential mothers, and an inherently more vulnerable group than men. When the U.S. Supreme Court conceded the constitutionality of special hours laws for female workers in 1908, reformers pressed successfully for a wide range of protective labor legislation for women. This legislation, however, tended to marginalize women in the labor market, divide the constituency that challenged employer prerogatives, and reinforce the notion that family wages depended (and should depend) on male breadwinners. In the case of gender, then, the very arguments that allowed policymakers to break the institutional logjam of the American policymaking process also drove a wedge in the working class, dividing the interests of male and female workers.[58] As historian Vivien Hart explains, "A struggle to redefine the civil, economic, and social status of women, and to match the language of constitutional interpretation to the circumstances of women's lives," became "central to American policy history."[59]

For organized labor, then, American public policy was an exceptionally expensive and unreliable instrument for labor market power. Even if unions successfully lobbied Congress for a law, they could not be sure that executives would effectively implement the law or that courts would uphold it. Unions grew cynical about the gap between hard-won statutory protections on the one hand and lax implementation and court reversals on the other. Regulatory laws often produced the illusion, not the reality, of governance.

How Political Institutions Obstructed Coalition-Building

One way of overcoming these institutional obstacles was to build an inclusive trade union movement or political party that could push on all the pressure points of the policymaking process simultaneously. Abroad, unions gained strength as industrial workers in the steel, auto, and other mass production industries swelled membership. New working-class political parties helped transform politics when they emerged in Germany after the lifting of the anti-socialist laws in 1890 and in Great Britain and France with the emergence of the British Labour Party and the French Socialist party (Section Française de l'Internationale Ouvrière, SFIO) in the first decade of this century. These parties expanded the policy agenda, created new party structures and techniques, and shifted the agendas of existing parties to the Left, making them more inclined to promise increases in social benefits and business regulations in order to win a share of working-class votes.[60] These economic and political developments were closely related. Crafts workers in many nations preferred to exercise labor market power through their own union organizations without government aid[61] but turned to politics when their efforts fell short of their goals.[62] In continental Europe, intense repression of trade unions made labor movements focus on political reform as a rallying point for worker protection. The struggle for the right to vote became a central organizing tactic in nations such as Germany, Norway, and Sweden. Winning the franchise required labor to develop political parties to achieve this goal.[63]

In the United States, however, neither industrial unionism nor a labor party emerged in the early twentieth century. Union growth was stunted, and uniquely among the industrialized nations, no mass-based working-class party sustained electoral support.[64] Much like the path of policy development, the path of unionization in the United States diverged from that of Great Britain and Germany immediately after the turn of the century. The United States did not endure the sustained boost of unionization that corresponded to a qualitative change in labor market policy and the emergence of successful, mass-based labor parties. Potential support for using labor market regulation, management, trade union law, and work insurance to limit employers' prerogatives was weak and divided in the crucial early years of labor market policy development.

American political institutions diminished the strategic practicality of mass membership unions and political movements. Until the turn of the century,

Americans joined unions in numbers that were very similar to those abroad. In 1886, when the membership of the Knights of Labor peaked, American trade union membership included as many as seven hundred thousand Knights of Labor and two hundred and fifty thousand other trade unionists, a rate of unionization very close to that reported for Great Britain half a dozen years later.[65] After the depression of 1893, AFL membership exploded from about a quarter of a million in 1898 to well over a million and a half in 1904.[66] Comparative statistics, though necessarily rough estimates, suggest that American unionization rates did not differ substantially from those in Great Britain or Germany around 1900 (see figure 1.1). The gap between the United States and these nations widened between the early 1900s and the 1920s, closed in the 1940s, and widened again after 1950.

The flat development of American trade union growth in the early twentieth century reflects the exceptional anti-union counterattack mounted by American employers in the first and third decades of the twentieth century. American employers have opposed trade unions with a vehemence unequaled in other OECD nations.[67] As chapter 4 explains, American political institutions uniquely prevented the kinds of employer collaboration that would have moderated this employer opposition. Abroad, employers sometimes colluded with one another to stabilize prices and production. Unions facilitated this collusion by helping to police such agreements. The limited scope of federal power and

Figure 1.1: Comparative Unionization Rates, 1890–1932

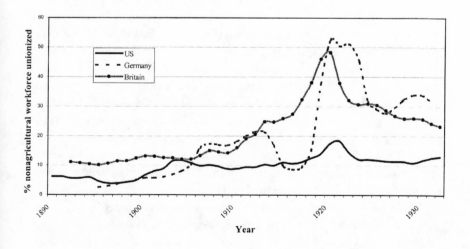

Sources: Gerald Friedman, "New Estimates of Union Membership: The United States, 1880–1914," *Historical* Methods 32, no. 2 (Spring 1999): 75–86; George Sayers Bain and Robert Price, *Profiles of Union Growth: A Comparative Portrait of Eight Countries* (Oxford: Blackwell, 1980): 39, 88, 133.

competitive American federalism made it impossible for American employers to organize markets or to collude in the same way.[68] Unlike Great Britain (where government tolerated cartels) or Germany (where government encouraged cartels), the American Sherman Anti-Trust Act, combined with the courts' interpretation of it, prevented cartels. Some American businesses adapted to their inability to collude by merging into single, dominant corporations, which exercised even more market power than a cartel[69] and had no need of unions to enforce price and production stability. Big business thus bypassed anti-trust laws, trade unions unsuccessfully sought exemption from them, and small firms used anti-trust to defeat unions.[70]

Because American employers could not collude, they had much less incentive to acquiesce to union demands. In the politically crucial steel and automobile industries, employment became concentrated in large firms that easily fended off the union shop drive. In less organized industries, smaller employers fiercely battled the union shop. Business historians such as Sanford Jacoby have explained the effect of American employers' strategic adjustment to the union shop drive. In Jacoby's view, it is not the weakness of labor, but the strength and hostility of employers, that explain the "low union density and the lack of labor radicalism in the United States."[71]

Why did the United States lack a working-class political party if it permitted propertyless men to vote so much earlier than comparable nations? American voters did not show an unusual hostility to socialist parties. Before World War I, similar percentages of American and British voters supported Socialist candidates. In 1912–13, twenty Socialists served in the legislatures of nine states. In 1914–15, thirty-four Socialist legislators served in fourteen states. Seventy-four American cities elected Socialist mayors in 1911.[72] In the 1912 presidential election, U.S. Socialist Party candidate Eugene Debs received 6 percent of the national vote.[73] In England's national elections at about the same time, the Labour Party received a maximum of 7 percent of the vote. This period constituted the most intensive early development of the British welfare state. During these years, the American Socialist Party increased its percentage of the popular vote between national elections at a faster rate than did the British Labour Party. This increase is more striking because laws in the South that prohibited African American citizens from exercising their franchise excluded a potential addition to the Socialist total.[74]

Political institutions are indispensable for understanding why the early extension of voting rights held back the development of a working-class socialist party in the United States. Several authors argue that the early extension of voting rights to American workers defused an issue that unified workers abroad. Without a campaign for suffrage to unify the working class, ethnic, racial, and gender animosities cleaved labor solidarity in America. Early suffrage itself, however, is not a necessary condition for the slow development of worker protections across nations. Some nations that became welfare states (Germany and France) had instituted a form of universal suffrage before 1880. The initiation of universal suffrage in nations could stimulate more demands for government intervention in markets, not less. For Australian labor, political involvement, along with labor scarcity, made government intervention attractive to labor early on.[75] Among seventeen developing capitalist nations in the late nineteenth and early twentieth centuries, "those that achieved full male suffrage earlier (including Germany, France, Denmark, and New Zealand) were also among the most precocious of welfare innovators."[76] Moreover, suffrage was not as universal in America as might be supposed. Only 15 percent of the adult population in the leading textile center of Lawrence, Massachusetts, was registered to vote in 1880. Residential and poll tax requirements, along with the absence of voting rights for women, minimized the working-class vote in Lawrence.[77] Election restrictions in southern states eliminated a potentially large part of the constituency for a labor party by 1900.[78]

Even with relatively widespread suffrage, American political institutions effectively contained the electoral power of workers by penalizing political movements representing national economic interests. The staggered election schedule for federal offices, and the lack of direct electoral control over most of the federal government, blunted the force of working-class votes and made it hard for a programmatic party to sustain its support.[79] At the state level, "winner-take-all" rules, the separation of executive and legislative powers, and malapportioned legislative districts disadvantaged left-wing parties that attracted city voters. The separation of public offices, constituencies, and interests would not permit disciplined cross-state party control of candidates, money, or philosophy.[80]

These circumstances caused the AFL to back away from political socialism while their British counterparts, similarly skeptical of political socialism in the 1890s but facing different political institutions and circumstances, reluctantly embraced it. Samuel Gompers and other labor leaders discovered through experience that it was more effective to support sympathetic officials in the two major parties than to commit labor support to one party or the other.[81] The limited practical impact of elected labor leaders in the 1880s and the failure of the Populist movement in the 1890s drove home the futility of efforts to bypass the Democratic and Republican Parties.[82] The third party that won the most votes in an election during this era, Theodore Roosevelt's Progressive Party, had a stronger worker protection agenda than its opponents in 1912. This "Bull Moose" party could not win and retain a large number of seats as a third party, however. Its supporters for the most part gravitated back to the Republican Party.

American labor leaders learned from successes and failures to be opportunistic and not ideological. Political parties naturally were stronger at the state and local levels rather than at the national level. State political parties naturally tailored their policy agendas to suit local constituencies, rather than national working-class interests. Candidates who nominally were Democrats or Republicans had both the means and the motive to tailor labor market policy positions to the local balance of power between employers and workers. Progressive Era politicians who supported worker protection, such as Robert La Follette of Wisconsin and Robert Wagner of New York, could more easily run as Republicans or Democrats (respectively) in their states than mount an assault on the two-party system. Political parties became diverse and ideologically incoherent coalitions that attracted participants of diverse labor market views.[83] Regional factions within the same party took diverse positions on divisive issues such as immigration and the free coinage of silver. Many close votes in Congress more clearly divided along lines of regional economic interest than political party.[84] The spoils system, rather than a coherent policy agenda, became the critical instrument for party building in the United States. Without a common policy agenda, the control of offices and the distribution of "pork barrel" benefits provided the only glue that held political parties' members together.[85] Unions found that they could exchange support for laws benefiting specific groups of workers and that politicians in both parties were interested in labor votes.

This very political opportunism, though, cleaved the constituency for labor market policy. Incremental, small-scale reforms arrested the development of an inclusive policy agenda. Florence Kelley, a vigorous and effective organizer of campaigns for child labor laws, women's hour restrictions, and minimum wage laws for women, viewed protective labor legislation for women as an "entering wedge" for inclusive, universal labor laws.[86] The extension of protective labor legislation for women and children, however, reinforced the AFL's inclination to secure labor protections for men through the union shop rather than legislation. When the highly skilled railway operating workers (engineers, conductors, brakemen) won battles for programs that protected their interests almost exclusively, they turned their back on less skilled workers in the railway industry, who lacked comparable protections.

Fragmented policy institutions made it hard to sustain coalitions among potential allies, such as progressive reformers, reform-minded civil servants, and labor leaders. Professional civil servants designed and implemented many active labor market programs abroad. In the United States, local machine bosses opposed civil service reforms and professional policy administration because these reforms threatened patronage prerogatives and the yields of corruption. Far from discouraging labor market policy reformers, machine politics spurred on efforts to professionalize labor market administration to remove it from partisan control. In the 1910s, the progressive social reformers who sought to emulate foreign policy development became creative and accomplished architects of alternative public institutions. They developed independent agencies, juvenile courts, and other new bodies. These institutions had substantial capacity to redistribute resources. When some reformers abandoned the European idea of municipal ownership because American urban machines made the idea too tempting to local bosses, they developed the notion of independent regulatory commissions.[87] The establishment of the U.S. Forest Service and emerging public universities demonstrate reformers' willingness to support heavy public sector investments under the right circumstances. Patronage politics merely increased the resolve to insulate these new institutions from political influence.

When reformers explicitly designed new labor market policy institutions (such as state industrial commissions and public employment offices), however, these institutions often posed a serious threat to the AFL's union shop strategy. In proposing the creation of a permanent federal industrial commission, John R. Commons and his colleagues advocated an exceptionally powerful new federal agency. This commission, funded by inheritance taxes, would regulate workplace conditions, manage job services and apprenticeship, mediate labor disputes, and potentially manage a large social insurance system.[88] Labor leaders such as Gompers understandably saw these commissions as a potential threat to their labor market power. Such commissions, in the hands of unsympathetic officials, could be potent tools for undermining labor autonomy and the union shop. Gompers broke permanently with these reformers over this issue.

STRATEGY AND STRUCTURE

American labor market policy was not decisively different from that of comparable nations in the mid-1890s. It became unambiguously exceptional in the early twentieth century. This divergence corresponds to narrowing policy strategies of labor, oppositional strategies of employers, and the relative weakness of unions. These changes in the battle for American labor markets, in turn, were rooted in the lessons that labor and employers learned as they gained experience in attempting to use American political institutions to achieve their ends. Labor's most important lessons were learned in battles to extend labor market regulation.

NOTES

1. B. L. Hutchins and A. Harrison, *A History of Factory Legislation* (London: Frank Cass, 1903; reprint by August M. Kelley, 1966).

2. Gary Cross, *Worktime and Industrialization: An International History* (Philadelphia: Temple University Press, 1988); David R. Roediger and Philip S. Foner, *Our Own Time: A History of American Labor and the Working Day* (New York: Greenwood Press, 1989).

3. William A. McConagha, *Development of the Labor Movement in Great Britain, France, and Germany* (Chapel Hill: University of North Carolina Press, 1942).

4. Francis G. Castles, *The Working Class and Welfare: Reflections on the Political Development of the Welfare State in Australia and New Zealand, 1890–1980* (Wellington, NZ: Allen and Unwin, 1985), 82–84.

5. John A. Garraty, *Unemployment in History: Economic Thought and Public Policy* (New York: Harper and Row, 1978).

6. Elizabeth Brandeis, "Labor Legislation," in *History of Labor Legislation in the United States,* 4 vols., ed. John R. Commons et al. (New York: Macmillan, 1935), 3: 570.

7. This list also excludes the important but temporary programs for managing labor markets established during World War I. The general effect of Progressive Era war mobilization for each area of labor market policy is discussed briefly in chapters 4–9. Although the lessons learned in these years demonstrably shaped the design of New Deal programs, most of the World War I agencies were not themselves part of an enduring institutional policy development.

8. An accounting of each requires that one identify their place in proponents' strategic calculations. This identification may require extended discussion, as in the case of child labor laws, or brief mention, as in the case of the specialized eight-hour laws.

9. David Brian Robertson, "Governing and Jobs: America's Business-Centered Labor Market Policy," *Polity* 20, no. 3 (Spring 1988): 426–56.

10. U.S. Industrial Commission, *Report on . . . Foreign Legislation,* 22–23.

11. U.S. Industrial Commission, *Report on . . . Foreign Legislation,* 81–118.

12. E. H. Phelps Brown and M. H. Browne, "Carroll D. Wright and the Development of British Labour Statistics," *Economica* 30, no. 119 (August 1963): 277–86.

13. U.S. Department of Labor, "The Public Employment System in the United States, 1933–1953," 4.

14. Darrell Hevenor Smith and H. Guy Herring, *The Bureau of Immigration: Its History, Activities, and Organization* (Baltimore: Johns Hopkins University Press, 1924); Kitty Calavita, *U.S. Immigration Law and the Control of Labor: 1824–1924* (London: Academic, 1984); Alexander Sexton, *The Indispensable Enemy: Labor and the Anti-Chinese Movement in California* (Berkeley: University of California Press, 1971); Gwendolyn Mink, *Old Labor and New Immigrants in American Political Development: Union, Party, and State, 1875–1920* (Ithaca, N.Y.: Cornell University Press, 1986), 94. On Canada, see Freda Hawkins, *Canada and Immigration: Public Policy and Public Concern,* 2nd ed. (Kingston, Ontario: McGill–Queen's University Press, 1988). On Australia, see H. I. London, *Non-White Immigration and the "White Australia" Policy* (New York: New York University Press, 1970).

15. Victoria Hattam, "Reply to Lovell: Politics of Commitment or Calculation?" *Studies in American Political Development* 8 (1994): 103–10.

16. Brandeis, "Labor Legislation," 570; Flora and Alber, "Modernization, Democratization, and the Development of Welfare States in Western Europe," 59, provide an alternative chronology of European programs based on specific program features.

17. Peter J. Coleman, *Progressivism and the World of Reform: New Zealand and the Origins of the American Welfare State* (Lawrence: University Press of Kansas, 1987); Brandeis, "Labor Legislation," 501–39.

18. J. Joseph Huthmacher, *Senator Robert F. Wagner and the Rise of Urban Liberalism* (New York: Athenum, 1968), 3–5; Brandeis, "Labor Legislation," 421, 453.

19. U.S. Bureau of Labor Statistics, *Workers' Compensation Legislation of the United States and Canada, 1919*, Bulletin 272 (Washington, D.C.: GPO, 1919); Brandeis, "Labor Legislation," 575–77; Ruth Kellogg, *The United States Employment Service* (Chicago: University of Chicago Press, 1933), 16; Daniel J. Nelson, *Unemployment Insurance: The American Experience, 1915–1935* (Madison: University of Wisconsin Press, 1969).

20. Derek C. Bok, "Reflections on the Distinctive Character of American Labor Laws," *Harvard Law Review* 84, no. 6 (April 1971): 1394–463.

21. Frederic Meyers, *Ownership of Jobs: A Comparative Study* (Los Angeles: Institute for Industrial Relations, University of California, Los Angeles, 1964); Bok, "Reflections on the Distinctive Character of American Labor Laws"; Bob Hepple, "Flexibility and Security of Employment," in *Comparative Labour Law and Industrial Relations,* 2 vols., ed. Roger Blanpain (Deventer, Netherlands: Kluwer, 1990), 1: 167–95; Lawrence E. Blades, "Employment at Will vs. Individual Freedom, on Limiting the Abusive Exercise of Employer Power," *Columbia Law Review* 67 (December 1967): 1404–36; Alan B. Krueger, "The Evolution of Unjust-Dismissal Legislation in the United States," *Industrial and Labor Relations Review* 44 (July 1991): 644–60; Barbara Presley Noble, "When Employers Rule by Whim," *New York Times,* March 1, 1992: C33; Organization for Economic Cooperation and Development (OECD), *The OECD Jobs Study: Evidence and Explanations,* 2 vols. (Paris: OECD, 1994), 2: 74.

22. On interest in the living wage, see John A. Ryan, *A Living Wage: Its Ethical and Economic Aspects* (New York: Macmillan, 1906); and L. T. Hobhouse, "The Right to a Living Wage," in *The Industrial Unrest and the Living Wage,* ed. William Temple (London: P. S. King, c. 1914). On the eight-hour day movement, see Cross, *Worktime and Industrialization.*

23. Brandeis, "Labor Legislation," 632.

24. Commons and Andrews, *The Principles of Labor Legislation,* 122. The British Trade Disputes Act did not prevent employers from hiring permanent replacements for striking workers, a practice that increased in the United States and in the U.K. in the 1980s; see Jeffrey A. Spector, "Replacement and Reinstatement of Strikers in the United States, Great Britain, and Canada," *Comparative Labor Law Journal* 13 (Winter 1992): 184–232.

25. The precise impact of court decisions on labor activities and the timing of that impact is contested by, among others, Victoria C. Hattam, *Labor Visions and State Power: The Origins of Business Unionism in the United States* (Princeton: Princeton University Press, 1993); and William Forbath, "The Shaping of the American Labor Movement,"

Harvard Law Review 102 (April 1989): 1111–256, and "Law and the Shaping of Labor Politics in the United States and England," in *Labor Law in America: Historical and Critical Essays,* ed. Christopher J. Tomlins and Andrew J. King, (Baltimore: Johns Hopkins University Press, 1992), 201–30.

26. Sanford M. Jacoby, "The Duration of Indefinite Employment Contracts in England and the United States: An Historical Analysis," *Comparative Labor Law* 5 (Winter 1982): 85–128; Felix Frankfurter and Nathan Greene, *The Labor Injunction* (New York: Macmillan, 1930).

27. Frankfurter and Green, *The Labor Injunction,* 165, appendixes I and II.

28. Ira Katznelson and Margaret Weir, *Schooling for All: Class, Race, and the Decline of the Democratic Ideal* (Berkeley: University of California Press, 1985), 150–77.

29. Bernard Elbaum, "Why Apprenticeship Persisted in Britain but Not in the United States," *Journal of Economic History* 49 (June 1989): 337–49.

30. Brandeis, "Labor Legislation," 581; Margaret S. Gordon, "Industrial Injuries Insurance in Europe and the British Commonwealth before World War II" and "Industrial Injuries Insurance in Europe and the British Commonwealth since World War II," in *Occupational Disability and Public Policy,* ed. Earl F. Cheit and Margaret Gordon (New York: John Wiley, 1963), 203, 224.

31. Brandeis, "Labor Legislation," 570; Flora and Alber, "Modernization, Democratization, and the Development of Welfare States in Western Europe," 59. The U.S. Social Security Act was amended to provide insurance against disability.

32. John R. Commons referred to organizational customs as the "working rules" of going concerns. The "repeated, duplicated and expected transactions of many individuals" is "another name for custom evolving into the working rules of organized concerns"; *Institutional Economics* (New York: Macmillan, 1934), 241–42.

33. William H. Riker, "Implications from the Disequilibrium of Majority Rule for the Study of Institutions" and "Comments and Replies" by Peter C. Ordeshook, Douglas W. Rae, and Riker, *American Political Science Review* 74 (June 1980): 432–58.

34. I do not claim that federal structures per se inherently impede redistributive policies or protective labor legislation. The argument here only pertains to American federalism. Many political scientists identify America's federal system as a key to its unique politics and public policy: Theodore J. Lowi, "Why Is There No Socialism in the United States? A Federal Analysis," in *The Costs of Federalism,* ed. Robert T. Golembiewski and Aaron Wildavsky (New Brunswick, N.J.: Transaction Press, 1984), 37–53; Robert Salisbury, "Why No Corporatism in America?" in *Trends toward Corporatist Intermediation,* ed. Philippe Schmitter and Gerhard Lembruch (Beverly Hills, Calif.; Sage, 1979); Morton Grodzins, *The American System: A New View of Government in the United States* (Chicago: Rand McNally, 1966), 254–60; Grant McConnell, *Private Power and American Democracy* (New York: Knopf, 1966), 178; James L. Sundquist, "A Comparison of Policy-Making Capacity in the United States and Five European Countries: The Case of Population Distribution," in *Population Policy Analysis,* ed. Michael E. Kraft and Mark Schneider (Lexington, Mass.: Lexington Books, 1978); David Brian Robertson and Dennis R. Judd, *The Development of American Public Policy: The Structure of Policy Restraint* (Glenview, Ill., and Boston: Scott Foresman/Little, Brown, 1989).

35. On interstate competition in the Progressive Era, see David A. Moss, *Socializing Security: Progressive-Era Economists and the Origins of American Social Policy* (Cambridge: Harvard University Press, 1996); William Graebner, "Federalism in the Progressive Era: A Structural Interpretation of Reform," *Journal of American History* 64 (September 1977); 351–77; David Brian Robertson, "The Bias of American Federalism: The Limits of Welfare State Development in the Progressive Era," *Journal of Policy History* 1 (1989): 261–91. For more contemporary perspectives, see Dennis O. Grady, "State Economic Development Incentives: Why Do States Compete?" *State and Local Government Review* 19 (Fall 1987): 86–94; Daphne A. Kenyon, *Interjurisdictional Tax and Policy Competition: Good or Bad for the Federal System?* (Washington, D.C.: Advisory Commission on Intergovernmental Relations, 1991); Daphne A. Kenyon and John Kincaid, eds., *Competition among State and Local Governments: Efficiency and Equity in American Federalism* (Washington, D.C.: Urban Institute, 1991).

36. In effect, the constitution imposed a free trade zone on semi-independent states. When nation-states are truly independent, they enjoy a full range of economic powers and can help business by erecting tariffs that shelter domestic business from foreign competition. European governments could compensate employers with tariff protections when their worker protection policies cut into business profits. If worker protections raised employer costs, higher tariffs could keep prices for foreign competitors' goods high as well. Thus, tariff protections could allow businesses to raise prices and pass these higher costs on to domestic consumers. European government officials, then, could expand protections for workers and employers simultaneously with a tacit "logrolling" agreement, uniting employers and workers by giving advantages to both. But American states lacked similar powers, and were helpless to compensate employers when they extended worker protections. Assistant Attorney General (and later Supreme Court Justice) Robert H. Jackson explained succinctly why American federalism made it so difficult to extend worker protections at the expense of employer autonomy:

> Let us assume each State as completely sovereign as a nation could be. No State would then have any right to send its goods into another State. Each State would have the right to stop all incoming goods at its borders, to exclude any goods unfairly competing in its own market, or to lay a tariff on those admitted to equalize any advantage that the incoming goods had over its own producers.... The exercise by the several States of their own parochial and conflicting rules to protect their own markets was a powerful incentive to formation of our Government.
>
> Each State, therefore, largely surrendered its sovereignty over incoming goods to the National Government. This was not intended to surrender the home market place to the under-cutting competitor States. The power was granted to the National Government that the rule of the market place should be fixed by a national policy for the common good.
>
> A State may wish to meet advancing wealth of production with advancing standards of life for those who work in production. But if its own market place, as well as outside markets, are overrun with goods cheapened by child labor or sweated labor it has lost its power over its own working conditions. Is it then confined to appeals to its competitors for protection from such unfair competition?

In Senate Committee on Education and Labor and House Committee on Labor, Joint Hearings on *Fair Labor Standards Act of 1937* (Washington, D.C.: GPO, 1937), 6–7.

37. A famous example is the editorial by William Allen White attacking populist state officials; see "What's the Matter with Kansas?" *Emporia Gazette*, August 15, 1896.

38. Louis Brandeis, dissent in *Liggett Co. v. Lee*, 288 U.S. 517 (1933).

39. In *Politics and Markets: The World's Political-Economic Systems* (New York: Basic, 1977), Charles E. Lindblom argues that private business enjoys special influence in the policy-making and implementation process by virtue of its contribution to economic prosperity, employment, and tax revenues (170–88). Neil J. Mitchell extensively reviews, critiques, and tests this assertion with survey data in *The Conspicuous Corporation: Business, Public Policy, and Representative Democracy* (Ann Arbor: University of Michigan Press, 1997).

40. Florence Kelley, "The Federal Government and the Working Children," *Annals* 27 (February 1906): 289–92. The staff of the U.S. Commission on Industrial Relations was preparing extensive and comprehensive research on the problem in 1914, but disagreement between the commission members and the research chief terminated much of this research in early 1915; see Alexander M. Daly, "Preliminary Report," in *Reports of the United States Commission on Industrial Relations, 1912–1915*, National Archives Microfilm Publication T4, Roll 13, U.S. National Archives, College Park, Maryland.

41. J. Lynn Barnard, *Factory Legislation in Pennsylvania: Its History and Administration* (Philadelphia: University of Pennsylvania, 1907), 18; Clara M. Beyer, *History of Labor Legislation for Women in Three States*, U.S. Department of Labor, Women's Bureau, Bulletin 66 (Washington, D.C.: GPO, 1929), 18–33; Fred Rogers Fairchild, *The Factory Legislation of the State of New York* (New York: American Economic Association, 1905), 45.

42. David Montgomery, *Beyond Equality: Labor and the Radical Republicans* (New York: Knopf, 1967), 312; Testimony of George Blair, in Senate Committee on Education and Labor, *Relations between Labor and Capital*, vol. 2: 40 (see also testimony of George M. Weston, vol. 1: 1059); Marion Cotter Cahill, *Shorter Hours: A Study of the Movement since the Civil War* (New York: Columbia University Press, 1932), 24–25.

43. *Congressional Record*, December 7, 1906: 173.

44. Susan Lehrer, *Origins of Protective Labor Legislation for Women, 1905–1925* (Albany: State University of New York Press, 1987), 209–10.

45. U.S. Industrial Commission, *Final Report*, 19 vols. (Washington, D.C.: GPO, 1902) 19: 922; *Congressional Record*, April 2, 1908: 4484; House Committee on Labor, *Child-Labor Bill*, Report No. 1400, 63rd Cong., 3rd sess. (February 13, 1915), 7–8; Elizabeth Davidson, *Child Labor Legislation in the Southern Textile States* (Chapel Hill: University of North Carolina Press, 1939), 55.

46. "Labor Legislation," 509; Vivian Hart, *Bound by Our Constitution: Women, Workers, and the Minimum Wage* (Princeton: Princeton University Press, 1994), 70.

47. Thomas I. Parkinson, "Problems and Progress of Workmen's Compensation Legislation, *American Labor Legislation Review* 1 (January 1911), 55–71; Weiss, "Employers' Liability and Workmen's Compensation," 600.

48. Robertson, "The Bias of American Federalism."

49. U.S. Industrial Commission, *Final Report*, 775.

50. "Business done in such States [with protective labor legislation for women] may be at an economic disadvantage when compared with States which have no such regulations"; *Hammer v. Dagenhart et al.* 247 U.S. 251 (June 3, 1918).

51. F. B. Gordon, "Georgia's Tempting Invitation to Mill-Man and Immigrant," *American Industries* 3, no. 2 (September 1, 1904): 13.

52. C. Vann Woodward, *Origins of the New South, 1877–1913* (Baton Rouge: Louisiana State University Press, 1951), 318–19.

53. Edward F. McSweeney, "New England's Opportunities and Needs," *American Industries* 17, vol. 7 (February 1917): 27. Mitchell discusses the conditions under which businesses "lose" policy battles in *The Conspicuous Corporation*.

54. Graebner, "Federalism in the Progressive Era: A Structural Interpretation of Reform"; Robertson, "The Bias of American Federalism."

55. Hattam, *Labor Visions and State Power*, 165; see also 139, 152.

56. Forbath, *Law and the Shaping of the American Labor Movement* (Cambridge: Harvard University Press, 1991), 7–8.

57. See also George Lovell, "The Ambiguities of Labor's Legislative Reforms in New York State in the Late Nineteenth Century," *Studies in American Political Development* 8 (1994): 81–102.

58. For arguments about the role of gender in the American labor market and public policy toward the labor market, see, among others, Alice Kessler-Harris, *Out to Work* (New York: Oxford University Press, 1982); Ava Baron, "Gender and Labor History: Learning from the Past, Looking to the Future," in *Work Engendered: Toward a New History of American Labor*, ed. Ava Baron (Ithaca, N.Y.: Cornell University Press, 1991), 1–46; Suzanne Mettler, *Dividing Citizens: Gender and Federalism in New Deal Public Policy* (Ithaca, N.Y.: Cornell University Press, 1998).

59. Hart, *Bound by Our Constitution*, xi.

60. Maurice Duverger, *Political Parties: Their Organization and Activity in the Modern State* (London: Methuen, 1964 [1951]); Anthony Downs, *An Economic Theory of Democracy* (New York: Harper and Row, 1957), 128.

61. David Montgomery, *The Fall of the House of Labor: The Workplace, the State, and American Labor Activism, 1865–1925* (New York: Cambridge University Press, 1987).

62. Gary Marks, *Unions in Politics: Britain, Germany, and the United States in the Nineteenth and Early Twentieth Centuries* (Princeton: Princeton University Press, 1989), 120–94.

63. Everett M. Kassalow, *Trade Unions and Industrial Relations: An International Comparison* (New York: Random House, 1969), 9–10; Martin Shefter, *Political Parties and the State: The American Historical Experience* (Princeton: Princeton University Press, 1994), 101–68; Marks, *Unions in Politics*, 73.

64. Duverger, *Political Parties*, 22–23; see also Werner Sombart, *Why Is There No Socialism in the United States?* (London: Macmillan, 1976); Giovanni Sartori, *Parties and Party Systems: A Framework for Analysis* (New York: Cambridge University Press, 1976), 1; Seymour Martin Lipset, *American Exceptionalism: A Double-Edged Sword* (New York: Norton, 1997).

65. The number of union members in Britain has been estimated at six hundred thousand in 1859, eight hundred thousand in 1867, and 1.6 million in 1876; W. Hamish Fraser, *Trade Unions and Society: The Struggle for Acceptance, 1850–1880* (Totowa, N.J.: Rowman and Littlefield, 1974), 16.

66. Montgomery, *The Fall of the House of Labor*, 269.

67. Sanford M. Jacoby, "American Exceptionalism Revisited: The Importance of Management," in *Masters to Managers: Historical and Comparative Perspectives on American Employers,* ed. Sanford Jacoby (New York: Columbia University Press, 1991), 173–200; Christopher Tomlins, *The State and the Unions: Labor Relations, Law and the Organized Labor Movement in America, 1880–1960* (New York: Cambridge University Press, 1985); Kassalow, *Trade Unions and Industrial Relations*; John T. Dunlop, "Have the 1980's Changed U.S. Industrial Relations?" *Monthly Labor Review* 11 (May 1988): 29–34.

68. John P. Heinze, Edward O. Laumann, Robert L. Nelson, and Robert H. Salisbury make a similar point in *The Hollow Core: Private Interests in National Policymaking* (Cambridge: Harvard University Press, 1993), 308:

> the government apparatus is less powerful in the United States and is thus less able to modify the groups' perceptions of self-interest. Note that we are not arguing that European governments function as neutral mediators. Rather, we believe that they act as major players in political struggles. But the power of the European governments may be sufficient to alter the calculations of advantage of the business and labor interest aggregations, so that they perceive mutual benefit in a settlement of the policy issues.

Colleen A. Dunlavy examines this development in *Politics and Industrialization: Early Railroads in the United States and Prussia* (Princeton: Princeton University Press, 1994).

69. Martin J. Sklar, *The Corporate Reconstruction of American Capitalism, 1890–1916: The Market, the Law, and Politics* (Cambridge: Cambridge University Press, 1988), 164–65; quote, 168.

70. Tony Freyer, *Regulating Big Business: Antitrust in Great Britain and America, 1880–1990* (Cambridge: Cambridge University Press, 1992), 7–9.

71. Jacoby, "American Exceptionalism Revisited"; note the parallel between Jacoby's emphasis on business and the emphasis given by Castles and others to the strength of the conservative opposition in explaining social welfare policy. For both, it is the strength or weakness of anti-reform forces, not the strength or weakness of pro-reform forces, that determines outcomes. Jacoby's study, however, does not extend to *policy* outcomes. For a more local perspective on the impact of employer opposition on the Knights of Labor, see Kim Voss, *The Making of American Exceptionalism: The Knights of Labor and Class Formation in the Nineteenth Century* (Ithaca, N.Y.: Cornell University Press, 1993).

72. James Weinstein, "The Problems of the Socialist Party before World War I," in *Failure of a Dream? Essays in the History of American Socialism*, ed. John H. M. Laslett and Seymour Martin Lipset (Garden City, N.Y.: Anchor, 1974), 332–34.

73. *Congressional Quarterly's Guide to U.S. Elections*, 2nd ed. (Washington, D.C.: Congressional Quarterly, 1985), 347–48; Peter Flora, *State, Economy, and Society in Western Europe 1815–1975* (Frankfurt: Campus Verlag, 1983), 151.

74. J. Morgan Kousser, *The Shaping of Southern Politics: Suffrage Restrictions and the Establishment of the One-Party South, 1880–1910* (New Haven, Conn.: Yale University Press, 1974).

75. Francis Castles, *The Working Class and Welfare*, 83.

76. A. John Williamson and Fred C. Pampel, *Old Age Security in Comparative Perspective* (New York: Oxford University Press, 1993), 23–24; Christopher Pierson, *Beyond the Welfare State?* (College Park: Pennsylvania State University Press, 1991), 109.

77. Montgomery, *The Fall of the House of Labor*, 167.

78. Kousser, *The Shaping of Southern Politics*, 12–13. Additional research on the relationship between federalism and American political parties includes Grodzins, *The American System: A New View of Government in the United States*; William H. Riker, *Federalism: Origin, Operation, Significance* (Boston: Little, Brown, 1964); David B. Truman, "Federalism and the Party System," in *Federalism: Mature and Emergent,* ed. Arthur Macmahon (New York: Columbia University Press, 1962), 115–36.

79. Richard Oestreicher, "Urban Working Class Political Behavior and Theories of American Electoral Politics, 1870–1940," *Journal of American History* 74 (1988): 1257–86.

80. Kenneth Janda, "The American Constitutional Framework and the Structure of American Political Parties," in *The Constitution and American Political Development: An Institutional Perspective*, ed. Peter F. Nardulli (Urbana: University of Illinois Press, 1992), 179–206.

81. Marks, *Unions in Politics,* 220.

82. On the importance of the cooperation of farmers and workers in advancing reforms in this period, see Elizabeth Sanders, *Roots of Reform: Farmers, Workers, and the State, 1877–1917* (Chicago: University of Chicago Press, 1999).

83. James L. Sundquist, *Dynamics of the Party System: Alignment and Realignment of Political Parties in the United States*, 2nd ed. (Washington, D.C.: Brookings, 1983); V. O. Key Jr., *American State Politics: An Introduction* (New York: Knopf, 1955), 51.

84. Richard Franklin Bensel, *Sectionalism and American Political Development, 1880–1980* (Madison: University of Wisconsin Press, 1984).

85. Stephen Skowronek, *Building a New American State: The Expansion of National Administrative Capacities, 1877–1920* (Cambridge: Cambridge University Press, 1982).

86. Kathryn Kish Sklar, "Two Political Cultures in the Progressive Era: The National Consumers' League and the American Association for Labor Legislation," in *U.S. History as Women's History: New Feminist Essays*, ed. Linda A. Kerber, Alice Kessler-Harris, and Kathryn Kish Sklar (Chapel Hill: University of North Carolina Press), 51, 59.

87. Daniel T. Rogers, *Atlantic Crossings: Social Politics in a Progressive Age* (Cambridge: Belknap, 1998), 155–56.

88. U.S. Commission on Industrial Relations, *Final Report and Testimony,* 64th Cong., 1st sess., Senate Doc. 415 (Washington, D.C.: GPO, 1915), 221–26.

2

LABOR AND REGULATION,
1865–1900

Senator William Henry Blair (R, New Hampshire): "Here is this
law, more than a dozen years old, still on the statute-book . . . and
yet not only is its principle not adopted among the people at large,
but even the Government itself fails to enforce its own edict."

Samuel Gompers: "It is a very peculiar Government in that
respect."

—U.S. Senate Hearings on the Relations between Capital and
Labor, 1883[1]

In the late nineteenth century, American labor leaders above all demanded
simple, clear, public regulations on employers' unlimited control of employment and the work environment. Workers frequently and intensely lobbied
public officials to limit hours and improve working conditions. Labor nominally
succeeded. Despite determined opposition, American legislatures enacted many
laws regulating hours, factories, mines, and the work of women and children.

In practice, however, these regulations bitterly disappointed many labor
leaders. Laws that established eight hours as the legal workday did not benefit
workers materially. Few states put serious effort into enforcing laws limiting the
work of women and children. Illinois enacted a very ambitious law regulating
sweatshops, but when officials tried to enforce it, the state courts nullified it.

Such experiences taught American Federation of Labor (AFL) leaders,
notably President Samuel Gompers, that they could not rely on American government for help in rolling back employers' labor market prerogatives. American policymaking institutions made the legislative route to worker protection
slow, expensive, and highly uncertain. Lobbying demanded scarce resources as
well as vigilance. Public officials sometimes failed or refused to implement reg-

ulations effectively. Courts sometimes refused to validate these regulations when employers challenged them. Labor conditions prohibited on one side of a state border often could continue unregulated on the other side of the border. American government, in short, could not make a credible commitment to protect American workers. Shorter hours, better pay, and safer workplaces could be achieved more effectively, AFL leaders came to believe, through direct trade union confrontation with employers and the establishment of union shops.

TRADE UNIONS' EXPERIMENTS
WITH GOVERNMENT PROTECTION

As the Union subdued the Confederacy, American workers' fight for shorter hours and better working conditions was becoming more focused and organized.[2] Trade unions became the dominant force pressing for labor regulation in the late nineteenth century. Like unions abroad, American unions sought shorter hours and better working conditions through union–employer agreements, not legislation.

American unions pursued the eight-hour day and other goals as aggressively as their European comrades. Massive railroad strikes in 1877 paralyzed much of the American transportation system. A general strike for the eight-hour day on May 1, 1886, conservatively involved nearly two hundred thousand strikers and one hundred fifty thousand demonstrators nationwide. Acrimonious strikes in Coeur d'Alene, Idaho; Homestead, Pennsylvania; and against the Pullman company flared in the 1890s. Between 1891 and 1900, nearly twenty-three thousand strikes occurred in the United States. Strikes involved slightly more American than British workers in these years, and far more American workers than German, French, or Italian workers.[3]

American unions used militant tactics similar to those employed by German unions.[4] American labor organized consumer boycotts of recalcitrant employers' products, for example. Citing American workers' militancy, some European Marxists viewed the United States as the home of the world's most advanced labor movement. Friedrich Engels introduced an American edition of *The Condition of the Working Class in England* in 1887 with an enthusiastic note about the advanced state of American class consciousness relative to that in Europe. Eduard Bernstein believed in 1890 that the United States confirmed the Marxist belief that the advance of capitalism brought about modern socialism.[5]

In the mid-1860s, the 1880s, and the late 1890s, American union membership surged. Local trade unions created by carpenters, cigar-makers, typographers, and other crafts workers joined regional and national craft associations. Twenty-nine national craft unions existed at the end of the 1870s, seventy-nine at the end of the 1880s, and one hundred and twenty by the turn of the century.[6] In many cities, building trades councils organized workers in the construction trades. Broad city labor assemblies included workers in diverse local industries.[7] State labor federations, organized to lobby state legislatures, originated in New York (Workingmen's Assembly of the State of New York) in 1865. State labor federations emerged in New Jersey and Massachusetts in 1879; in Illinois, Indiana, Connecticut, and Michigan in the 1880s; and in rest of the industrialized states by 1904.[8]

Trade unions struggled to create an overarching national organization. The National Labor Union (NLU) of the immediate post–Civil War years marked the first such effort. The NLU, however, dissolved in the economic downturn of the 1870s. The Knights of Labor's membership peaked at nearly three-quarters of a million in the mid-1880s before it, too, faded in the 1890s.[9] The Federation of Organized Trades and Labor Unions (FOTLU), renamed the American Federation of Labor in 1886, clearly emerged as the leading national voice of organized labor by the 1890s. The AFL represented over a million workers by 1901.[10]

Labor's policy agenda in this period seems somewhat unfocused and mercurial at first glance. Disputes about tactics and priorities cleaved many unions. Some workers favored "pure and simple" unionism that shunned political activity. Others insisted on the necessity of an independent labor party. Some pressed for socialism, others for the greenback, single-tax, or populist programs.[11]

Though labor leaders disagreed among themselves about political philosophy, they agreed that government should enforce specific public regulations when direct economic pressure could not protect workers.[12] The NLU of the 1860s, the Knights of Labor and the AFL each pursued a similar policy agenda: the eight-hour day; public bureaus of labor; and an end to competition from convict labor and immigrants, particularly Chinese contract labor.[13] AFL leaders opposed forming an independent labor party with a coherent and encompassing worker rights platform,[14] but they consistently supported specific regulations in convention speeches and testimony before congressional committees. AFL president Samuel Gompers apparently did not view legislative lobbying as inconsistent with "pure and simple" economic unionism (in contrast to the creation of an independent labor party) and may have equated the two.[15]

More important, individual state labor organizations often pursued very ambitious political agendas that went well beyond the national AFL leadership. For example, the New Jersey Federation of Trades and Labor Unions conducted forceful campaigns of legislative endorsements and pressure for factory laws. The Illinois State Federation of Labor in the 1890s called for laws establishing compulsory education, direct legislation, the eight-hour day, sanitary workshop inspection, the abolition of "sweating," municipal ownership of utilities, the nationalization of railroads, and "collective ownership of the means of production and distribution."[16]

Legislatures often responded favorably to this lobbying. States enacted laws restricting hours and immigrant and convict labor, as well as statutes regulating factories, railroads, mines, and private employment offices. Many legislators had good reason to vote for these laws. In this era of intense party competition, labor votes could provide them a decisive electoral margin. Legislators who voted for labor legislation gambled that gains in labor support could offset the loss of business support.[17]

Figure 2.1 illustrates the substantial amount of state legislation produced in this period. The figure represents the number of each of eight types of state labor

Figure 2.1: State Labor Market Policy Enactments, 1865–1900

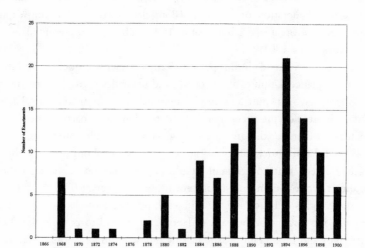

Sources: General eight-hour laws: John R. Commons and John B. Andrews, *The Principles of Labor Legislation* (New York: Harper and Brothers, 1916), 229 and discussion in this chapter, below. *Eight-hour laws on public works, arbitration, and anti-yellow-dog contract laws:* U.S. Industrial Commission, *Labor Legislation,* vol. 5 (Washington, D.C.: Government Printing Office, 1900), 5, 25, 128; U.S. Bureau of Labor, Second Special Report of the Commissioner of Labor, *Labor Laws of the United States,* 2nd ed. (Washington, D.C.: GPO, 1896), passim. *Factory inspection:* W. F. Willoughby, *The Inspection of Factories and Workshops in the United States,* U.S. Department of Labor, Bulletin 12, (Washington, D.C.: GPO, 1897); U.S. Industrial Commission, *Labor Legislation. Bureaus of labor statistics:* U.S. Bureau of Labor, Bulletin 54, *Bureaus of Labor in the United States,* (Washington, D.C.: GPO, 1904), 994–99. *State public employment offices:* J. E. Conner, *Free Public Employment Offices in the United States,* U.S. Bureau of Labor Statistics, Bulletin 68 (Washington, D.C.: 1907). *Employers' liability laws:* Robert Asher, "Failure and Fulfillment: Agitation for Employers' Liability Legislation and the Origins of Workmen's Compensation in New York State, 1876–1910," *Labor History* 24 (Spring 1983): 198–222.

laws enacted during biennial periods (roughly corresponding with legislative sessions) from 1865 to 1900. The statutes include laws declaring eight hours the legal workday, eight hours as the legal workday on state government work, bureaus of labor statistics, public employment offices, factory inspectors, trade union incorporation, state arbitration laws, and limitations on employers' liability defenses.

The drop-off after the 1893–94 biennium reflects the saturation of some of these statutes in states with substantial labor organization and the shift in agenda to other legislative reforms (such as the eight-hour day for specific occupations). Legislative activity and union militancy subsided as the national economy slumped in 1893.

Labor leaders themselves moved in and out of government with remarkable facility. They helped forge new American labor regulations when in office. In a sample of ninety-six labor leaders prominent in the period from 1860 to 1875, historian David Montgomery found that forty-four served as officials of labor reform parties or stood as candidates for elective office. Historian Leon Fink estimated that Knights of Labor candidates ran in one hundred eighty-nine cities and towns in thirty-four states between 1885 and 1888. The Knights took credit for the election of a dozen U.S. representatives in 1886. Terence V. Powderly served most of his six-year tenure as the mayor of Scranton, Pennsylvania, while also leading the Knights of Labor from 1879 to 1893. Powderly sought the position of first commissioner of labor statistics when the federal bureau was created. Powderly became commissioner of immigration (1897–1902) and head of the Immigration Bureau's Division of Information in 1907. Voters elected Eugene Debs as Terre Haute, Indiana, city clerk and as an Indiana state legislator before he assumed the leadership of the American Railway Union in the 1890s. Trade union leaders often became leaders in state labor bureaus (see chapter 3).[18]

Organized labor, then, counted on protective labor legislation as a fallback position for economic pressure. American legislators often responded positively to labor's demands. American government's structure, however, enabled determined opponents of legislation to neutralize it in other arenas. The campaign for eight-hour legislation illustrates how the results of its policy efforts embittered many American labor leaders.

THE EIGHT-HOUR DAY:
THE "QUESTION OF QUESTIONS"[19]

By the end of the Civil War, unions made the eight-hour day the central goal of organizing drives in the United States and abroad. Shorter hours persisted into the twentieth century as a predominant labor demand.[20] The leaders of embryonic labor organizations who gathered in Baltimore in 1866 to founded a national labor union all advocated "the enactment of a law making 'eight hours' a legal day's work by the national Congress and the several state legislatures, and the election of men pledged to sustain and represent the interests of the industrial classes."[21] *Fincher's Trades' Review*, then the most widely read American labor newspaper, carried the eight-hour demand on its masthead. Despite their rivalry in the 1880s, both the AFL and the Knights of Labor agreed on the centrality of the goal of the eight-hour day.

The eight-hour goal inspired unprecedented labor lobbying. State and local Eight-Hour Leagues, roused by labor leaders such as the Massachusetts machinist Ira Steward, his associate George McNeill, and Detroit Trades Assembly president Richard Trevellick, organized workers explicitly with the goal of shorter hours. As early as 1863, the Boston Trades Assembly and Steward, a member of the Machinist's and Blacksmith's International Union, campaigned for an eight-hour law in Massachusetts. The goal of an eight-hour day sparked the creation of the New York Workingmen's Assembly, the nation's first state-level labor federation.[22]

Labor pressure put the issue on the policy agenda. The Grand Eight-Hour League of Massachusetts successfully lobbied for the creation in 1865 of a Massachusetts legislative committee to investigate an eight-hour law. The following year, several state legislatures seriously weighed the eight-hour legislation demanded by workers. The lower house of the state legislatures in Pennsylvania, Ohio, and California passed eight-hour bills, but supporters could not win final legislative approval.[23]

In 1867 and 1868, intense trade union pressure had stimulated legislatures to pass the world's first eight-hour laws. Seven states and the national government enacted laws making eight hours a legal day's work when no contract set a different workday.[24] William Jessup, president of the state Workingmen's Assembly, led the legislative battle for New York's eight-hour law of 1867. The vice president of Connecticut's branch of the National Labor Union played a leading role in securing that state's law the same year. Indiana's state Eight-Hour League influenced the Democratic Party to include a plank in the party platform endorsing an eight-hour law. California trades unions petitioned and lobbied for that state's law.[25]

Legislators and newspapers readily acknowledged labor's influence in enacting these laws. In leading congressional debate in favor of the eight-hour law for federal employees in 1868, Senator Thomas Hendricks (D, Indiana) said that "I have supported this measure because in very large numbers the working men of the United States have petitioned Congress for it."[26] In the same year, the San Francisco Trades Union lobbyist reported that the average state legislator believed that "If they [the laboring people] were satisfied that the bill would benefit them he would vote to let them try it."[27] The *New York Times*, which opposed the laws vigorously, credited "agents of working-men's associations . . . in some half-dozen States" with "getting [these] Laws passed."[28]

Two kinds of evidence support the contention that these laws constituted substantial legislative victories. First, labor leaders passionately defended their importance.[29] Even in 1883, Samuel Gompers refused to concede that the 1867 federal law was a meaningless gesture. The law would "set an example to be imitated by private employers, to be requested by the employed, to be agitated for, to be organized for, to be attained." Asked if private employers would be much influenced by such "sentimental considerations," Gompers responded, "Probably not at all; but I know that a good many employees would."[30] Gompers' call to the Knights of Labor to join in the AFL's general strike for the eight-hour day on May 1, 1890, was couched in terms of the "enforcement of the 8-hour rule."[31]

The laws seemed to inspire workers to demand the eight-hour day. In 1867 and in the mid-1880s, workers demonstrated and struck for the eight-hour day on May 1, the effective date of the 1867 Illinois and Missouri laws.[32] In the 1880s, Ohio, Michigan, and Indiana enacted hours laws nearly identical to those of 1867–68 despite the laws' status as "dead letters" in neighboring states. Ohio's eight-hour law, enacted in April 1886, spurred Cincinnati workers militantly to demand an eight-hour working day. In 1890, many union locals in New York state still supported the eight-hour day law.[33]

A second reason for concluding that the eight-hour laws mattered is the intensity with which employers and their allies opposed the laws. Employers resisted demands for shorter hours more fervently than demands for higher pay. Hours mandates imposed more limitations on workplace control than wage demands. Paying workers the same wages for a shorter workday threatened profit margins. A shorter and more regular workday reduced employer discretion in the use of workers' time, forced investment in new machinery, or required the buildup of inventories.[34] Legislative battles in California, New York, and Massachusetts indicate that employers and economic conservatives took the eight-hour laws very seriously. Ten years after the enactment of the New York eight-hour law, the New York state legislature took the law seriously enough to attempt to repeal it. Gompers took the law seriously enough to rally unionists "to avert that catastrophe."[35]

Though labor leaders successfully overcame employers' resistance and won the enactment of these laws, American political institutions frustrated their efforts to make the laws effective. Loopholes, poor implementation, and adverse court decisions made these laws ineffectual.

First, legislators had included loopholes that made each of the eight-hour laws unenforceable. The laws permitted longer hours when the employer and worker agreed. Employers generally viewed an agreement to work longer hours as implicit in every hiring decision. Labor had intended to shorten hours without cutting pay. When confronted by demands to abide by the laws, employers frequently threatened to cut pay along with hours and to switch to hourly, rather than daily, pay schedules. In the late 1860s unions in New York and Pennsylvania tried to persuade state legislatures to remove the loophole permitting contracts for more than eight hours (at least without overtime pay). These legislatures, however, refused to make the laws enforceable.[36]

Second, public officials often refused to implement the laws effectively. New York and California, where labor movements constituted an unusually strong constituency for the laws, offered striking lessons in the difficulty of enforcement. New York's Governor Reuben E. Fenton refused to direct state administrators to enforce the 1867 law despite the support of the Workingmen's Assembly. The governor explained his refusal by stating that such laws were "obligatory by their nature." The San Francisco city council in 1867 enacted an eight-hour ordinance for workers under city contract. When the Mechanics' State Council demanded the enforcement of the San Francisco law, however, the city attorney claimed that "the city is not a party to the contracts made by the Superintendent of Streets." When the superintendent of streets finally stipulated an eight-hour day in city contracts, contractors sued for a restraining order. The California Supreme Court obliged, holding that the laws "permitted a workday of more than eight hours when such an agreement had been entered into by the employer and his employees." (The state acted to remedy the problem in 1870 by declaring that no work on state buildings should be done under contract.[37])

The federal government's failure to enforce the eight-hour law for its own employees may have given labor its most embittering experience with the legislative route to worker protection (as the quotation opening this chapter indicates). Federal officials repeatedly refused to enforce this most visible of the American eight-hour laws of 1867. The attorney general equivocated on whether pay would be cut for those working eight-hour days. The War Department permitted wage cuts to coincide with shorter hours at federal arsenals and navy yards. In 1869 and in 1872, President Ulysses S. Grant issued proclamations that reduced hours should not result in wage cuts. These proclamations, however, had very limited impact.[38] In 1892, Congress enacted a new federal eight-hour bill with more explicit enforcement provisions. The War Department and the Corps of Engineers, however, interpreted the law in a way that exempted them from its provisions. These officials constructed the Panama Canal in violation of the law and despite the protests of the AFL.[39] When the House unanimously passed a new bill in 1898 to guarantee enforcement of the eight-hour law, the bill died in the Senate. Gompers later recounted the political tricks used to defeat the measure.[40]

Third, the courts often eviscerated these statutes when employers challenged them. In 1868, the Connecticut Supreme Court rendered that state's eight-hour law ineffective. The Connecticut court interpreted the law to mean that a worker could go home at the end of eight hours, provided that he did not agree to work longer and that the employer did not ask him to stay. A worker who sued for overtime under the federal executive order lost his appeal to the U.S. Supreme Court in 1876. In this case, the Court effectively nailed shut the coffin of the federal eight-hour law by concluding that workers implicitly contracted for longer hours by performing a particular federal job. An 1891 Nebraska eight-hour law eliminated the contract loophole by requiring employers to double workers' pay for any time over eight hours. The Nebraska Supreme Court quickly struck down this approach.[41]

Lawmaking and implementation, however, rather than judicial interpretation, had more impact on the eight-hour laws' ineffectiveness. Courts did not always uphold the employer in disputes over eight-hour laws. The courts supported narrower and more clearly written eight-hour laws of the late nineteenth century. When the post office evaded a federal eight-hour statute of 1888 by counting only time spent in carrying the mail, the Supreme Court upheld a strict interpretation of the statute. In 1899, a U.S. District Court fined a contractor five hundred dollars for violating the provisions of the federal eight-hour law. This decision invited federal administrators to take a more aggressive role in enforcing the law.[42]

These difficulties with the American policymaking process induced workers to narrow the scope of their demands. Labor lobbying resulted in thirteen states enacting laws limiting hours on public works under contract from state government.[43] States also enacted laws limiting hours for specific occupations. Several limited the workday on street railways,[44] on railroads,[45] and in mines.[46] The federal government enacted laws in 1888 limiting hours for postal workers and for the public printer.[47] Courts generally upheld these laws. In *Holden v. Hardy* (1898), the landmark case that upheld Utah's hour law for miners, the Court recognized that workers had less bargaining power than employers and that laws could rectify that bargaining inequality.[48]

By 1900, it was clear that *some* workers could win the eight-hour day in some industries in some states. It also was clear that labor could win the eight-hour day more easily by directly bargaining with employers than by depending on government legislation. Factory legislation was confirming organized labor's skepticism about government.

REGULATING WORKING CONDITIONS
FOR WOMEN AND CHILDREN

In the nineteenth century, many women and children worked long hours for little pay in dangerous and unhealthy workshops. One in eight boys between the ages of ten and fifteen worked for pay in the United States in 1890. So did one in six females. Textile mills in the South and sweatshops in the North particularly depended on these workers.[49]

The exploitation of women and children in the workplace induced female workers and middle-class reformers to demand legislative protection. Female textile workers had taken the initiative in petitioning state legislators for hours restrictions in the 1840s, and thereafter they played a more autonomous role in the drive for hours limitation than did their British counterparts.[50] Factory, mill, and tenement work hurt children physically, mentally, and morally. Unsanitary and dangerous conditions threatened women's health. The low wages received by women created a host of social temptations and ills that appalled moral sensibilities.[51] Female employment inevitably became complicated by the common assumption that males should earn the family wage and play the role of breadwinner. Regulation of female employment, then, became enmeshed in ambivalence about the desirability of women's participation in the labor market.

Trade unions backed public regulation of working conditions for women and children for several reasons. Inhumane working conditions tapped unions' reflexive demand for worker protection. Exploitation of women and children undermined unions' economic power—underpaid and overworked women and children were hard to unionize. Male craftsmen protested the unfair competitive advantage enjoyed by the employers of these workers.[52] Laws regulating hours for women and children could create an opening wedge for inclusive limitations on hours. In effect, "women's petticoats" could advance the cause of the universal eight-hour day. Laws regulating hours for women and children also could buttress eight-hour contracts that male craft unions had obtained through collective bargaining.[53]

Trade unions played an indispensable role in securing these factory laws in the industrial states, including Massachusetts, New York, and Illinois.[54] Support for the Massachusetts landmark factory act of 1879 sprang directly from the eight-hour movement. This law marked the nation's first enforceable factory act. Hundreds of eight- to fourteen-year-old children worked eleven-hour days in the textile mills of Fall River, Massachusetts, at the end of the Civil War. The state's 1866 investigating commission called child labor "the most marked and inexcusable evil" it uncovered. In the wake of demonstrated public support, the lower house of the state legislature approved a ten-hour limitation for female and child workers in 1871, 1872, and 1873. The state senate refused to concur until proponents accepted a weaker version in 1874 (the penalty would apply only if the employer "willfully" broke the law). Massachusetts courts upheld the law in 1876. Only in 1879 did the legislature make the law enforceable by removing the loophole term "willfully" and by authorizing the hire of factory inspectors. Efforts to tighten these limits continued at a glacial pace. The state limited the workday to fifty-eight hours for these workers in 1892 and fifty-six hours in 1908.[55]

New York's Workingmen's Assembly initiated demands for limits on women's hours in that state. The New York Society for the Prevention of Cruelty to Children and public health advocates independently mounted a reform effort aimed at child labor. In the 1870s the child labor reform lobby crafted a bill that was passed by the state senate but ultimately defeated in the lower house. The state bureau of labor statistics, in effect a vehicle for policy agenda of the Workingmen's Assembly, helped break the impasse. The Workingmen's Assembly requested that the labor commissioner investigate child labor and recommend a factory law covering both women and children. Intense electoral competition in New York in the mid-1880s helped motivate candidates to embrace proposed factory legislation. The New York factory law won unanimous approval in the legislature in 1886. It banned children under thirteen from working in manufacturing. It also limited men under eighteen and women under twenty-one to a sixty-hour workweek. The law, however, included a loophole requiring that law breaking occur "knowingly" (comparable to the original Massachusetts statute). It provided for only two inspectors to monitor over forty-two thousand establishments covered by the law.

New York's factory inspectors became active lobbyists for tighter factory regulations after 1886. In 1889, 1890, 1892, and 1896, amendments recommended by the factory inspectors expanded the law's coverage and tightened enforcement.[56] In 1895 pressure from the New York Working Women's Society, the New York City Consumers' League, and state factory inspectors resulted in the appointment of a new investigating committee. This coalition successfully lobbied to extend labor regulations to mercantile establishments.[57] The factory inspectors also played the lead role in the 1899 New York law that finally limited hours for adult women in factories. Trade union support had prompted Governor Theodore Roosevelt to endorse the measure in 1899.[58]

The Chicago Women's Clubs originated the drive for the Illinois Factory Act of 1893, the most ambitious nineteenth-century regulatory law in the United States. Illinois, like other states, had enacted unenforceable statutes in

1877 and 1891 that limited child labor in places other than mines. The reformer Florence Kelley directed the battle for a broader, enforceable anti-sweatshop law in 1893. The Chicago Trades and Labor Assembly worked with the Illinois Women's Alliance, a coalition that included women's labor organizations, suffragettes, church groups, and professional organizations to support enactment. Though reformers led the battle in Illinois, Kelley herself credited labor unions for providing the political muscle necessary to ensure legislative success. When Governor John Peter Altgeld appointed Kelley as the state's chief factory inspector, it seemed that the Illinois law would be enforced more vigorously than any other such regulation. Kelley and her inspectors were determined to implement the law aggressively. The state's manufacturers, however, challenged the law in court. The Illinois Supreme Court struck down the law in *Ritchie v. The People* (1895). The Illinois legislature enacted a new child labor law in 1897 but did not enact new restrictions on women's hours until 1909.[59]

By 1899, twenty states had enacted laws limiting the hours that women worked in factories. Twenty-eight states had enacted some protection for child wage earners. Massachusetts, New York, Illinois, Connecticut, and Indiana set a minimum age of fourteen for workforce participation, a limit identical to that in Great Britain and Germany. Twenty-five states complemented these laws with compulsory school attendance requirements.[60]

Effective factory laws depended on a force of qualified factory inspectors. These inspectors could investigate conditions, enforce the laws, and advocate the expansion and strengthening of the laws. Factory inspectors worked closely with trade unionists, who acted as monitors for industrial conditions. In New Jersey, Lawrence Fell, appointed as first state factory inspector in 1883, collaborated with labor leader Joseph Patrick McDonnell and the state federation of labor to push labor's reform agenda.[61]

Most states did not provide for effective factory inspection, however. By the 1910s, a leading American expert in the field described the inferior quality of American factory inspection: "the rank and file of European inspectors are far above the rank and file of our own inspectors" because of merit selection and professional training. American inspectors often were poorly trained, poorly paid, and subject to frequent removal from office when elected executives changed.[62] By the end of the century, only sixteen states provided for any factory inspectors. Even where the states authorized factory inspectors, the task far exceeded their numbers. Kelley thought that five hundred inspectors were necessary to police Illinois factories, if tenement manufacturing were abolished. New York's thirty-seven factory inspectors could check less than one-third of the state's factories in 1900.[63]

GOMPERS'S LESSON IN GOVERNMENT UNRELIABILITY

Trade unions' experiences with hours and factory legislation were teaching labor leaders that they could not rely on America's fragmented government to shore up their labor market position. The most important of those leaders, AFL president Samuel Gompers, had absorbed the lesson of American government unreliability during his own union's campaign against tenement house cigar production in New York City. In a chapter of his autobiography describing these efforts (tellingly, titled "Learning Something of Legislation"), Gompers narrated the tortuous and ultimately elusive effort to enlist government against tenement employers. Several authors today point to this case as a decisive moment because of its effect on Gompers's view of government.[64]

The manufacture of cigars in tenements in New York City posed a growing threat to Gompers's Cigar Makers' International Union (CMIU) in the 1870s. The union began to campaign against tenement cigar production. Efforts to enlist government help in this campaign immediately proved frustrating. Gompers and CMIU president Adolph Strasser tried to persuade the New York City health commissioner to close the tenement shops. This approach failed. In 1879, Gompers and Strasser lobbied the U.S. Congress to authorize a tax on tenement house manufacture. This effort succeeded in the House of Representatives, but the Senate narrowly rejected the tax on a 28-to-25 vote.

The CMIU leaders next began to lobby New York's state lawmakers for relief. Despite union support for sympathetic legislative candidates, the state legislature rejected bills to ban tenement house manufacture in New York City in 1880, 1881, and 1882. In the last case, a bill approved by the Senate was stolen from the desk of the assembly clerk before its final reading. In 1883, the legislation passed, and the governor finally signed it.

The new law only applied to tenement house cigar making in New York City, however. Its limited reach prompted some tenement house cigar manufacturers to abandon the city in favor of unregulated Brooklyn and Long Island. When the cigar makers themselves undertook to detect violations of the law, some employers remaining in the city challenged the statute in court. The New York Court of Appeals ruled the law unconstitutional in 1883. The legislature reenacted the law in 1884, and the appeals court struck it down again as an interference with property rights.

This final exasperating obstacle, according to Gompers, convinced him that legislative protection of workers was futile. Self-reliance, or "organization work," offered the only effective means of worker protection under American circumstances.[65]

After the Appeals Court declared against the principle of the [second] law, we talked over the possibilities of further legislative action and decided to concentrate on organization work. Through our trade unions we harassed the manufacturers by strikes and agitation until they were convinced that . . . it would be less costly for them to abandon the tenement manufacturing system and carry on the industry in factories under decent conditions. Thus we accomplished through economic power what we had failed to achieve through legislation.[66]

This crucial case illustrates the many structural impediments that convinced American labor leaders that government could not offer workers reliable protection. It gave the most influential American labor leaders a powerful motive to design a worker protection strategy based on union self-reliance and to minimize dependence on government.

POLICYMAKING INSTITUTIONS
AND LABOR REGULATION

American governments, at least those in the nation's industrial regions, nominally enacted labor regulations that addressed the highest priorities of organized labor's nineteenth-century policy agenda. Despite the enormous time and effort that unions invested in them, however, these legislative victories did not result in effective worker protection policy. As John B. Lennon, the tailors' union leader and AFL treasurer, put it, "If one half of these [current] laws were enforced, the condition of the wage earners would be fairly good; but this, unfortunately, is not the case."[67] The leaders of organized labor became greatly disenchanted with legislative effort because the institutional policy obstacles identified in chapter 1 taught them to discount legislative assistance in their battle with employers.

The Constricted Policy Agenda

In this period, policymakers took for granted that the limited jurisdiction of the national government prevented it from regulating most workplaces. Constitutional limits were more than a convenient fiction that judges erected to advance their philosophical views. Few questioned the assumption that the federal government lacked authority to regulate state, local, and private hours contracts. Federal authority extended to only a small fraction of the labor market, such as railroads and ports, the District of Columbia, and federal employees. Beyond these areas, federal jurisdiction seemed too limited to test.

In the post–Civil War congressional debate over the federal eight-hour law, proponent Senator Thomas Hendricks (D, Indiana) conceded that the bill "does not propose to regulate the number of hours which shall constitute a legal day's work except in the employment of the Government of the United States. That, sir, we clearly have the right to provide for." Senator John Conness (R, California) also acknowledged that "the passage of this bill cannot control the labor of this country." [68] Leading students of the movement for hours legislation concluded that "limitations in the Constitution of the United States have restricted very narrowly the field in which the National Government can enact hours legislation."[69]

In congressional testimony in 1894, Gompers bitterly complained that "[w]hen labor goes to the various legislatures or goes to Congress and asks for remedial or beneficial legislation, the answer is that it is unconstitutional. The fact that it is beneficial or necessary is not denied, but it is said that it is unconstitutional." (Gompers accused *legislators* of making such claims, and did not blame courts exclusively.) The "marvelous" number of laws that legislators identified as constitutionally unacceptable "simply makes men who usually look upon the bright side ... become pessimistic," said Gompers.[70] Whatever their motive, participants used the claim that the federal government could only touch activities in its jurisdiction, and they usually behaved as if this were true. The AFL's support for a constitutional amendment "so that Congress may be empowered to legislate on the subject of the hours of labor for women and children" indicates that they conceived of limited federal jurisdiction as a real problem.[71]

Apart from the railroads, employers who wanted national rules did not find the national government any more capable of addressing their demands than did workers. The 1892 Massachusetts law limiting women's workweek to fifty-eight hours prompted Massachusetts employers to support federal hours regulation. These employers complained that they had to abide by hours limitations while "their competitors in other states have longer hours of labor, and in southern and western States the manufacturers can run as they please. . . ."[72] Some employers joined forces with trade unionists to oppose convict labor, Chinese immigrants, and other workers who in effect subsidized low-cost production. Manufacturers in the North created the National Anti-Convict Contract Association to battle low-cost contracts for prison labor. By 1899, this employer–labor coalition successfully had lobbied thirty-five states to halt the practice of contracting convicts' work to private employers beyond the prison walls. These changes could not reach goods made by convicts in other states. Courts struck down as an interference with interstate commerce any state laws that required labels for goods or licenses for sellers of goods made by convicts in other states.[73]

Competitive American federalism created strong disincentives for states to implement regulations that would harm their industries. Labor journalist Jonathan Fincher blamed interstate competition for the failure of the 1867–68 eight-hour laws. He indicated that Illinois employers could not agree to the eight-hour demand because competitors from other states could undersell them. A New York box manufacturer testified in 1883 that no one state could reduce the hours of labor because "Just as soon as men engaged in manufacture asked and struck for eight hours other States secured the trade where ten and twelve hours per day prevailed."[74] John Andrews also laid the failure of labor laws to the federal system, which "made it necessary to break the movement up into as many independent parts as there were state legislatures." He noted that, "[i]n England, a legislative movement had the advantage that Parliament was the only body upon which labour needed to bring pressure in order to attain results."[75]

Employers and their allies used interstate competition as a weapon to defeat every type of state labor regulation proposed. Even before the Civil War, employers in Pennsylvania complained that, if the state imposed a special burden of child labor laws on them, they would relocate to Camden, New Jersey. Massachusetts textile manufacturers consistently opposed that state's factory laws because the laws would disadvantage them and benefit firms in other New England states (and, after 1885, with competitors in the South). Evidence of the importance of this claim lies in the fact that Massachusetts textile workers helped counterparts in other New England states to lobby for comparable statutes. New York manufacturers "threatened personally to take their own factories out of the state if the bills are passed, and it was this argument more than any other which proved fatal from year to year."[76]

While industrial states in the North and Midwest provided some regulations for workers, states in the South were using labor laws to advantage their employers and to subjugate African American workers in particular. Almost all of the latter states eventually enacted contract labor laws to enforce property owners' authority over sharecroppers. Under a law adopted by Alabama in 1885, if a laborer signed a contract, obtained an advance in money, and then left the job without repaying it, he could be punished "as if he had stolen it." Peonage in the American South continued until the late 1940s, when the Supreme Court voided the contract labor laws of Georgia and Florida.[77] Southern states leased convicts to industrial employers, using state power to supply black workers for what were, in effect, white employers' labor cartels. Leased convicts helped physically reconstuct the South's economy by making bricks, laying rails, mining coal, and draining swamps.[78]

The Cost and Reliability of Regulation

As an early twentieth-century analyst of labor regulation observed, the federal government had "made neither extensive nor daring use of its power" even within the limits of its constitutional authority.[79] The same could be said for most of the states. The cumbersome policymaking process and federalism help explain why these governments did not use fully their authority to regulate labor markets.

Organized labor bore exceptionally high costs in maintaining pressure to win legislative support for laws in two branches of a legislature and across many states. The course of labor regulation in state after state slowed or stopped when a bill enacted by one house failed in the other, or when a governor vetoed the bill.[80] To win the approval of the other legislative house or the executive branch, legislators often weakened regulations. Within legislative houses, committees bottled up desired legislation, such as the 1898 amendment proposed for the U.S. Constitution to permit federal hours laws for women and children.[81]

The complexity of the political system also invited occasional fraud and deception, as in the case of the stolen tenement house cigar bill. It was alleged a New York employers' liability bill was misprinted in 1899 to ensure its defeat. In Colorado either a mistake or bribery caused a bill banning payment in scrip (instead of cash) to arrive at the governor's desk without an enacting clause.[82] While the complexity of the legislative process usually complicated labor's agenda, occasionally it created an opportunity for the defense of laws already won. In New York, unions worked the legislative process to fend off the repeal of labor laws. At the turn of the century, when conservative legislators introduced compulsory arbitration bills, Gompers and other leaders often successfully maneuvered to ensure that the bills died in committee.[83]

The gap between legislation and implementation especially deepened labor leaders' cynicism. States seemed to enact laws, such as the declaratory eight-hour statutes, without any capacity or interest in enforcement.[84] The federal government's reluctance to enforce its own eight-hour law constituted perhaps labor's most bitter disappointment in the late nineteenth century.

State enforcement often seemed worse than federal efforts. "Overwhelming" evidence existed that the New York School Attendance Laws of 1874 and 1876 were "a dead letter throughout the state." New York's Ainsworth bill of 1896, regulating the employment of women and children in mercantile establishments, was "absolutely unenforced" as late as 1905. Local health boards, charged with implementing the law, had been "practically unanimous in allowing the law to become a dead letter." Pennsylvania's fire commissioners did little to enforce the state fire escape laws of the 1870s and 1880s. In Illinois, various bans on child labor in mines between 1872 and 1887 had no enforcement provision. Utah's attorney general originally refused to enforce the 1896 state's eight-hour day for mining workers, which was later upheld in the *Holden v. Hardy* decision.[85]

The Courts and the Policymaking Process

The courts provided the veto point of last resort for opponents of labor market legislation, as Victoria Hattam and others argue.[86] Courts could prevent the implementation of statutes. Even in those situations where labor had aligned support in diverse parts of the legislature and the executive branch, courts exercised the power to strike down the result through judicial review. The ban on tenement house cigar manufacture in New York, the aggressive factory inspection of Florence Kelley in Illinois, and a host of other labor laws may well have laid a foundation for substantial limits on employers prerogatives if courts had not struck them down.

Courts were not independent and arbitrary actors, however. In the case of *Ritchie v. The People* and in many other cases, the courts reacted to lawsuits generally initiated by employers. When courts struck down labor laws, they were responding positively to employers' claims for managerial freedom. Courts, then, must be understood in large part as the instruments of employer opposition to labor.

Courts were only one of many institutions that undermined labor regulation after it was enacted into law. The 1884 AFL platform acknowledged that implementation problems involved more than the courts: "A united demand for a shorter working day, backed by thorough organization, will prove vastly more effective than the enactment of a thousand laws depending for *enforcement upon the pleasure of aspiring politicians [and] sycophantic department officials*" [emphasis added].[87] As historian Melvin Urofsky argues, the courts upheld the constitutionality of a large share of labor market legislation and did so in highly publicized cases such as *Holden v. Hardy*. A contemporary student of factory laws argued in 1902 that judicial review had affected factory legislation only at the margins.[88]

The executive branch contributed at least as much as the courts to labor leaders' frustration with government. Child labor offered the most poignant example. Neither New York, with a conservative supreme court, nor any other state invalidated laws limited to child labor regulation through World War I. A majority of the states enacted bans on child labor between the 1870s and 1900. Poor enforcement of these laws, however, resulted in an increased number of child workers in the United States.[89]

Patronage politics further undermined enforcement. Kelley was replaced as Illinois state factory inspector in part because her vigorous enforcement of the 1893 Factory Act sparked political opposition. Her successor, Louis Arrington, had been associated for many years with the Illinois Glass Bottle Company (the glass industry was a major employer of children). An expert on New York's factory laws had no doubt that the New York factory inspectors would do a better job "if the department could be removed from political influence and doubtless a more efficient corps of inspectors could be obtained if larger salaries were authorized."[90] Organized labor of course supported "political" appointments when labor loyalists received them. When trade unionists did not staff these offices, labor's stake in them diminished.

REGULATION AND STRATEGIC SELF-RELIANCE

In 1886, some European radicals envied the energy and the militancy of American labor. In the world's most democratic nation, state governments had enacted legislation responsive to much of labor's agenda. This legislation included the world's first laws enshrining the universal goal of the eight-hour day. Factory laws reflected the successful cooperation between unions and reformers toward enhanced worker protection.

By 1900, though, American labor regulation had bitterly disappointed workers and the leaders of their unions. Despite their arduous efforts, legislative success did not result in reliable government worker protections. Success in a legislature could be undermined by unsympathetic presidents or governors, resistant administrators, or recalcitrant courts. Worker protections enacted in one state could be imperiled by arguments that the pioneering states would lose business to neighboring jurisdictions.

Direct regulation was the most important and obvious way for labor leaders to enlist government as an ally in the battle for the labor market. Disappointments with American government drove these leaders to rely on a militant strategy of self-reliance.

NOTES

1. U.S. Senate Committee on Education and Labor, *Report of the Committee of the Senate on the Relations between Labor and Capital,* 4 vols. (Washington, D.C.: Government Printing Office, 1885), 1: 297.

2. David Montgomery, *Beyond Equality: Labor and the Radical Republicans* (New York: Knopf, 1967).

3. U.S. Industrial Commission, *Final Report*, vol. 19 (Washington, D.C.: GPO, 1902), 864–65. P. K. Edwards statistically analyzes strike data since 1881 in *Strikes in the United States, 1881–1974* (Oxford: Basil Blackwell, 1981). On the 1877 railroad strikes, see Robert V. Bruce, *1877: Year of Violence* (Indianapolis: Bobbs-Merrill, 1959) and Philip S.

Foner, *The Great Labor Uprising of 1877* (New York: Monad, 1977). On Homestead, see Paul Krause, *The Battle for Homestead, 1880–1892: Politics, Culture, and Steel* (Pittsburgh: University of Pittsburgh Press, 1992). On Pullman, see the literature reviewed by Richard Schneirov, Shelton Stromquist, and Nick Salvatore, "Introduction," in *The Pullman Strike and the Crisis of the 1890s*, ed. Richard Schneirov, Shelton Stromquist, and Nick Salvatore (Urbana: University of Illinois Press, 1999), 1–19.

4. On the use of the boycott, see John R. Commons, "European and American Unions," in John R. Commons, *Labor and Administration* (New York: Macmillan, 1913), 149–57.

5. R. Laurence Moore, *European Socialists and the Promised Land* (New York: Oxford University Press, 1970), 12–15, 70–71. This ardor cooled in the 1890s.

6. Examples include the Brotherhood of Locomotive Engineers (1864), the Bricklayers' and Masons' International Union of America (1865), the Brotherhood of Carpenters and Joiners of America (1881; it became the United Brotherhood in 1888), and the Cigar Makers' International Union (1864). See Lloyd Ulman, *The Rise of the National Trade Union: The Development and Significance of its Structure, Governing Institutions, and Economic Policies* (Cambridge: Harvard University Press, 1955).

7. City Trade Assemblies existed by the end of the Civil War in leading industrial centers including Boston, New York, Chicago, Philadelphia, Pittsburgh, Detroit, Cincinnati, St. Louis, and San Francisco. One of the earliest and strongest building trades councils was Chicago's Amalgamated Council of Building Trades, established in 1887. On the former, see Montgomery, *Beyond Equality*, 160–64; on the latter, see Philip Taft, *Organized Labor in American History* (New York: Harper and Row, 1964), 205–7.

8. Eugene Staley, *History of the Illinois State Federation of Labor* (Chicago: University of Chicago Press, 1930), 561–62. Labor historian Philip Taft asserts that state federations were "from the beginning, the political arm" of organized labor (*Organized Labor in American History*, 233). The New York's Workingmen's Assembly coexisted for a time with the New York State Federation of Labor, which was established in 1888, and they merged in 1898.

In *Protecting Soldiers and Mothers: The Political Origins of Social Policy in the United States* (Cambridge, Mass.: Belknap, 1992, 572, note 117), Theda Skocpol criticizes the characterization of the Progressive Era AFL as a loose, state-based confederation. It is true that "state federations were not at all important constituent units within the national AFL." But states, not the federal government, were the main locus of labor market and social insurance legislation in this period. The national AFL was not all that important in the state policymaking process (even in the notorious Western state referenda on eight-hour laws; see chapter 6, below). State labor federations, large city labor federations, and strong union locals were the predominant labor influence in state capitals. Philip Taft writes about California:

> The leaders of the AFL seldom tried directly to steer the political activities of the central bodies they chartered. While not enthusiastic about the occasional attempts of local unions and central labor bodies to launch labor parties, the most drastic steps normally taken against

such ventures was persuasion. . . . The decision on political tactics was always made at the local level, and maximum freedom existed for local organizations to follow the policy their leaders believed would serve the interests of the movement and its members. . . . It cannot be overstressed that the decisions of the AFL and even the international unions on the kind of political policies the workers of the United States should follow were not significant in shaping the decisions of the labor organizations in their own "backyards." The California State Federation of Labor became the political arm of the workers of the state not because of any ideological commitments or because of the opposition to an independent program, but because the tactics used were the only ones that could gain results. The failure of European and American writers to recognize the significance of the state federation of labor as a political institution is perhaps the chief reason for their inability to understand American labor's political behavior.

Philip Taft, *Labor Politics American Style: The California State Federation of Labor* (Cambridge: Harvard University Press, 1968), 4–5. In 1911 John R. Commons wrote that a comparison of the British Trades Union Congress (TUC) with the American Federation of Labor "misses the point." The state labor federations constituted the organizations most comparable to the TUC; Commons, "European and American Unions," 154.

9. Leon Fink, *Workingmen's Democracy: The Knights of Labor and American Politics* (Urbana: University of Illinois Press, 1983); Kim Voss, *The Making of American Exceptionalism: The Knights of Labor and Class Formation in the Nineteenth Century* (Ithaca, N.Y.: Cornell University Press, 1993).

10. Norman J. Ware, *The Labor Movement in the United States, 1860–1895: A Study in Democracy* (New York: Appleton-Century-Crofts, 1959); Philip Taft, *The A.F. of L. in the Time of Gompers* (New York: Octagon, 1970); Stuart Bruce Kaufman, *Samuel Gompers and the Origins of the American Federation of Labor, 1848–1896* (Westport, Conn.: Greenwood, 1973).

11. David Montgomery, *The Fall of the House of Labor: The Workplace, the State, and American Labor Activism, 1865–1925* (Cambridge: Cambridge University Press, 1987). Socialists advocated economic collectivism through increased government ownership and direction of production and distribution. The Greenback Party of the 1870s and 1880s sought continued use of paper money ("greenbacks") issued during the Civil War, as well as the eight-hour day, an income tax, and additional government control of commerce. The "single tax" movement, associated most closely with the economist Henry George, advocated government funding from a tax on rent from land as a way to achieve fairness in the distribution of resources; George ran for mayor of New York but lost in 1886. Populism was a late nineteenth-century political movement strongest in farming areas of the South and Great Plains; the People's Party of 1892 and the Democratic presidential campaign of William Jennings Bryan in 1896 represented populist influence in national politics.

12. Gary Marks, *Unions in Politics: Britain, Germany, and the United States in the Nineteenth and Early Twentieth Centuries* (Princeton: Princeton University Press, 1989).

13. On the National Labor Union platforms, see *A Documentary History of American Industrial Society,* ed. John R. Commons et al. (New York: Russell and Russell, 1958), 9: 126–274.

14. Mary O. Furner, "The Republican Tradition and the New Liberalism: Social Investigation, State Building, and Social Learning in the Gilded Age," in *The State and Social Investigation in Britain and the United States*, ed. Michael J. Lacey and Mary O. Furner (Washington, D.C.: Woodrow Wilson Center Press, 1993), 206; U.S. Senate Committee on Education and Labor, *Relations between Labor and Capital*, vol. 1: 2, 10, 85–87, 271, 328–34, 377–79, 404, 461–62, 1172–73 (the hearings were conducted in 1883).

15. For example, in his memoirs, Gompers recalls sending a union committee "to present our position and needs" to New York's governor and New York City's mayor as early as 1876; he concluded that "[s]uch experiences strengthened my conviction in the *economic* work of my union"; Samuel Gompers, *Seventy Years of Life and Labour*, 2 vols. (New York: Dutton, 1925), 1: 137 [emphasis added].

16. Furner, "The Republican Tradition and the New Liberalism," 206. On New Jersey, see Herbert G. Gutman, *Work, Culture, and Society in Industrializing America: Essays in American Working-Class and Social History* (New York: Knopf, 1976), 281–90; on Illinois, see Ernest Ludlow Bogart and John Mabry Matthews, *The Centennial History of Illinois; The Modern Commonwealth, 1893–1918* (Springfield: Illinois Centennial Commission, 1920), 5: 161.

17. Montgomery, *Beyond Equality*, 86–87, 242–45, 298–99.

18. Montgomery, *Beyond Equality*, 208–29; Fink, *Workingmen's Democracy*, 26–29; William E. Wilson, *Indiana: A History* (Bloomington: Indiana University Press, 1966), 120.

19. As described by Gompers in 1883; Senate Committee on Education and Labor, *Relations between Labor and Capital*, 1: 299.

20. On the persistent interest in shorter working hours, see U.S. Industrial Commission, *Final Report*, 947. On the eight-hour movement of the post–Civil War years, see Montgomery, *Beyond Equality*, particularly 176–85 on the "Baltimore Program." On demands for reduced worktime generally, see Marion Cotter Cahill, *Shorter Hours: A Study of the Movement since the Civil War* (New York: Columbia University Press, 1932); David R. Roediger and Philip S. Foner, *Our Own Time: A History of American Labor and the Working Day* (Westport, Conn.: Greenwood, 1989); *Worktime and Industrialization: An International History,* ed. Gary Cross (Philadelphia: Temple University Press, 1988); Benjamin Kline Hunnicutt, *Work without End: Abandoning Shorter Hours for the Right to Work* (Philadelphia: Temple University Press, 1988).

21. Proceedings of the Baltimore Congress of the National Labor Union (1864), in *A Documentary History of American Industrial Society*, 9: 135–36.

22. *Labor Laws and Their Enforcement, with Special Reference to Massachusetts*, ed. Susan M. Kingsbury (New York: Longmans, Green, 1911), 106–7; James Leiby, *Carroll Wright and Labor Reform: The Origins of Labor Statistics* (Cambridge: Harvard University Press, 1960), 44; Montgomery, *Beyond Equality*, 163, 238, 249–60, 278 ff.

23. John B. Andrews, "Nationalisation," in *History of Labor in the United States*, 4 vols., ed. John R. Commons et al. (New York: Macmillan, 1918 and 1935); 45, 91; Leiby, *Carroll Wright and Labor Reform*, 47, 107; Roediger and Foner, *Our Own Time*, 93; Kingsbury, *Labor Laws and their Enforcement*, 102; Montgomery, *Beyond Equality*,

125, 242; Ira B. Cross, *History of the Labor Movement in California* (Berkeley: University of California Press, 1935), 37–38; Cahill, *Shorter Hours*, 96.

24. Illinois, Missouri, Wisconsin, New York, Connecticut, California, and Pennsylvania. The federal law covered federal employees only.

25. On New York and Connecticut, see Andrews, "Nationalisation," 107–9; on Indiana, see Montgomery, *Beyond Equality*, 242. On California, see A. M. Kenaday, *The Record of the Eight-Hour Bill in the California Legislature, Session 1866–1867* (San Francisco: n.p., 1867); and Cross, *History of the Labor Movement in California*, 37–38.

26. *Congressional Globe*, June 24, 1867: 3424.

27. Kenaday, *The Record of the Eight-Hour Bill in the California Legislature*, 18.

28. *New York Times*, June 8, 1867: 4; see also *New York Times*, May 8, 1867: 4, and *The Nation* 1 (October 26, 1865): 517.

29. David R. Roediger, "Ira Steward and the Anti-Slavery Origins of American Eight-Hour Theory," *Labor History* 27 (Summer 1986): 410–26.

30. Senate Committee on Education and Labor, *Relations between Labor and Capital*, 1: 297.

31. Reprinted in New York Bureau of Statistics of Labor, *Eighth Annual Report* (Albany: James B. Lyon, 1891), 509–11.

32. Montgomery, *Beyond Equality*, 308–10; Roediger and Foner, *Our Own Time*, 139; John H. Keiser, *Building for the Centuries: Illinois, 1865–1898* (Urbana: University of Illinois Press, 1977), 223.

33. Doris B. McLaughlin, *Michigan Labor: A Brief History from 1818 to the Present* (Ann Arbor: Institute of Labor and Industrial Relations, 1970), 33–34; Steven J. Ross, *Workers on the Edge: Work, Leisure, and Politics in Industrializing Cincinnati, 1788–1890* (New York: Columbia University Press, 1985), 274; New York Bureau of Statistics of Labor, *Eighth Annual Report*, 736–42.

34. Cross, *Worktime and Industrialization*, 11.

35. Gompers, *Seventy Years of Life and Labour*, 1: 137.

36. In New York, the law was characterized as a "dead letter"; Fred Rogers Fairchild, *The Factory Legislation of the State of New York* (New York: American Economic Association, 1905), 4; Montgomery, *Beyond Equality*, 303–4.

37. Montgomery, *Beyond Equality*, 325; Andrews, "Nationalisation," 109; Cross, *A History of the Labor Movement in California*, 54.

38. Cahill, *Shorter Hours*, 68–77; Montgomery, *Beyond Equality*, 320, 328–29; Andrews, "Nationalisation," 124–25.

39. Cahill, *Shorter Hours*, 72–75. The House debate on the 1892 bill includes criticisms of the previous laws' ineffectiveness; see *Congressional Record*, July 1, 1892: 5723–37.

40. American Federation of Labor, *Proceedings* of the Eighteenth Annual Convention, 1898: 22, and *Proceedings* of the Nineteenth Annual Convention, 1899: 12. Hereafter, cited as *AFL Proceedings*, [date].

41. Montgomery, *Beyond Equality*, 303–4, 312–23; *U.S. v. Martin*, 94 U.S. 400 (1876); *Low v. Rees Printing Co.*, 59 N.W. 762; 41 Neb., 127 (1894). See F. J. Stimson, *Handbook to the Labor Law of the United States* (New York: Charles Scribner's Sons, 1896), 43–44.

42. *United States v. Post*, 148 U.S. 124 (1893). See Cahill, *Shorter Hours*, 75–76.

43. New York (1853), California (1868), Indiana (1889), Massachusetts (1890), Idaho (1890–91), Kansas (1891), Nebraska (1891), Colorado (1893), Utah (1894), Pennsylvania (1897), West Virginia (1899), Washington (1899), Ohio (1900). Wyoming included such a provision in its 1889 constitution. Elizabeth Brandeis, "Labor Legislation," in *History of Labor Legislation in the United States*, 3: 560–61.

44. Louisiana (1886); Pennsylvania, New York, California, and New Jersey (1887); Ohio (1892); Michigan (1893); Massachusetts (1894); Washington (1895); South Carolina (1897); and Maryland (1898); Brandeis, "Labor Legislation," 561–62.

45. Ohio and New York (1892), Michigan (1893), Nebraska (1899); Brandeis, "Labor Legislation," 561.

46. Utah (1896), Montana (1897), Missouri and Colorado (1899); Brandeis, "Labor Legislation," 562.

47. Cahill, *Shorter Hours*, 72.

48. *Holden v. Hardy*, 169 U.S. 66, 18 Sup. Ct. 383 (1898). In reaction to this favorable court decision, Colorado enacted an eight-hour law identical to Utah's. The Colorado Supreme Court struck it down as inconsistent with Colorado's constitution; see *In re Morgan*, 26 Colo. 415, 58 Pac. 1071 (1899).

49. U.S. Industrial Commission, *Final Report*, 915–16, 923–26. In Great Britain, one in three women was gainfully employed in 1891.

50. Kathryn Kish Sklar, "'The Greater Part of the Petitioners Are Female': The Reduction of Women's Working Hours in the Paid Labor Force, 1840–1917," in *Worktime and Industrialization*, 106–7.

51. U.S. Industrial Commission, *Final Report*, 917–18, 927.

52. Adolph Strasser complained about competition from women, children, coolies, and convicts in Senate testimony; see the Senate Committee on Education and Labor, *Relations between Labor and Capital*, 1: 452–53.

53. P. J. McGuire's testimony in *Relations between Labor and Capital*, 1, 333; Clara M. Beyer, *History of Labor Legislation for Women in Three States*, U.S. Department of Labor, Women's Bureau, Bulletin 66 (Washington, D.C.: GPO, 1929), 2–3.

54. Trade union influence on protective labor legislation for women and children is also documented in J. Lynn Barnard, *Factory Legislation in Pennsylvania: Its History and Administration* (Philadelphia: University of Pennsylvania, 1907), 51–59; Florence P. Smith, *Chronological Development of Labor Legislation for Women in the United States*, U.S. Department of Labor, Women's Bureau, Bulletin 66 (Washington, D.C.: GPO, 1929), 243–44; and Brandeis, "Labor Legislation," passim. For a cross-national perspective, see Ulla Wikander, Alice Kessler-Harris, and Jane Lewis, eds., *Protecting Women: Labor Legislation in Europe, the United States, and Australia, 1880–1920* (Urbana: University of Illinois Press, 1995).

55. Kingsbury, *Labor Laws and their Enforcement*, 112–25; Carl Siracusa, *A Mechanical People: Perceptions of the Industrial Order in Massachusetts, 1815–1880* (Middletown, Conn.: Wesleyan University Press, 1979), 187–98; Sklar, "The Greater Part of the Petitioners Are Female," 112; Beyer, *History of Labor Legislation for Women in Three States*, 20, 30–31.

56. Fairchild, *The Factory Legislation of the State of New York*, 44–45; Jeremy P. Felt, *Hostages of Fortune: Child Labor Reform in New York State* (Syracuse, N.Y.: Syracuse University Press, 1965), 17–21.

57. Beyer, *History of Labor Legislation for Women in Three States*, 7.

58. Brandeis, "Labor Legislation," 468; Beyer, *History of Labor Legislation for Women in Three States*, 66–71; Howard Hurwitz, *Theodore Roosevelt and Labor in New York State, 1880–1900* (New York: Columbia University Press, 1943), 192–93.

59. Sklar, "The Greater Part of the Petitioners Are Female," 118; Kathyrn Kish Sklar, *Florence Kelley and the Nation's Work, 1830–1900* (New Haven: Yale University Press, 1995), 206–85; Meredith Tax, *The Rising of the Women: Feminist Solidarity and Class Conflict, 1880–1917* (New York: Monthly Review Press, 1980), 67–89; Beckner, *A History of Labor Legislation in Illinois* (Chicago: University of Chicago Press, 1929), 152–62; *Ritchie v. The People*, 155 Ill. 98 (1895); William R. Brock, *Investigation and Responsibility: Public Responsibility in the United States, 1865–1900* (Cambridge: Cambridge University Press, 1984), 177; Brandeis, "Labor Legislation," 466.

60. Smith, *Chronological Development of Labor Legislation for Women*, 135–285; Hayes Robbins, "The Necessity for Factory Legislation in the South," *Annals* 20 (1902): 181–88; Elizabeth Sands Johnson, "Child Labor Legislation," in *History of Labor Legislation in the United States*, 3: 403–37.

61. U.S. Industrial Commission, *Final Report*, 899–900; on New Jersey, see Herbert G. Gutman, *Work, Culture, and Society in Industrializing America*, 280–84.

62. George M. Price, *Administration of Labor Laws and Factory Inspection in Certain European Countries*, U.S. Bureau of Labor Statistics Bulletin 142 (Washington, D.C.: GPO, 1914), 25; John R. Commons and John B. Andrews, *Principles of Labor Legislation*, (New York: Harper and Brothers., 1916), 418.

63. W. F. Willoughby, *The Inspection of Factories and Workshops in the United States*, U.S. Department of Labor Bulletin 12 (Washington, D.C.: GPO, 1897), 557; U.S. Industrial Commission, *Labor Legislation*, 100; Felt, *Hostages of Fortune*, 63.

64. William E. Forbath, *Law and the Shaping of the American Labor Movement* (Cambridge: Harvard University Press, 1991); Eileen Boris, "A Man's Dwelling House Is His Castle": Tenement House Cigarmaking and the Judicial Imperative," in *Work Engendered: Toward a New History of American Labor*, ed. Ava Baron (Ithaca, N.Y.: Cornell University Press, 1991), 114–41; Eileen Boris, *Home to Work: Motherhood and the Politics of Industrial Homework in the United States* (New York: Cambridge University Press, 1994); Victoria Hattam, *Labor Visions and State Power* (Princeton: Princeton University Press, 1993); *The Samuel Gompers Papers, Vol. 1: The Making of a Union Leader, 1850–86*, ed. Stuart B. Kaufman (Urbana: University of Illinois Press, 1986), 169–70. In 1915, Gompers linked voluntarism to the failure of the eight-hour laws of 1867 and 1868; see *Our Own Time*, Roediger and Foner, 336, note 13.

65. Gompers, *Seventy Years of Life and Labour*, 1: 183–98; Kaufman, *The Samuel Gompers Papers*, vol. 1: 169–70; Fairchild, *The Factory Legislation of the State of New York*, 11–23; Hurwitz, *Theodore Roosevelt and Labor in New York State*, 87–88; Senate Committee on Education and Labor, *Relations between Labor and Capital*, 1: 452.

66. Gompers, *Seventy Years of Life and Labour*, 197; See also U.S. Strike Commission, *Report on the Chicago Strike of June–July, 1894*, U.S. Senate Executive Document 7, 53rd Cong., 3rd sess. (Washington, D.C.: GPO, 1895), 203.

67. Quoted in Melvin I. Urofsky, "State Courts and Protective Legislation during the Progressive Era: A Reevaluation," *Journal of American History* 72 (June 1985): 63–91.

68. *Congressional Globe*, June 3, 1867: 2802; June 24, 1867: 3424.

69. Cahill, *Shorter Hours*, 93.

70. U.S. Strike Commission, *Report on the Chicago Strike*, 203–4.

71. *AFL Proceedings*, 1897: 85.

72. Beyer, *History of Labor Legislation for Women in Three States*, 27.

73. Stephen P. Garvey, "Freeing Prisoners' Labor," *Stanford Law Review* 50 (January 1998): 339–70; Glen A. Gildemeister, *Prison Labor and Convict Competition with Free Workers in Industrializing America, 1840–1890* (New York: Garland, 1987).

74. Montgomery, *Beyond Equality*, 312; testimony of George Blair, in Senate Committee on Education and Labor, *Relations between Labor and Capital*, 2: 40 (see also testimony of George M. Weston, 1: 1059).

75. Andrews, "Nationalisation," 109.

76. Barnard, *Factory Legislation in Pennsylvania*, 18; Beyer, *History of Labor Legislation for Women in Three States*, 18–33, esp. 18 for 1865–74 and 26–27 for 1879–92; Fairchild, *The Factory Legislation of the State of New York*, 45.

77. Pete Daniel, *The Shadow of the Slavery: Peonage in the South, 1901–1969* (Urbana: University of Illinois Press, 1972), 24–25, 66, 78–81.

78. Garvey, "Freeing Prisoners' Labor"; Jennifer Roback, "Southern Labor Law in the Jim Crow Era: Exploitative or Competitive?" *University of Chicago Law Review* 51 (1984): 1161–62; Alex Lichtenstein, *Twice the Work of Free Labor: The Political Economy of Convict Labor in the New South* (London: Verso, 1996); Matthew J. Mancini, *One Dies, Get Another: Convict Leasing in the American South, 1866–1928* (Columbia: University of South Carolina Press, 1996); Martha A. Myers, *Race, Labor, and Punishment in the New South* (Columbus: Ohio State University Press, 1998).

79. Cahill, *Shorter Hours*, 93.

80. In 1828, Pennsylvania's lower house approved legal limitations on child labor in the textile industry in 1828, but the bill was twice defeated in the state senate. Had Pennsylvania enacted such a law, it would have preceded the British Parliament in establishing the first factory act. See Barnard, *Factory Legislation in Pennsylvania*, 2–4.

81. *AFL Proceedings*, 1898: 22.

82. Asher, "Failure and Fulfillment," 210; David Lawrence Lonsdale, "The Movement for an Eight-Hour Law in Colorado, 1893–1913" (unpublished Ph.D. dissertation, University of Colorado, Department of History, 1964), 75.

83. Gompers, *Seventy Years of Life and Labour*, 1: 137; AFL *Proceedings*, 1901: 26.

84. George Lovell, "The Ambiguities of Labor's Legislative Reforms in New York State in the Late Nineteenth Century," *Studies in American Political Development* 8 (1994): 81–103.

85. Montgomery, *Beyond Equality*, 304–5; Beckner, *A History of Labor Legislation in Illinois*, 151; Fairchild, *The Factory Legislation of the State of New York*, 8–9, 65; Barnard, *Factory Legislation in Pennsylvania*, 34; AFL *Proceedings*, 1897: 86.

86. Hattam, *Labor Visions and State Power*.

87. Hattam, *Labor Visions and State Power*, 139. See also Cahill, *Shorter Hours*, 71.

88. Sarah S. Whittelsey, "Tendencies of Factory and Inspection in the United States," *Annals* 20 (1902): 235–53.

89. Urofsky, "State Courts and Protective Legislation during the Progressive Era." In New York, however, Fairchild reported that the percentage of children under sixteen employed in manufacturing establishments fell 8.4 percent in 1887 to 2.1 percent in 1903. Fairchild, *The Factory Legislation of the State of New York*, 128.

90. Beckner, *A History of Labor Legislation in Illinois*, 154; Florence Kelley, "Child Labor Legislation," *Annals* 20 (1902): 155–65; Fairchild, *The Factory Legislation of the State of New York*, 107.

3

THE AMERICAN FEDERATION OF
LABOR CONFRONTS EMPLOYERS

"[W]e have come to the conclusion that wherever we can help
ourselves we will do it, without asking the aid of the Government, and if we want to make a law we will make it in our own
trades unions and try to enforce it through them by contracts
with our employers."

—Carpenter P. J. McGuire, 1883[1]

Frustrated by ineffective regulation, America's labor leaders concluded that
they could not depend primarily on their government to protect workers.
This conclusion toughened labor's instinctive resolve to rely on union power.
Leaders of the American Federation of Labor (AFL) argued that if unions
organized workers in every employer's shop, labor itself could unilaterally establish and enforce the eight-hour day, higher wages, and better working conditions. This union shop strategy obligated the AFL militantly to demand concessions from employers. It also obligated the organization, in principle, to bring
virtually the entire American nonfarm workforce into unions.

The AFL's union shop strategy included an important, if secondary, role for government regulation, labor market management, and trade union policy. As chapters 2 and 6 explain, labor leaders lobbied government to regulate those parts
of the labor market that were unorganized and difficult to organize, such as
shops that employed a large number of children. Unions also sought government protection of their economic weapons, such as the strike, picket line, and
boycott. Finally, unions also supported new public labor market institutions,
such as bureaus of labor statistics and public employment offices, that held out
the prospect of union-staffed public agencies, giving unions more leverage in
disputes with employers.

As public labor market regulation frustrated American labor leaders, however, their experiences with trade union policy and public labor market institu-

tions disillusioned them further. American employers grew ever more skillful in using public institutions, especially courts, to disarm unions and nullify state laws protecting union powers. Although public labor agencies were created, they did not give unions the expected advantages in the battle for the labor market. Labor statistics bureaus generally failed to press the union agenda effectively, and public employment offices did not weaken employers' hiring power. Nineteenth-century immigration controls had little apparent impact on the flood of foreign job seekers.

For all these setbacks, the United States in 1900 had not decisively abandoned the path to substantial limitations on employer prerogatives. Had the union shop strategy met with success, limitations on employer prerogatives would have developed as they did in Germany rather than as in Great Britain. Collective bargaining, rather than statute law, would have established protection for most of the workforce. It was not the union shop strategy, but the employer reaction to it, that decisively caused the United States to deviate from the path of labor market policy that other nations were about to follow.

VOLUNTARISM IN 1900: THE AFL'S THREAT TO EMPLOYER AUTONOMY

Leaders of the AFL had committed the federation to a strategy of "voluntarism" by the turn of the century. Voluntarism held that unions were private and voluntary institutions. They sought nothing from the state and sought absolute freedom from state regulation. This view emphasized "pure and simple" material gains for labor, particularly better wages, hours, and working conditions. AFL leaders repudiated socialism and alliances with existing political parties.[2] Compared to a more self-consciously Marxist trade union movement, such as that in Germany, voluntarism seemed relatively tame. Unlike the Knights of Labor, the AFL seemed little interested in building working-class solidarity.[3]

The voluntarism espoused by AFL leaders in 1900, however, posed a sweeping, confrontational, and credible challenge to employers' prerogatives in the labor market. AFL leaders sought no less than a fully unionized industrial capitalist economy. A blanket of union rules, argued the dominant voices in the AFL, would protect the nation's nonagricultural workforce. This union shop[4] economy would do no less than place unions, rather than employers, in control of the terms of employment and worker security in the United States.

In July 1900 the AFL Executive Council called on the nation's "wealth producers to unite and federate regardless of whether they are located East,

West, North or South; irrespective of sex, politics, color or religion." These workers should "organize unions where such do not now exist, to join those already organized ... and to affiliate in one common bond of labor upon the broad platform and under the proud banner of the American Federation of Labor." The unity and consequent solidarity of American labor would permit workers to confront the "oppressor," the "possessors of wealth," whose combination and concentration allowed "no sectional or state lines to interfere with their power."[5]

This union shop strategy would establish inclusive worker protection and universal restraints on employers without direct government help. AFL leaders had argued for union self-reliance from the federation's inception. By the turn of the century, AFL leaders had turned this principle into a broad-based strategy for increasing workers' labor market power. AFL president Samuel Gompers articulated this vision in his address to the 1901 AFL convention in Scranton, Pennsylvania:

> The first convention of our Federation declared that it is absolutely essential to a successful resistance to the combined power of capital that the laboring element of the whole population should be joined in one united federation of labor, based on the broadest principles of justice to all men of good will who contribute to the general welfare of humanity by useful labor. ... [W]e will not cease our effort until every wage-earner in our land is a member of the grand army of labor, and we shall have left in our whole social life not a vestige of the wrongs from which the workers have suffered from time immemorial.[6]

"The trade union is not a Sunday-school," Gompers wrote later. It should be militant and inclusive in pursuit of its self-interest. If men and women "are good enough to be employed for profit by the employer they are good enough for us to accept as members into the trade unions for their and our common protection."[7]

With a workforce that was fully unionized (including all female and minority workers),[8] the labor movement could impose maximum hours, minimum wages, employment security, and self-funded social insurance without regard to state lines or the separation of powers. Stonecutter and AFL vice president James Duncan argued that the experience with regulation proved that unions should themselves legislate worker protection. He wrote that "the delays, obstacles, machinations and even duplicity" with which Congress handled the federal eight-hour bills had exasperated labor. A union contract that bound employers to the eight-hour day provided a "more permanent, safe, and honest enactment" of this principal labor goal than any statute.

AFL leaders frequently asserted that union contracts could constitute a more effective form of legislation than a public statute (see the McGuire quote, above). Duncan observed that the Granite Cutters established the eight-hour day through collective bargaining with employers on May 1, 1900. They governed the workplace far more effectively than American government ever could, according to Duncan, because

> They know no veto by one man could stampede them; they had no fears of governmental parasites side tracking their "act." There were no horrors of questions of jurisdiction being raised. They had no fear of a capitalistic judge deciding the question as unconstitutional; they lost no sleep about what the Supreme Court might do about it. Their own Supreme Court had decided the question was constitutional. . . . The law's delay was conspicuous by its absence. . . . [T]he granite cutters present the object lesson to their fellow-workers that they, in the short period of 12 years, have gained by trade union-ism what Congress had failed to accomplish in 32 years' agitation, namely, a permanent 8-hour workday that is not subject to be knocked out in municipal, State or federal courts. . . .[9]

The AFL and its leaders, of course, would enjoy tremendous power if this vision became reality. This enhanced AFL power also stoked the leaders' passionate support for the union shop economy.

It has been easy to view as disingenuous Gompers's later claim to socialists that "we go further than you."[10] The AFL's goal of monopolizing control over labor skills and the conditions of employment unambiguously posed a direct challenge to employers' right to manage their firms, however. Moreover, American unions pressed the goal of union shops with a force and vigor unparalleled in other nations such as Great Britain.

At its Scranton, Pennsylvania, convention in 1901, the AFL formalized the union shop strategy as its predominant approach to worker protection in America. Both socialism and independent labor politics constituted potential alternatives to the union shop strategy. Supporters of these approaches introduced resolutions endorsing them. In response, AFL leaders substituted a resolution that identified the trade union movement as "the most practical, safe, and legitimate channel" for workers "to continue to seek redress for their wrongs." The resolution unambiguously made unionization a priority. It relegated policy lobbying to a distinctly secondary role. A union "can strengthen [workers'] economic position until it will control the political field, and thereby place labor in full possession of its inherent rights," it stated.

The AFL's union shop strategy posed a substantial threat to employers. The employers' need for scarce skilled labor constituted their greatest economic vulnerability. The union shop strategy aimed to exploit that vulnerability to the fullest. The highly skilled crafts, such as the building trades, had already demonstrated that this craft monopoly could cement union strength. The Scranton convention established crafts skills as the basis for union organizing. "The future success, permanency, and safety" of the AFL and the trade unions depended on the principle of craft autonomy. In principle, the dominant craft unions would organize workers in the large enterprises, such as steel plants (or the carriage factories that would soon produce automobiles). Closely allied crafts would work together toward a common goal of a stronger trade union movement.[11] For a generation, AFL leaders invoked the Scranton resolution as the authoritative federation position that crafts should be the basis of organization.[12]

Establishing such economic power also required the unions to monopolize control of the potential material incentives—higher wages, shorter hours, and collateral benefits—necessary for attracting and retaining union membership. If workers could enjoy better hours, wages, working conditions, and work insurance as union members, most would be likely to join unions freely. If business or government established better working conditions, however, such benefits could hurt unions. Workers would avoid unions because they could "free ride," enjoying higher benefits without paying the costs of union dues. When a committee recommended against public pensions at the 1902 AFL convention, it explained that "the conditions, wages, and other concerns of the working people should be arranged through the efforts of organized labor."[13]

American employers had good reason to take the union shop as a credible threat, especially given the unions' established willingness to use strikes and other economic weapons to win labor disputes. The AFL was growing rapidly. Its membership exploded from about a quarter of a million in 1898 to well over a million and a half in 1904. By the fall of 1903, Chicago had a quarter of a million trade union members, nearly matching London as center of trade unionism.[14] Comparative statistics, though necessarily rough estimates, suggest that American unionization rates did not differ substantially from those in Great Britain or Germany around 1900 (figure 1.1).

The organization of the industrial labor force, the backbone of labor parties and employer limitations abroad, had not been decisively delayed. As the following chapter documents, employers behaved as if the AFL's strategy constituted a serious threat to the control of both skilled and unskilled workers.

The federation pursued its goals in the political realm with a determined and opportunistic nonpartisanship. The AFL's top policy priorities in 1900— a stronger federal eight-hour law that would cover government contractors, and a law protecting the widest possible use of unions' economic weapons— constituted plausible threats to the balance of labor market power.[15] The AFL, trying to maximize the direct political impact of workers, endorsed the direct election of the president and the U.S. Senate, as well as the use of the initiative and referendum.[16]

Headquartered in Washington, D.C., beginning in 1897, the AFL Executive Council met with key congressional and executive leaders in order to influence committee and executive agency appointments, the legislative agenda, the details of specific bills, and the implementation of existing federal laws. In February 1901, AFL lobbying was credited with the defeat of an injunction bill objectionable to the federation.[17] Gompers's influence with American workers, both union and nonunion, was sufficient for President Theodore Roosevelt to ask House Speaker Joseph Cannon to stop criticizing Gompers by name in the 1906 congressional campaign.[18] Even in the 1908 presidential election, when the AFL generally supported the national Democratic ticket, AFL vice president Daniel J. Keefe endorsed Republican presidential candidate William Howard Taft because of his support for the eight-hour day when he was secretary of war.[19]

Leaders of German and British unions in 1900 articulated the same key strategic premises as the AFL leaders. "Ambivalence toward the state ran hard, indeed, through all the workers' institutions of the Atlantic economy," in Daniel Rogers's words.[20] Successful labor leaders abroad primarily concerned themselves with strengthening their economic bargaining power. German and British crafts workers were among the strongest unions, and like American crafts workers they sought to monopolize control over hours, wages, benefits, and other conditions of employment. Gary Marks demonstrates that German, British, and American printing unions were much more similar than different in their emphasis on economic independence, political nonpartisanship, and reluctance to turn to government for help in gaining labor market leverage.[21]

Key leaders in both the British and German union movements also embraced political independence in the 1890s. British machinists in 1891 voted by a two-to-one margin to seek the eight-hour day "by voluntary trade union action rather than by legislation." This vote represented a decisive victory for the many British machinists who viewed legislation as interference with the "natural liberties" of "free adult males."[22] In the late 1890s German trade union leader Carl Legien told the emerging peak organization of the German trade union movement that "In the economic struggle all forces need to be concentrated without enquiring into the political creed of the individual."[23]

This union shop strategy constituted a realistic and rational response to the circumstances that American trade unions faced at the turn of the century. The separation of powers and federalism had foreclosed the effective establishment of comprehensive worker protections through legislation. Gompers often entered statements of his frustration with American government in the public record, as he did before the U.S. Industrial Commission in 1900.[24]

The president of the United Mine Workers of America (UMWA) expressed similar frustrations with government, especially with federalism. Compared to the skilled workers who dominated many other AFL unions, the coal miners had much less bargaining power for securing shorter hours and other benefits. Few groups of workers needed statutory protection more than the miners. In Great Britain, miners constituted a powerful force for legislative protection. Nevertheless, UMWA president John Mitchell argued that its federal structure foreclosed the possibility of legislative protection available to miners abroad.

> Unlike England, France, Belgium, and other countries, the United States is not a single, unified nation, but its powers of government are divided between the nation and the several states. . . . A victory gained in one state may sometimes be nullified by the failure to gain a like victory in neighboring states. A British law regulating hours of labor in the cotton factories applied to all the cotton factories in the United Kingdom; but a Massachusetts law has no validity in Pennsylvania. Whenever legislation for benefiting the workman is sought in one state, it is contested on the ground that its passage and enforcement will drive the industry in question from that state. [Uniform state laws have] never been possible and legislation in one state has been hampered by the failure to secure similar legislation in another. The ordinary advantage of labor laws as compared with reforms obtained by strikes or negotiation is their more general application and validity. This, however, is very much less the case in the United States than in other countries, owing to the subdivision of the powers of government and, sometimes, to inefficient and even dishonest administration. Many laws tending to improve the conditions of workingmen remain a dead letter, or are enforced so unequally and unfairly that benefits which might otherwise arise from them are lost.[25]

Contemporary labor experts did not question either the reasonableness of the AFL's private pursuit of worker protection or the organization's militancy. The foremost labor economist of the day, John R. Commons, concluded that "a kind of natural selection" had instilled in American unions "a more 'pragmatic' or 'opportunistic' philosophy, based on the illogical variety of actual conditions, and immediate necessities."[26]

Labor was not an indiscriminate opponent of government. It was a very discriminating proponent of particular government action. The AFL, its headquarters newly relocated to the nation's capital, had not abandoned the political field. It continued to support legislation that strengthened its bargaining position, protected hard-to-organize workers, and established public offices that could further its goals.[27] It selectively supported candidates for office. Its demand for the wider use of the initiative and referendum seemed, considering union growth, a reasonable device for maximizing labor's electoral power.

Today, many experts view the AFL's crafts-based, union shop strategy as a sensible adaptation to structural limitations. The wide gap between the letter of the law and the reality of policy, according to labor historian David Montgomery, "made the administrative task of translating statutory prescription into public practice revert to the trade unions."[28] William Forbath, a historian of labor law, concludes that the crafts-based strategy "was a matter of necessity and grudging accommodation." Trade union leaders "had concluded that legislation was a distressingly unreliable engine."[29]

The AFL's expressed attitude toward women and African American workers was consistent in principle with the AFL's crafts-based, union shop strategy. Theoretically, the union shop strategy required the organization of both groups of unorganized workers. Despite substantial opposition from male crafts workers, the AFL leadership maintained its rhetorical commitment to these workers in the early twentieth century. When a delegate at the 1898 AFL convention offered a resolution calling on the federal government to ban women from the workplace, advocates of "pure and simple" unionism angrily sank it. They substituted a call for the unionization of women workers.[30] The AFL remained a consistent advocate of the unionization of women and invested resources in organizing them.

Critics, however, blamed the AFL for failing to match its rhetoric with adequate resources necessary for unionizing female workers. These critics have substantial evidence. Several international unions maintained constitutional bars to the admission of women; the UMWA did so until 1942.[31] More important, the deeply held identification of craftsmanship as a masculine virtue undermined the theoretical imperative of union shop solidarity between men and women.

Race posed an even more formidable obstacle to American worker solidarity than gender.[32] The AFL adapted the union shop strategy to African American workers by accommodating segregation. The AFL constitution prohibited unions from barring black members. Gompers had insisted that the International Association of Machinists (IAM) remove formal racial discrimination from its charter before it joined the AFL.[33] Though the IAM dropped its whites only policy when it joined the AFL in 1895, its locals retained effective power to exclude blacks. In 1900, the AFL convention altered its constitution to permit African American unions to create separate central bodies in cities where whites had already established such bodies. By the end of World War II, twenty AFL international unions with two and a half million members still had constitutions, bylaws, or established practices that explicitly denied admission to blacks.[34] At the same time, interracial unionism persisted in some places and in some unions, such as the UMWA.[35]

Undoubtedly, the AFL's willingness to accommodate racial discrimination limited American trade unions' ability to mobilize the workforce. Racism does not distinguish the AFL's initial *policy* strategy from that of counterparts abroad, however. Race and gender discrimination obstructed working-class solidarity in the United States, but did not make the decisive difference in the AFL's strategy for labor market power, or in the way the AFL adapted to economic and political defeats.

TRADE UNION LAW

The union shop strategy made it imperative that government fully protect unions' ability to strike, boycott, and picket employers. These weapons permitted unions to squeeze employer profits and weaken employer resistance to the union shop and the demands for better pay, hours, and working conditions. When government limited strikes, picketing, or boycotts, it limited unions' effectiveness in securing benefits from employers. When government permitted employers to sue unions for financial damages resulting from these activities, it jeopardized critically needed union resources.

Though most nations treated unions as illegal conspiracies in the early 1800s, American courts had pioneered legal tolerance of trade unions. The Massachusetts Supreme Court in 1842 ruled that employers could enter into an agreement with a union to establish a union shop and that workers could lawfully strike against an employer to require his employees to join the union.[36] This decision acknowledged that workers could advance their collective self-interest as long as they used lawful means to do so. By the 1850s and 1860s, jurists in other American states cited the Massachusetts case in similar rulings. In the late 1800s, however, other nations put trade unions on a firmer legal footing than did the United States. The British Parliament swept away the conspiracy doctrine with statutes in 1871 and 1875. These new laws legalized trade unions, protected their funds, and permitted peaceful picketing.[37]

American labor leaders sought similar laws to protect trade union powers, economic weapons, and resources. Unlike the government of Great Britain, however, no single American governing body had authority to enact and enforce such a law. The national government lacked authority to do so. The states reacted with predictable diversity when union leaders demanded statutory protection. Several states enacted laws that aimed to prevent the courts from returning to the conspiracy doctrine.[38] Other states legally permitted workers to act collectively to protect or advance their wages; state courts, however, defined these laws narrowly.[39] When union militancy increased in the late 1870s and 1880s, courts began to reassert the conspiracy doctrine to limit strikes and picketing.[40] Most states did not respond at all to demands for laws protecting unions from adverse court rulings.

Some labor leaders initially believed that incorporation and arbitration laws could protect unions. They changed their minds, however, as public officials proved themselves increasingly untrustworthy in the 1880s and 1890s. A number of union leaders felt that American government should permit trade unions to incorporate, much like private businesses. Incorporation protected business in a number of ways. For example, it limited the liability of those participating in the business. One of the initial demands of the New York Workingmen's Assembly was a state incorporation law for unions. The Iron Molders' International Union petitioned Congress for national incorporation in 1874.[41] Asked about remedies for labor's problems in 1883, union leader P. J. McGuire named "the legalization, by incorporation, of the trade and labor unions" as his first priority. Gompers advocated the British trade union law as a model before the same committee.[42] American legislators responded supportively to this union demand. Advised that the Federation of Organized Trades and Labor Unions (FOTLU) supported the bill, the U.S. Congress enacted a trade union incorporation law in 1886 for the District of Columbia and the federal territories. Four states had done the same by 1900.[43]

American labor leaders reversed their position on incorporation over the next decade as anti-trust law exposed unions to government legal action. The Sherman Anti-Trust Act of 1890 outlawed conspiracies among businesses to limit prices and production that "restrained" free trade (see the following chapter). The Sherman Act initially posed little threat to trade unions. The violent 1894 strike against the Pullman Palace Sleeping Car Company, however, prompted some federal courts to define union activities, such as strikes, as illegal conspiracies to restrain trade outlawed by the Sherman Act.

As courts and business lawyers reinterpreted anti-trust laws, they became anti-union weapons, making union incorporation risky. If they incorporated, unions' assets could be more vulnerable to adverse legal decisions. From labor leaders' perspective, incorporation would merely give employers a new way to defeat unions. In a survey in the early 1900s, the Massachusetts Bureau of Labor reported that a majority of the labor leaders believed that union incorporation would be "inimical to [union] interests."[44] No prominent national union had incorporated under the federal law by 1900.[45] Instead, the AFL began to lobby for legislation that would decisively exempt trade unions from the Sherman Anti-Trust Act.

In the 1880s, many union members also advocated government arbitration of labor disputes because arbitration promised to force employers to deal with unions as worker representatives. When two hundred union members testified on behalf of state arbitration in 1885, the New York Bureau of Labor Statistics concluded that "the workingmen want it." Gompers and other labor leaders, wary of state compulsion, were unenthusiastic about government arbitration but conceded its value under the right circumstances. In hearings in New York in 1885, Gompers expressed conditional agreement with the idea of a state arbitration board. The main obstacle to arbitration in the 1880s, reported the New York bureau, was not worker opposition but "the hostile attitude, or contemptuous indifference, of many employers to the wants and needs of their employees."[46] Opposition to arbitration in Massachusetts came from employers who objected to it as an intrusion into business privacy.[47]

In the 1880s, American governments enacted many arbitration laws perceived as part of the union agenda. New Jersey, Pennsylvania, Ohio, Kansas, and Iowa established arbitration at the county level. New York and Massachusetts created the nation's first state-level arbitration boards in 1887. The federal government's first labor relation law, the Arbitration Act of 1888, established a voluntary process for arbitrating railroad disputes. The act provided for presidential boards to investigate the causes of such disputes. Only President Grover Cleveland used this provision, after the Pullman strike. Its arbitration features never were used.[48]

In the early 1890s, however, trade unionists abandoned arbitration while employers embraced it. Employers came to view compulsory arbitration as a tool for preventing strikes. The Pullman strike prompted seven states to enact arbitration laws in 1894 or 1895. In these states, notably in Illinois, support for this legislation came from conservatives reacting against the disorder resulting from the strike. By 1900, twenty-three states had enacted arbitration machinery.[49] As states reacted to the Pullman strike with arbitration laws, labor leaders' opposition to state arbitration intensified.[50]

When the U.S. Congress deliberated arbitration for railroads in the wake of the Pullman strike, only the conservative railroad brotherhoods supported the proposal. These brotherhoods—representing the locomotive engineers, the firemen, trainmen, and conductors—sought narrow advantages for the skilled craftsmen they represented. From the brotherhoods' perspective, a national railroad labor relations law could ratify their preeminent status in the industry and protect their large insurance funds. The railroad unions collaborated with the chair of the House Labor Committee and with the U.S. labor commissioner to draft an acceptable railroad arbitration bill.[51]

The railroad arbitration bill passed in 1898 only when the AFL abandoned opposition to it. The law, the Erdman Act of 1898, initiated a federal mediation process in the railroad industry and encouraged voluntary arbitration. It prevented railroads from requiring new employees to sign "yellow–dog" contracts (in which they agreed not to join a trade union). The law also prohibited discrimination against workers who were members of unions.[52] The Erdman Act protected the railroad brotherhoods' insurance funds and established national mediation mechanisms that ratified their bargaining status. This law, then, channeled railway brotherhoods toward an emphasis on private benefits for their members.[53]

As labor leaders abandoned their flirtation with incorporation and arbitration, the courts were expanding their power to limit unions' use of economic weapons.[54] With increasing frequency in the 1880s and early 1890s, federal courts began to issue injunction orders prohibiting unions from striking. By the mid-1890s, Gompers called attention to the increasing use of court injunctions to frustrate and defeat unionization drives.[55] Courts used injunctions even more aggressively as the century turned and the union shop drive gained momentum. The injunction issue rose to the top of the AFL agenda by 1902. For many years federation lobbyists unsuccessfully sought congressional legislation to sterilize the conspiracy doctrine and to limit injunctions.

Many judicial rulings that were adverse to labor would not have had much effect without support from the American military and police. The railroad strikes of 1877 prompted New York, Pennsylvania, New Jersey, and Connecticut to transform their militias into effective riot and strike control forces. Business often provided officers for these militia units. By the turn of the century these state militias had become "a formidable internal police force of over 100,000 men, most of whom were located in the industrial states."[56] Federal courts did not implement the injunctions against Pullman strikers; federal bayonets did. Strikes "are an education to the working classes," commented McGuire, "in showing us what we have to expect from the Government, when it uses its police and soldiers at the instant bidding of the capitalists to imprison us or to shoot us down."[57]

"IN CLOSE TOUCH WITH ORGANIZED LABOR": LABOR MARKET MANAGEMENT

In the late nineteenth century, trade union leaders viewed new government institutions as a way to level the playing field with employers. Unions lobbied for labor statistics bureaus, public employment offices, and licensing arrangements that promised them leverage in the labor market. Though legislatures favorably responded to these demands, these new labor market institutions were relegated to the margins of political and economic influence.

As the initial fervor for the eight-hour day peaked in the 1860s, the U.S. House of Representatives signaled labor's importance when it established a Committee on Education and Labor in 1867. The resolution establishing the House committee announced that the protection of workers constituted a natural next step after the defeat of slavery in the South.[58] The Senate created a similar committee in 1870. The rise of the Knights of Labor coincided with the creation of a separate House Labor Committee in 1883. Representative John O'Neill (D, Missouri) described the new body as one "to which the representatives of the laboring element can submit their claims."[59]

Congress also created special committees to investigate labor issues. The Senate Committee on the Relations between Labor and Capital publicized labor's grievances in 1883. Special congressional committees investigating individual strikes showed considerable sympathy to the strikers' point of view.[60] The United States Industrial Commission, established in 1898, produced nineteen volumes of material on labor issues. Its final report anticipated much of the Progressive Era labor reform agenda.[61]

Labor leaders, however, had a much greater interest in permanent labor agencies than in investigative commissions. They lobbied intensely for these new offices. Bureaus of labor and, to a lesser extent, public employment offices, could give unions control of public offices that could break the labor market logjam created by the separation of powers. If unionists staffed these offices, they could use them to legitimate and advance union priorities and the spread of union shops. By the turn of the century, however, labor leaders' experiences with bureaus of labor statistics, public employment offices, and immigration controls further underscored the limited utility of American government for the union shop strategy.

Bureaus of Labor Statistics

American governments created labor bureaus before other nations created them because unions demanded these bureaus. All the major national labor organizations of the period—the National Labor Union in 1867, the Knights of Labor in 1878, and the FOTLU in 1881—lobbied for the creation of national and state bureaus of labor statistics. These labor organizations envisioned these bureaus as agencies for exposing employer greed and labor market injustice.

Labor leaders and reformers led the fight for the first state labor bureau in Massachusetts, for example. When that state's eight-hour commission of 1866 rejected an eight-hour law, it recommended the creation of a fact-finding bureau. This new public agency annually would provide "reliable statistics in regard to the condition, prospects, and wants of industrial classes." In 1869, when a Labor Reform party won 10 percent of the vote in statewide elections, the state legislature approved a bill creating a state labor statistics bureau.[62] Reform-minded Henry Oliver became the bureau's first chief, and George McNeill, Ira Steward's associate and the president of the Boston Eight-Hour League, became deputy chief. Oliver initially aspired to report facts about labor conditions that would produce "mingled surprise, shame, and indignation" and thus demands for reform. The bureau soon drew criticism for its excessive partiality to the eight-hour movement.[63] Even the more neutral Carroll Wright, who replaced Oliver in 1873, described the bureau's goal as "giving information of real conditions" with the hope "that, through public sentiment or legislation, conditions that are not favorable may be improved."[64]

Trade unions led the legislative campaign for labor statistics bureaus in other states as well. The New York State Workingmen's Assembly received credit for persuading New York legislators to approve the bureau in that state. Labor leaders also influenced legislative approval of bureaus in Colorado, Illinois, Iowa, Kansas, Louisiana, Maine, Maryland, Michigan, Minnesota, New Hampshire, North Carolina, Ohio, Oregon, Pennsylvania, Virginia, Washington, and West Virginia.[65] Once established, organized labor often staffed these bureaus and provided their agenda. McGuire, later an organizer of the United Brotherhood of Carpenters and Joiners of America and vice president of the AFL, briefly served as deputy commissioner of the Missouri Bureau of Labor Statistics. John McBride, a founder and second president of the UMWA (and in 1894 the only labor leader to defeat Gompers for the AFL presidency), served for a time as commissioner of the Ohio Bureau of Labor Statistics. The understaffed New York bureau relied on trade unionists to investigate labor conditions.[66]

The U.S. Congress explicitly acknowledged labor's influence when it approved the creation of a similar federal agency in 1884.[67] Many Knights of Labor and other unionists lobbied President Chester A. Arthur to appoint Terence Powderly, the Knights of Labor leader and the nation's most prominent union spokesman, to direct the bureau. Instead Arthur nominated John Jarrett, a Republican, the leader of the Amalgamated Association of Iron and Steel Workers, and a founder of the embryonic AFL. When Arthur later withdrew Jarrett's name and instead nominated Wright, the head of the Massachusetts bureau, labor newspapers applauded the choice. Wright served as U.S. commissioner of labor statistics for a generation. He often worked closely with Gompers, who consulted with Wright on setting up the New York and federal labor statistics bureaus. Gompers also helped encourage Congress to grant the bureau more autonomy in 1888, recommended the publication of a regular bulletin in the 1890s, and provided a sounding board for bureau investigations.[68]

Labor's strong support for these bureaus rested on three expectations. First, the bureaus would provide unions with direct access to the policy process. Louis F. Post, of the New York City Central Labor Union, expressed the hope that such an agency would have "a man at its head who will not only be competent to administer such a bureau, but also in sympathy with the laboring classes." In retrospect, a turn of the century commentator observed that many of the bureaus had, like New York State's, furnished "a certain official mouthpiece for organized labor in the state." The Missouri Bureau of Labor Statistics said as much in its 1899 report: "Being in close touch with organized labor this department should take cognizance of its just demands."[69] In some states these bureaus had assumed responsibility for factory inspection, free public employment offices, and mediation services by 1900.

Second, trade unionists believed that the bureaus could arm labor with politically potent information about the unfair distribution of profits and wages in the United States. Gompers relied on census data to argue in 1883 that labor did not get a fair share of business profits. Jarrett sought a national bureau that would provide information on profits, investment, and wages. This information, he said, would allow workers to "know exactly what they pay for their labor and for everything that enters into the manufacture of iron and steel, and the same in other manufactures."[70] U.S. Bureau of Labor Statistics reports on the "cost of production" in the early 1890s aimed to advertise the gap between profits and wages.[71] These reports constituted a preliminary step in justifying militant labor action and the redistribution of income. State bureau reports also pursued information on this gap between profits and wages.[72]

Third, union-inspired bureau investigations of unfair practices and poor conditions would further the union policy agenda. Responding to a union resolution, the New York State bureau spent 1884 investigating child labor. This study laid the groundwork for New York's factory act. Florence Kelley's meticulous investigation of "sweating" for the Illinois bureau in the early 1890s similarly shaped the anti-sweatshop provisions of the Illinois Factory Act of 1893. Reports by the Ohio bureau included investigations of slums in Cincinnati, "scrip" money redeemable only in company stores, and yellow-dog contracts. State labor commissioners helped mediate some of the 1885 Knights of Labor strikes to the strikers' advantage. Missouri's labor commissioner, Lee Meriwether, used the 1896 report to expose abuses by the street railway companies in St. Louis, stimulating a reform movement in that city.[73]

Under Wright's direction, the U.S. Bureau of Labor published reports that reflect an ambitious reform agenda. These reports included macroeconomic concerns (*Industrial Depressions*, its first report) and strikes and lockouts in peak years of industrial conflict (1887 and 1894). The bureau's reports on vocational education, social insurance, prohibition, and municipal socialism questioned the fundamental assumptions of laissez-faire and anticipated the Progressive Era agenda. Wright's 1893 report on compulsory social insurance in Germany brought that option to policymakers' attention two generations before the U.S. Social Security Act of 1935.[74]

Though the labor statistics bureaus met unions' expectations to some degree, the bureaus could neither enact laws nor ensure that enacted laws would be implemented effectively. The bureaus could not compel employers to provide them with information or prevent employers from forbidding employees from providing information.[75] Some of the bureaus were losing both their militancy and their influence by 1900. The New York bureau's annual report, eagerly purchased in the mid-1880s, was so complex that it was "practically unread" by 1900. Many bureaus followed the lead of Massachusetts and installed statistical experts rather than labor officials at the helm of these offices. By replacing trusted labor comrades with neutral experts, states undermined labor's faith in the offices. Labor analyst Fred Rogers Fairchild commented that the New York bureau had devoted itself "almost exclusively to the interests of *organized* labor" (emphasis in the original). Middle-class reformers discounted the neutrality of bureaus that remained under trade union control.[76]

State Employment Services

Private employment offices became prime targets of trade unions and bureaus of labor statistics by the 1880s. Some for-profit employment agencies used fraudulent advertising to extract fees from desperate job seekers (often immigrants), and then sent these unfortunate individuals to distant, nonexistent jobs or to serve as strikebreakers. Labor leaders described the offices as "leeches engaged in sucking the life blood from the poor." Labor bureau investigations built support for state regulation of these private agencies. By 1910, twenty-five states had enacted private employment agency regulations.[77]

In the mid-1880s some labor leaders argued that public employment offices could provide an effective remedy for the private employment agency problem. Cincinnati's labor congress drafted state legislation to establish public employment offices in Ohio's major cities. The Ohio legislature enacted this law, authorizing the nation's first state-level public employment offices in April 1890. A letter by the Ohio secretary of state to a national weekly claimed that "the duty of the State to lessen as much as possible the number of unemployed is the strongest reason for the establishment of free employment agencies."[78]

Other cities and industrial states created public employment offices because state labor commissioners, organized labor, and settlement house activists pressed them to do so. Five states (Montana, New York, Nebraska, Illinois, and Missouri) and two cities (Los Angeles and Seattle) emulated Ohio and created similar public bureaus in the 1890s.[79] Without legislative authorization, the California labor commissioner opened a free public employment office in San Francisco in 1895 as a model for the state. The Illinois Bureau of Labor Statistics drafted that state's 1899 law, and both organized labor and settlement house activists from Chicago's Hull House lobbied successfully for its enactment. Missouri's labor commissioner established its offices without formal authorization in 1898. Connecticut's commissioner of labor recommended such offices in his 1899 report, and the state federation of labor instructed its legislative committee to lobby for them in 1900. In 1892, a national convention of labor commissioners passed a resolution recommending the spread of public employment office legislation. The Knights of Labor endorsed the idea at their national convention in the same year.

Trade unionists initially staffed many of these offices. The state commissioner of labor statistics selected employment office superintendents and clerks in Wisconsin (1901), Illinois, Missouri, and Michigan. By one estimate early in the twentieth century, as many as three-quarters of the employment office superintendents were trade unionists.[80]

Soon after the turn of the century, though, it was becoming clear that these offices were not much help for union members or much of a threat to private employment agencies. Skilled workers, particularly in the construction trades, preferred to control placement through business agents and hiring halls. These unions had little reason to surrender placement in their industry to public officials, even if they were fellow unionists. In Wisconsin, labor leaders expressed some fear that the offices would interfere with their prerogatives. Other crafts workers felt that it would be degrading to search for work in the company of unskilled workers.[81] Trade unions' stake in the offices shrank even more when courts struck down laws in Wisconsin and Illinois that prohibited the use of the offices for breaking strikes. When it became possible for the public employment offices to serve as labor centers for scabs (workers hired to replace union members who were on strike), many unionists also lost interest in the offices. By the early twentieth century, American public employment offices were being orphaned by their potential clients and becoming marginal players in labor markets.[82]

Apprenticeship and Licensing

American trade unions had little interest in government-sponsored apprenticeship programs. In the volatile construction industry, small-scale employers, fixed-term projects, and seasonal unemployment made it difficult to sustain labor solidarity. Union-controlled apprenticeship seemed a natural tool for strengthening unions. Building trades workers carried their own tools from job to job, and employers preferred workers trained in a variety of tasks (in contrast to their mass production counterparts). By 1888, the United Brotherhood of Carpenters and Joiners endorsed a union-controlled apprenticeship system to all its locals.[83] Public laws concerning apprenticeship had fallen into "complete disuse" by the late nineteenth century.[84]

By the end of the century, craft licensing seemed to be replacing apprenticeship as a tool for controlling the supply of skilled labor. By 1900, thirteen states (including New York, Pennsylvania, Massachusetts, Illinois, and California) licensed plumbers or gas fitters. Four states licensed stationary engineers. Six states licensed horseshoers. Two states licensed barbers. An 1889 Pennsylvania law required miners to have a certificate of competency. Local boards of miners examined prospective miners under oath about evidence that they had two years of practical experience. Missouri also provided that miners produce evidence of two years' experience and competency.[85] Other specific rules about construction and crafts work also strengthened the unions' power over the skilled workforce. In New York State, unions successfully lobbied for thirty-four building trades laws and thirteen metal trades laws, enacted between 1894 and 1918, affecting safety and protecting union apprenticeship.[86]

Managing Immigration

Immigration constituted one policy area in which the national government unquestionably could exercise jurisdiction. The federal government had encouraged immigration during the Civil War. Though the government reversed its wartime immigration policy in 1868, the Republican platform that year advocated immigration. The Republican administration's Burlingame treaty with China guaranteed travel rights to Chinese citizens in the United States.[87] Court decisions in the 1870s lodged responsibility for immigration control squarely with the federal government. The states had long imposed restriction on the immigration of potential paupers and those posing health risks, and now coastal states enacted new, far-reaching limitations on immigration.[88] In 1876, the U.S. Supreme Court declared unconstitutional the New York, California, and Louisiana immigration taxes on incoming aliens.[89] These Supreme Court decisions swept away his state's "feeble barriers" protecting native workers, declared a California senator.[90]

Trade unions, especially in the western states, intensely resented these perceived Asian rivals and began to lobby for immigration restrictions. As many as a quarter of San Francisco's 1870 wage earners were Chinese. By 1867, leaders of eight-hour leagues in San Francisco helped create "anti-coolie" organizations in the state. Hostility to Chinese workers helped Democrats defeat Republicans in the gubernatorial campaign of that year. When some Chinese began to manufacture shoes, clothing, cigars, and other products on a small scale, the opposition to Chinese labor broadened to include white employers who owned small manufacturing shops.[91] Chinese labor became a national issue when Massachusetts employers transported Chinese coolies across the country to break an 1870 shoemakers strike. By 1880, the Republican Party platform promised to "limit and restrict" Chinese immigration. The Democrats went much further. Their 1880 platform promised "no more Chinese immigration except for travel, education, and foreign commerce, and that even carefully guarded."[92]

As state authority over immigration evaporated, labor's opposition to Chinese workers concentrated on Congress. Congress amended the Burlingame treaty in 1880 to permit restrictions on Chinese labor. Bills to implement these restrictions flooded Congress the following year. By 1882, debate turned on how long Chinese workers would be banned, rather than whether they would be banned. Senator John Miller (R, California) proposed a twenty-year ban. Lead by fervent support in the West, close votes in the Senate (21–20) and the House (131–100) turned back amendments to reduce the term to ten years. President Arthur vetoed the bill and then agreed to a compromise that shortened the ban to ten years.[93] Congress extended Chinese exclusion for another decade in 1892 and extended it indefinitely in 1902.

Organized labor also successfully pressured Congress to enact the Alien Control Labor (Foran) Act of 1885. The Foran Act aimed to eliminate the presumably widespread practice whereby employers signed contracts to import low-wage European craftsmen into American shops. The window glass workers union took the lead in formulating the proposal. In 1879–80, American glass manufacturers had imported Belgian craftsmen under contract to break strikes. Representative Martin Foran (D, Ohio) championed the bill in Congress and spoke for it at labor gatherings. Both the Knights of Labor and AFL crafts workers also supported the bill. Gompers expressed the hope that the ban would prevent the future importation of strikebreakers. Congress passed the Foran Act with little opposition. Employers generally did not oppose the bill, a fact that suggests the unimportance of contract labor for business. Supporters of a high tariff supported the measure as consistent with the argument that protection benefited workers as well as business.[94]

The Foran Act provided labor with yet another lesson in American government's unreliability, however. The law proved hard to enforce and easy to evade. Originally, the law failed to provide for any enforcement at all. Only in

1890 did the secretary of the treasury receive authority to deport violators. The following year, the government established a new Bureau of Immigration. Powderly headed the new bureau. Until 1909, however, the bureau had only two inspectors to police the Atlantic seacoast and Canadian border. The law exempted labor contracts arranged by immigration bureaus run by the states. Courts interpreted the statute narrowly enough to acquit many defendants. A loophole permitted contract labor for "new" industries, and administrators and courts usually accepted employers' definition of "new."[95] Though Congress strengthened the Foran Act several times (1887, 1888, 1891, 1893, 1903, and 1907) in response to labor pressure, immigrants continued to pour into the United States. It became apparent that the act could do little to stem the tide. Most European workers did not immigrate with contracts to work for specific employers; 6,291 contract laborers were deported from 1889 through 1899, years in which two hundred thousand to six hundred thousand immigrants were arriving annually.

In the 1890s, a coalition of workers and other interests gradually formed around further immigration restriction. Conservative Henry Cabot Lodge (R, Massachusetts) proposed a literacy test as a tool for excluding immigrants, arguing that "we have the right to exclude illiterate persons from our immigration." Congress approved such a test, but President Cleveland vetoed it in 1897. Late that year, the AFL took a much stronger anti-immigration stand than it had before. The federation, previously divided over immigration, overwhelmingly passed a resolution supporting the literacy test. After this, the federation grew increasingly supportive of strict immigration limits.[96]

NOT THE TURNING POINT

Many writers argue that the ascendance of the AFL and its voluntarist strategy marked the turning point in American labor exceptionalism. Kim Voss argues that the decline of the Knights of Labor after 1887 removed from American politics a labor organization that advocated an expansive and inclusive labor strategy comparable to those abroad. The erosion of the Knights' influence left the field of labor advocacy to the more resilient, but more narrow and conservative, AFL.[97] Martin Shefter also argues that the ascendance of voluntarism constituted the turning point in American labor development. In Shefter's view, the emergence of craft unions and political machines defused American working-class radicalism by channeling worker action into the pursuit of pure and simple material benefits (through unions representing white craftsmen) and political patronage (through urban political machines).[98] Historian Julie Greene attributes labor conservatism to the leadership of Gompers, who consolidated control of the AFL as the Knights of Labor retreated. In her view Gompers's leadership ensured a conservative labor strategy geared to white, male-dominated crafts unions. Gompers steered the AFL down a path that benefited its members at the expense of women, blacks, new immigrants, socialists, and industrial workers.[99]

This chapter and the preceding one argue that the ascendance of the AFL did not mark the turning point in American labor exceptionalism. The AFL's strategy of a union shop economy, forged in part by frustration with American political institutions, posed a militant, sweeping, and credible challenge to employers' prerogatives. AFL leaders sought to place unions in control of the terms of employment and worker security in the United States, and redoubled their efforts to achieve worker protection by unionizing the American economy. Given the growth of unionization at the turn of the century, and employers' response to that growth, this strategy seemed credible.

Substantial limitations on employers' labor market power now depended on one of two events, however. Either labor had to win the battle and substantially extend the union shop in the American economy, or it had to change its mind about the government establishment of worker protection and successfully lobby for comprehensive labor market policy. For over thirty years, neither event occurred. During that time, employers came to dominate American labor markets.

NOTES

1. U.S. Senate Committee on Education and Labor, *Report of the Committee of the Senate on the Relations between Labor and Capital*, 4 vols. (Washington, D.C.: Government Printing Office, 1885), 1: 340. McGuire later served as AFL secretary, second vice president, and first vice president.

2. Victoria C. Hattam, *Labor Visions and State Power: The Origins of Business Unionism in the United States* (Princeton: Princeton University Press, 1993), 3; Michael Rogin, "Volunteerism: The Political Functions of an Antipolitical Doctrine," *Industrial and Labor Relations Review* 15 (July 1962): 521–35; Ruth L. Horowitz, *Political Ideologies of Organized Labor* (New Brunswick, N.J.: Transaction, 1978); Derek C. Bok, "Reflections on the Distinctive Character of American Labor Laws," *Harvard Law Review* 84 (April 1971): 1394–463; Seymour Martin Lipset, "North American Labor Movements: A Comparative Perspective," in *Unions in Transition: Entering the Second Century*, ed. Seymour Martin Lipset (San Francisco: Institute for Contemporary Studies, 1986), 421–52.

3. Kim Voss, *The Making of American Exceptionalism: The Knights of Labor and Class Formation in the Nineteenth Century* (Ithaca, N.Y.: Cornell University Press, 1993).

4. Conventionally, a closed shop is one in which hiring is closed to those who are not union members. A union shop refers to a shop in which one must join a union as a condition of retaining employment. Gompers in 1902 carefully emphasized that the AFL sought union shops rather than closed shops; American Federation of Labor, *Proceedings of the Twenty-second Annual Convention*, 1902: 20; hereafter, cited as *AFL Proceedings* [date].

5. Minutes of the Executive Council of the American Federation of Labor, in *American Federation of Labor Records: The Samuel Gompers Era* (Microfilm Corporation of America, 1979; hereafter *AFL Executive Council Minutes*), Reel 2, July 21, 1900.

6. *AFL Proceedings*, 1901: 9.

7. Samuel Gompers, *Seventy Years of Life and Labour*, 2 vols. (New York: Dutton, 1925), 1: 338. For Christopher Tomlins, Gompers's earlier assertions of militant autonomy resembled syndicalism; see Tomlins, *The State and the Unions: Labor Relations, Law, and the Organized Labor Movement in America, 1880–1960* (Cambridge: Cambridge University Press, 1985), 56.

8. By arguing that the AFL espoused a fully unionized workforce as a strategic premise, I am not claiming that it follows that the AFL placed a priority on organizing African American and female workers. Far from it. The degree to which the federation actually backed up its goal of inclusiveness with organizational resources, and the degree to which it tolerated racial segregation of organized workers, will attract continuing research. See Julie Greene, *Pure and Simple Politics: The American Federation of Labor and Political Activism, 1881–1917* (New York: Cambridge University Press, 1998), 36–47.

9. James Duncan, "The Law's Delay," *American Federationist* 7 (September 1900): 270–72. Duncan was the Granite Cutters' general secretary, second vice president of the AFL from 1894 to 1899, and first vice president from 1900 to 1928. *The Carpenter* made a similar argument in 1891: "Eight-Hour Laws made by politicians will never be observed by the employers. The only eight-hour law that will ever have binding force in this country will be made and enforced by the workingmen." Quoted in *Our Own Time: A History of American Labor and the Working Day*, David R. Roediger and Philip S. Foner (Westport, Conn.: Greenwood, 1989), 154.

10. As is the conclusion of Horowitz, *Political Ideologies of Organized Labor*, 42. This is also the thrust of Greene's argument in *Pure and Simple Politics*. Richard Schneirov describes the drive for control of employment in Chicago in this period in *Labor and Urban Politics: Class Conflict and the Origins of Modern Liberalism in Chicago, 1864–1897* (Urbana: University of Illinois Press, 1998), esp. 311–12. On the importance of the union shop in the United States relative to Great Britain, see John R. Commons, *Labor and Administration* (New York: Macmillan, 1913), 85–105.

11. *AFL Proceedings*, 1901: 232–35, 240.

12. For a generation, AFL leaders invoked the Scranton resolution as the authoritative AFL position that the crafts should be the basis of the organization. *AFL Proceedings*, 1922: 337–38.

13. Horowitz, *Political Ideologies of Organized Labor*, 32; *The Samuel Gompers Papers, Vol. 6: The American Federation of Labor and the Rise of Progressivism, 1902–6*, ed. Stuart B.

Kaufman, Peter J. Albert, and Grace Palladino (Urbana: University of Illinois Press, 1997), 58–60; Daniel Nelson, *Unemployment Insurance: The American Experience, 1915–1935* (Madison: University of Wisconsin Press, 1969), 65–67, 77.

14. David Montgomery, *The Fall of the House of Labor: The Workplace, the State, and American Labor Activism, 1865–1925* (New York: Cambridge University Press, 1987), 269.

15. In 1898, the AFL clearly ranked the eight-hour law at the top of unions' legislative agenda, with injunction and seamen's bills ranked second, immigration restriction third, and convict labor limitation fourth. See *AFL Executive Council Minutes,* April 21, 1897, and December 21, 1897. Just as clearly, the rising tide of injunctions and Gompers's own potential liability in the case of *Loewe v. Lawler* was making injunctions a top priority by mid-1902; see *AFL Executive Council Minutes*, April 19, 1902; January 21, 1903; and on *Loewe*, September 21, 1903.

16. *AFL Executive Council Minutes*, March 21, 1900; September 20, 1901.

17. See reports of such meetings in *AFL Executive Council Minutes*, April 20, 1897; February 22, 1898; February 13, 1899; October 16, 1899; December 20, 1899; February 18, 1901. On the injunction bill vote, see *Congressional Record*, February 18, 1901: 2589–98.

18. Theodore Roosevelt to Joseph Cannon, letter, September 16, 1906, in Joseph G. Cannon Papers, Illinois State Historical Library.

19. Daniel J. Keefe to the editor of the *Buffalo Republic*, letter, October 5, 1908, in Oscar Straus Papers, U.S. Library of Congress, Box 10.

20. Daniel T. Rogers, *Atlantic Crossings: Social Politics in a Progressive Age* (Cambridge, Mass.: Belknap, 1998), 18.

21. Gary Marks, *Unions in Politics: Britain, Germany, and the United States in the Nineteenth and Early Twentieth Centuries* (Princeton: Princeton University Press, 1989), 120–94.

22. Keith Burgess, "New Unionism for Old? The Amalgamated Society of Engineers in Britain," in *The Development of Trade Unionism in Great Britain and Germany, 1880–1914*, ed. Wolfgang J. Mommsen and Hans-Gerhard Husung (London: Allen and Unwin, 1985), 176; U.S. Commissioner of Labor, *Regulation and Restriction of Output,* Eleventh Special Report (Washington, D.C.: GPO, 1904), 751; Henry Pelling, *A History of British Trade Unionism* (London: Penguin, 1963), 123–27; H. A. Clegg, Alan Fox, and A. F. Thompson, *A History of British Trade Unions since 1889*, 2 vols. (Oxford: Clarendon, 1964), 1: 374.

23. John A. Moses, *Trade Unionism in Germany from Bismarck to Hitler, 1869–1933*, 2 vols. (Totowa, N.J.: Barnes & Noble, 1982), 1: 133–37.

24. From U.S. House of Representatives hearings on *Hours of Labor for Workmen . . . ,* 1900, quoted in Kaufman, Albert, and Palladino, eds., *The Samuel Gompers Papers, Vol. 5: An Expanding Movement at the Turn of the Century, 1898–1902* (Urbana: University of Illinois Press, 1995), 227–28.

25. John Mitchell, *Organized Labor: Its Problems, Purposes and Ideals and the Present and Future of American Wage Earners* (Philadelphia: American Book and Bible House, 1903), 219–20.

26. John R. Commons, "Introduction," in *History of Labour in the United States*, 4 vols., John R. Commons et al. (New York: Macmillan, 1918 and 1935), 1: 17.

27. Schneirov, *Labor and Urban Politics.*

28. David Montgomery, *Beyond Equality: Labor and the Radical Republicans* (New York: Knopf, 1967), 326.

29. William E. Forbath, *Law and the Shaping of the American Labor Movement* (Cambridge: Harvard University Press, 1991), 168–69.

30. *The Samuel Gompers Papers*, 5: 37–38.

31. Clyde Summers, "Admission Policies of Labor Unions," *Quarterly Journal of Economics* 61 (1946): 66–107.

32. Eric Arnesen, "Up from Exclusion: Black and White Workers, Race, and the State of Labor History," *Reviews in American History* 26 (1998): 146–74.

33. Mark Perlman, *The Machinists: A New Study in American Trade Unionism* (Cambridge: Harvard University Press, 1962), 16.

34. Montgomery, *The Fall of the House of Labor,* 200–201; Samuel Gompers to William Smith, letter, September 12, 1900, in *The Samuel Gompers Papers,* 5: 261–62; Summers, "Admission Policies of Labor Unions." See also Herbert Hill, "The Problem of Race in American History," *Reviews in American History* 24 (June 1996): 189–207.

35. Daniel Letwin, *The Challenge of Interracial Unionism: Alabama Coal Miners, 1878–1921* (Chapel Hill: University of North Carolina Press, 1998).

36. *Commonwealth of Massachusetts v. Hunt*, 4 Metcalf 3 (1842).

37. The two most important British laws were the Trade Union Act (1871) and Employers and Workmen Act (1875); Pelling, *A History of British Trade Unionism*, 72–76.

38. States that modified the common law conspiracy doctrine included Illinois (1873), Maine (1883), Maryland (1886), Minnesota, New Jersey (1883), New York (1870, 1881, 1882), and Pennsylvania (1869, 1872, 1876). Felix Frankfurter and Nathan Greene, *The Labor Injunction* (New York: Macmillan, 1930), 137; Hattam, *Labor Visions and State Power*, 144–49. F. J. Stimson held that New York, Minnesota, Mississippi, North and South Dakota, Montana, and Oklahoma had repealed the common law doctrine of conspiracy by statute; in U.S. Industrial Commission, *Labor Legislation*, vol. 5 (Washington, D.C.: GPO, 1900): 129–33.

39. Frankfurter and Greene, *The Labor Injunction*, 137. The states were Illinois, Maine, Maryland, Minnesota, New Jersey, New York, and Pennsylvania.

40. John R. Commons and John B. Andrews, *Principles of Labor Legislation*, (New York: Harper and Brothers, 1916), 95.

41. George Gorham Groat, *Trade Unions and the Law in New York: A Study of Some Legal Phases of Labor Organizations* (New York: Columbia University Press, 1903), 89; Melvyn Dubofsky, *The State and Labor in Modern America* (Chapel Hill: University of North Carolina, 1994), 5.

42. Senate Committee on Education and Labor, *Relations between Labor and Capital*, 1: 340, 378–81, 402–3.

43. *Congressional Record*, June 9, 1886: 5447; and June 11, 1886: 5565–66. States with incorporation laws were Massachusetts (1888), Louisiana (1890), Michigan (1897), and

Kansas (1899); *Second Special Report of the Commissioner of Labor, Labor Laws of the United States,* 2nd ed. (Washington, D.C.: GPO, 1896), passim; and U.S. Industrial Commission, *Labor Legislation,* vol. 5 (Washington, D.C.: GPO, 1900), 148–50.

44. Massachusetts Bureau of Statistics of Labor, *The Incorporation of Trade Unions,* part 3 of the *Annual Report* for 1906 (Boston: Wright and Potter, State Printers, 1906), 147, 149, 156, 160–161, 190. Edwin Witte, in *The Government in Labor Disputes* (New York: McGraw-Hill, 1932), 149, states that unions also came to fear lawsuits against them by their own members if they incorporated.

45. U.S. Industrial Commission, *Final Report,* vol. 19 (Washington, D.C.: GPO, 1902), 951.

46. New York Bureau of Labor Statistics, *Third Annual Report,* 1885 (Albany: The Argus Company, 1886), 365–66, 439, 450; Gompers quoted in Senate Committee on Education and Labor, *Relations between Labor and Capital,* 1: 377, 404.

47. "Notes and Memoranda," *Quarterly Journal of Economics* 6 (October 1886): 86–91 and (July 1887): 487–98.

48. *Quarterly Journal of Economics* 6 (July 1887): 487–98; Robert F. Koretz, ed., *Statutory History of the United States: Labor Organization* (New York: Chelsea House, 1970), 12.

49. Illinois State Board of Arbitration, *First Annual Report* (Springfield: Ed. F Hartman, 1896), 16–17; *Labor Laws of the United States,* passim; U.S. Industrial Commission, *Labor Legislation,* 148–50.

50. Though arbitration became the normal way to resolve disputes in the building trades, private arbitration of building trade disputes rarely involved any public official; Robert Max Jackson, *The Formation of Craft Labor Markets* (Orlando: Academic, 1984), 228–32.

51. U.S. House of Representatives, "Carriers Engaged in Interstate Commerce," House Report 1754, 53rd Cong., 3rd sess., February 2, 1895 (Washington, D.C.: GPO, 1895).

52. Koretz, ed., *Statutory History of the United States: Labor Organization,* 13.

53. Karen Orren, *Belated Feudalism: Labor, the Law, and Liberal Development in the United States* (Cambridge: Cambridge University Press, 1992), 185–88.

54. Hattam, *Labor Visions and State Power,* 162. Still, in 1894, federal judge John Harlan of the Seventh Circuit Court of Appeals upheld the legality of unions and strikes in *Arthur et al. v. Oakes et al.* (63 *Federal Reporter,* 1894), 310–29.

55. Gompers, *Seventy Years of Life and Labour,* 2: 195.

56. Stephen Skowronek, *Building a New American State: The Expansion of National Administrative Capacities, 1877–1920* (Cambridge: Cambridge University Press, 1982), 103–7.

57. Senate Committee on Education and Labor, *Relations between Labor and Capital,* 1: 322; Jerry M. Cooper, *The Army and Civil Disorder: Federal Military Intervention in Labor Disputes, 1870–1900* (Westport, Conn.: Greenwood, 1980).

58. *Congressional Globe,* March 20, 1867: 225.

59. Quoted in Mary O. Furner, "The Republican Tradition and the New Liberalism: Social Investigation, State Building, and Social Learning in the Gilded Age," in *The State*

and Social Investigation in Britain and the United States, ed. Michael J. Lacey and Mary O. Furner (Washington, D.C.: Woodrow Wilson Center Press, 1993), 201; for original quote, see *Congressional Record*, 1883: 194–95.

60. Furner, "The Republican Tradition and the New Liberalism," 210. Examples of these reports include "Labor Troubles in the Anthracite Regions of Pennsylvania, 1887–1888," House Report 4147, 50th Cong., 2nd sess. (Washington, D.C.: GPO, 1889); "Investigation of Labor Troubles in Missouri, Arkansas, Kansas, Texas, and Illinois," House Report 4174, 49th Cong., 2nd sess. (Washington, D.C.: GPO, 1887); "Investigation of the Employment of Pinkerton Detectives," Senate Report 1280, 52nd Cong., 2nd sess. (Washington, D.C.: GPO, 1893); "Employment of Pinkerton Detectives," House Report 2447, 52nd Cong., 2nd sess. (Washington, D.C.: GPO, 1893).

61. Clarence E. Wunderlin Jr., *Visions of a New Industrial Order: Social Science and Labor Theory in America's Progressive Era* (New York: Columbia University Press, 1992).

62. Montgomery, *Beyond Equality*, 262–68; Jonathan Grossman and Judson MacLaury, "The Creation of the Bureau of Labor Statistics," *Monthly Labor Review* 98 (February 1975): 27. See also William R. Brock, *Investigation and Responsibility: Public Responsibility in the United States, 1865–1900* (Cambridge: Cambridge University Press, 1984), 148–84.

63. James Leiby, *Carroll Wright and Labor Reform: The Origins of Labor Statistics* (Cambridge: Harvard University Press, 1960), 48–61; Montgomery, *Beyond Equality*, 306; Susan M. Kingsbury, ed., *Labor Laws and Their Enforcement, with Special Reference to Massachusetts* (New York: Longmans, Green, 1911), 109; Brock, *Investigation and Responsibility*, 148–84.

64. Senate Committee on Education and Labor, *Relations between Labor and Capital*, 3: 280.

65. On New York, see Fred Rogers Fairchild, *The Factory Legislation of the State of New York* (New York: American Economic Association, 1905), 24–25; Gompers, *Seventy Years of Life and Labour*, 1: 194. On Ohio, see Ohio Bureau of Labor Statistics, *Second Annual Report* (Columbus, Ohio: Nevins and Myers, State Printers, 1879), 37–41. On the labor role generally, see U.S. Bureau of Labor, *Bureaus of Labor in the United States*, Bulletin 54 (Washington, D.C.: GPO, 1904): 994–99.

66. On McGuire, see Walter Galenson, *The United Brotherhood of Carpenters: The First Hundred Years* (Cambridge: Harvard University Press, 1983), 24–25. On New York, see Jeremy P. Felt, *Hostages of Fortune: Child Labor Reform in New York State* (Syracuse, N.Y.: Syracuse University Press, 1965), 13–14.

67. *Congressional Record*, March 7, 1884: 1676.

68. Leiby, *Carroll Wright and Labor Reform*, 70; Jonathan Grossman and Judson MacLaury, "The Creation of the Bureau of Labor Statistics, *Monthly Labor Review* 98 (February 1975): 25–31; Judson MacLaury, "The Selection of the First U.S. Commissioner of Labor," *Monthly Labor Review* 98 (April 1975): 16–19; Joseph P. Goldberg and William T. Moye, "The AFL and a National BLS: Labor's Role Crystallized," *Monthly Labor Review* 105 (March 1982): 21–29.

69. Senate Committee on Education and Labor, *Relations between Labor and Capital*, 1: 791; Fairchild, *The Factory Legislation of the State of New York*, 26; Missouri Bureau of

Labor Statistics and Inspection, *Twenty-first Annual Report* (Jefferson City: Tribune Company, 1899), 117.

70. Senate Committee on Education and Labor, *Relations between Labor and Capital*, 1: 363–64, 1142.

71. U.S. Commissioner of Labor, *Cost of Production: Iron, Steel, Coal, etc.*, Sixth Annual Report (Washington, D.C.: GPO, 1891), and *Cost of Production: The Textiles and Glass*, Seventh Annual Report (Washington, D.C.: GPO, 1892).

72. Ohio Bureau of Labor Statistics, *Second Annual Report*, 38; and *Fourteenth Annual Report . . . For the Year 1890* (Columbus, Ohio: Westbote Co., 1891), 3–4.

73. Fairchild, *The Factory Legislation of the State of New York*, 44–45; J. Lynn Barnard, *Factory Legislation in Pennsylvania: Its History and Administration* (Philadelphia: University of Pennsylvania, 1907), 51–53; Kathyrn Kish Sklar, "'The Greater Part of the Petitioners Are Female': The Reduction of Women's Working Hours in the Paid Labor Force, 1840–1917, in *Worktime and Industrialization: An International History,* ed. Gary Cross (Philadelphia: Temple University Press, 1988), 115; Illinois Bureau of Labor Statistics, *Seventh Biennial Report, 1892* (Springfield: H.W. Rokker, 1893), 355–443; Brock, *Investigation and Responsibility*, 156–58; Ohio Bureau of Labor Statistics, *Tenth Annual Report*, 1886 (Columbus, Ohio: Westbote Co, State Printers, 1887), 55; Furner, "The Republican Tradition and the New Liberalism," 210; David Thelen, *Paths of Resistance: Tradition and Democracy in Industrializing Missouri* (Columbia: University of Missouri Press, 1986).

74. U.S. Commissioner of Labor, *Industrial Depressions,* First Annual Report, (Washington, D.C.: GPO, 1886); *Strikes and Lockouts,* Third Annual Report (1888); *Compulsory Insurance in Germany,* Fourth Special Report (1893); *Industrial Education,* Eighth Annual Report (1893); *Strikes and Lockouts,* Tenth Annual Report (1895); *Municipal Ownership,* Fourteenth Annual Report (1900).

75. Fairchild, *The Factory Legislation of the State of New York*, 122; Senate Committee on Education and Labor, *Relations between Labor and Capital*, 1: 343.

76. Fairchild, *The Factory Legislation of the State of New York*, 26; Clara M. Beyer, *History of Labor Legislation for Women in Three States*, in U.S. Department of Labor, Women's Bureau, Bulletin 66 (Washington, D.C.: GPO, 1929), 6.

77. Ohio Bureau of Labor Statistics, *Fourteenth Annual Report*; J. E. Conner, *Free Public Employment Offices in the United States*, U.S. Bureau of Labor Statistics, Bulletin 68 (Washington, D.C.: GPO, 1907), 53–54, 58; see also Udo Sauter, *Three Cheers for the Unemployed: Government and Unemployment before the New Deal* (Cambridge: Cambridge University Press, 1991), 55; Shelby Harrison and Associates, *Public Employment Offices: Their Purpose, Structure, and Methods* (New York: Russell Sage Foundation, 1924).

78. Charlotte Erickson, *American Industry and the European Immigrant, 1860–1885* (New York: Russell and Russell, 1957), 152; Conner, *Free Public Employment Offices in the United States*, esp. 6, 57; Ohio Bureau of Labor Statistics, *Fourteenth Annual Report*, 21–25.

79. Conner, *Free Public Employment Offices*, 1–115, esp. 5, 53.

80. Conner, *Free Public Employment Offices*, 6–8, 31–45, 57, 83, 90; Earl R. Beckner, *A History of Labor Legislation in Illinois* (Chicago: University of Chicago Press, 1929), 387–89.

81. Conner, *Free Public Employment Offices*, 47, 60, 73.

82. Conner, *Free Public Employment Offices*, p 15, 89; Erickson, *American Industry and the European Immigrant*, 179.

83. James M. Motley, "Apprenticeship in the Building Trades," in *Studies in American Trade Unionism*, ed. Jacob H. Hollander and George E. Barnett (New York: Henry Holt, 1912), 263–91; Galenson, *The United Brotherhood of Carpenters: The First Hundred Years*, 156–57.

84. Stimson in U.S. Industrial Commission, *Labor Legislation*, 125.

85. U.S. Industrial Commission, *Labor Legislation*, 243, 268.

86. Philip Taft, *Organized Labor in American History* (New York: Harper and Row, 1964), 234.

87. Darrell Hevnor Smith and H. Guy Herring, *The Bureau of Immigration: Its History, Activities, and Organization* (Baltimore: Johns Hopkins University Press, 1924), 2–3.

88. See Benjamin Klebaner, "State and Local Immigration Restriction in the United States before 1882," *International Review of Social History* 3 (1958): 269-95; Gerald L. Neuman, "The Lost Century of American Immigration Law, 1776–1885" *Columbia Law Review* 93 (December 1993): 1833–901.

89. *Henderson v. Mayor of the City of New York*, 92 U.S. 259 (1876); and *Chy Lung v. Freeman et al.* 92 U.S. 275 (1876); see also Elmer Sandmeyer, "California Anti-Chinese Legislation and the Federal Courts," *Pacific Historical Review* 5 (Summer 1936): 189–211.

90. Gwendolyn Mink, *Old Labor and New Immigrants in American Political Development: Union, Party, and States, 1875–1920* (Ithaca: Cornell University Press, 1986), 85–86; Senator Aaron Sargent (R, California), in *Congressional Record*, May 1, 1876: 2852–53, 2856. Despite their limited control over immigration, states with influential union movements enacted any restrictions on Chinese labor that had a hope of surviving judicial review. California, Idaho, New York, and Wyoming banned the employment of Chinese aliens on public works. See F. J. Stimson, *Handbook to the Labor Law of the United States* (New York: Charles Scribner's Sons, 1896), 120.

91. Alexander Saxton, *The Indispensable Enemy: Labor and the Anti-Chinese Movement in California* (Berkeley: University of California Press, 1971), 3–16, 78–81, 104; Selig Perlman, "Upheaval and Reorganization," in *History of Labor in the United States*, 2: 253; Mink, *Old Labor and New Immigrants in American Political Development*, 71–112; Neil Larry Shumsky, *The Evolution of Political Protest and the Workingmen's Party of California* (Columbus: Ohio State University Press, 1991); Keith Fitzgerald, *The Face of the Nation: Immigration, the State, and the National Identity* (Stanford: Stanford University Press, 1996).

92. John B. Andrews, "Nationalisation," in *History of Labor in the United States*, 137, 149; Donald Bruce Johnson, ed., *National Party Platforms*, rev. ed., 2 vols. (Champaign: University of Illinois Press, 1978), 1: 57, 62.

93. *Congressional Record*, March 9, 1882: 1752; and March 21, 1882: 2127. See also Saxton, *The Indispensable Enemy*, 178. On the Chinese Exclusion Act, see Andrew Gyory, *Closing the Gate: Race, Politics, and the Chinese Exclusion Act* (Chapel Hill: University of North Carolina Press, 1998).

94. Erickson, *American Industry and the European Immigrant*, 148–66; E. P. Hutchinson, *Legislative History of American Immigration Policy, 1798–1965* (Philadelphia: University of Pennsylvania Press, 1981), 85–91.

95. Erickson, *American Industry and the European Immigrant*, 167–96; U.S. Industrial Commission, *Immigration*, vol. 15 (Washington, D.C.: GPO, 1901), xciv–cxvi, and *Final Report*, 957–58, 977–1012. Smith and Herring, *The Bureau of Immigration*, 7; Terence V. Powderly, *The Path I Trod* (New York: AMS, 1968; Orig. 1940), 298.

96. Henry Cabot Lodge, "The Restriction of Immigration," *North American Review* 152 (January 1891): 27–36; Erickson, *American Industry and the European Immigrant*, 184–85; A. T. Lane, *Solidarity or Survival? American Labor and European Immigrants, 1830–1924* (Westport, Conn.: Greenwood, 1987), 95–113; *AFL Proceedings*, 1897: 94.

97. Kim Voss, "Disposition Is Not Action: The Rise and Demise of the Knights of Labor," *Studies in American Political Development* 6 (1992): 272–321, and *The Making of American Exceptionalism*.

98. Martin Shefter, "Trade Unions and Political Machines: The Organization and Disorganization of the American Working Class," in *Political Parties and the State: The American Historical Experience*, ed. Martin Shefter (Princeton: Princeton University Press, 1994), 101–68.

99. Julie Greene, *Pure and Simple Politics*, 36–47.

4

THE EMPLOYERS COUNTERATTACK

> Heretofore organized labor has had only the individual
> employer to combat, but its growing power now demands a
> counter-organization strong enough to resist its encroachments.
>
> —David M. Parry, president of the National Association of
> Manufacturers, 1903[1]

The union shop drive directly challenged employers' control over their own enterprises. Motivated by profits, survival, principle, or pride of personal proprietorship, employers instinctively opposed the surrender of their managerial independence. Abroad, however, many employers had strong reason to subdue these anti-union instincts. In other nations, independent employers often could cooperate with each other for mutual gain, agreeing to keep prices, production, and wages at levels profitable to all. Because they could manage their competition, these employers often engaged unions to help in policing employers' agreements and to establish uniform conditions within an industry. This employer–union collaboration created a role for trade unionism and eventually for public worker protections. In the United States, such employer–union collaboration occurred much less frequently. Instead, many American employers resisted the union shop drive with a ferocious anti-union, "open shop" counterattack.

This employer counterattack marked the turning point in the battle for American labor markets. It was driven by two unique developments that distinguished labor market relationships in the United States: first, dominance of large corporate employers in key industries and second, the vehement anti-unionism of many smaller manufacturers. Both these uniquely American labor market characteristics became pronounced as the union shop drive peaked at the turn of the century.

Like the American Federation of Labor (AFL)'s union shop strategy, American employers' aggressive anti-union strategy was a rational choice under the circumstances. American policymaking institutions helped instill this strong, sustained anti-unionism because they made it so difficult for competing employers to cooperate with one another and therefore with unions. The vacuum in American political authority allowed large corporations to consolidate whole industries in steel, automobiles, and other key parts of the economy. These large corporations unilaterally exercised sufficient power over prices, production, and costs in their industry and had the means and motive to beat back the union shop drive. Smaller manufacturers could not collaborate with each other because no American government had the authority to enforce their agreements. While the Sherman Anti-Trust Act did not obstruct corporate consolidations, it prohibited independent employers from cooperating with each other to set prices. At the beginning of the twentieth century, then, smaller manufacturers found themselves squeezed by growing corporate power on one hand and the union shop drive on the other. Leaders of some of these firms organized the full force of their frustration into a virulent open shop counterattack against the AFL. Employer hostility largely stopped the advance of American unions in the early 1900s and diminished their power after World War I.

COLLABORATION AMONG
EMPLOYERS AND UNIONS

Like employers abroad, American employers made many attempts to agree to limit their competition over prices and output in the nineteenth century. Competing hatmakers, stove manufacturers, coal mine operators, and other employers experimented with "gentlemen's agreements" to limit production, set similar prices, and pay similar wages. Without any means of enforcement, however, these gentlemen's agreements invariably collapsed over time.

Though employers inherently resisted unions as a challenge to managerial authority, when employers cooperated with each other, they often moderated their initial anti-union outlook and acquiesced in multiemployer collective bargaining. Employers in industrializing nations found that trade unions could help enforce these agreements when they could not themselves.[2] Bargaining with unions provided the least unacceptable means of stabilizing industrial relations. It also provided a way to limit labor's influence in the workplace. Cooperating employers could engage unions in helping to police employers' agreements and establish uniform conditions within an industry. Unions could also help centralize the management of labor disputes, expanding the geographical coverage of employer cooperation and setting limits on local wildcat strikes and other job actions. Unions could provide these policing services in return for tolerance of unions in the workplace or, under more favorable conditions, for collective bargaining and concessions on wage and hours. Finally, collective bargaining in an organized industry could set a floor under employers' competition to pay the lowest wages.[3] In Great Britain, for example, employers who refused to join the nut and bolt trade association were forced to do so when the association instructed the union to strike the stubborn holdouts.[4]

European governments made it much easier than the United States did for employers to join together in collective agreements that served their economic interests. Abroad, governments tolerated or even encouraged employers' collective action to keep prices, production, and wages at favorable levels. Such collusion permitted employers in competitive industries such as machinery, coal, or textiles to set limits on price and output competition in an industry, permitting all the firms to enjoy higher profits.[5] When European governments explicitly or tacitly supported multiemployer agreements, employers could collaborate with trade unions for a prolonged period. Organized labor eventually became an integral partner in managing key sectors of the European economy in this way.[6] Employers' intense antipathy to unions faded as they grudgingly built working relationships with organized labor.

The German government explicitly promoted cartels. By 1905, more than four hundred cartels dominated coal, iron, steel, chemicals, textiles, paper, glass, and other basic industries in Germany. Though large steel and iron firms bitterly resisted unions, collective bargaining was widespread in the German building, woodworking, clothing, printing, food, drink, and tobacco industries by 1913. More important, smaller and less concentrated firms engaged in light manufacturing and consumer goods organized against the tough anti-labor heavy industries of the Ruhr Valley. Geographically dispersed and with fragile employer cooperation, small and medium manufacturing firms found that working with the growing unions provided some potential advantages. Small and medium-sized German metalworking enterprises frequently agreed to metalworkers' union demands, giving that union a foundation for future growth and influence in the German labor movement.[7]

British courts explicitly vindicated employer cooperation to manage production and prices. British courts were no less supportive of laissez-faire than American courts. British jurists, though, viewed laissez-faire as a doctrine that permitted employers freely to cooperate to control markets. In Great Britain, the machinists union gained an industrial foothold even when they suffered a humiliating loss in a protracted strike in 1897–98. Though the engineering employers won the agreement decisively, they did not attempt to destroy all vestiges of the machinists union, the Amalgamated Society of Engineers. Instead, the employers, working through an effective national trade association, used the 1898 agreement to nationalize dispute settlement and crafts practices, putting district disputes under national control. National union leaders helped ensure that disputes were settled without local strikes.[8]

The end of World War I marked a major expansion of employer–union collaboration in many European nations. In postwar Germany, the large Ruhr Valley industrial concerns altered their calculations about anti-unionism and entered into a rapprochement with union leader Carl Legien. The Stinnes–Legien agreement of 1918 extended collective bargaining, trade unions, and the eight-hour day in German heavy industry. It also created a Central Working Community that would institutionalize employer–labor cooperation in economic and social issues.[9]

European employers were neither more nor less benevolent than American employers. European employers and American employers behaved in similar ways under similar circumstances. British and German employers extensively used lockouts, strikebreakers, local police, spies, and legal harassment in their battle with unions.[10] In these countries, however, employers had less compelling reasons to resist union demands than their American counterparts because they could more easily work together with each other and with unions to establish a degree of stability and control over profits. Employer cooperation with unions, then, spread more widely in Europe because government permitted employers to cooperate with each other and to use unions as a tool for enforcing that cooperation.

Many American employers also had tried to work with unions to stabilize their industries. The New York State cigar makers' first convention in 1856 included employers and established a set of uniform prices for the state.[11] In the 1860s, anthracite miners in Schuylkill County, Pennsylvania, helped operators of small mines reduce overproduction by restricting tonnage during periods of adequate profits and pay. At the turn of the century, railroads bought up most of the area coal mines and developed a full cartel that managed anthracite prices until World War I.[12] The Stove Founders' National Defense Association, which represented 80 percent of U.S. stove production in the early 1900s, originally opposed the stove molders union. These stove manufacturers, however, came to embrace the union when it helped them establish national price and wage scales that stabilized the industry. In the window glass industry, unions helped employers to restrict output.[13] Building contractors and printers commonly made local agreements to stabilize prices and wages.

Many union leaders publicly advocated such cooperation with employers. In 1883, the carpenters union's leader P. J. McGuire told a Senate committee that wage cuts resulted from the employer's failure to "combine with others like him and organize industry so that there would not be any such competition or any such [market] fluctuations" that in turn forced payroll reductions.[14] In court testimony in a landmark labor case before World War I, the secretary of the United Hatters of North America explained "that the manufacturers had tried for many years to control this industry, but that they had failed." United Hatters union officials had stepped in to provide order and stability.[15]

Interest in employer–union collaboration in the United States peaked as union membership grew at the turn of the century. In May 1900, the International Association of Machinists (IAM) and the National Metal Trades Association (NMTA) concluded the portentous "Murray Hill" agreement at the New York City hotel of that name. Earlier, the settlement of a Chicago machinist strike had resulted in employer agreements to abandon blacklists, arbitrate grievances, and establish a fifty-four hour week. The Murray Hill agreement expanded these terms nationwide. The agreement acknowledged the NMTA as the bargaining agent for all metal trades employers, whether members of the association or not. It established one of the key union goals, a workday reduction to nine hours (effective the following year). It provided extra compensation for overtime.[16]

The National Civic Federation (NCF), established in 1900, actively promoted further employer–union cooperation. The NCF explicitly recruited industrialists, AFL officials, and public leaders to cement employer–union collaboration to solve "the labor question." The NCF's membership included Grover Cleveland; William Howard Taft; Louis Brandeis; John R. Commons; Andrew Carnegie; directors of J. P. Morgan, the International Harvester Company, and other large enterprises; and AFL leaders Samuel Gompers, John Mitchell (president of the United Mine Workers of America, UMWA), and McGuire. Republican senator and leading party strategist Marcus Hanna served as the first NCF president; Gompers briefly served as his successor after Hanna's death in 1904.

The industrialists participated in the NCF in the hope of securing labor peace and more uniform production costs.[17] AFL leaders defended their participation as a pragmatic effort to ensure labor influence in industrial decision making. In return for meeting with these "captains of industry," Gompers insisted that they recognize "the same rights of organization . . . which they demanded for themselves." The NCF at least symbolically acknowledged unions' right to bargain.[18] In the early 1900s, the chair of its Executive Council and guiding spirit, Ralph Easley, emphasized the importance of business and labor cooperation and industrial peace.

Conceivably, American employers could have followed the path of their European counterparts and extended employer–union collaboration, as the NCF advocated. President Taft's secretary of commerce and labor even suggested modeling American efforts to promote such collaboration on Austria's corporatist Permanent Advisory Council on Labor.[19] Some progressive reformers advocated "tripartite" industrial commissions in which representatives of labor, business, and the public together would manage specific labor policies. Such a path might well have laid a foundation for extending labor protection, union political power, and substantial restrictions on managerial prerogatives.

Government in the United States, however, displayed "exceptional enmity" toward price and production associations.[20] U.S. policymaking institutions made collaboration among employers and unions nearly impossible to sustain across state lines.[21] After the turn of the century, employer interest in collaborating with unions receded, and hostility to unions intensified. Large manufacturing corporations did not need to collaborate with unions to establish market power. In many industries smaller firms could not alleviate competitive market pressures even when they did attempt to collaborate with unions.

THE LARGE CORPORATION
AGAINST THE UNION SHOP

The large manufacturing corporation became a distinguishing feature of the American economy at the century's outset, and corporations quickly became the primary bulwark of employer rights in key industries. American economic circumstances facilitated the growth of large corporations. The vast size of the American domestic market enabled many businesses to profit from production on a scale impractical in any other industrializing nation. The relative scarcity of skilled labor increased entrepreneurs' incentive to mechanize and subdivide work into tasks requiring minimal skills. The Singer Sewing Machine and the McCormick Harvesting Machine Companies exemplified the way that huge consumer demand and standardized production could facilitate the growth of large enterprises in nineteenth-century America. National economic circumstances uniquely favored the creation of corporations such as Standard Oil, the United States Steel Corporation, International Harvester, General Electric, and American Telephone & Telegraph. The large companies were larger and more dominant in their industries than were comparable business enterprises abroad.[22]

American economic circumstances encouraged the *growth* of such large corporations in many markets, but the vacuum of political authority, rather than sheer size, permitted the corporations to exercise incomparable market power. American public policy discouraged the cartel, the form of employer cooperation that encouraged employers to deal with trade unions in managing the labor market. Instead of the cooperation of individual employers, gaps in American political authority permitted entrepreneurs to develop firms large enough to dominate markets unilaterally. This dominance freed these firms from the need for unions. The large corporations used their singular economic power to resist the union shop, institute production techniques that undermined the crafts power of unions, and undermine the attractiveness of independent unions by offering corporate welfare benefits.

Unlike European firms, American firms could not use government to enforce collaborative agreements among themselves. American state and federal courts would not enforce gentlemen's agreements to maintain prices. An Illinois court, for example, refused to help a grain dealer enforce a secret arrangement with his partners, explaining simply that common law prohibited contracts in restraint of trade.[23] Unlike British courts, American courts interpreted laissez-faire as a mandate for competition rather than business freedom to collude.

More important, even if states attempted to protect employer collusion, they had no authority to protect colluding employers from predatory competitors outside the state's jurisdiction. Some American states tried to alter their tax codes and other parts of the law to protect businesses inside their borders. Courts struck down these laws as interference with interstate commerce. The 1869 U.S. Supreme Court decision in *Paul v. Virginia* had the effect of limiting state power to discriminate against "foreign" (that is, out of state) corporations in favor of in-state enterprise. The states retained some powers to tax "foreign" companies, but interstate economic competition frequently made such discrimination impractical. In 1901, the president of the NAM advised his members that they were not liable for the fees sometimes demanded by state officials and that "State authorities [have] thus far failed to persist in their demands whenever resistance by this Association has been offered. . . ."[24]

American employers, then, found the cartel impractical. They could not turn to the state governments for effective protection from out-of-state competitors. Some entrepreneurs, searching for a way to manage competition, attempted to overcome limitations by legally binding competing firms in "pools." The trust, then, constituted an alternative to the cartel better suited to American circumstances.

Carnegie and John D. Rockefeller personified the strategy of pooling many competitors in an industry such as steel or oil into a single, loosely organized "trust." These trusts transcended political boundaries and could dominate production and prices in an industry. For example, the oil trust emerged in 1882 when Standard Oil and forty other corporations turned over their common stock to nine trustees. These trustees managed the pooled firms in a way that minimized competition among them. The steel, oil, sugar, whiskey, cordage, lead, and other trusts could raise prices and cut production when times were bad and raise both prices and output when the economy improved. Neither citizens nor public officials had access to the secret arrangements that established these trusts. Their market power also enabled these large enterprises to buy raw materials, finished goods, and labor on favorable terms from smaller, competing suppliers.[25]

The trusts fueled increasing public wrath in the 1880s, and state officials struggled to find the authority to bring them under control. By 1890, twenty-one states had enacted constitutional or statutory prohibitions on trusts. Some state officials tried to prosecute state-chartered corporations that participated in these trusts. California and New York, for example, filed suit against firms affiliated with the Sugar Trust (incorporated as the American Sugar Refining Company in 1891).[26]

The states' limited power to regulate the trust catapulted anti-trust legislation onto the national agenda. Only federal law could reach some of the interstate trust practices that fell between the cracks of the many state laws. In 1890, Congress passed the Sherman Anti-Trust Act, declaring illegal "[e]very contract, combination in the form of trust or otherwise, or conspiracy, in restrain of trade or commerce among the several states. . . ." Proponents of the Sherman Act conceded before it was passed that it could not reach *intra*state conspiracies in restraint of trade. Senator John Sherman (R, Ohio) emphasized that state courts "are admitted to be unable to deal with the great evil that now threatens us."[27] Supporters, then, justified the Sherman Act as a federal intervention to address only those trust activities that were beyond the reach of the states.

With the trust under attack, entrepreneurs sought a more suitable structure for bringing markets under control. They found it in the form of the corporation. Most state anti-trust laws prohibited two manufacturers of a product in the state from agreeing on prices and production. State laws, however, permitted manufacturers to absorb competitors into a single corporation that could set prices and production. Reinvented as a single corporation, a "trust" could transform itself from an illegal combination into a single, legal enterprise chartered by a state government. Since the Sherman Anti-Trust Act had conceded that states controlled corporate law, any state could create a legal shelter for these enterprises. Moreover, a state with relatively lax corporate laws could attract firms from other states to incorporate under its laws.

New Jersey immediately seized the opportunity to attract large firms. Its revised statutes in 1889 diminished corporate liability, reduced legal restrictions on corporate behavior, and allowed corporations to hold stock in other corporations. This latter change made it possible for large businesses allied in a trust simply to merge into a single, large corporation with a New Jersey charter. The number of corporations that incorporated in New Jersey dramatically increased in the four years following the change in its corporate law. These firms paid additional state taxes, reducing the burden on New Jersey's taxpaying voters. This tactic proved very successful in the short run. By 1893 the state's governor credited the policy for allowing the state to eliminate its property tax.[28]

New Jersey thus positioned itself as a magnet for large corporations seeking to maximize their market power and legal autonomy. New Jersey gave corporations unprecedented latitude to govern markets themselves with minimal public oversight or interference. Elihu Root and other corporate lawyers urged clients to accept the state's invitation and incorporate their property holdings under the New Jersey law. Business flowed into the state.[29]

Because other states could not reach businesses incorporated in New Jersey, New Jersey's corporate and economic gains brought pressure in other states to follow its lead in a race "not of diligence but of laxity." Its law particularly made it difficult for neighboring New York, a leading home of industry, to sustain its more extensive corporate regulations. Pressured by the loss of firms, states began to match New Jersey by loosening their corporate laws and offering more autonomy to corporations. The NAM, hardly a proponent of business regulation, acknowledged that the relaxation of corporate law invited deception. Employers were "seeking that State and the aid of those laws which are most lax, which give to them the greatest opportunity for mis-statement without personal danger, which render it most easy for them to appear to be heavily capitalized with the investment probably of comparatively a few dollars."[30]

Two significant U.S. Supreme Court decisions validated the movement from trust to corporation. The case of *United States v. E. C. Knight* (1895) tested the reach of the Sherman Anti-Trust Act in the case of the reviled Sugar Trust. The Court ruled that whatever the degree to which the trust had monopolized the manufacture of sugar, it had not monopolized *interstate* commerce in sugar. The Sherman Anti-Trust Act, then, did not permit the federal government to regulate a company that manufactured goods in a given state, even if the company later shipped the goods across state lines. In 1899, the Supreme Court's ruling in *United States v. Addyston Pipe and Steel* ruled that the Sherman Act could strike down an agreement among separate companies to fix prices, but that it did not permit the federal government to reach a single manufacturing corporation in a particular state that did the same thing.[31]

State and federal regulation of large business now drained through the cavities of American political authority. Merger into a single legal entity opened the irresistible prospect of unprecedented market control. Corporate consolidation rapidly accelerated after the mid-1890s depression. Nationwide, thirteen competing industrial concerns consolidated from 1895 through 1897. Sixteen such consolidations occurred in 1898, sixty-three in 1899, and fifty-seven more between 1901 and 1903. In one-half of these cases, the consolidation absorbed more than 40 percent of the industry. In a third of these cases, the consolidated corporation absorbed at least 70 percent of the industry. Most of these newly consolidated corporations, and all the largest ones (including U.S. Steel, American Sugar Refining, and Standard Oil), incorporated in New Jersey. From 1899 to 1902, New Jersey incorporated 1,100 large corporations, while much larger industrial states incorporated far fewer (Pennsylvania incorporated 131, Ohio eighty, Massachusetts eighty-two, and Illinois forty-two).[32]

American governments, then, presided over the development of large corporations that could exercise more unilateral power over prices, production, and labor markets than the American trusts or European cartels.[33] The large corporation became the distinguishing feature of the American economy and the key to its labor markets soon after the century's turn.[34] While other countries had large firms, none had the singular market power enjoyed by U.S. Steel or Standard Oil. By 1904, corporations owned about one in four manufacturing establishments and produced about three-quarters of the value of manufactured products. They controlled at least one-half of output in seventy-eight industries in the United States. Not all the corporations survived. Those that did, however, provided an effective framework for managing prices, costs, and profits through the "visible hand" of mass production, mass marketing, and the managerial revolution.[35] Observers immediately recognized that these corporations enjoyed vast power in labor markets. By the 1920s, these corporations were using their market power in three ways to maintain employer sovereignty and defeat the union shop strategy.[36]

First, large corporations were powerful enough to defeat unionization drives directly. Large concerns such as McCormick Harvesting Machine Company and Carnegie Steel had battled unions well before the merger wave. By increasing the number of factories in the firm, mergers vastly increased the firm's power to sustain production even if a strike closed one or more factories. Unions commonly tried to focus their resources on organizing a particular factory. The corporations rendered this union tactic ineffective because managers could more easily shift production away from a factory targeted by unions to a nonunion factory.

The steel industry, a central battleground for capital and labor in industrial nations, shows how large American corporations defeated the union shop. Carnegie Steel had established at Homestead, Pennsylvania, in 1892 that the nation's largest steel maker literally would war against unions. The leaders of the U.S. Steel Corporation, formed in 1901, considered taking a moderate position toward the Amalgamated Association of Iron, Steel, and Tin Workers. The corporation offered to accept the union in plants that were already unionized, if the union would permit its other plants to remain nonunionized. In July 1901, the Amalgamated chose to strike to achieve complete unionization of the steel workforce. The corporation soundly defeated the union by rapidly training replacement workers and running production through its nonunion plants. When the Amalgamated conceded defeat in September of that year, it lost representation in fifteen steel mills and remained a force only in the least efficient plants. Whenever the economy slumped over the following decade, U.S. Steel shut down unionized mills first. After the panic of 1907, the union no longer served any purpose for U.S. Steel. On June 1, 1909, U.S. Steel announced that its twelve steel mills would all become nonunion shops. Remnants of the Amalgamated conducted a strike that dragged on for more than a year. The union ultimately capitulated. The corporation's ability to shift production from plant to plant gave it an insurmountable advantage in the battle with unions until the New Deal (except during periods of extreme labor shortage, notably during World War I). UMWA president John L. Lewis later characterized steel as "the Hindenburg line of [American] industry."[37]

Other large corporations also established open shops with little resistance. Less than a year after its formation, International Harvester closed for two weeks and reopened its factories as open shops in September 1903. Other corporations in meatpacking, electrical goods, automobiles, chemicals, and tobacco followed U.S. Steel's lead.[38] Theoretically, many of these large corporations supported unions. Many of their officers remained active in the NCF. They took an uncompromising anti-union stand regarding their own workforces, however.

Second, the large corporations initiated new mass production techniques that destroyed the market value of the crafts skills upon which the AFL's unions shop strategy depended. America's chronic labor shortages and the potential market for mass-produced goods already had inspired employers to mechanize and rationalize the division of labor. The threat of the union shop added urgency to the process of redesigning work to reduce dependence on skilled labor. Scientific management broke down skilled crafts into a series of smaller work steps that unskilled workers and machines could execute. These subdivided tasks permitted the mass production of huge quantities of goods. Industrial engineers assumed the decision-making authority once exercised by skilled craftsmen. Operatives who specialized in a small part of the process assumed responsibility for production.[39] By the mid-1910s many corporations had seized control of apprenticeship from the craft unions, some by creating their own industrial training schools as an alternative. Corporations also instituted personnel management techniques in these years.[40]

Mass production and scientific management undermined the value of crafts skills in the rapidly growing automobile industry. At the Ford Motor Company's Highland (Detroit) plant, the minute subdivision of tasks performed by unskilled workers became a model for other companies. Ford produced nearly half the nation's automobiles in 1914. The company explicitly sought employees who brought no previously learned skills to the job.[41]

Third, some large firms developed corporate welfare programs that diminished the value of the material benefits offered by unions. While social responsibility informed the development of these plans, corporate officials viewed them primarily as a defense against unions and government anti-trust initiatives. Judge Elbert H. Gary of U.S. Steel instructed steel company presidents to make sure that steelworkers were treated as well as union workers so that steelworkers came "to the conclusion that it is for their interests in every respect to be in your employ."[42] Soon after International Harvester secured effective monopoly control of its industry in 1907, more than a dozen state legislatures threatened to enact legislation aimed at reducing the company's power. After an exposé appeared in *Collier's* magazine in 1908, management drew up a plan for accident and sickness benefits. Internal company reports indicated that the former could save the company money by reducing its liability against lawsuits brought by injured workers. The company's pension plan rewarded workers for not joining unions.[43] Within a year after industrial warfare in Colorado, Rockefeller announced a program of corporate welfare and employee representation for the Colorado Fuel and Iron Company. When its annual turnover rate reached 416 percent in 1912–13, Ford Motor Company instituted the eight-hour day and a five-dollar day for employees. Ford investigated employees to certify that they were acceptably loyal to qualify for its benefits.[44]

The development of the large manufacturing corporation made the battle for control of the American labor market decisively different from similar battles being waged abroad. The AFL's crafts-based union shop strategy now confronted large mass-production organizations with the will and power to defeat it. Corporate power, along with the union shop strategy itself, forced the smaller firms to assume active leadership of the anti-union counterattack.

SMALLER EMPLOYERS
AGAINST THE UNION SHOP

Smaller manufacturers confronted the AFL's union shop strategy without the market power that the large corporations enjoyed. These manufacturers were much more difficult to consolidate into dominant firms. Anti-trust law precluded these smaller enterprises from forming cartels.[45] The corporate giants squeezed the profits of these smaller firms and sometimes threatened their independent existence.

The union shop posed a more immediate threat to many of these smaller employers than the corporations. The unions' efforts to expand economic conflicts increased the depth and breadth of these employers' opposition to the union shop strategy. Labor leaders strategically targeted particular small firms for organizing drives, often to unionize the workforce of the most recalcitrant employers. Unions used "secondary strikes" and boycotts to pressure these firms. Secondary strikes were aimed at other small employers who could pressure the targeted firm to bargain with the union. The AFL's "We Don't Patronize" list advocated that workers boycott these marked firms.[46] When a small firm agreed to bargain collectively while competitors remained nonunion, competitive pressures on unionized employers increased.

Threatened by the advance of the corporations on the one side and the unions on the other, many owners of smaller enterprises grew furious about what seemed to be a closing economic trap. Many joined in a ferocious "open shop" counterattack aimed at fortifying their labor market position against the unions. Combative anti-unionism was a rational response under the circumstances.[47] This anti-union hostility became a second distinguishing feature of the battle for American labor markets. Because these firms continued to employ a substantial part of the American workforce after the merger wave,[48] their counterattack altered the course of American labor history.

The militant leaders of small firms' open shop movement viewed unions as personal enemies that sought to seize control of their businesses. These employers owned and personally managed their firms.[49] They included St. Louis stove manufacturer James Van Cleave (president of Buck's Stove and Range Company), Indianapolis vehicle manufacturer David Parry, Michigan cereal manufacturer C. W. Post, and Dayton employer John Kirby. Van Cleave described the AFL boycott of his stove company as a "dastardly effort . . . to assassinate our business."[50] Post, who spent a million dollars a year in advertising his cereals in the early twentieth century, was outraged when printers in a New York strike demanded a boycott of the newspapers' advertisers.[51]

The leaders of the small firms' open shop drive based their opposition on clear, simple principles of employer sovereignty in labor markets. In a speech to fellow small employers in 1906, the president of the association of printing employers, George H. Ellis, warned that they "must pay more attention . . . if we are going to retain the control of our own lines of business. . . ." Employers were not antagonistic to unions, Ellis argued, but rather "[w]e are antagonistic to the control of our business by these unions."[52] "Labor is a commodity," declared Post; it should be graded, classified, and sold and bought by free individuals. Each "owner of labor" should enjoy the freedom to "sell and deliver his or her labor without interference."[53]

The union shop drive galvanized many smaller manufacturers to organize locally in their own defense. Kirby inspired one of the first such organizations, the Dayton Employers' Association, uniting thirty-eight local firms to resist the metal trades' organizing drive in 1901. Van Cleave similarly organized many St. Louis employers into a Citizens' Alliance. Henry Leland (the founder of the Cadillac Motor Company) helped create the formidable Detroit Employers' Association, a model for open shop proponents. Washington, D.C., Indianapolis, and Los Angeles became notable open shop cities.[54]

Local Citizens' Alliances frequently used the unions' methods against them. San Francisco members paid dues to the organization, tried to boycott union shops, and even carried "anti-union" cards. The Metal Manufacturers' Association of Philadelphia established a labor bureau that provided a ready supply of strikebreakers as well as an employment exchange for both skilled workers and employers. The Employers' Association of Detroit created a labor bureau that kept files on half of the city's workforce by 1906 and coordinated efforts to develop workers' skills through a trade school rather than union-controlled apprenticeships.[55]

Leaders of local open shop movements soon pooled their efforts nationally. Representatives of more than a hundred local organizations formed a national Citizens' Industrial Association in the fall of 1903. For a brief period under the leadership of C. W. Post, the Citizens' Industrial Association conducted an aggressive open shop drive nationally. It organized local employers and tried to rally communities against organized labor.[56]

The breakdown of the Murray Hill agreement deepened the intensity of the open shop drive and accelerated its nationalization. The Murray Hill agreement stipulated that metal trades employers would institute the nine-hour day in May 1901. The employers implemented the shorter day with proportionate wage cuts. Intending shorter hours for the same pay, the machinists struck to restore their wages. The NMTA swung to a vehement open shop position soon after the agreement collapsed. Guided by E. F. Du Brul, the NMTA provided its more than three hundred members with strategic and legal advice as well as private detectives and files on thirty-five thousand employees. The NMTA created the Independent Labor League of America, which provided machinists who would replace strikers. The NMTA, the National Founders' Association, and the National Erectors' Association became implacable foes of unions in response to rapid unionization of employees in those industries between 1900 and 1903.[57]

On the surface, American employers' unusual hostility to unions seemed driven by both the relative weakness of their adversaries and the technology that enabled American manufacturing to develop on a much larger scale. American employers, in short, "had both greater interest in attacking union controls at work and greater ease in doing so."[58]

The nationalization of the open shop drive, however, resulted from a more intricate sequence of events and strategic choices—the ineffectiveness of government authority for labor protection, the resulting militant union shop strategy of the AFL, and the concurrent growth of powerful corporations—whose course had been guided by American political institutions. Employers otherwise incapable of alleviating competitive price and production pressures could at least collaborate with each other against the unions.

President Theodore Roosevelt's administration seemed to validate the open shop impulse. In 1902, the UMWA struck in the anthracite mines of Pennsylvania. The strike caused grave public concern over the threat to an indispensable fuel. President Roosevelt intervened with an arbitration commission that forced employer concessions to the union.[59] The anthracite coal strike helped nationalize the anti-union resentments of the smaller manufacturers. At the same time, Roosevelt seemed to sanction the open shop by reinstating a fired federal employee in 1903.[60]

The NAM became the instrument for institutionalizing the open shop drive across industries on a national scale. In 1902, David Parry won the presidency of the NAM. Parry, Post, and Kirby declared war on organized labor on behalf of smaller businesses. The NAM's 1903 Declaration of Principles explicitly dedicated the organization to the protection of an employer's unlimited right to hire and fire employees and to set wages and hours. "Employers must be unmolested and unhampered in the management of their business," declared the NAM.[61] The open shop offensive invigorated the NAM. Its membership grew rapidly after the 1902 convention and tripled to three thousand between 1902 and 1904.[62] Van Cleave and Kirby succeeded Parry as NAM presidents.

NAM leaders often attacked the NCF, the representative of "Socialized or Centralized Industry," for accommodating unions. Parry criticized the NCF for encouraging "a combination of labor and capital combinations, and therefore of adopting policies foreign to the principle of our Constitution. . . ."[63] In turn, the NCF secretary Ralph Easley cautioned Secretary of Commerce and Labor Oscar Straus that the NAM was hostile to the NCF because "we believe in dealing with the unions."[64]

Other organizations broadened the open shop offensive still further. The American Anti-Boycott Association (AABA) originated in a boycott threatened in early 1901 by the hatters' union of Danbury, Connecticut, against Dietrich E. Loewe's hat firm. A year later, Loewe helped call a meeting of employers on the AFL's "We Don't Patronize List" to consider counteraction. By the middle of 1903, over a hundred smaller manufacturers on the list organized to oppose the union shop and the labor-sponsored boycott by pursuing litigation against the unions. In early 1908, representatives of the NAM and national employers' associations created the National Council for Industrial Defense (NCID), an organization designed to coordinate employer lobbying efforts.[65] Although they had no more success in establishing an open shop economy than the AFL had in establishing a union shop economy, these smaller employers substantially impaired the union shop drive and the implementation of many labor policy proposals. They did so by using three kinds of weapons against labor.

Publicity constituted the first of the NAM's main weapons against the union shop and the AFL's legislative agenda. In 1903, NAM president Parry acknowledged that the unions had gained the upper hand in the struggle for public opinion. He advised the members that the "chief work . . . of this Association is an educational one—the molding of public opinion." The NAM aimed to persuade a broader audience that the AFL constituted another sinister "trust" whose belligerence, corruption, and inclination to violence betrayed American values (figure 4.1). The characterization of the AFL as a trust was both a rhetorical and a legal tactic, consistent with employers' effort to bludgeon the unions with the Sherman Act (see chapter 7).

The open shop employers targeted opinion leaders in government, universities, churches, and industry. It broadcast its message in publications such as *Amer-*

Figure 4.1: *From* The Square Deal *(March 1908).*

The Chief Offender

ican Industries and *Open Shop*. The Citizens' Industrial Association published the open shop publication *The Square Deal* and even advertised in the *New York Times*. The AABA mailed bulletins, briefs, judicial opinions, and congressional testimony to six thousand companies, three hundred trade associations, many newspapers, four hundred colleges and universities, and a number of judges. The AABA also helped open shop employers by providing them a model yellow-dog contract.[66]

These employers used legislative lobbying as a second weapon against the unions and their agenda. In the early 1900s, individual employers and NAM leaders began to appear regularly to oppose federal labor legislation. They lobbied with "untiring persistency and unwavering earnestness."[67] AABA spokesman Daniel Davenport eventually took up residence in Washington, D.C., and routinely testified against labor proposals. The NAM made James Emery, a counsel for the Citizens' Industrial Association, its chief Washington lobbyist in 1907. Emery represented the NAM until his retirement forty years later.[68]

The NAM cultivated links with legislators such as House Speaker Joseph Cannon (R, Illinois) and House Judiciary Committee Chair Charles Littlefield (R, Maine). Both legislators were reliable opponents of AFL-endorsed labor legislation in the first decade of the century. These links included advice on appointments to key committees, such as the Labor and Judiciary Committees. At least one Judiciary Committee member lost his committee seat in 1905 because of his pro-labor sympathies. These employer groups also campaigned against pro-labor legislators and on behalf of their legislative allies. They coordinated efforts to deluge Congress with anti-labor policy telegrams, anticipating contemporary grassroots lobbying strategies. The organization took credit (and was given credit by the AFL) for derailing federal labor legislation.[69] State employers' groups, notably in Illinois, also gained a reputation for influential opposition to labor legislation.[70] Though the NAM's influence faded with the fall of Cannon in 1910 and the ascendance of a Democratic president (Woodrow Wilson) and Congress in 1913, it already had succeeded in halting the momentum of AFL proposals that might have substantially fortified union power.

Third, these employers aggressively used litigation to disarm unions and block the implementation of unfavorable laws. Inspired by the success of 1890s injunctions against railroad strikes, smaller employers asked courts to enjoin strikes, picketing, and boycotts. "Injunctive relief" required little employer investment (affidavits could be prepared quickly and simply) and no cooperation with other employers.[71] The most notable anti-union judicial decisions of this period resulted from the smaller employers' strategic and highly publicized challenge to the union shop. These two cases, *Loewe v. Lawlor* and *Buck's Stove and Range*, resulted primarily from employer resistance to unions, not the unilateral judicial seizure of labor market policy by laissez-faire judges.

The Danbury hatters' union strike against Loewe's hat firm in 1902 aimed to envelop an important segment of the hat industry in the union shop. Loewe, whose company was too financially strapped to meet the union's demand, refused to join other hatmakers in an industrywide collective bargaining agreement with the union. Daniel Davenport and the AABA took up Loewe's cause as a critical test case. It ultimately invested over $20,000 in prosecuting it. Davenport's lawsuit argued that the unionists had violated the Sherman Act by conspiring to restrict interstate commerce. The suit sought treble damages from the union. By choosing the Sherman Act, Davenport effectively removed the dispute from Connecticut courts and nationalized this legal assault on the AFL. The hatters' union lawyers, ironically, staked their defense in federalism: "We stand here for the State jurisdiction," they claimed, and tried to persuade the judges to leave alone the "autonomy of the states" in this particular case. In February 1908, the U.S. Supreme Court unanimously ruled that the Sherman Act applied to such union activity and remanded the case to lower federal courts for trial. The cases dragged on for nine years. By the time appeals were exhausted, the Danbury case cost the hatters' union and the AFL the substantial sum of $421,477 in fines, court costs, and attorney's fees.[72]

Like Loewe, stove manufacturer James Van Cleave refused to join in the collaborative agreement between his industry and the unions representing its workers. Unlike Loewe, Van Cleave was an enthusiastic leader of the national open shop movement. He assumed the NAM presidency in May 1906. When his employees struck for shorter hours in August of that year, the AFL added the company to its "We Don't Patronize" list. AFL leaders recognized that they were challenging the NAM directly. Van Cleave relished this opportunity to counterattack. At Davenport's request, the federal district court in Washington, D.C., enjoined the AFL from publishing its boycott list. The court issued the injunction on December 18, 1907, in the case "which both sides agree is the great test of strength between the National Manufacturers' Association and the Federation of Labor."[73] Though the AFL pulled the list from *American Federationist* in February 1908, the labor leaders complained bitterly about the injunction. The AABA lawyers urged the court to find the union leaders in contempt for these complaints. The court agreed with the AABA on December 23, 1908. Its decision included a sentence of a year in prison for Gompers (which he never served). While these cases eventually became moot after Van Cleave's death in 1910, the AFL's termination of the "We Don't Patronize" list ended a major union weapon in the union shop strategy.[74]

Gompers explicitly acknowledged the effectiveness of individual injunctions generally and the AABA efforts in particular. "The damage to trade union effort lies not only in the injunctions actually issued," he noted, "but also on occasions in the partial paralysis of union activity because of the threat of injunctions by employers"; the police also sometimes acted as if courts had already granted injunctions. Battling injunctions diverted money from strike funds and time from organizing efforts.[75] Though such court rulings helped to contain the expansion of unions, the courts were not slavish enforcers of employers' rights. Courts sometimes refused to grant employers' requests for injunctions. Most important, a series of state court decisions generally upheld the union shop as legally valid, a point that even Davenport conceded by 1915.[76]

The open shop counterattack indisputably put unions on the defensive in the century's first decade and suppressed union expansion in the United States (figure 1.1). From 1904 until 1915, unions found it hard to win strikes and recruit members. By 1904 over 12 percent of the American workforce belonged to trade unions, a level of unionization about the same as that in Great Britain and twice the rate of German unionization. Within two years, however, that growth stopped. Unions were stymied in the heartland of American manufacturing. Detroit, for example, rapidly was becoming the center of automobile manufacturing employment. In that city, the workforce more than doubled to 175,000 between 1904 and 1911. The number of union members in Detroit, however, barely increased in those years. On the eve of World War I in 1913, the percentage of British and German workers who belonged to unions was twice that of American workers.[77] As the threat of the union shop economy receded by 1909, so did the passion that fueled open shop campaigns.

Smaller manufacturers adapted their strategy for responding to economic threats within the constraints and opportunities that American political structure offered them. For many, opposition to the closed shop constituted a path of much less risk and resistance than cooperation with labor. Open shop employers renewed their drive in the wake of the union upsurge during World War I.

WAR AND NORMALCY

The war in Europe caused demand for American goods to soar. Unemployment plummeted. Unions took advantage of the strengthened economic position of workers. Now organizing drives were much more successful. Between 1917 and 1920, union membership increased from three million to five million. In 1920 nearly 20 percent of the labor force was unionized.

Briefly, the open shop fortifications buckled. Unions flourished in coal mining and railroads. Unions took root even in the meatpacking industry, previously an open shop bastion. With Gompers's blessing, a national organizing committee set about to organize the steel industry. The steel organizers established a beachhead in the Chicago area. The old Amalgamated Association reawakened as an industrial union. The drive to organize steel rapidly spread to Cleveland, Ohio; Youngstown, Ohio; Johnstown, Pennsylvania; and Wheeling, West Virginia. Steelworkers achieved the eight-hour day and wage increases.[78]

As the postwar economy slowed, labor market antagonism intensified. Wartime successes encouraged organized labor to take a militant stand with employers. In 1919, four million workers took part in more than three thousand strikes. As their labor market leverage grew after the war, however, employers resisted the invigorated unionization drives with increased determination. U.S. Steel and others had delayed efforts to recognize unions until the war's end. Now these firms resolved to defeat the unions and insisted that labor negotiations be conducted at the plant level, rather than at the industrial level between the corporation and national unions. This decentralized bargaining strengthened managers' control and diminished union strength by dividing union power.[79]

Employers began a new open shop offensive. Invoking wartime patriotism, its proponents labeled the open shop the "American Plan." Local "Law and Order" groups recalled the earlier "Citizens Associations." One postwar survey identified 540 open shop organizations in 240 cities. Emery recommended a renewed NAM commitment to the open shop, and the association created an open shop department in October 1920. The U.S. Chamber of Commerce, formed in 1912, originally distinguished itself from the NAM by taking a much more moderate position on cooperation with organized labor. Now, the Chamber joined the NAM in this second open shop counterattack. The membership of the Chamber nearly unanimously agreed with a referendum declaring "The right of open-shop operation . . . is an essential part of the individual right of contract possessed" by employers and workers.[80]

Employers now unequivocally won the postwar battle for control of American labor markets. Government swung to the employers' aid. State and local law officers (and in Gary, Indiana, the U.S. military) broke a massive 1919 steel strike.[81] Strikes around the nation were defeated. The steel and auto industries returned to the open shop. Even in the labor bastion of San Francisco, the building employers imposed the open shop. In 1920–21, unions lost a million and a half members.[82] Reformers described the perception that "promising efforts to bring about better industrial relations" were being "swept away by a tide of reaction."[83]

While the U.S. government helped employers repel the union shop, new levels of cooperation between employers and unions emerged abroad. The Stinnes–Legien agreement laid the groundwork for a social partnership between German capital and labor. The postwar crisis also led to the recognition of metalworkers in France with government support. In Great Britain, the postwar crisis served to reinforce trade agreements.[84]

By the 1920s, in contrast, employers controlled American labor markets to an extent unparalleled in comparable nations. Trade associations formed "open price" agreements to exchange information on prices, production, technology, and personnel.[85] These associations provided employers a legitimate (if weak) way to cooperate with each other. This form of collective action required little union participation. Instead, this form of employer collusion sometimes promoted additional anti-union counterattacks.

Neither trade associations nor the NAM nor the U.S. Chamber of Commerce spoke definitively for American business. No "peak" association effectively coordinated employers' response to strikes, voiced employers' concerns in the lawmaking process, or presented a unified business position to the public.[86] Such peak organizations would establish the kinds of cooperation among employers in some European countries that facilitated comprehensive worker protections and egalitarian programs. Coping with unions, under American circumstances, did not require systematic and inclusive collective action on the part of American employers.

THE TURNING POINT

Anti-trust probably made American labor market exceptionalism irreversible. It prompted the invention of large firms with substantial legal and economic autonomy. It stimulated anti-union hostility among smaller employers who could not cooperate. And it made unions retreat to the safer trenches of material benefits, eschewing social legislation that could not advance without the power of their support.

The decisive turning point in American labor market policy occurred in the first decade of the twentieth century. With the union shop drive defeated in most industries, the AFL could not establish broad-based protections for American workers. Because the open shop drive spilled into the legislative arena, employer opposition also helped to defeat or limit legislative efforts to limit their labor market authority.

Some corporations invented private labor market programs that protected employer sovereignty. These corporate activities provided models of private, employer-controlled labor market policy in regulation, active labor market management, collective bargaining, and work insurance. As the record of union and legislative frustrations lengthened, American proponents of worker protection increasingly embraced these corporate labor market programs and the employer sovereignty they protected.

NOTES

1. David M. Parry's first presidential address to the National Association of Manufacturers, in *Proceedings* of the Eighth Annual Convention, 1903: 16; hereafter, cited as *NAM Proceedings* [date].

2. Franz Traxler, "Two Logics of Collective Action in Industrial Relations?" in *Organized Industrial Relations in Europe: What Future?* ed. Colin Crouch and Franz Traxler (Aldershot, UK: Avebury, 1995).

3. Keith Sisson, *The Management of Collective Bargaining: An International Comparison* (Oxford: Basil Blackwell, 1987), 136; Peter Swenson, "Bringing Capital Back In, or Social Democracy Reconsidered: Employer Power, Cross-Class Alliances, and Centralization of Industrial Relations in Denmark and Sweden," *World Politics* 43, no. 4 (July 1991), 513–44.

4. Clarence E. Bonnett, *History of Employers' Associations in the United States* (New York: Vantage, 1956), 239.

5. U.S. House of Representatives, Committee on the Judiciary, Hearings on *Trust Legislation*, vol. 2 (Washington, D.C.: Government Printing Office, 1914), 1197–217; Henry R. Seager and Charles A. Gulick, *Trust and Corporation Problems* (New York: Harper and Brothers, 1929), 552–627; Hans B. Thorelli, *The Federal Antitrust Policy: Origination of an American Tradition* (Baltimore: Johns Hopkins University Press, 1955), 34. See also Morton J. Keller, "The Pluralist State: American Economic Regulation in Comparative Perspective, 1900–1930," in *Regulation in Perspective: Historical Essays*, ed. Thomas K. McCraw (Cambridge: Harvard University Press, 1981), 62–64; Martin J. Sklar, *The Corporate Reconstruction of American Capitalism, 1890–1916: The Market, the Law, and Politics* (New York: Cambridge University Press, 1988), 154–56. For a more formal presentation of collective action among capitalists, see John R. Bowman, *Capitalist Collective Action: Competition, Cooperation, and Conflict in the Coal Industry* (New York: Cambridge University Press, 1989), 1–31.

6. Swenson, "Bringing Capital Back In, or Social Democracy Reconsidered."

7. Bo Stråth, *The Organization of Labour Markets: Modernity, Culture and Governance in Germany, Sweden, Britain, and Japan* (London: Routledge, 1996), 36. Klaus Schönhoven, "Localism–Craft Union–Industrial Union: Organizational Patterns in German Trade Unionism," in *The Development of Trade Unionism in Great Britain and Germany, 1880–1914*, ed. Wolfgang J. Mommsen and Hans-Gerhard Husung (London: Allen and Unwin, 1985), 227; Sisson, *The Management of Collective Bargaining*, 147.

8. Sisson, *The Management of Collective Bargaining*, 165; Eric Wigham, *The Power to Manage: A History of the Engineering Employers' Federation* (London: Macmillan, 1973).

9. Sisson, *The Management of Collective Bargaining*, 138; John A. Moses, *Trade Unionism in Germany from Bismarck to Hitler, 1869–1933*, 2 vols. (Totowa, N.J.: Barnes & Noble, 1982), 1: 222–23; Gerald D. Feldman, *Iron and Steel in the German Inflation, 1916–1923* (Princeton: Princeton University Press, 1977), 82–83.

10. H. A. Clegg, Alan Fox, and A. F. Thompson, *A History of British Trade Unions since 1889,* 2 vols. (Oxford: Clarendon, 1964), 1: 161–68; Klaus Saul, "Repression or Integration? The State, Trade Unions, and Industrial Disputes in Imperial Germany," and Geoffrey Alderman, "The National Free Labour Association: Working-Class Opposition to New Unionism in Britain," in *The Development of Trade Unionism in Great Britain and Germany, 1880–1914,* 302–10, 338–56; W. L. Guttsman, *The German Social Democratic Party: From Ghetto to Government* (London: Allen and Unwin, 1981), 90.

11. U.S. Senate, Committee on Education and Labor, *Report of the Committee of the Senate on the Relations between Labor and Capital,* 4 vols. (Washington, D.C.: GPO, 1885), 1: 449.

12. U.S. Commissioner of Labor, *Regulation and Restriction of Output,* Eleventh Special Report (Washington, D.C.: GPO, 1904), 485–86; David Montgomery, *The Fall of the House of Labor: The Workplace, the State, and American Labor Activism, 1865–1925* (New York: Cambridge University Press, 1987), 159; David Brody, "Market Unionism in America: The Case of Coal," in *In Labor's Cause: Main Themes on the History of the American Worker,* ed. David Brody (New York: Oxford University Press, 1993), 131–37.

13. Bonnett, *History of Employers' Associations*, 229, 350–51; U.S. Commissioner of Labor, *Regulation and Restriction of Output*, 13, 178.

14. U.S. Senate, *Relations between Labor and Capital*, 1: 359.

15. Daniel Robinson Ernst, "The Lawyers and the Labor Trust: A History of the American Anti-Boycott Association, 1902–1919" (unpublished Ph.D. dissertation, Princeton University, Department of History, 1989), 139–40.

16. Mark Perlman, *The Machinists: A New Study in American Trade Unionism* (Cambridge: Harvard University Press, 1961), 25–27; Montgomery, *The Fall of the House of Labor*, 261–69.

17. On the NCF, see Marguerite Green, *The National Civic Federation and the American Labor Movement, 1900–1925* (Washington, D.C.: Catholic University of America Press, 1956); James Weinstein, *The Corporate Ideal in the Liberal State, 1900–1918* (Boston: Beacon, 1968); Montgomery, *The Fall of the House of Labor*, 257–69; Clarence E. Wunderlin Jr., *Visions of a New Industrial Order: Social Science and Labor Theory in America's Progressive Era* (New York: Columbia University Press, 1992).

18. Samuel Gompers, *Seventy Years of Life and Labour*, 2 vols. (New York: Dutton, 1925), 2: 105–15; American Federation of Labor, *Proceedings* of the Thirty-first Annual Convention, 1911: 218, 258; hereafter, cited as *AFL Proceedings*, [date]. Weinstein, *The Corporate Ideal in the Liberal State*, 18.

19. U.S. Department of Commerce and Labor, *Labor Conference: Proceedings of the Conference with the Representatives of Labor*, February 10–11, 1909 (Washington, D.C.: GPO, 1909).

20. Marc Schneiberg and J. Rogers Hollingsworth, "Can Transaction Cost Economics Explain Trade Associations?" in *The Firm as a Nexus of Treaties*, ed. Masahiko Aoki, Bo Gustafsson, and Oliver E. Williamson (London: Sage, 1990), 320–46 (quote 330).

21. J. Rogers Hollingsworth, "The Logic of Coordinating American Manufacturing Sectors," in *Governance of the American Economy,* ed. John L. Campbell, J. Rogers Hollingsworth, and Leon N. Lindberg (New York: Cambridge University Press, 1991), 35–73. For a specific and telling industry analysis, see Colleen A. Dunlavy, *Politics and Industrialization: Early Railroads in the United States and Prussia* (Princeton: Princeton University Press, 1994).

22. Alfred D. Chandler Jr. argues that American market conditions caused the growth of American corporations in *The Visible Hand: The Managerial Revolution in American Business* (Cambridge: Harvard University Press, 1977) and in *The Scale and Scope: The Dynamics of Industrial Capitalism* (Cambridge: Belknap/Harvard, 1990). See also H. J. Habakkuk, *American and British Technology in the Nineteenth Century: The Search for Labour-Saving Inventions* (Cambridge: Cambridge University Press, 1967).

23. Tony Freyer, *Regulating Big Business: Antitrust in Great Britain and America, 1880–1990* (Cambridge: Cambridge University Press, 1992), 23–26; Thomas McCraw, "Rethinking the Trust Question," in *Regulation in Perspective*, 1–55; *Craft et al. v. McConoughy*, 79 Ill., 346 (1875).

24. Christopher Grandy, *New Jersey and the Fiscal Origins of Modern American Corporation Law* (New York: Garland, 1993), 56; Harry N. Scheiber, "Federalism and the American Economic Order, 1789–1910," *Law and Society Review* 10, no. 1 (Fall 1975): 57–118; Henry N. Butler, "Nineteenth-Century Jurisdictional Competition in the Granting of Corporate Privileges," *Journal of Legal Studies* 14 (January 1985): 129–66; *Paul v. Virginia*, 75 U.S. (Wall.) 168 (1869); Alton D. Adams, "State Control of Trusts," *Political Science Quarterly* 18 (September 1903): 462–79; Seager and Gulick, *Trust and Corporation Problems*, 351–61; President Theodore Search, *NAM Proceedings*, 1901: 17–18.

25. Thorelli, *The Federal Antitrust Policy*, 72–79 (Sherman quote, 181).

26. Thorelli, *The Federal Antitrust Policy*, 79–83; Seager and Gulick, *Trust and Corporation Problems*, 53–57; Steven L. Piott, *The Anti-Monopoly Persuasion: Popular Resistance to the Rise of Big Business in the Midwest* (Westport, Conn.: Greenwood, 1985); Gretchen Ritter, *Goldbugs and Greenbacks: The Antimonopoly Tradition and the Politics of Finance in America, 1865–1896* (New York: Cambridge University Press, 1997).

27. Thorelli, *The Federal Antitrust Policy*, 79–83; William Letwin, *Law and Economic Policy in America: The Evolution of the Sherman Antitrust Act* (Chicago: University of Chicago Press, 1965), 55–70; Piott, *The Anti-Monopoly Persuasion*; Ritter, *Goldbugs and Greenbacks*.

28. Grandy, *New Jersey and the Fiscal Origins of Modern American Corporation Law*, 43–46; Butler, "Nineteenth-Century Jurisdictional Competition." Data on large company incorporations from George Heberton Evans, Jr., *Business Incorporations in the United States, 1800–1943* (New York: National Bureau of Economic Research, 1948), 123–40.

29. Richard W. Leopold, *Elihu Root and the Conservative Tradition* (Boston: Little, Brown, 1954), 16.

30. Louis Brandeis, dissent in *Liggett Co. v. Lee*, 288 U.S. 517 (1933); Report of the Committee on National Incorporation, *NAM Proceedings*, 1908: 226–28; Thorelli, *The Federal Antitrust Policy*, 84, 259–65; Lucian Arye Bebchuk, "Federalism and the Corporation: The Desirable Limits on State Competition in Corporate Law," *Harvard Law Review* 105 (May 1992): 1437–510. Delaware, with need for even fewer state revenues than New Jersey, eventually supplanted New Jersey as the most advantageous state environment for business incorporation; see William L. Cary, "Federalism and Corporate Law: Reflections upon Delaware," *Yale Law Journal* 83 (March 1974): 663–705.

31. *United States v. E. C. Knight Co.*, 156 U.S. 1 (1895); *United States v. Addyston Pipe and Steel Co., et al.*, 175 U.S. 211 (1899); Letwin, *Law and Economic Policy in America*, 121–24; Sklar, *The Corporate Reconstruction of American Capitalism*, 124–27. For a contemporary policymaker's perspective, see the speech of Representative George W. Ray (R, New York), in *Congressional Record*, May 31, 1900: 672–73.

32. Seager and Gulick, *Trust and Corporation Problems*, 60–67; Chandler, *The Visible Hand*, especially 317–19; Evans, *Business Incorporations in the United States, 1800–1943*, 123–40.

33. Alfred L. Bernheim, ed., *Big Business: Its Growth and Its Place* (New York: Twentieth Century Fund, 1937), 13; Mansel G. Blackford, *A History of Small Business in America* (New York: Twayne, 1991), 57; Sklar, *The Corporate Reconstruction of American Capitalism*, 164–65, 168. An argument along similar lines is made by William G. Roy, *Socializing Capital: The Rise of the Large Industrial Corporation in America* (Princeton: Princeton University Press, 1997); Roy emphasizes the merger of manufacturing and finance.

34. Naomi R. Lamoreaux, *The Great Merger Movement in American Business, 1895–1904* (New York: Cambridge University Press, 1985); Freyer, *Regulating Big Business: Antitrust in Great Britain and America*; Alfred D. Chandler, Jr., "The United States: Seedbed of Managerial Capitalism," in *Managerial Hierarchies: Comparative Perspectives on the Rise of the Modern Industrial Enterprise,* ed. Alfred D. Chandler and Herman Daems (Cambridge: Harvard University Press, 1980), 9–40.

35. Chandler, *The Visible Hand*.

36. "[I]t will absolutely control labor in that given industry," Rep. L. F. Livingston (D, Georgia), in U.S. Industrial Commission, vol. 1, *Trusts and Industrial Combinations* (Washington, D.C.: GPO, 1900), 289.

37. Jonathan Rees, "Managing the Mills: Labor Policy in the American Steel Industry, 1892–1937," (unpublished Ph.D. dissertation, University of Wisconsin–Madison, 1997); Gerald G. Eggert, *Steelmakers and Labor Reform, 1886–1923* (Pittsburgh: University of Pittsburgh Press, 1981), 34–38; Lewis quoted in Robert H. Zieger, *The CIO, 1935–1955* (Durham: University of North Carolina Press, 1995), 54. The AFL upbraided President Taft's Justice Department for instigating anti-trust proceedings against American Tobacco and Standard Oil while ignoring U.S. Steel. It endorsed state investigations of the company in 1909. See *AFL Proceedings*, 1910: 308.

38. Robert Ozanne, *A Century of Labor-Management Relations at McCormick and International Harvester* (Madison: University of Wisconsin Press, 1967), 70; Don D. Lescohier, "Working Conditions," in *History of Labor Legislation in the United States* 4 vols., ed. John R. Commons et al. (New York: Macmillan, 1935), 3: 297–98.

39. Montgomery, *The Fall of the House of Labor*, 112–256.

40. Daniel Jacoby, "The Transformation of Industrial Apprenticeship in the United States," *Journal of Economic History* 51 (December 1991): 887–910; Sanford Jacoby, *Employing Bureaucracy: Managers, Unions, and the Transformation of Work in American Industry, 1900–1945* (New York: Columbia University Press, 1985).

41. Stephen Meyer III, *The Five Dollar Day: Labor, Management, and Social Control in the Ford Motor Company, 1908–1921* (Albany: State University of New York Press, 1981); David Gartman, *Auto Slavery: The Labor Process in the American Automobile Industry, 1897–1950* (New Brunswick, N.J.: Rutgers University Press, 1986); Montgomery, *The Fall of the House of Labor*, 214–35; Perlman, *The Machinists*, 28; Ton Korver, *The Fictitious Commodity: A Study of the U. S. Labor Market, 1880–1940* (Westport, Conn.: Greenwood, 1990), 107–22.

42. Stuart D. Brandes, *American Welfare Capitalism, 1880–1940* (Chicago: University of Chicago, 1976), 30–37. Gary quoted in Robert Wiebe, *Businessmen and Reform: A Study of the Progressive Movement* (Cambridge: Harvard University Press, 1962), 166.

43. Ozanne, *A Century of Labor-Management Relations at McCormick and International Harvester*, 71–84.

44. Wiebe, *Businessmen and Reform*, 167; Montgomery, *The Fall of the House of Labor*, 235; Daniel M. G. Raff, "Ford Welfare Capitalism in Its Economic Context," in *Masters to Managers: Historical Perspectives on American Employers,* ed. Sanford M. Jacoby (New York: Columbia University Press, 1991), 90–105.

45. Chandler, *The Visible Hand*, 320–44; see also McCraw, "Rethinking the Trust Question."

46. Montgomery, *The Fall of the House of Labor*, 265.

47. Cynthia L. Estlund makes a similar argument about current employer efforts to avoid unions in "Economic Rationality and Union Avoidance: Misunderstanding the National Labor Relations Act," *Texas Law Review* 73 (April 1993): 921–91.

48. Establishments that employed a hundred workers or less constituted about 39 percent of the American workforce in 1904, a percentage that fell to 29 percent in 1919 (and was the same in 1929). In 1919, about three out or every four members of the labor force worked in an establishment that employed a thousand or fewer people. Mark Granovetter, "Small Is Bountiful: Labor Markets and Establishment Size," *American Sociological Review* 49 (June 1984): 323–34.

49. The theme of proprietary capitalists is emphasized by Ernst in "The Lawyers and the Labor Trust"; see also Ernst, "The Closed Shop, The Proprietary Capitalist, and the Law, 1897–1915," in *Masters to Managers*, 132–52.

50. *NAM Proceedings*, 1908: 115.

51. "C. W. Post and the National Association of Manufacturers," manuscript, in National Association of Manufacturers Papers [hereafter NAM Papers], Vada Horsch collection, Box 852.3, "Emery, James A." folder 2, Accession 1411, Hagley Museum and Library.

52. *NAM Proceedings*, 1906: 173–74.

53. C. W. Post, in *NAM Proceedings*, 1903: 123.

54. Philip Taft, *Organized Labor in American History* (New York: Harper and Row, 1964), 212–13, 221–24; Pamela Terpack Rose, "Design and Expediency: The Ohio State Federation of Labor as a Legislative Lobby, 1883–1935," (unpublished Ph.D. dissertation, Ohio State University, 1975), 54; Stephen Amberg, *The Union Inspiration in American Politics: The Autoworkers and the Making of a Liberal Industrial Order* (Philadelphia: Temple University Press, 1994), 44–45; Frank T. Stockton, *The Closed Shop in American Trade Unions* (Baltimore: Johns Hopkins University Press, 1911), 49, 56; Sidney Fine, *Without Blare of Trumpets: Walter Drew, the National Erectors' Association, and the Open Shop Movement, 1903–57* (Ann Arbor: University of Michigan Press, 1995).

55. Michael Kazin, *Barons of Labor: The San Francisco Building Trades and Union Power in the Progressive Era* (Urbana: University of Illinois Press, 1987), 116; Howell Harris, "Getting It Together: The Metal Manufacturers Association of Philadelphia, c. 1900–1930," in *Masters to Managers*, 111–31; Amberg, *The Union Inspiration in American Politics*, 45–49; Steve Babson, *Working Detroit: The Making of a Union Town* (New York: Adama Books, 1984), 20–21.

56. Taft, *Organized Labor in American History*, 212–13.

57. Bonnett, *History of Employers' Associations in the United States*; Ernst, "The Lawyers and the Labor Trust," 49; Montgomery, *The Fall of the House of Labor*, 270; Taft, *Organized Labor in American History*, 219–20. According to IAM president William H. Johnston, the NMTA came to assume a defensive position later in the decade, and the employers and unions engaged in a battle of attrition in the early 1910s; Johnston to Secretary of Labor William B. Wilson, letter, May 13, 1914, in File 20/158, General Records, 1907–1942 (Chief Clerk's Files), General Records of the Department of Labor, RG-174, U.S. National Archives, College Park.

58. Jeffrey Haydu, "Trade Agreement vs. Open Shop: Employers' Choices before WWI," *Industrial Relations* 28, no. 2 (Spring 1989): 159–73.

59. Melvyn Dubofsky, *The State and Labor in Modern America* (Chapel Hill: University of North Carolina Press, 1994): 40–44; Perry K. Blatz, "Workplace Militancy and Unionization: The UMWA and the Anthracite Mine Workers, 1890–1912," in *The United Mine Workers of America: A Model of Solidarity?* ed. John H. M. Laslett (University Park: Pennsylvania State University Press, 1996), 51–71.

60. Daniel R. Ernst, *Lawyers against Labor: From Individual Rights to Corporate Liberalism* (Urbana: University of Illinois Press, 1995), 52.

61. "Declaration of Principles," in *NAM Proceedings*, 1903: 288–89. James A. Emery attributed the NAM open shop declaration to the anthracite coal strike and the strike commission's refusal to endorse the closed shop; James A. Emery, "Outline: Circumstances under which the National Association of Manufacturers Adopted the Declaration of Labor Principles at the Annual Convention, New Orleans, April 1903," NAM papers, Accession 1411, Vada Horsch Collection, Box 852.3, Folder 1, Hagley Museum and Library.

62. *NAM Proceedings*, 1903: 96; Wiebe, *Businessmen and Reform*, 25–26.

63 *NAM Proceedings*, 1907: 80–81.

64. Ralph M. Easley to Oscar S. Straus, letter, March 25, 1907, in Oscar Straus Papers, U.S. Library of Congress, Box 6.

65. James A. Emery, "The National Council for Industrial Defense," *American Industries* 7, no. 8 (June 1, 1908), 22–23.

66. Parry to *NAM Proceedings*, 1903: 16–17; Albion G. Taylor, *Labor Policies of the National Association of Manufacturers* (Urbana: University of Illinois, 1928), 63, 66–67; Ernst, *Lawyers against Labor*, 47–68; Wiebe, *Businessmen and Reform*, 168. See also *New York Times*, July 12, 1905: 4; and March 11, 1906: 7.

67. U.S. House of Representatives, Lobby Investigation Select Committee, *Charges against Members of the House and Lobbying Activities*, Report 113, 63 Cong., 2nd sess., December 9, 1913: 15.

68. On Emery's activities, see NAM papers, Accession 1411, Vada Horsch Collection, Box 852.3, Folder 4, Hagley Museum and Library. In a 1938 speech critical of the pro-union bias he observed in the National Labor Relations Act, Emery noted that "English law permits a far greater degree of cooperation between competitors in marketing their goods, than we tolerate." Emery was making the point that British tolerance of union independence was relatively fair because both unions and employers could cooperate. "Collective Employment Relations in Great Britain and the United States," in NAM papers, Accession 1411, Vada Horsch Collection, Box 852.3, Folder 3, Hagley Museum and Library.

69. *NAM Proceedings*, 1909: 112; Ernst, *Lawyers against Labor*, 132; Albert K. Steigerwalt, *The National Association of Manufacturers, 1895–1914: A Study in Business Leadership* (Ann Arbor: Bureau of Business Research, University of Michigan, 1964), 128–35. The intensive lobbying activities of the NAM are documented in U.S. Senate, Subcommittee of the Committee on the Judiciary, Hearings on *Maintenance of a Lobby to Influence Legislation*, 63 Cong. 1 sess., (Washington, D.C.: GPO, 1913). See also Richard W. Gable, "NAM: Influential Lobby or Kiss of Death?" *Journal of Politics* 15 (May 1953): 254–73.

70. Wiebe, *Businessmen and Reform*, 20–21; Earl R. Beckner, *A History of Labor Legislation in Illinois* (Chicago: University of Chicago Press, 1929), 188–89.

71. Ernst, *Lawyers against Labor*, 59–60

72. *Loewe v. Lawlor*, 208 U.S. 274 (1908); Taft, *Organized Labor in American History*, 217–19; Ernst, *Lawyers against Labor*, 57, 110–16, 269 fn. 22.

73. *New York Times*, December 18, 1907: 2.

74. Ernst, "The Lawyers and the Labor Trust," 182–90; Ernst, *Lawyers against Labor*, 124–46; *Gompers v. Buck's Stove and Range Company*, 221 U.S. 418 (1911); William E. Forbath, *Law and the Shaping of the American Labor Movement* (Cambridge: Harvard University Press, 1991), 94.

75. Gompers in *AFL Proceedings*, 1911: 53–55.

76. Ernst, *Lawyers against Labor*, 90–109.

77. On Detroit, see Babson, *Working Detroit*, 19–21; on comparative unionization in 1913, see figure 1.1.

78. David Brody, *Steelworkers in America: The Non-Union Era*, (New York: Harper and Row, 1969), 214–26; Dubofsky, *The State and Labor in Modern America*, 74–75.

79. Jean Tripp McKelvey, *AFL Attitudes toward Production, 1900–1932* (Ithaca, N.Y.: Cornell University Press, 1952), 48–50.

80. Weibe, *Businessmen and Reform*, 36–38; Allen M. Wakstein, "Origins of the Open-Shop Movement, 1919–1920," *The Journal of American History* 51 (December 1964): 460–75; Selig Perlman and Philip Taft, "Labor Movements," in *History of Labor in the United States*, 4: 489–514; Taft, *Organized Labor in American History*, 364–71; Letter, James A. Emery to NAM President Stephen C. Mason, February 12, 1920, and National Industrial Council, "Report on Open Shop Department, National Association of Manufacturers," May 14, 1921, in NAM Papers, Accession 1411, Vada Horsch Collection, Box 852.3, Folder 4, Hagley Museum and Library; Chamber of Commerce of the United States, "Referendum Number Thirty-one: Employment Relations, 1920," Special Bulletin, September 1, 1920, in Chamber of Commerce Records, Accession 1960, Series I, Box 12, 1920 Volume, Hagley Museum and Library.

81. In some states, state police forces emerged as tools for controlling labor conflict. See Gerda Ray, "'We Can Stay until Hell Freezes Over': Strike Control and the State Police in New York, 1919–1923," *Labor History* 37 (Summer 1985): 403–25, and "From Cossack to Trooper: Manliness, Police Reform and the State," *Journal of Social History* 28 (Spring 1995): 565–86.

82. Kazin, *Barons of Labor*, 245–64; Dubofsky, *The State and Labor in Modern America*, 62, 78–79.

83. Letter, John B. Andrews, AALL, to "OUR MEMBERS AND FRIENDS," November 23, 1920, in U.S. National Archives, RG 174, General Records of the Department of Labor, Box 79, File 20/156.

84. Sisson, *The Management of Collective Bargaining*, 138; Moses, *Trade Unionism in Germany from Bismarck to Hitler*, 2: 222–23; Gerald D. Feldman, *Iron and Steel in the German Inflation, 1916–1923* (Princeton: Princeton University Press, 1977), 82–83; Jeffrey

Haydu, *Making Industry Safe for Democracy: Comparative Perspectives on the State and Employee Representation in the Era of World War I* (Urbana: University of Illinois Press, 1997).

85. Seager and Gulick, *Trust and Corporation Problems*, 304–38, esp. 308. See also Robert F. Himmelberg, *The Origins of the National Recovery Administration: Business, Government, and the Trade Association Issue, 1921–1933* (New York: Fordham University Press, 1976).

86. Colin Gordon, *New Deals: Business, Labor, and Politics in America, 1920–1935* (New York: Cambridge University Press, 1994), 128–65; Joel Rogers, "Divide and Conquer: Further 'Reflections on the Distinctive Character of American Labor Laws,'" *Wisconsin Law Review,* 1990 (January/February): 1–147.

5

THE AMERICAN FEDERATION OF LABOR'S STRATEGIC RETREAT AND ITS CONSEQUENCES

> We believe in being moderate in our demands, but absolutely radical in our determination to achieve them.
>
> —Samuel Gompers, to the 1904 American Federation of Labor (AFL) Convention[1]

The employers' counterattack checked the pace of unionization in the United States. Open shop tactics hit machinists, industrial workers, and coal miners especially hard. These workers formed a natural constituency for public labor protections, and their setbacks muted support for inclusive labor market programs in the United States. Craftsmen in the construction and other skilled trades withstood the open shop assault more readily than the miners or machinists. The open shop drive helped the craft union leaders of the AFL reinforce their strength as organized labor's strategists.

The open shop drive, then, severely retarded the unions' will and ability to enlist government as an ally in their challenge to employer sovereignty. The weakness of machinists, miners, and industrial unions in the AFL reduced support for industrywide union organizing, an independent labor party, and comprehensive labor legislation. In 1900, the AFL had not decisively rejected social insurance or government regulation of working conditions for men in the private sector. It did so over the course of the next fifteen years. By rejecting these universal protections, the AFL in effect ceded labor market dominance to employers by the 1930s.

Lacking labor support, facing business resistance, and coping with a fragmented political structure, Progressive Era policy reformers made the best of the growing employer dominance of labor markets. These reformers backed away from challenging employer prerogatives. They came to view policy innovations that protected employer control of the labor market as virtues that suited

125

"American circumstances." Their proposals increasingly conceded, rather than questioned, employer sovereignty in American labor market policy.

THE MUTED VOICE OF MACHINISTS, MINERS, AND INDUSTRIAL UNIONS

The union shop drive and the obstacles inherent in competitive American federalism hit machinists, industrial unions, and coal miners harder than other unions.[2] The corporations beat back the machinists' efforts to organize key industries. American federalism precluded the national cooperation of coal producers that was a necessary condition for sustaining the strength of the United Mine Workers of America (UMWA).

Machinists

No group of American workers occupied a more critically important position in the battle for the labor market than the machinists. They bore the brunt of the assault of mass production on specialized skills, of scientific management on craft power, and of the open shop drive on the union shop strategy. Armed with indispensable metalworking skills, the machinists worked at key jobs in vital industries: railroad maintenance shops; mass production plants (including automobiles); and smaller, owner-run shops that worked metal. They ran increasingly complicated machinery. Their job required diverse skills, involved diverse products, and created diverse working arrangements and methods of pay. Employers recognized that machinists exercised unusual power in the workplace. American employers especially welcomed new management techniques that reduced that power. Machinery became the "nursery" of scientific management. Time and motion studies and the subdivision of tasks struck directly at the machinists' craft power and solidarity.[3]

These occupational changes caused many machinists to question the crafts-based strategy of the AFL. The fate of machinists in large firms and of the growing army of unskilled workers became increasingly interdependent. Many machinists gravitated toward broader-based strategies for worker protection: industrial unionism, political socialism, and universal labor laws. Machinists thus served as the front line in the battle for the labor market. In the United States, as in every industrializing nation, their position made machinists natural leaders of campaigns to restrict employer power.

British and German machinists gradually came to lead their nations' union movements into universal worker protections and labor politics. Like their

American counterparts, British and German machinists were skeptical of industrial unionism and wary of politics in the late nineteenth century. Before 1900, Great Britain's Amalgamated Society of Engineers leaned toward a crafts-based union strategy similar to that of the AFL. In 1891, the British machinists voted by a two-to-one margin to seek the eight-hour day "by voluntary trade union action rather than by legislation." This vote represented a decisive victory for the many British machinists who viewed legislation as interference with the "natural liberties" of "free adult males." In July 1901, however, the British House of Lords jeopardized British trades unions in its Taff Vale decision. In this decision the Lords, acting as a supreme court, ruled that unions were liable for triple damages when they inflicted harm on employers by striking and picketing. This decision fundamentally threatened union finances, autonomy, and existence. The British machinists' union dropped its previous reluctance to engage in political action. It committed itself to independent labor politics by affiliating with the Labour Representation Committee, a predecessor of the British Labour Party.[4]

German machinists also advocated political neutrality at the turn of the century. As factories enlarged, the machinists understood that their bargaining power depended on cooperation with other metalworkers, including the unskilled. Out of self-interest, then, German machinists helped to create an economically powerful federation of several metalworking craft unions. This federation laid the foundation for industrial unionism in Germany. Though large firms in heavy industry continued to resist the unions before World War I, the small and medium-sized metal working enterprises (unlike the American metal shops) frequently agreed to metalworkers' union demands. By 1916, the German metalworkers' federation constituted the nation's most powerful force for industrial unionism, a strong component of the Socialist Party, and a potent constituent for labor market policy in Germany.[5]

American machinists also came to support industrial unionism strongly, for the same reasons that British and German machinists came to support it. The International Association of Machinists (IAM), formed in 1888, primarily enrolled machinists on the southern and western railroad lines at first. Machinists in urban areas began to shift the core union membership north in the 1890s. By century's turn several IAM leaders were active socialists. While highly skilled machinists in small shops remained true to crafts-based unionism, machinists in railroad shops and larger plants found the crafts approach ineffective. Many favored the nationalization of the railroads and other industries. Many also favored government arbitration of labor disputes.[6] In contrast to the AFL policy, these American machinists wanted to unionize workers of different skill levels within the same industry. Industrywide unionization would increase their economic power to deal with corporations (though, as a self-defined "manly" craft, their inclusiveness rarely extended across established boundaries of race and gender).

American employers acknowledged the pivotal role of the machinists by targeting open shop tactics against them. Large corporations singled out the machinists as they battled unions. In preparation for its change to the open shop, International Harvester's general manager of manufacturing indicated that "We consider it probable that we shall have trouble with machinists, pattern makers, and some of the other skilled trades," but that the trouble could be overcome in reasonable time with reasonable expense and was worth the effort even at a high cost.[7] After the breakdown of the Murray Hill agreement, the National Metal Trades Association (NMTA) became a leader in the smaller firms' open shop drive.

The open shop counteroffensive took a heavy toll on the IAM's organizing momentum. While the number of IAM members rapidly increased to more than fifty thousand (or more than one in six American machinists) by the middle of 1901, the employer counteroffensive brought this expansion to a near standstill. The IAM represented a smaller percentage of American machinists' membership in 1910 than it had before the employer counterattack.

Much as Taff Vale had done in Britain, the failure of Murray Hill and the open shop drive further convinced many IAM members of the futility of the AFL's crafts-based approach. In a 1903 IAM referendum, three-quarters of the respondents endorsed industrial unionism over craft unionism. A majority also endorsed socialism. In 1911 the membership replaced IAM president James O'Connell, a chief author of the Murray Hill agreement, ally of Gompers, and proponent of the crafts approach who opposed opening the IAM to less skilled

Table 5.1:   Machinists and Membership in the International Association of Machinists, 1890–1930

Year	Number of U.S. Machinists	Membership in International Association of Machinists	Percentage Unionized
1890	186,828	N/A	–
1900	283,145	22,500	8
1910	461,344	60,970	13
1920	801,901	282,496	35
1930	640,289	69,397	11

Sources: David Montgomery, *The Fall of the House of Labor: The Workplace, the State, and American Labor Activism, 1865–1925* (New York: Cambridge University Press, 1987), 181; Mark Perlman, *The Machinists: A New Study in American Trade Unionism* (Cambridge: Harvard University Press, 1961), 206.

workers. The new IAM president, William H. Johnston, had run for governor of Rhode Island as a Socialist. Under Johnston, the union pursued industrial organization more aggressively.[8] The strengthening economy and growing membership of the mid-1910s seemed to validate the IAM's commitment to industrial unionism. The machinists emerged from World War I with more than a quarter of a million members and represented more than a third of the nation's machinists.

Yet the IAM could not make the metal trades into the kind of potent economic force that existed in Germany. Many of the other American metal trades, including the Boilermakers, Steamfitters, Sheet Metal Workers, and Blacksmiths, retained their craft focus. They stayed loyal to the crafts-based unionism of the AFL leadership. These unions obstructed efforts to create the kind of metal trades federation that German machinists had forged. Instead, when the AFL loosely collected the unions in a "Metal Trades" department, these unions retained their independence. Gompers appointed former IAM president O'Connell to head the Metal Trades Department as a check on the IAM. The craft-centered AFL leadership and the industrial IAM continued to fight bitterly into the 1920s.[9]

Corporations constituted a much greater problem for the IAM than the AFL craftsmen. Even at the height of its strength, the IAM could not dent the resistance of many of the largest corporations. Lead by a fledgling industrial union and the IAM (and with the blessing of the AFL), an alliance of workers of varied skills and ethnic backgrounds conducted an organizing strike against the Westinghouse works near Pittsburgh in mid-1916. Labor leaders viewed Westinghouse as a critical case. Unionizing the plant would create a union foothold in the large businesses that were reshaping the American economy. But a bloody battle with plant guards turned the tide. The strike collapsed. Westinghouse's East Pittsburgh works remained free of unions until the 1930s.[10] While other corporations made concessions to the machinists during the war, these concessions generally proved short-lived.

After the war, the IAM tried, but failed, to forge a "middle way" between narrow craft unionism and the mass-movement Industrial Workers of the World (IWW). General Electric defeated an organizing drive spearheaded by the IAM in 1920. The increasingly conservative AFL Executive Council turned back new efforts to amalgamate the metal trades. In 1922, the union lost a two-year strike against the American Can Company, which was closely associated with U.S. Steel. In the same year, the IAM participated in the railroad shopmen's strike that ended disastrously for the unions involved. In 1922 IAM membership shriveled to less than half the wartime peak and to less than a quarter of it in 1925.[11]

Though employers and AFL leaders blunted the IAM's drive for inclusive industrial unionism, the IAM itself abandoned independent party politics. The Clayton Act of 1914 and other lobbying successes persuaded many machinists that direct legislative influence would have more certain and immediate benefits than an effort to elect a labor slate to office. Strongly supportive of Socialist Party presidential candidate Eugene V. Debs in 1912, machinists shifted to Woodrow Wilson and the Democrats by the end of Wilson's first term. Much like the AFL leadership, the IAM had concluded by the early 1920s that the nonpartisan support for "labor's friends" would bring results more quickly and surely than the path of independent politics.[12]

The experience of the IAM shows how the union shop and open shop strategies constricted organized labor's influence on American public policy. The AFL's commitment to crafts, the strength of the large corporations, and the anti-unionism of smaller employers decisively altered the way that American machinists struggled to secure their goals. Historian Jeffrey Haydu argues that the experience of the American machinists is a crucial case. American machinists had far less economic and political success than their British counterparts, he rightly argues, because of more intense and effective employer opposition.[13]

Coal Miners

Coal fueled the nation's economy. Rich fields of bituminous coal stretched from northwestern Pennsylvania through Ohio, Indiana, Illinois, Tennessee, Kentucky, West Virginia, and Alabama. Thousands of mine owner–operators produced coal in these fields. These owners, trying to eke out profits in a market they could not control, frequently engaged in cutthroat competition.[14]

American coal miners had strong reasons to demand government action on their behalf. Since wages constituted two-thirds of the cost of producing American coal, operators vigorously resisted union demands for recognition, shorter hours, and higher pay. Scattered in small mining communities distant from large cities, miners were hard to organize and easy to divide. Miners' skills were mastered with relative ease, so that potential strikebreakers were abundant. Mine operators intentionally lured immigrants to the mines to make miner solidarity more difficult to sustain. Company stores and housing increased miners' dependence on the operators. Wages based on tonnage invited operators to cheat in weighing the coal that miners produced. Explosions and cave-ins entombed hundreds of miners yearly.[15]

The miners thus lacked the labor market advantages of the skilled crafts workers. Crafts-based unionism made much less sense for advancing unionism in the coal industry. Labor laws were a more practical way to limit hours, raise wages, and ensure safe mines. Initially reluctant to turn to government, miners abroad came to support political solutions to the problem of worker protection. The Miners Federation in Britain affiliated with the Labour Party when it became practical to do so.[16] The mine workers' union, in turn, became a foundation for building British trade union power. More than half of all British miners were unionized in 1900, and 70 percent were unionized a decade later. The Miners' Federation, with over half a million members, enrolled one in four British union members in 1910.[17]

Coal miners in the United States, like those abroad, were drawn to a broader political strategy than the crafts-based union shop. The UMWA asserted more aggressively than did the AFL the need for broad industrial organization and government action. They sought a legal floor for wages and a ceiling on hours, with unions negotiating for improvements on these basic standards. They sought laws that would reduce competition from immigrants and children and guarantee safe working conditions. The UMWA supported the nationalization of communication, transportation, and coal mines as well as protective legislation for miners.[18] Mine union leaders were at the forefront of lobbying for expanding state regulation, public labor market management, and work insurance.

When confronted by concerted union action, many bituminous mine operators offered to collaborate with each other and the union for their mutual economic advantage. In 1897, coal operators revived an interstate coal mining agreement that set prices and wages in much of the "central competitive field" in Ohio, Illinois, Indiana, and Pennsylvania. The agreement stipulated that the union would enforce the agreement and police wildcat strikes. More important, the UMWA agreed with midwestern operators in 1897 that they would launch a drive to unionize the West Virginia coal fields. Cheaper West Virginia coal gradually was gaining a larger and larger share of the urban and factory energy market. Until the West Virginia producers joined the agreement, they could underprice the unionized mines in the states north of them. UMWA president John Mitchell described West Virginia as the prime threat to the cooperative agreement in the central field.[19]

West Virginia's operators, however, had no interest in the agreement and fought to maintain union-free mines. Especially in southern West Virginia, employers relished their competitive advantage and growing market share. The UMWA's organizing drives in West Virginia in 1897, 1902, and 1907 had limited success. The UMWA expanded the unionization of West Virginia miners to about 16 percent of the state's tonnage produced in 1905. The operators' open shop counterattack dropped the tonnage produced under union contract to 7 percent in 1912. Union contracts covered about half the West Virginia coal mined during World War I. Postwar depression and the ruinous mine strikes of the early 1920s devastated the union, however. By the mid-1920s the UMWA had completely disappeared from the state. It did not return until 1933.[20]

The failure to organize West Virginia had disastrous consequences for the union nationally and muted a potentially strong voice for universal worker protections. The nature of mining in West Virginia partially explains the UMWA's failure to organize its mines. The state's operators were particularly hostile to the union. West Virginia miners were unusually mobile and skeptical of the union. Virtually all the southern West Virginia miners lived in company towns. These miners depended completely on coal operators for not only income but also housing and basic supplies, and they hesitated to join the union. In the 1920s, many of the state's coal operators instituted the "American Plan" to combat unions.[21]

Competitive American federalism also is indispensable for explaining the UMWA's failure in West Virginia. West Virginia governed its own mining industry, free of federal interference. Primarily a coal and railroad economy, West Virginia exercised its authority primarily for the benefit of the coal operators. The state's coal and rail interests and its public officials worked closely together. The state's legislators were reluctant to regulate the coal industry, and its judges were quick to enjoin UMWA organizers. Industry leaders such as Stephen B. Elkins dominated the state's politics. Clarence Watson, president of Consolidated Coal, exemplified coal industry dominance when he was appointed U.S. senator in 1911.

West Virginia, then, provided minimal legal protection to its coal miners. Though the legislature passed some mine laws, coal operators routinely ignored those laws that were on the books. The state committed fewer resources to mine inspection than other coal states. Laws regulating payments and coal weights were rarely enforced. Indeed, miners were more likely to face prosecution for violating safety laws than were operators. Company towns lacked state charters, so that coal operators served as surrogate city officials. Local law enforcement officials permitted the coal operators free reign in the use of private guards (notably the brutal Baldwin–Felts guards). The legislature enacted a law prohibiting the use of private mine guards in 1913, but it omitted any penalty for violation. The operators continued to use private guards until 1933. Officials generally declared martial law to combat union organizers.[22]

West Virginia state government, in short, was put at the service of the coal industry just as New Jersey law was put at the service of the corporations. Both state governments acted rationally to exploit the opportunities for competitive economic advantage afforded by the American federal system. Both states contributed profoundly to maintaining employer sovereignty in American labor market policy.

The UMWA's failure in West Virginia weakened the union's attraction to employers elsewhere. Without the West Virginia mines in the union agreement, northern operators lost market share to their nonunion competitors to the south. Coal operators and labor leaders unsuccessfully sought to establish minimum standards of mining competition that would limit the advantages of the nonunion mines. Since the federal government had no authority to set such standards, however, proponents of mining regulation had to rely on the much more difficult uniform state law approach. Efforts to create uniform state coal mining laws fared no better than the campaign for uniform state corporation laws, however. By 1924, a federal official concluded that constitutional obstacles made nationwide labor standards in bituminous coal mining virtually impossible to implement in any effective way.[23]

The federal government temporarily nationalized the industry during World War I, and it imposed some national standards for the duration. The postwar collapse of the economic boom refueled the open shop. Southern mines cut wages quickly. Many northern owners who had signed contracts with the union went out of business in 1921. Those operators that remained in business turned against the interstate agreement and the union. After a prolonged strike in 1922, the UMWA fell from half a million members in the bituminous fields to fewer than a hundred thousand (mainly in Illinois and Indiana) in 1928.[24]

Even though its strength did not match that of British miners' unions, the UMWA remained a powerful force in the American labor movement through the Progressive Era. However, it could not bring about either national laws or uniform state laws. American political institutions foreclosed both the legislative and the economic routes for protecting coal miners and diluted the strength of an important constituency for broader worker protection.

Industrial Workers

Chapter 4 demonstrated that the U.S. Steel Corporation had the power to resist the unionization of workers in the pivotal steel industry. Automobile production, a fast-growing industry in America, also generated enough employment to lay the basis for industrial unions and labor politics. Instead, unions had little impact in the industry until the 1930s. The U.S. auto industry emerged in Detroit, a bastion of the open shop. Detroit employers beat back the union shop with unusual success. Between 1902 and 1910, employment in the Detroit auto plants grew rapidly. During these years the membership of the AFL-affiliated Carriage, Wagon, and Automobile Workers' Union (CWAWU) declined from 5,500 to 1,100.[25]

In 1913–14, the CWAWU, many of the other AFL craft unions, and the IWW cooperated in an attempt to organize the auto industry in Detroit. Now one large corporation—the Ford Motor Company—overshadowed other automakers. The coalition specifically targeted Ford for its unionization drive. Like other open shop employers, Henry Ford refused to surrender managerial control to union negotiators. He denied that workers could gain anything from unions that his factories could not provide. Ford expanded both corporate welfare and corporate surveillance to defeat the unions. Ford's five-dollar day, instituted in January 1914, created a profit sharing plan for which workers could qualify if they demonstrated efficiency and company loyalty. Ford also established a Sociological Department to investigate the personal lives of Ford employees. Ford investigated workers' faithfulness, productivity, and union sympathies. When union militancy increased again during the war, the corporate welfare aspect of the Ford plan began to fade. Ford cultivated an extensive network of industrial spies and informants successfully to break strikes.

War temporarily facilitated unionization in the auto plants. The CWAWU became a more militant and socialist union during World War I. The AFL, ever more firmly under the control of the craft unions, revoked its charter in 1918. The sharp economic depression of the early 1920s weakened the autoworkers' union and permitted the automakers to counter strikes with production cuts and strikebreakers. The autoworkers' union evaporated after 1921, shrinking to 1,500 members in 1929, when the industry employed 450,000 workers. While the auto industry continued to grow in importance as an employer in the 1920s, unions had virtually no presence in the industry until the sitdown strikes of 1936–37. Ford's workforce was not organized until 1941.[26]

THE STRENGTHENED POSITION OF THE CRAFT UNIONS

Craft unions in the industries "least exposed . . . to the geographical competition of industry"[27] weathered the open shop assault comparatively well. By the mid-1920s, the strength of the American trade union movement lay in construction and printing, two economically localized industries, and in the railroad operating jobs (engineers, firemen, conductors, and brakemen). These craft unions enjoyed natural labor market power. Without the direct help of government, they could limit the number of available workers, compel employer concessions, and ensure a measure of protection for their members. Access to jobs became as important a resource for craft unions as patronage jobs were for elected officials.

Persuaded that their fortunate circumstances reflected superior strategy, the craft unions defined AFL strategy in ever narrower terms. The leaders of these unions distilled the militancy and inclusiveness of the AFL's union shop strategy

at the turn of the century. Because they could win worker protections directly
from employers, they advocated that all workers do so. Thus, they abandoned
most workers to the protection of their employers.

The Building Trades

The AFL's strongest unions were in industries where employers had little
alternative to skilled labor and no opportunity to relocate production. Construction epitomized these circumstances. Building a facility is a highly specialized enterprise. Construction involves small firms contracting for specific tasks.
Builders tailor each product to individual customers. Buildings are not portable,
and little construction work can be done at distant, nonunion plants. Interstate
competition is a marginal factor in construction, compared to manufacturing.
It requires highly specialized skills (such as bricklaying) that cannot easily be
mechanized. Building craftsmen, however, could easily move among job sites.

These conditions favored employer–union cooperation on terms relatively
favorable to labor. Without some form of discipline, small contractors could
compete ruthlessly. Unlike many manufacturing firms, however, virtually all
builders competed only in local markets. In many areas, builders favored strong
unions that could enforce agreements and thereby impose some stability on an
otherwise chaotic local construction market. The union shop established a floor
under labor costs (the largest cost component for these contractors) for all competitors. Given their market advantages and often superior organization, the
construction unions could pressure recalcitrant builders to join the agreement
and enforce exclusive contracts that allowed the local construction union to
monopolize its services.[28]

Unlike the machinists or the coal miners, the building craftsmen could and
did achieve their goals mainly though the union shop. By controlling apprenticeships, the building trades limited the supply of workers and increased their
value. In San Francisco, construction workers enjoyed high wages. Even hod
carriers enjoyed higher wages than machinists.[29] The building trades required
limited and local legislation, rather than inclusive national standards. In cities
such as San Francisco, as much as half of the municipal labor force in the early
1910s consisted of construction jobs. The municipal code required that work
on public building and repair projects be conducted by union members. This
local provision furnished substantial protection for these craftsmen.[30]

The building trades exerted much more influence in the American labor
movement than did their counterparts in Great Britain. Membership in building construction unions constituted 15 percent of American union membership
in 1897, 21 percent in 1910, and 27 percent in 1929. In 1939, more than three-

quarters of American construction workers were unionized. This figure was more than one and a half times higher than that of any other American industry and more than double the unionization rate of British construction workers.[31] This growth, in combination with the difficulties experienced by the machinists and the miners, considerably strengthened the influence of the building trades and the craft perspective in the AFL. By the mid-1920s, William L. Hutcheson, the head of the United Brotherhood of Carpenters and Joiners of America, was a dominant American labor leader.[32]

Printers

As in the case of the building trades, the printers retained substantial bargaining power in the early twentieth century. Like construction, printing was intensely competitive and very localized. Employers could not stockpile newspapers and could ill afford a work stoppage.

The printing craftsmen made sure that the introduction of new machinery strengthened rather than weakened their market position. Instead of resisting the introduction of the Linotype machine in the late nineteenth century, the International Typographical Union (ITU) helped manage the changeover to the new presses. In return, the printing employers granted the union control of apprenticeships that trained workers for the new technology. The printers, then, staked their future on limiting entry into the trade. Their gamble succeeded. The ITU helped stabilize the industry. When printers in Zanesville, Ohio, went off the job on an unauthorized strike at the turn of the century, for example, the union president sent union typesetters from other cities to replace the striking workers. The American Newspaper Publishers' Association concluded a collective agreement with the ITU in 1901 that conceded control of work rules to the union in return for union policing of work conditions and wildcat strikes.[33]

Printers, then, rarely needed the support of other unions to improve their hours, wages, and job conditions. They generally declined to support wider enforcement of the union shop across the printing trades. Despite the pleas of other crafts for help, the ITU rejected demands that it seek the "joint closed shop" for all jobs in the printing industry.[34]

The printers joined the building trades as leaders of the AFL as the high tide of unionization receded after World War I. By 1920, unions enrolled half of American printers, a level comparable to the 58 percent of British printers in unions. By 1930, the printers and the building craftsmen together constituted two-fifths of the AFL membership, but only 10 percent of the American labor force.[35]

Railroad Brotherhoods

Four brotherhoods—locomotive engineers, firemen, trainmen, and conductors—organized the elite workers of the railroad industry. The insurance policies they offered members strongly attracted skilled workers to join the brotherhoods. All these workers were engaged in the highly dangerous work of moving trains, and private insurance companies rarely found it profitable to write policies for them. Aloof from less skilled railroad workers, these unions were conservative even by the standards of the AFL, and they refused to join the federation.[36] The defeat of the industry-inclusive American Railway Union in the 1894 Pullman strike ensured the brotherhoods' dominant role in representing railroad workers. By the outset of World War I, the Brotherhood of Locomotive Engineers and the Order of Railway Conductors enrolled over 90 percent of their potential members. The four brotherhoods together, though, represented only about one-fifth of railroad workers.[37]

The brotherhoods had little interest in making common cause with less-skilled railroad workers or other crafts workers in the AFL. They sought state laws setting qualifications for conductors, engineers, and telegraphers, hoping to control and limit the supply of skilled labor in their own occupations. These unions, however, largely had ignored earlier pleas by less-skilled railroad workers for state laws mandating weekly pay. They claimed that such laws constituted an unwarranted state interference in the federally governed industry.[38]

Federal jurisdiction over railroads encouraged the brotherhoods to lobby for legislation narrowly beneficial for themselves. The Erdman Act of 1898, an early lobbying success, reinforced the brotherhoods' conservatism. That law protected the brotherhoods' insurance funds and established national mediation mechanisms that ratified the brotherhoods' industrial position. The brotherhoods won the eight-hour day when Congress passed the Adamson Act of 1916. The brotherhoods, however, refused to join the IAM and other unions in the railroad shop crafts strike of 1922.[39]

THE AFL'S NARROWING AGENDA

The uneven development of unions in the wake of the open shop counterattack fortified crafts-based unionism in the AFL. Natural selection seemed to be producing the survival of the fittest American unions. When craft unions fought and won labor market battles, as did the printers in securing the venerated eight-hour day, Gompers held up their success as a model.[40] Such a union, organized to take advantage of natural craft divisions and fueled with material benefits for members, stood a much greater chance of withstanding economic vicissitudes and employer counterattacks than any alternative. No other national labor movement in the world could compare with the AFL for "thoroughness and clearness in scope of purpose, militancy of spirit, soundness in finances . . . or continuity and rapidity of development," Gompers wrote after touring Europe.[41]

The AFL leaders espoused craft unionism while defending the federation from the centrifugal forces that it set in motion. Jealously protecting their turf, strong craft unions skirmished to control the unionization of overlapping tasks. Jurisdictional battles dissipated union energy in huge amounts. Carpenters disputed shipwrights' claim to control ship carpentry. Boilermakers clashed with ironworkers. Plumbers battled steamfitters. Brewery workers contended with steam engineers. Upholsterers disputed autoworkers. Internally, the craft unions bureaucratized themselves more than their counterparts in western Europe.[42]

The union shop strategy had an unanticipated effect: it made organizational durability a key concern for the leaders of the AFL. Independent of their personal stake in the labor bureaucracy, Gompers and his allies developed a stake in fending off every imagined challenge to the dominance of their organization. The open shop drive and its allies in government hardened this attitude irreversibly.

Gompers and other AFL leaders took an increasingly hard line against proponents of other approaches to worker protection. Gompers argued that the sad experiences of the Knights of Labor and the American Railway Union proved that industry-wide unions lacked the resilience for sustained worker protection.[43] He was incensed by his socialist critics. He presented the German case as an example of government unreliability, arguing that German Socialists elected to that nation's parliament had failed to amend Germany's backward labor legislation. The leadership narrowly won a test vote committing the AFL to socialism (4,897–4,171) in 1902, as the open shop counterattack gathered momentum. Growing craft union power strengthened the leadership's ability to fend off the socialists. Even in 1912 and 1913, when socialist strength in the AFL peaked with firm support among the miners, machinists, brewery workers, and garment workers, socialists still constituted only a third of the AFL convention vote. These AFL socialists failed to end Gompers's leadership.[44]

Over the course of the first thirty years of the twentieth century, the original militancy of the AFL's union shop, crafts-based strategy eroded. "Voluntarism" ossified into a defense of craft control over jurisdiction and benefits, to the exclusion of broader worker protections.[45] The AFL leadership increasingly came to accommodate employer rights and reconstituted its demands accordingly, tacitly conceding the superior power of business after the open shop drive. The AFL in the 1910s gradually surrendered the aspiration to control production. It scaled back its ambitions and began to emphasize the distribution of profits. It made wages the top union priority. By the 1920s, under the leadership of Gompers's successor William Green, the unions had fallen back to the position of hoping that they could persuade employers that cooperation with independent unions could increase business profits. Vehemently opposed to scientific management before World War I, the AFL came to support improvements in efficiency during the 1920s.[46]

The AFL, in effect, strategically abandoned much of the field of labor protection to employers. British and German unions in the 1890s displayed much the same sentiment for a narrow craft union approach to securing labor market power that American unions displayed. In these nations, however, adversity and opportunity propelled the growth of industrial unions and independent labor politics. The AFL, in contrast, became primarily concerned with the protection of the prerogatives of the craft unions that dominated it, even at the cost of expanded union membership and worker protection. The result was a Pyrrhic victory for the strategy that had been formulated during the battles of the last decades of the nineteenth century.

The AFL's hardening commitment to the crafts-based strategy increasingly restricted its legislative vision. Though the federation developed long lists of legislative priorities for the federal government in the Progressive Era, these lists included many specific initiatives aimed at protecting particular groups of (usually unionized) employees. Its political tactics emphasized pressure group activities such as endorsements, lobbying, and campaign aid.[47] The AFL increasingly opposed those government efforts that undermined their control of the material benefits that gave them leverage against hostile employers, antagonistic courts, and capricious officeholders.

Some of the state labor federations pursued more ambitious political agendas in defiance of the AFL leadership. The AFL had encouraged the growth of the state federations, recognizing the importance of state laws for protecting workers and their unions.[48] Several of the state labor federations eluded national AFL direction. Some of the most important state federations, such as those in New York, Illinois, and California, ignored the AFL's strictures against support of far-reaching regulatory and social insurance measures. These state federations pushed worker protection further along the national policy agenda than did the AFL itself.[49]

PROGRESSIVE REFORMERS, BUSINESS, AND THE AFL

Civil servants, university professors, settlement house leaders, social reformers, lawyers, and lobbyists turned general labor market hopes, fears, and animosities into specific labor market policy proposals. These policy entrepreneurs advised elected officials about the appropriate priorities for the public agenda. They brought new aspects of labor market problems to policymakers' attention. They crafted what they viewed as specific, appropriate, and politically feasible solutions to these problems.[50] The alternatives that these policy reformers offered to legislators, administrators, judges, and interest group leaders constituted the concrete options for the course of American labor market policy.

In the first thirty years of the century, these American reformers adapted their proposals to expanding employer power, shrinking labor aspirations, and gaps in constitutional authority. Florence Kelley, head of the National Consumers' League, sought constitutional loopholes through which to advance labor market regulations that could later be expanded to the entire workforce. Confronted by the growing imbalance in labor market power that favored business, some of these reformers made a virtue of business power. University of Wisconsin economist John R. Commons, for example, promoted solutions that used employer sovereignty itself to increase worker protection.

The group of reformers surrounding Commons constituted America's most influential labor market experts. Commons commanded national respect as a labor market authority in these years. He wrote definitive works on labor markets, unions, and legislation. He helped design progressive legislation in Wisconsin that other states emulated. He participated in the era's most important public investigations. Appointed to the U.S. Commission on Industrial Relations in 1913, Commons shaped its agenda, staffed it with his graduate students, secretly brought together leading industrialists and the AFL, and wrote a minority report that articulated his vision of national labor problems.[51] Commons also was one of the most potent intellectual forces behind the American Association for Labor Legislation (AALL, 1906–42). The AALL was the most self-conscious and active organization that promoted the expansion of labor market policy in the United States during the Progressive Era.[52]

Commons (like Gompers) believed that existing labor market arrangements had merit because they had evolved slowly and naturally. Trade unions had, by securing collective bargaining agreements across state lines, "enact[ed], by the power of organization, uniform laws which our federal system and our written constitutions have prevented the states from enacting."[53] Government, Commons believed, should take a cautious and indirect role in steering these natural labor market developments, prescribing a regimen for preventing social ills rather than intervening surgically to correct them. Business, the engine of prosperity, should be induced to become the engine of worker protection. In the United States, capitalism had produced a strong economy and a standard of living higher than that in Europe. American businessmen, the architects of this prosperity, "are ingenious, alert, they take chances. . . . They are also quite superior to our politicians and other government officials."[54] U.S. Steel's accident prevention work inspired Commons to craft programs that would build on the best corporate practices. Commons sought to "regulate but not destroy the system," to "save Capitalism by making it good."[55]

Public policy toward labor markets, Commons concluded, should try to induce business itself to prevent problems such as industrial accidents, and even disease and joblessness. Labor law relies too heavily on "penalties and punishment" and not enough on business incentives, Commons wrote. Public policy should leave business and labor free and should "endeavor to widen and enlarge the opportunities for their employment."[56] To do so, policy should reward business for preventing social problems and penalize business for causing them.[57] Commons's extensive work with the National Civic Federation (NCF) also manifested this faith in business self-regulation. So did his affirmative answer to the question, *Can Business Prevent Unemployment?* (in his coauthored book of that title).

In this view, labor markets would constitute the foundation of American social policy. It is significant that an "American Association for *Labor* Legislation" led so many battles for social programs in the Progressive and New Deal Eras. This title indicates that these reformers viewed even health insurance as a remedy for *labor* market failure. Arthur Altmeyer, another Commons student and architect of the Social Security Act, accounted for the differences between American and British social security provision in terms of the former's origins in labor legislation rather than the Poor Law reforms.[58]

America's labor market reformers insisted that the impartial and professional administration of labor laws was essential for business trust in government. AALL leaders such as Henry Farnam deplored the patronage appointment of factory inspectors and other labor officials.[59] Commons championed the idea of "industrial commissions" as a new form of governance for the corporate age. These commissions would remove industrial relations from patronage politics and laissez-faire judges. Such commissions were not simply a defense against patronage. They constituted a positive vision of an American form of corporatist management of the labor market. In spite of the separation of powers, such commissions could align labor policy: they could legislate, execute, and adjudicate the laws of worker protection.[60]

The reformers' insistence on neutral labor market administration drove a wedge between them and organized labor. The issue of industrial commissions decisively alienated the AFL leadership from the AALL. The industrial commission concept directly challenged the AFL's long-standing support for public offices controlled by labor itself. Top labor leaders did not want neutral administrators. These union officials wanted administrators who were sympathetic to the unions. Gompers viewed the notion of industrial commissions as an effort by intellectuals to establish a bureaucracy that would control workers. In New York, the AALL poured its resources into a successful campaign for an industrial commission. When the bill passed, Gompers quit the AALL.[61]

When the AALL championed health insurance, Gompers bitterly attacked the proposal as a fundamental attack on the union strategy of self-reliance. Trade unions, in helping to provide a living wage, had established a far more effective health insurance plan than the "would-be 'uplifters'" could devise. Compulsory insurance, however, would undermine trade union activity by removing a reason for workers to join unions. Just as bad, they would require a new bureaucracy that would threaten union independence.

> the American labor movement . . . will not yield any field of activity directly affecting the workers to *any agency other than the workers themselves*. We commend to the consideration of the self-constituted guardians of labor, the fact that the American labor movement has had to contend with organized antagonism of no mean caliber; with enemies avowed and pseudo; with hypocritical pretenders; with subsidized institutions and associations, and that the labor movement has never run away from the battle or the contest, and is now in a stronger, more powerful and influential position for service than at any time in its history. Though desirous of avoiding any conflict or contest which can be avoided, the men in control of the so-called American Association for Labor Legislation are respectfully but insistently advised that in any struggle which that association may desire to inaugurate or maintain, they will find the American labor movement an adversary worthy of any combatant, and that after the smoke of the battle shall have cleared away, the American labor movement will still be marching along the road to triumph in the protection and promotion of the rights, interests, welfare and freedom of the toilers. (Italics added)[62]

In this statement, Gompers reveals the scars of government betrayal, battles for the union shop, and the open shop counterattack. His choice of words reveals his view of the AFL as an organization that had survived a protracted siege, its union shop strategy intact and its aspiration for union-established worker protection alive. In this moment of AFL confidence, with the Clayton Act a year old and union membership expanding again, the AFL decisively broke with potential allies in the fight for universal public worker protections.

Reformers and unions should have been natural allies in the battle for public labor market protections. As the battle for American labor markets unfolded, however, they sometimes became irreconcilable rivals for labor market control. Their mutual distrust strengthened the hand of business. As chapters 8 and 9 detail more fully, reformers adapted to business power and trade union rivalry by proposing programs for labor market management and social insurance that further strengthened the position of employers and invented a uniquely American path to labor market governance.

Florence Kelley of the NCL had a better understanding of the AFL's fears of new labor market institutions placed beyond labor's influence. She also had a particularly acute understanding of the policy constraints and opportunities imposed by the American constitution. Kelley worked to build coalitions, especially at the state and local level, that could successfully exploit constitutional loopholes to enact enforceable regulations for women and children. These coalitions involved women's groups, social reformers, and often state and local labor federation. Protective labor legislation for special groups, it was thought, would lay a foundation for more inclusive labor protections.[63] The success of the NCL and other groups in securing protection for groups of workers that generally were difficult to unionize, however, may have made it easier for Gompers and other AFL leaders to oppose universal hours and wage regulations.

POLITICIANS AND THE BATTLE FOR LABOR MARKETS

Partisan politics facilitated progressive labor legislation from about 1905 to 1916. Even in the conservative 1920s, partisan considerations worked against the repeal of those labor laws passed in the Progressive Era. For most of the period from 1900 to 1932, Republicans firmly controlled the national government and many states. Employers expected the Republicans to champion employer freedom, and indeed Theodore Roosevelt in his first term showed little interest in labor reform. From 1903 to 1910, Speaker Joseph Cannon (R, Illinois), a strong conservative and instinctive supporter of employers, firmly controlled the House of Representatives and its agenda. Cannon largely agreed with the NAM on labor proposals. Gompers viewed Cannon as "the strategic center to the opposition to labor."[64]

Roosevelt's reelection in 1904 marked a political opening for labor reform as the AFL entered partisan politics and the Republican coalition came under stress. Frustrated by its failure to secure even modest labor protections from the federal government, the AFL laid a "Bill of Grievances" before the president and Congress in early 1906. The federation asked for the long-sought eight-hour law for government contractors, restrictions on immigration, a convict labor law, and relief from injunctions. In that year's November election, the AFL campaigned to defeat prominent Republican enemies, including Cannon.[65] When an AFL delegation lead by Gompers met with the Republican Party platform committee before the 1908 presidential election, NAM leaders in attendance mocked their platform requests. The federation forged a link with the Democrats in the 1908 campaign that persisted despite the AFL's formal "nonpartisan" position.[66] Republican officials in industrial areas became torn between their party's support for employers and their constituents' demands for labor reform.

Growing popular support for reform even more strongly persuaded some Republicans to break with uncritical support for employer rights. Labor conditions once unquestioned now seemed intolerable. Newspapers and magazines exposed shocking stories of corruption that swelled personal fortunes at the expense of unfortunate workers.[67] State and local reform groups proliferated.[68]

Some Republicans responded favorably to this growing progressive constituency. Progressive Republicans, particularly in the Midwest, enjoyed considerable success in elections. Robert La Follette (R, Wisconsin), elected to the U.S. Senate in 1905, immediately became a leader of a growing progressive faction among Republican legislators. Formerly stalwart Republicans, such as Albert Beveridge (R, Indiana), embraced progressive positions around the same time. After the 1904 presidential election, Theodore Roosevelt increasingly offered aid and comfort to the insurgent Republican agenda. He endorsed new protective labor laws and lobbied Congress to pass them. He rejected the NAM's opposition to "every rational and moderate measure for benefiting workmen."[69]

In 1912, Roosevelt led many insurgent Republicans into a Progressive Party. The party platform provided an explicit blueprint for an expansive labor market strategy. It promised legislation to prevent industrial accidents, diseases, and unemployment; the extension of minimum federal standards for safety and health; the prohibition of child labor; a minimum wage for working women and a "living wage" for all industrial occupations; the extension of the eight-hour day for all women and in continuous twenty-four-hour industries such as steel; abolition of convict labor; and "the protection of home life against the hazards of sickness, irregular employment and old age through the adoption of social insurance adapted to American use."[70]

The Democrats had a greater stake in labor support than the Republicans. To win national elections, the Democrats needed to be competitive in the northern urban states to complement their southern base. The Democrats welcomed the AFL and Progressives.[71] The political successes of the Democrats in the 1910s, along with divisions in the Republican Party, gave advocates of worker protection an effective majority in the federal and many state governments. In 1910, the Democrats won a majority of seats in the U.S. House of Representatives and established a working coalition with insurgent Republicans in the Senate. The 1912 election gave the Democrats control of Congress and the presidency for the rest of the 1910s. Business influence hit a nadir, and state and federal labor legislation flowed in unprecedented volume. Before the 1910 election, the AFL counted seven legislative successes in the 59th Congress (1905–7), eleven in the following Congress, and sixteen in the next. After 1910, the federation counted twenty-nine legislative successes in the 62nd Congress (1911–13), thirty-five in the 63rd Congress (1913–15), and thirty-two in the 64th Congress (1915–17).[72]

Progressivism weakened during World War I. Business began to reassert itself in the state capitals. The Republicans regained undisputed control over Congress and the presidency during the 1920s. The AFL's shrinking base and prior commitment to the Democrats reduced its political influence. Many Republican elected officials, however, including Presidents Warren G. Harding, Calvin Coolidge, and Herbert Hoover, avoided direct confrontations with unions and curbed the most extreme anti-labor sentiments in their party. They did not repeal the labor laws of the Wilson years. They also refused to endorse the renewed open shop drive of the 1920s or to make it the central Republican theme of the 1924 presidential campaign.[73]

Political competition, then, tended to work moderately in favor of the worker protection agenda, rather than against it. American political structure, and the interest strategies that it shaped, explain why the Progressive Era modernized employer sovereignty instead of creating a labor market policy that substantially restricted employers' prerogatives.

STRATEGIC INTERESTS IN THE BATTLE
FOR AMERICAN LABOR MARKETS

By the 1910s, the dynamic interaction of American employers, workers, and reformers had shaped their labor market policy strategies in a way distinctly different from their counterparts abroad. Employers did not eliminate the closed shop, but they checked its expansion. The open shop counterattack especially weakened those unions that advocated more inclusive government labor protection and a more mass-based, industrial union movement. The AFL increasingly represented white, male craftsmen of Northern European extraction. It steadily lost touch with the majority of the workforce that was assembling automobiles, forging steel, mining coal, serving customers, and attending to the clerical complexity of the marketplace. Reformers, recognizing the economic strength of employers and the limitations of government, elevated the fact of business strength into the virtue of business proprietorship of labor protection.

In doing so, the prospective proponents of an expansive and inclusive labor market policy retreated. They conceded to employers their prerogatives in the labor market. Their strategic adaptation reflected the peculiar circumstances set in motion by American policymaking institutions. Corporations, intransigent open shop employers, craft-unions labor "barons," and "pragmatic" policy reformers all benefited from limited national authority, competitive American federalism, and the complex policy process. These American political institutions impeded employer–union cooperation, socialism, and public restraints on employers. U.S. policymaking institutions did not determine that labor market programs that were exceptionally protective of employer rights would be implemented. These institutions, however, made the behavior that resulted in the policy that was the most reasonable course of action for the most influential participants in the battle for the American labor market.

Employers did not win every policy battle. By the 1920s, however, they largely had won the war. The interests of American labor market combatants had permanently and decisively deviated from that in most comparable nations. Between 1912 and 1922, the fundamental elements of worker protection—child labor protection, public employment offices, the Clayton Act, and health insurance—had failed. By the start of the New Deal, the institutional legacy of these years made it difficult to sustain a substantive challenge to employers' prerogatives.

NOTES

1. American Federation of Labor, *Proceedings* of the Twenty-fourth Annual Convention, 1904: 6; hereafter, cited as *AFL Proceedings*, [date]. In his welcoming address to the delegates, Gompers was reflecting on the open shop drive.

2. Frank T. Stockton, *The Closed Shop in American Trade Unions* (Baltimore: Johns Hopkins University Press, 1911).

3. John H. M. Laslett, *Labor and the Left: A Study of Socialist and Radical Influences in the American Labor Movement, 1881–1924* (New York: Basic Books, 1970), 144–81; David Montgomery, *The Fall of the House of Labor: The Workplace, the State, and American Labor Activism, 1865–1925* (New York: Cambridge University Press, 1987), 178–91. On scientific management and the unions, see Samuel Haber, *Efficiency and Uplift: Scientific Management in the Progressive Era, 1890–1920* (Chicago: University of Chicago Press, 1964); Ton Korver, *The Fictitious Commodity: A Study of the U.S. Labor Market, 1880–1940* (Westport, Conn.: Greenwood, 1990).

4. Keith Burgess, "New Unionism for Old? The Amalgamated Society of Engineers in Britain," in *The Development of Trade Unionism in Great Britain and Germany, 1880–1914*, ed. Wolfgang J. Mommsen and Hans-Gerhard Husung (London: Allen and Unwin, 1985), 176; U.S. Commissioner of Labor, *Regulation and Restriction of Output*, Eleventh Special Report (Washington, D.C.: Government Printing Office, 1904), 751; Henry Pelling, *A History of British Trade Unionism* (London: Penguin, 1963), 123–27; H.

A. Clegg, Alan Fox, and A. F. Thompson, *A History of British Trade Unions since 1889,* 2 vols. (Oxford: Clarendon, 1964), 1: 374.

5. "Labor Organizations," *Monthly Review of the U. S. Bureau of Labor Statistics* 6 (February 1918): 427–31; John A. Moses, *Trade Unionism in Germany from Bismarck to Hitler, 1869–1918,* 2 vols. (Totowa, N.J.: Barnes and Noble, 1982), 1: 138; Michael Schneider, *A Brief History of the German Trade Unions,* (Bonn: Verlag J. H. W. Dietz Nachf, 1991), 103; Klaus Schönhoven, "Localism–Craft Union–Industrial Union: Organizational Patterns in German Trade Unionism, " in *The Development of Trade Unionism in Great Britain and Germany, 1880–1914,* 227.

6. Jeffrey Haydu, "Trade Agreement vs. Open Shop: Employers' Choices before WWI," *Industrial Relations* 28 (Spring 1989): 159–73; Montgomery, *The Fall of the House of Labor,* 171–213.

7. Quoted in Robert Ozanne, *A Century of Labor-Management Relations at McCormick and International Harvester* (Madison: University of Wisconsin Press, 1967), 56–57.

8. Laslett, *Labor and the Left,* 158; Montgomery, *The Fall of the House of Labor,* 281, 290–91.

9. Laslett, *Labor and the Left,* 165

10. Montgomery, *The Fall of the House of Labor,* 317–27.

11. Perlman, *The Machinists,* 35–37, 56–60; Philip Taft, *Organized Labor in American History* (New York: Harper and Row, 1964), 376–82; Montgomery, *The Fall of the House of Labor,* 450–52.

12. Laslett, *Labor and the Left,* 167.

13. Haydu, "Trade Agreements vs. Open Shop." See also Sanford M. Jacoby, "American Exceptionalism Revisited: The Importance of Management," in *Masters to Managers: Historical Perspectives on American Employers,* ed. Sanford M. Jacoby (New York: Columbia University Press, 1991), 173–200.

14. David Brody, "Market Unionism in America: The Case of Coal," in *In Labor's Cause: Main Themes on the History of the American Worker,* ed. David Brody (New York: Oxford University Press, 1993), 131–37; Testimony of Charles Van Hise in U.S. House of Representatives, Committee on the Judiciary, Hearings on *Trust Legislation,* vol. 2 (Washington, D.C.: GPO, 1914), 554.

15. Brody, "Market Unionism in America: The Case of Coal," 131–37.

16. Gary Marks, *Unions in Politics: Britain, Germany, and the United States in the Nineteenth and Early Twentieth Centuries* (Princeton: Princeton University Press, 1989), 173–79. Marks finds that German coal miners' unions were relatively weaker than British counterparts, opposed by better organized coal operators, and internally divided by ethnicity and religion. Nevertheless, the German miners also came to demand legislative solutions to the problem of labor protection (179–84).

17. Clegg, Fox, and Thompson, *A History of British Trade Unions since 1889,* 2: 1; Richard Hyman, "Mass Organization and Militancy in Britain: Contrasts and Continuities," in *The Development of Trade Unionism in Great Britain and Germany, 1880–1914,* 256.

18. Marks, *Unions in Politics,* 170, 184–94.

19. David Allen Corbin, *Life, Work, and Rebellion in the Coal Fields: The Southern West Virginia Miners, 1880–1922* (Urbana: University of Illinois Press, 1981); William Graebner, *Coal Mining Safety in the Progressive Period: The Political Economy of Reform* (Lexington: University Press of Kentucky, 1976), 102.

20. William M. Boal, "Estimates of Unionism in West Virginia Coal, 1900–1935," *Labor History* 35 (Summer 1994), 3: 429–41.

21. John C. Hennen, *The Americanization of West Virginia: Creating a Modern Industrial State, 1916–1925* (Lexington: University Press of Kentucky, 1996), 99–118.

22. Corbin, *Life, Work, and Rebellion in the Coal Fields*, 1–18, 114–15; Graebner, *Coal Safety in the Progressive Period*, 73–76, 86–91; Otis K. Rice, *West Virginia: A History* (Lexington: University Press of Kentucky, 1985), 165–69, 185–92, 205–33; U.S. Industrial Commission, *Capital and Labor in the Mining Industries*, vol. 12 (Washington, D.C.: GPO, 1912), xxvi–xxvii, 699. For western miners, see, for example, George G. Suggs, Jr., *Colorado's War on Militant Unionism: James H. Peabody and the Western Federation of Miners* (Detroit: Wayne State University Press, 1972), 82–83.

23. Brody, "Market Unionism in America," 139–44; Frederick P. Lee, "Possibilities of Establishing a National Minimum of Safety in the Coal Industry," *American Labor Legislation Review* 14 (March 1924): 71–80; Daniel J. Curran, *Dead Laws for Dead Men: The Politics of Federal Coal Mine Health and Safety Legislation* (Pittsburgh: University of Pittsburgh Press, 1993).

24. Brody, "Market Unionism in America," 144–53; Montgomery, *The Fall of the House of Labor*, 409.

25. Joyce Shaw Peterson, *American Automobile Workers, 1900–1933* (Albany: State University of New York Press, 1987), 112–13.

26. Peterson, *American Automobile Workers*; Stephen Meyer III, *The Five Dollar Day: Labor, Management, and Social Control in the Ford Motor Company, 1908–1921* (Albany: State University of New York Press, 1981).

27. This observation was made by Leo Wolman, *Ebb and Flow in Trade Unionism* (New York: National Bureau of Economic Research, 1936), 96.

28. U.S. Commissioner of Labor, *Regulation and Restriction of Output*, 270–84; William Haber, *Industrial Relations in the Building Industry* (Cambridge: Harvard University Press, 1930), 238; Stockton, *The Closed Shop in American Trade Unions*, 133–34.

29. Michael Kazin, *Barons of Labor: The San Francisco Building Trades and Union Power in the Progressive Era* (Urbana: University of Illinois Press, 1987), 151, 305.

30. Haber, *Industrial Relations in the Building Industry*, 197–256, 351–56; Alexander Keyssar, *Out of Work: The First Century of Unemployment in Massachusetts* (New York: Cambridge University Press, 1986), 210–11; Stockton, *The Closed Shop in American Trade Unions*, 133–34.

31. Wolman, *Ebb and Flow in Trade Unionism*, 87; George Sayers Bain and Robert Price, *Profiles of Union Growth: A Comparative Statistical Portrait of Eight Countries* (Oxford: Basil Blackwell, 1980), 171. On the British building trades unions, see Richard Price, *Masters, Unions, and Men: Work Control in Building and the Rise of Labour, 1830–1914* (Cambridge: Cambridge University Press, 1980).

32. Irving Bernstein, *The Lean Years* (Boston: Houghton Mifflin, 1966), 109–17.

33. Marks, *Unions in Politics*, 120–54; U.S. Commissioner of Labor, *Regulation and Restriction of Output*, 35–36.

34. Stockton, *The Closed Shop in American Trade Unions*, 113.

35. U.S. Commissioner of Labor, *Regulation and Restriction of Output*, 35–36; Marks, *Unions in Politics*, 145–51; Haydu, "Trade Agreements vs. Open Shop"; J. David Greenstone, *Labor in American Politics* (Chicago: University of Chicago Press, 1969), 28–29.

36. Helen Marot, *American Labor Unions* (New York: Henry Holt, 1914), 29–47.

37. Taft, *Organized Labor in American History*, 156; Marot, *American Labor Unions*, 34; Montgomery, *The Fall of the House of Labor*, 365.

38. James H. Ducker, *Men of the Steel Rails: Workers on the Atchison, Topeka, and Santa Fe Railroad, 1869–1900* (Lincoln: University of Nebraska Press, 1983), 92–93.

39. Montgomery, *The Fall of the House of Labor*, 365–66, 399–404, 422–24.

40. The printers' success in winning the eight-hour day was held up as a special victory in 1905; see *AFL Proceedings*, 1905: 25, 79.

41. "President Gompers in Europe," *American Federationist* 17 (February 1909): 146–51.

42. Warren R. Van Tine, *The Making of the Labor Bureaucrat: Union Leadership in the United States, 1870–1920* (Amherst: University of Massachusetts Press, 1973), 82, 119, 124; Keyssar, *Out of Work*, 218–19; Derek C. Bok, "Reflections on the Distinctive Character of American Labor Laws," *Harvard Law Review* 84 (April 1971): 1394–463; John T. Dunlop, "Have the 1980s Changed U.S. Industrial Relations?" *Monthly Labor Review* 111 (May 1988): 29–34.

43. Samuel Gompers, *Seventy Years of Life and Labour*, 2 vols. (New York: Dutton, 1925), 1: 406; *AFL Proceedings*, 1907: 28–29; Kazin, *Barons of Labor*, 240–44.

44. Montgomery, *The Fall of the House of Labor*, 292–93.

45. Michael Rogin, "Voluntarism: The Political Functions of an Antipolitical Doctrine," *Industrial and Labor Relations Review* 15 (July 1962): 521–35.

46. Jean Tripp McKelvey, *AFL Attitudes toward Production, 1900–1932* (Ithaca, N.Y.: Cornell University Press, 1952), 9–12, 80–98; see also John R. Commons, "Organized Labor's Attitude towards Industrial Efficiency," *American Economic Review* 1 (September 1911): 463–72. On the 1920s and William Green, see Craig Phelan, "William Green and the Ideal of Christian Cooperation," in *Labor Leaders in America,* ed. Melvyn Dubovsky and Warren Van Tine (Urbana: University of Illinois Press, 1987), 134–59.

47. Julie Greene, *Pure and Simple Politics: The American Federation of Labor and Political Activism, 1881–1917* (New York, Cambridge University Press, 1998), 81–88.

48. *AFL Proceedings*, 1905: 243.

49. Matthew Woll, in *AFL Proceedings*, 1910: 296; Eugene Staley, *History of the Illinois State Federation of Labor* (Chicago: University of Chicago Press, 1930); Irwin Yellowitz, *Labor and the Progressive Movement in New York State, 1897–1916* (Ithaca, N.Y.: Cornell University Press, 1965); Kazin, *Barons of Labor*, 151–53.

50. John Kingdon, *Agendas, Alternatives, and Public Policies*, 2nd ed. (New York: Harper Collins, 1995).

51. David Brian Robertson, "Policy Entrepreneurs and Policy Divergence: John R. Commons and William Beveridge," *Social Service Review* 62 (September 1988): 504–31; Lafayette G. Harter Jr. *John R. Commons: His Assault on Laissez-Faire* (Corvallis: Oregon State University Press, 1962), 57–67, 73, 89–159; James Weinstein, *The Corporate Ideal in the Liberal State* (Boston: Beacon, 1968), 172–213; Clarence E. Wunderlin, Jr., *Visions of a New Industrial Order: Social Science and Labor Theory in America's Progressive Era* (New York: Columbia University Press, 1992); U.S. Commission on Industrial Relations, *Final Report and Testimony,* 64th Cong., 1st sess., Senate Document 415, (Washington, D.C.: GPO, 1915); H. M. Gitelman, "Management's Crisis of Confidence and the Origin of the National Industrial Conference Board," *Business History Review* 58 (Summer 1984): 153–177.

52. David A. Moss, *Socializing Security: Progressive-Era Economists and the Origins of American Social Policy* (Cambridge: Harvard University Press, 1996).

53. John B. Andrews and John R. Commons, *Labor and Administration* (New York: Macmillan, 1913), 153; John R. Commons, *The Legal Foundations of Capitalism* (New York: Macmillan, 1924), 361.

54. John R. Commons, *Institutional Economics* (New York: Macmillan, 1934), 106.

55. John R. Commons, *Myself* (New York: Macmillan, 1934), 118, 143; on the inspiration by U.S. Steel, see 141–43.

56. John R. Commons and John B. Andrews, *The Principles of Labor Legislation* (New York: Harper and Brothers, 1916), 454; John R. Commons, *Industrial Goodwill* (New York: McGraw-Hill, 1919), 77–79; John R. Commons, *The Distribution of Wealth* (New York: Macmillan, 1893), 258; Commons, *The Legal Foundations of Capitalism*, 363.

57. Moss, *Socializing Security*, 59–76.

58. Arthur J. Altmeyer, *The Formative Years of Social Security* (Madison: University of Wisconsin Press, 1966), vii.

59. Henry W. Farnam, "Practical Methods in Labor Legislation," *American Labor Legislation Review* 1 (January 1911): 5–15.

60. Commons and Andrews, *The Principles of Labor Legislation*, 443–48.

61. Moss, *Socializing Security*, 29–32; Yellowitz, *Labor and the Progressive Movement in New York State*, 120, see also 139–40.

62. Samuel Gompers, "Labor vs. Its Barnacles," *American Federationist* 13 (May 1916): 268–74).

63. Kathryn Kish Sklar, "Two Political Cultures in the Progressive Era: The National Consumers' League and the American Association for Labor Legislation," in *U. S. History as Women's History: New Feminist Essays*, ed. Linda A. Kerber, Alice Kessler-Harris, and Kathryn Kish Sklar (Chapel Hill: University of North Carolina Press), 36–62.

64. Blair Bolles, *Tyrant from Illinois: Uncle Joe Cannon's Experiment with Personal Power* (New York: Norton, 1951), 11; U.S. House, Lobby Investigation Select Committee, *Charges against Members of the House and Lobby Activities of the National Association of Manufacturers of the United States and others,* House Report 113, 63rd Congress, 2nd. sess. (Washington, D.C.: GPO, 1913), 31; Gompers, *Seventy Years of Life and Labour*, 2:239.

65. Gompers, *Seventy Years of Life and Labour*, 2: 245; Mark Karson, *American Labor Unions and Politics, 1900–1918* (Carbondale: Southern Illinois University Press, 1958), 42–49; Greene, *Pure and Simple Politics*, 107–41.

66. Gompers, *Seventy Years of Life and Labour*, 2: 262; Karson, *American Labor Unions and Politics*, 51–64; Greene, *Pure and Simple Politics*, 142–80.

67. A study of the *Reader's Guide to Periodical Literature* of topics such as poverty, child labor, slums, and philanthropy showed that articles on them were most numerous in the years from 1905 to 1914 and peaked in 1909, with articles declining steadily to 1930. Report of the President's Committee on Social Trends, *Recent Social Trends* (New York: 1933), cited by Katharine Du Pre Lumpkin and Dorothy Wolff Douglas, *Child Workers in America* (New York: Robert M. McBride, 1937), 260. On the link between business and corruption, see Richard L. McCormick, "The Discovery That Business Corrupts Politics: A Reappraisal of the Origins of Progressivism," *American Historical Review* 86 (1981): 247–74.

68. Theda Skocpol, *Protecting Soldiers and Mothers: The Political Origins of Social Policy in the United States* (Cambridge: Belknap, 1992), 373–401; Walter I. Trattner, *Crusade for the Children: A History of the National Child Labor Committee and Child Labor Reform in America* (Chicago: Quadrangle Books, 1970).

69. Theodore Roosevelt to Charles Mitchell Harvey, letter, August 29, 1908, in *The Letters of Theodore Roosevelt*, ed. Elting E. Morison, (Cambridge: Harvard University Press, 1952), 6: 1203. On Albert Beveridge, see John Braeman, *Albert J. Beveridge: American Nationalist* (Chicago: University of Chicago Press, 1971), 98–111.

70. Donald Bruce Johnson, ed., *National Party Platforms*, rev. ed., 2 vols. (University of Illinois Press, 1978), 1:177.

71. Karson, *American Labor Unions and Politics, 1900–1918*, 58–62; Greene, *Pure and Simple Politics*, 242–73.

72. *AFL Proceedings*, 1916: 85–90, 1917: 105–7.

73. Robert H. Zeiger, *Republicans and Labor, 1919–1929* (Lexington: University Press of Kentucky, 1969); John D. Hicks, *Republican Ascendancy, 1921–1933* (New York: Harper and Brothers, 1960).

6

LIMITATIONS OF LABOR
MARKET REGULATION

It is only necessary to state the [child labor] situation to make
clear how fatuous is the attempt to deal with the textile industries through the legislatures of a dozen different states; and with
the glass industries through the legislatures of a second dozen
states. . . . When it is a question of the nation checking, even
indirectly, their cruel robbery of the cradle, [the industries that
oppose it] urge that it is with West Virginia or with New Jersey
that the friends of the children should deal, the state legislatures
having been hitherto, on the whole, satisfactory to employers.

—Florence Kelley, 1905[1]

If we can get an eight-hour law for the working people, then you
will find that the working people themselves will fail to have any
interest in your economic organization.

—Samuel Gompers, 1914[2]

States and the national government enacted hour, wage, and child labor regulations in abundance between the late 1890s and World War I. These
efforts, however, did not result in effective national protection for children or
effective national limits on hours or wages. The poignant crusade against child
labor demonstrates the way that American political institutions obstructed the
most fundamental and widely supported form of worker protection of this era.
Support for national child labor standards forged a large coalition of leading
reformers, the American Federation of Labor (AFL), and politicians of both parties. The coalition secured the enactment of two federal child labor laws and
later prodded Congress to present the states with a child labor amendment to
the constitution. Key employers, notably textile manufacturers in the South,
successfully used the opportunities afforded by American federalism and sepa-

153

rated powers to frustrate the implementation of these child labor standards and the adoption of the amendment.

The campaigns for shorter hours and minimum wages illustrate the way that political institutions and the union shop strategy conspired to protect employers' labor market power. Proponents of shorter work hours exploited whatever political opportunities they could. New and stronger hours laws covered women, children, government workers, and workers in dangerous occupations. Some states enacted minimum wage laws for particular groups. The AFL rejected universal wage and hours laws for all workers, however. Its craft unions jealously guarded wages and hours as material benefits that legislation would undermine. The failure to achieve uniform standards weakened support for legislation, largely undermined enforcement, diminished reform expectations, and left employers in control of labor standards. New Deal wage, hour, and child labor statutes established a narrow floor of labor regulations but did not challenge employer prerogatives above that floor or beyond its scope.

CHILD LABOR

If any issue united labor reformers in the Progressive Era, it was the plight of the child worker.[3] The child labor problem worsened as America urbanized and industrialized. By 1900, 280,000 American children between the ages of ten and fifteen worked in manufacturing. Even in New York, where a factory act limited child labor, thousands of children worked in dangerous factories and sweatshops. Children shared with adults the risks of burns, amputated limbs, and accidental death. Another 420,000 children worked in domestic and personal services, street trades, and message delivery.[4]

The textile industry especially depended on child labor. Children constituted a quarter of the textile mill labor force in the leading southern textile states of Alabama, Georgia, North Carolina, and South Carolina. A large majority of the southern mills sampled in 1907 employed children under twelve, and some were as young as six. Southern textile workers labored for an average eleven and a half hours a day. In the North as well as the South, most of the cotton mills had poor ventilation, lighting, and sanitation. Clouds of toxic cotton dust filled the majority of these mills.[5]

The states' economic competition had inhibited effective child labor protection throughout the nation. Southern leaders celebrated the mills as magnets for industrial growth in their states. Southern industries publicized the relative laxity of their regulations when they invited northern investors to build plants in their region.[6] Southern industrialists opposed public regulation of mill labor because such limitations would reduce their economic advantage in competition with northern mills. The U.S. Industrial Commission in 1902 acknowledged that child labor gave the southern textile plants an economic advantage in competing with the New England mills.[7]

The child labor problem excited the deepest passions of the swelling reform spirit. Exposés of child labor multiplied in magazines and journals. Reformers organized to battle the problem. Southern reformer Edgar Gardner Murphy worked with an AFL organizer to strengthen Alabama's child labor restrictions and formed the nation's first Child Labor Committee in Alabama in 1901. Murphy, Florence Kelley of the National Consumers' League (NCL), and other reformers created a National Child Labor Committee (NCLC) that convened in 1904.[8] The NCLC formed the hub of a coalition that pressed for stricter child labor regulations nationwide.

Even the most visionary of the child labor reformers initially conceded that the federal government could not regulate children's work because it could not reach most private workplaces. "Obviously, Congress has no power without a constitutional amendment to legislate directly on this subject," the U.S. Industrial Commission observed in its final report. Federal law could only reach the District of Columbia, the territories, and a few industries (such as the railroads). Even Kelley, a determined proponent of national standards and worker protection, at first asked only that the federal government establish a new bureau to investigate the child labor problem. President Theodore Roosevelt called for an investigation of the problem in his annual message after his 1904 election.[9]

The child labor reformers resolved to battle for child labor protection state by state. By 1902, Massachusetts, New York, Connecticut, Illinois, and Indiana had legally limited work to children aged fourteen or over, a limit comparable to that in Great Britain and Germany.[10] The reformers developed a uniform state child labor bill and began to lobby for its adoption by all the states. Competitive American federalism made the task daunting, however. Poverty expert Robert Hunter told the NCLC in 1905 that "we have about as much legislation now as we are likely to get until the more backward states, that is, the southern states, are brought up more nearly to the standard of Massachusetts, New York, and a few other states. . . ."[11]

In 1906, Senator Albert J. Beveridge (R, Indiana) challenged the assumption that the federal government could do nothing about child labor when he introduced a federal child labor bill. Beveridge, acting independently of the NCLC, argued that only a federal law could surmount the problem of interstate economic competition and the "clumsy, ineffectual tangle of state statutes." The proposal aimed to prohibit goods made by child labor from entering interstate commerce. Beveridge held the Senate floor for three days, calling attention to the problem and to the states' helplessness to "stop this evil." The uniform law strategy was doomed, he concluded. Beveridge reminded his colleagues that "[i]f one State passes good laws and enforces them and another State does not, then the business men in the former State are at a business disadvantage with the business men in the latter state."[12]

The Beveridge bill sank under the weight of profound doubt and an aroused opposition. The AFL supported the abolition of child labor, but Gompers waxed indignant about the NCLC's claim to leadership on the issue. AFL leaders divided on the issue of federal authority to regulate the problem. Roosevelt refused to support the bill, citing the noncommittal stand of the AFL.[13] Louis Brandeis and Woodrow Wilson complained that the Beveridge plan went beyond the reasonable limits of federal power.[14] Beveridge's bill even split the NCLC. When it endorsed the bill, Edgar Murphy resigned in protest and campaigned against it. Internally divided and losing external support, the NCLC withdrew its endorsement of the Beveridge plan in November 1907.[15]

Even if the Beveridge bill had been enacted in the Senate, it almost certainly would have died in Speaker Joseph Cannon's House of Representatives. The House Judiciary Committee advised against the bill: "Congress has . . . no authority to suppress any abuses of [women and child] labor or ameliorate conditions surrounding the employment of such laborers." *American Industries* assured its readers that the report meant that the federal government "has no power to prescribe the hours of labor or any other condition of employment." The *Iron Age*, the organ of the metal and machine industries, advised its readers that this report would put an end to the child labor bill. For more than a decade, opponents of federal child labor legislation used this Judiciary Committee report as legal ammunition.[16]

The pressure for federal action increased as evidence of the child labor problem mounted and the states' shortcomings became more obvious. Indignation rose after the White House Conference on Dependent Children in 1909, the publication of the multivolume federal report on women and child wage earners in America, and the appearance of photographer Lewis Hine's images of children at work in southern textile mills. Still, as late as 1912, only nine states had met the standards laid out in the NCLC's 1904 model state law. No state's child labor law met the higher standards of the NCLC's Uniform Child Labor Law of 1910. Overall, state child labor provisions had become less uniform over time.[17]

As progressivism peaked, heartened reformers moved for definitive federal standards. The NCLC and other reformers had designed the Progressive Party's plank favoring the federal prohibition of child labor. President Woodrow Wilson indicated that he continued to oppose federal child labor regulation, and he reminded reformers of the Democrats' strong "states' rights feeling." Wilson agreed, however, not to oppose the bill. Representative A. Mitchell Palmer (D, Pennsylvania) and Senator Robert Owen (D, Oklahoma) introduced the NCLC bill in 1914. The Palmer–Owen bill banned from inter-state commerce products produced in factories, workshops, and canneries by children under the age of fourteen (or in mines and quarries by children under the age of sixteen). It also banned products made by children under sixteen when they worked more than eight hours a day or worked at night.[18]

The House Labor Committee unanimously endorsed the bill, arguing that the states had proven their inability to do the job.

> Session after session the friends of the children, approaching the legislatures of their respective States, have been met by the plea of the manufacturers that legislation State by State was unfair; that it was unjust to ask them to com-pete with other States of different standards; that if they must advance they should be permitted to advance in the company of their neighbors and com-petitors.[19]

The problem, then, "must be faced and solved only by a power stronger than any state." Kelley testified that one of the bill's greatest benefits "would be the transfer of cases [of local child labor violations] from local courts, terrorized by local large manufacturers, to Federal courts, where such terrorism does not occur."[20] Though strongly opposed by legislators from the southern textile states, the bill passed the House by a large margin, only to be killed in the Sen-ate by the objection of Senator Lee Overman (D, North Carolina).[21]

The following Congress passed the bill (now the Keating–Owen bill) despite more effective opposition. David Clark, the aggressively anti-labor editor of a trade publication for the southern textile industry, mobilized southern mill oper-ators against it. National Association of Manufacturers' (NAM) lobbyist James Emery joined the textile operators in opposing this federal labor regulation.[22]

House and Senate debates on the Keating–Owen bill in 1916 largely turned on the conflict between northern and southern textile states. States' rights to govern labor markets became the central issue. The chair of the House Judiciary Committee, Representative Edwin Webb (D, South Carolina) held that the bill "brings before us, in boldest form, the constitutional question of states' rights, in all its seriousness and importance. . . ." Representative Peter Tague (D, Massachusetts) stated that the issue "is whether the nation should per-mit any State, no matter where it is, to do the things that are unfair to the rest of the Nation."[23]

Opponents cited the 1907 Judiciary Committee report as evidence of the bill's unconstitutional expansion of federal power over labor markets. They revived the past opposition of Wilson and William Howard Taft as authoritative statements of its doubtful constitutionality.[24] Southern Democrats criticized their party for abandoning its "fundamental doctrine" of states' rights in order to "coquette with the Bull Moose" constituency in a presidential election year.[25]

Proponents of federal regulation hammered home the problem of unfair competition as the justification for federal action. "It is true that some States have dealt with it," said Senator Paul Husting (D, Wisconsin), but "in my State and in my legislature when the child-labor proposition was approached . . . it was held up to us that we were going to ruin our own manufacturers" by reducing the profits of businesses in the state while increasing those of neighboring states.[26] Self-interest, as well as altruism, motivated some northern legislators. Representative Augustus Gardner (R, Massachusetts), frankly observed that "We prohibit child labor in Massachusetts and so it is clearly to our interest to prohibit child labor in States which compete with us." Even supporters, however, conceded the bill's questionable constitutionality. [27]

The political appeal of the bill ensured the enactment of the first federal effort to regulate private workplaces on a large scale. Warned that "many Southern Senators will oppose it but . . . that the failure to pass that bill will lose us more votes in the close states than our Southern Senators appreciate," Wilson was persuaded to urge senators to pass the bill. The bill passed the Senate 52–12, with senators from Georgia and the Carolinas casting half the dissenting votes. Wilson signed the bill two months before the 1916 election (it would go into effect a year later, on September 1, 1917). The AFL Executive Council ranked the federal child labor bill as its top legislative achievement of the year.[28]

Once Congress enacted the Keating–Owen bill, however, Clark and the militant textile employers turned to the courts to defeat the federal child labor standard.[29] With funds provided by mill operators, Clark hired a phalanx of corporate lawyers to challenge the law. They settled on a test case involving fifteen-year-old Reuben and thirteen-year-old John Dagenhart, both legally able to work eleven hours under current North Carolina law, but restricted by the Keating–Owen Act. The legal team filed its challenge before a like-minded judge who presided in the Federal District Court of Western North Carolina, in the heartland of the southern textile industry. The district judge ruled against the law, and the ruling was appealed to the U.S. Supreme Court.[30]

The Supreme Court invalidated the child labor law in June 1918, by a 5-to-4 vote. The majority explicitly rejected the claim that Congress could prevent unfair economic competition among the states. "The Commerce Clause was not intended to give to Congress a general authority to equalize such conditions," they wrote. If this principle of federal regulation were conceded, "all freedom of commerce will be at an end, and the power of the States over local matters may be eliminated, and thus our system of government be practically destroyed."[31]

Some manufacturers immediately restored longer workdays for child workers and began to hire children again. Child labor abuses increased during World War I.[32] Progressives reacted with defiance. Senator Owen reintroduced the bill. The new Owen proposal declared that any federal justice who officially denied its constitutionality must vacate his office. The child labor reformers developed a different proposal. This alternative approach taxed employers' net profits an additional 10 percent each year that they failed to conform to the child labor standards in the original Keating–Owen Act. Congress passed this new child labor scheme as an amendment to the revenue bill of 1918. Rather than mount a futile effort to defeat it, senators from southern textile states included statements in the *Congressional Record* intended to cast doubt on its constitutionality. The tax took effect in April 1919.[33]

Clark returned to the strategy that had worked effectively in the Dagenhart case. Clark's legal team located a western North Carolina furniture firm, the Drexel Manufacturing Company, that had been penalized under the new tax. They arranged for Drexel to pay its tax under a carefully arranged protest and then challenged the constitutionality of the federal government to levy the tax.[34]

As the constitutional challenge to the second federal child labor law advanced in the courts, the law's chances of legal survival faded. The Republicans returned to power in 1921, installing more conservative policymakers in the Department of Justice and on the Supreme Court. Taft became chief justice in 1921. The Republican solicitor general worked with the textile manufacturers to expedite the case.[35] In May 1922, the Supreme Court struck down the child labor tax in an 8-to-1 vote. Even Oliver Wendell Holmes and Brandeis joined the majority voting against this second federal effort to bypass the constitutional limitation on child labor. Writing for the Court, Taft held that if the Court upheld such federal regulation, it would "break down all constitutional limitation of the powers of Congress and completely wipe out the sovereignty of the States." He described the "good sought in unconstitutional legislation" as "an insidious feature" that led well-meaning citizens and officials to forget "the serious breach it will make in the ark of our covenant or the harm which will come from breaking down recognized standards."[36]

Within days of the Supreme Court decision, resolutions calling for a constitutional amendment banning child labor appeared in the U.S. Congress. Gompers convened the child labor reform coalition at a meeting in the AFL headquarters. The coalition resolved to pursue a constitutional amendment permitting Congress to ban the labor of persons under the age of eighteen. Republican president Warren G. Harding and Commerce Secretary Herbert Hoover endorsed the amendment. The 68th Congress approved it by large margins of 297–69 in the House and 61–23 in the Senate.[37]

Opposition to the federal regulation of child labor had expanded and intensified, however. While Clark and Emery led the opposition, now the Sentinels of the Republic (formed by an officer of United Shoe Machinery Company) battled against expansion of federal power embodied in the amendment. The amendment used the term "labor" instead of "employment," which made it possible to persuade farmers that the amendment threatened family farm labor.[38] The congressional debate included a more emotional opposition to federal power and support for states' rights than occurred in the previous child labor debates. Charges of socialism and communism were common. Opponents now ridiculed the claim that interstate competition would inhibit child protection.[39]

Though they failed to stop the proposed amendment in Congress, the employer-led opposition blocked its approval by the states. The NAM designated the amendment's defeat as its top priority for 1924. Clark's "Farmers' States Rights League" circulated anti-amendment propaganda to farm states, and the American Farm Bureau Federation joined the opposition. In Massachusetts, Cardinal William O'Connell opposed it as an interference with church prerogatives and parental control over children. In New York, some manufacturers made their charitable contributions contingent on an organization's opposition to the amendment. This coalition of business, agriculture, and religious groups dealt a devastating blow when it helped defeat the amendment in the two most industrialized and progressive states, New York and Massachusetts.[40] By March 1925, a dozen states had rejected the child labor amendment, and only four (Wisconsin, California, Arkansas, and Arizona) had ratified it. Between 1925 and the beginning of 1933, only two more states (Colorado and Montana) ratified it. By then, thirty-five states had explicitly considered and rejected the amendment in one or both houses of the legislature.[41]

In the early 1930s, then, child labor regulation remained a state responsibility. For that reason, child labor laws remained unevenly drawn and administered. Between 1923 and 1932, new state child labor law reforms occurred very infrequently. By 1932, only half of the states met the NCLC minimum standards for child labor legislation set in 1925.[42]

SHORTER HOURS

Shorter working hours remained a top priority for trade unions and many reformers in the early twentieth century. Employers still considered hours laws a most serious intrusion on their prerogatives. Unlike the drive for national child labor regulation, however, shorter hours proponents fought separate battles for regulations of limited scope. The AFL sought for limitations on hours for public workers and contracts. The NCL lobbied for limiting the working hours of women and children. The railroad brotherhoods pressured for hours laws in their industry.

A patchwork of hours regulations resulted. AFL leaders refused to expand their program to include a law limiting hours for all manufacturing workers. By the 1920s, some private firms demonstrated that employers themselves could cut working hours without union pressure or formal regulation impinging on their labor market sovereignty.

Hours on Public Works

In 1897, the AFL's highest legislative priority remained the eight-hour day on public works.[43] Federal courts had upheld the principle of the eight-hour day for federal workers, though the interpretation was narrow and enforcement lax. As federal contract work expanded, the AFL became increasingly determined to expand the eight-hour law to workers employed on these contracts. An eight-hour day for federal contracts would give more leverage to the craftsmen who constructed federal buildings, built ships, and fashioned armor plate. A new federal eight-hour law, said Gompers, would shore up the union shop strategy by supplementing "our private efforts to secure a universal eight-hour day for all wage earners in America."[44] United Mine Workers of America (UMWA) president John Mitchell anticipated that such a law "would reach out and eventually include all of the industries of this country."[45]

Prior to the open shop drive, Congress moved toward enacting the AFL's eight-hour law. The House passed the bill unanimously in 1898, but it died in the Senate's end-of-session rush.[46] The eight-hour bill easily survived a procedural test in the House in the following Congress, despite more forceful lobbying from shipbuilders and metalworking companies. The House debate turned primarily on which political party had been more supportive of labor, rather than on the strengths and weaknesses of the proposal. The Senate, on a close procedural vote, permitted a watered-down version to die in 1900.[47]

The employer counteroffensive clearly undercut support for the federal contract hour law during 1902. In May of that year, the House of Representatives again passed the bill on a voice vote. After the election of David Parry as NAM president, the open shop employers joined steelmakers, shipyards, and other contractors to oppose the bill in the Senate.[48] Business lobbyists attacked the bill as despotism, socialism, and an unconstitutional intrusion on the states. One shipbuilder insisted that "our relations to our employees are regulated purely by the laws of [Virginia]."[49] At Parry's urging, NAM members lobbied federal legislators directly. The eight-hour bill never came to a vote in the Senate in that session of Congress. Parry described the NAM's lobbying success in 1902–3 "as the first decisive defeat of the socialistic forces which have of late years had such surprising growth."[50] In the following Congresses (until 1910), House Speaker and NAM ally Joseph Cannon ensured that the House Committees would prevent the AFL's eight-hour bill and other labor legislation from coming to the House floor.[51]

Organized labor fared little better in the states. In the 1890s, several of the states most influenced by populism enacted eight-hour laws for public works. State courts, however, ruled against the constitutionality of such eight-hour laws in the key industrial states of Ohio (1903), New York (1904), Pennsylvania (1911), and Illinois (city ordinances, 1900).[52] The U.S. Supreme Court upheld the constitutionality of state and local eight-hours on public works in *Atkin v. Kansas* in 1903. By 1917, all the western and mountain states had such laws, as did the largest eastern and midwestern industrial states other than Illinois. Nearly all of these states had enacted these laws before the 1903 Supreme Court decision, however.[53]

Cannon's fall and the Democrats' political gains in 1910 created the first opportunity to advance the federal hours bill since the start of the open shop drive. Congress added the eight-hour requirement to a naval appropriations bill after the revolt against the Speaker. President Taft endorsed new eight-hour legislation after the 1910 election.[54]

The more Democratic Congress that convened in 1911 debated the AFL hours bill for the first time in nine years. Its chastened proponents, however, had scaled back their claims about its impact. When conservatives expressed concerns about its reach, Representative (and UMWA leader) William B. Wilson (D, Pennsylvania) responded in Gompers's name "that the Federal government had no power and no right to interfere between a private employer and employees on the question of hours of labor" or wages.[55] The bill passed the House unanimously. The Senate turned back a proposal to change the bill to a nine-hour law on a 35-to-14 vote. The bill became law in 1912, forty-four years after the enactment of the initial federal eight-hour law.[56]

Woodrow Wilson's administration implemented the law in a way that generally satisfied the AFL. William B. Wilson, who became secretary of the new Department of Labor in 1913, lobbied other cabinet officers to apply it strictly. Though the administration suspended the eight-hour law in some war-related efforts in 1917, the government by and large upheld the eight-hour day and union standards in war production and paid time and a half for overtime.[57] The Republican administrations of the 1920s did not repeal it.

Hours on Railroads and on Ships

The federal government indisputably had jurisdiction over interstate railroads and waterborne commerce. Some railroad engineers and brakemen worked exhausting continuous shifts of forty hours or more. Horrifying rail accidents put a spotlight on the dangers of railroad work. By the early years of the twentieth century, the railroad brotherhoods and the seamen's union were urging Congress to limit hours in their industries.

The railroad brotherhoods in 1904 prepared legislation that limited the railroad operating employees to sixteen continuous hours of service. Comfortably elected in his own right and increasingly responsive to progressive reform, Roosevelt called for legislation limiting work hours on railroads.[58] Senator Robert La Follette (R, Wisconsin) introduced the brotherhoods' bill, and Roosevelt backed it. La Follette, demonstrating mastery of the Senate rules, secured narrow approval of the bill. Roosevelt interceded with Speaker Cannon to win the bill's approval in the House.[59] The Hours of Service Act of 1907 constituted the first Progressive Era law establishing a national worker protection. It was unambiguously a union victory. Legislative supporters had invoked the brotherhoods' demand for the law in debates. It gave legal support to contracts the brotherhoods already had concluded with some of the railroads. Congress strengthened the law in 1916.[60]

The Seamen's bill, first introduced in Congress in 1904, combined several types of regulations sought by the sailors' unions and particularly by Andrew Furuseth, the AFL's leading lobbyist. The bill in effect limited seamen's hours in port and at sea. It protected seamen's pay and limited the supply of merchant ship labor by mandating that crews include experienced sailors. Highly publicized marine disasters and support by the NCL propelled the bill forward in the more progressive Congress elected in 1912. In 1915, Congress finally enacted the bill in strengthened form. Gompers ascribed its success to "our political activity and our economic powers."[61]

The Adamson Act of the following year showed how national jurisdiction could produce even national eight-hour legislation, if only in a single industry. With the economy healthy and a presidential election looming in 1916, the railroad brotherhoods demanded the eight-hour day. Negotiations between the brotherhoods and the railroads broke down in August. President Wilson proposed the enactment of a law establishing the eight-hour day for railroad operating employees. Wilson told railroad presidents that he would influence the Interstate Commerce Commission (ICC) to permit higher railroad charges if the eight-hour law unduly burdened the lines. Wilson's mediation failed; the nation faced a paralyzing rail strike on September 4, two months before the presidential election. Wilson, claiming that "the whole spirit of the time and the preponderant evidence of recent economic experience" supported the eight-hour day, proposed that Congress establish it by law for operating employees. The ICC would have approval to raise rates to meet the additional costs of the change. Though reluctant to accede to government protection, the brotherhoods agreed to call off the strike if Congress enacted the eight-hour law for the industry. A bitterly divided Congress passed the law in time to avert the strike.[62]

The Adamson Act of 1916 marked the first legal eight-hour day for male workers in the private sector and the only such federal regulation until the New Deal. Its enactment reflected the unusual circumstance of federal regulatory authority over both working conditions and industry pricing. Senator Albert Cummins (R, Iowa), criticized the bill because its costs would be passed on to consumers.[63] Federal power to permit this price increase enabled the federal government to accede to the brotherhoods' eight-hour demand. In effect, the Adamson Act constituted a reluctant "logrolling" agreement that awarded workers protection with minimal cost to employers. In no other national industry could American industry engineer a similar logrolling agreement.

Hours Regulation for Women Workers

In 1905, the Supreme Court seemed to put a decisive limit on government regulation of hours in private employment. In the previous seven years, the Court had upheld as constitutional both Utah's hours law for miners and Kansas's hours limit on public works. In *Lochner v. New York*, however, the Court ruled that "the limit of police power has been reached and passed" by New York's state law limiting the working day for bakers. Unlike the mining statute, the New York law illegally interfered with employers' and employees' right to make labor contracts freely. Though the NAM hoped that *Lochner* would permanently check the growth of labor regulation, the decision had a very limited impact on statutory limitation on hours.[64] *Lochner*, however, reinforced the AFL's union shop strategy. After *Lochner*, Gompers told AFL delegates that "it is gratifying to say, that what the court declared was unconstitutional in law has been successfully maintained and achieved in fact; and the ten-hour work-day limit is enforced by the organized bakers of New York by agreement with their employers."[65]

Only three years later, the Supreme Court, in *Muller v. Oregon*, seemed to reverse its position again by sustaining Oregon's ten-hour limit on the workday for women.[66] But gender differences played a decisive role in the Muller case; in effect the Court paved the way for the segregation of labor market protection. In a landmark legal brief supporting the law, Brandeis and Josephine Goldmark painstakingly laid out the case that special health hazards and threats to the reproduction of the labor force justified women's hour restriction. The Court agreed unanimously. The female, concluded the majority, "is properly placed in a class by herself, and legislation designed for her protection may be sustained, even when like legislation is not necessary for men and could not be sustained." The husbandry of motherhood and women's reproductive capacity were of critical importance to the Court: "as healthy mothers are essential to vigorous offspring, the physical well-being of woman becomes an object of public interest and care in order to preserve the strength and vigor of the race."[67]

Muller v. Oregon energized support for the legal limitation on women's working hours just as the progressive impulse was peaking. In 1908–9, immediately after *Muller*, thirty-two states enacted laws regulating the employment of women and children. The movement crested in 1911. By 1917, four-fifths of the states had enacted women's hour laws that persisted until the New Deal.[68] Theda Skocpol demonstrates that these laws resulted from coalitions of trade unions and progressive women's groups, notably the NCL and the General Federation of Women's Clubs.[69]

Florence Kelley and Goldmark drafted a model law for the District of Columbia that they hoped would spread nationwide. Opposed only by smaller establishments that claimed that "certain work would be sent to neighboring states,"[70] Congress passed the District hours bill in 1914. Representative Augustus P. Gardner (R, Massachusetts), the pragmatic son-in-law of Senator Henry Cabot Lodge, cautioned that it was easier to vote for the District hours bill than for hours regulation in the states. "All such laws," Gardner reminded colleagues, "handicap manufacturers in those States where such laws do not exist. . . ." Gardner, who had not supported similar legislation in Massachusetts the previous year, voted for the District bill "where the question is not complicated by competitive textile industries."[71]

Gardner's caution proved well founded as the progressive tide began to ebb. The momentum for hours regulation faltered as business regained its policy footing. Though the Illinois Manufacturers' Association (IMA) had failed to defeat a ten-hour bill for women during the progressive upsurge of 1909, for example, IMA lobbying turned back further limitations proposed in 1913, 1915, and 1917. By 1926, Illinois hours regulations were less stringent than those of other industrial states.[72]

Virtually all the states had some restrictions on women's working hours by the mid-1920s, but these laws varied enormously. In some states, such hours laws compared favorably to those in Europe. The leading industrial states of New York, Ohio, and Massachusetts limited the working day to nine hours and the workweek to fifty-four, fifty, and forty-eight hours, respectively. California and three other states (as well as the District of Columbia) had a limit of eight hours per day.[73] However, in 1933 Alabama, Florida, Georgia, Indiana, Iowa, and West Virginia had no laws limiting women's weekly or daily hours. Seventeen other states (including Illinois and Minnesota) permitted work in excess of fifty-four hours a week.[74] Enforcement also differed vastly across the states.

Universal Hours Regulation for All Workers

As the hours agenda advanced piecemeal, its successes shaved off potential constituents for hours laws covering the whole workforce. The enactment of protective labor laws for women reinforced the will of AFL leaders to pursue hours reductions for male breadwinners through the union shop. An eight-hour law including men as well as women seemed constitutionally impossible in any case. Representative Hiram Fowler (D, Illinois) proposed to amend the District of Columbia hours bill of 1914 to cover men as well as women. The proposal had no support, and Fowler was instructed that the law undoubtedly would be held unconstitutional.[75]

State labor federations on the West Coast directly challenged the assumption that hours laws could not be extended to men. Fueled by recession and goaded by the open shop, socialists and unionists in California, Oregon, and Washington used the initiative and referendum to put general eight-hour laws before West Coast voters in 1914. California's open shop employers campaigned aggressively against the bill. Employers in all three states circulated materials indicating Gompers's opposition to the proposal. Farmers also opposed the reduction of working hours in agriculture. Each of the state measures lost by large margins.[76] Frustrated by the use of Gompers's words against the three states' eight-hour proposals, supporters of universal eight-hour protections proposed a resolution supporting them at the following AFL convention in late 1914 and again in 1915. As late as 1912, the federation had not expressly rejected a general hours law covering both men and women.[77]

The eight-hour resolutions forced the AFL to choose explicitly between legislation and the crafts-based union shop strategy. The UMWA and the International Association of Machinists (IAM) strongly supported the legal route to hours limitation. The IAM argued that it had spent $800,000 in a failed effort to reduce the workday in the metal trades since 1910. One delegate pointed out that "the plumbers, the firemen, the engineers, the electricians and half a dozen other organizations in the building trades . . . used licensing laws in many states to leverage eight hour agreements."[78]

The AFL leaders unambiguously supported the union shop approach and opposed universal eight-hour laws, however. In earlier congressional testimony, Gompers stated that he regarded "women workers and minors as particularly the concern of the Government. I want the men to secure the eight-hour day by . . . their own individual and their associated effort."[79] The states had the right to fix hours for women and children as "wards of State," argued William B. Wilson, but men, who were "a part of the State," should earn hours protection privately.[80]

In the 1915 AFL debate, molder John P. Frey, speaking for a committee that opposed the eight-hour law resolution, reminded the delegates of the frustration of trying to gain worker protection through the American government. Granite cutter James Duncan restated the labyrinthine story of the federal eight-hour day legislation. An eight-hour law, he suggested, would authorize the state to set the hours of labor, and an unfriendly legislature could later raise the hours of labor. Maryland had passed a nine-hour law on public works and then insisted that its granite cutters work the legal nine rather than the union eight hours per day. Gompers argued that the AFL's strength and material incentives depended on defeating the proposal (see quote at the beginning of this chapter).[81]

The AFL rejected these resolutions calling for a general eight-hour day by virtually identical percentages of 58 percent in 1914 (11,237 to 8,107) and 57 percent in 1915 (8,500 votes to 6,396).[82] The UMWA and the IAM formed the primary voting bloc in favor of the eight-hour day by legislation. Neither the miners nor the machinists enjoyed the leverage to alter the AFL's position on these votes. The construction trades (carpenters, painters, plumbers, electrical workers, hod carriers), typographers, and hotel and restaurant workers constituted the largest blocs of support for rejecting the legislative route.[83] Organized labor, still nominally committed to hours regulation through the union shop, abandoned the field of general hours protection until the Depression. Marion Cahill, in an authoritative study of hours laws published in 1932, concluded that "A general federal hours statute is a Utopian hope."[84]

It is not clear that American courts would have obstructed universal hours laws if the AFL had fought for them. Oregon and Mississippi enacted general hours laws for all workers. The Supreme Court upheld Oregon's ten-hour law for male as well as females in 1918 (*Bunting v. Oregon*). Elizabeth Brandeis concluded that, although some doubt about the constitutionality of such laws remained after the Bunting decision, such laws did not spread because "no group was interested in conducting the campaigns necessary to secure [them]."[85]

Employers' Self-Regulation of Working Hours

As the AFL withdrew behind its craft fortifications, and the progressive spirit ebbed, neither legal nor union limitations on working hours seemed capable of reducing hours effectively. Yet employers seemed to be cutting hours on their own. In the 1910s, many employers had already cut the hours of labor in their firms before hours laws took effect.[86] By the 1920s, employer self-regulation became the best hope for shorter working hours for American workers outside the unionized crafts.

Concern about the working hours of male workers focused on the nonunionized steel industry. Steel companies employed workers for twelve-hour shifts. Producing steel required continuous operation, and steel plants accordingly ran twenty-four hours a day. The workday, then, could not easily be reduced in one or two hour increments. To shorten hours, the plants had to go to three eight-hour shifts. No state, wrote John R. Commons, "can afford to take the lead in reducing hours [in the steel industry] abruptly from twelve to eight. Manufacturers in one state might work eight hours in competition with others working nine or ten hours, but they cannot generally compete with those working twelve hours." It was believed that only federal legislation could solve the problem.[87]

Representative William B. Wilson introduced a bill to reduce hours in the steel industry in 1912, soon after Gompers renewed the federation's pledge to help the steelworkers organize.[88] Congress never seriously considered the bill during the Progressive Era. By 1920, over half of the 300,000 workers in the steel industry worked twelve-hour shifts, and the labor conditions of the steel plants were becoming a public concern.[89]

The steel companies now demonstrated that employers could reduce hours unilaterally without the force of law (though not without informal government intervention). In 1922, Commerce Secretary Herbert Hoover prodded the steel executives to cut normal steelmaking shifts from twelve to eight hours. The steel employers balked. When Hoover threatened to make their hesitancy public, the steelmakers gave in. By the end of the year, the steel industry unilaterally had largely instituted the eight-hour day.[90] Other firms also demonstrated that "responsible" employers could cut worktime. In October 1926, Henry Ford announced the five-day workweek in his plants.[91] In 1930 and 1931, several firms—including Sears, Roebuck; Kellogg's; Standard Oil; General Motors at Tarrytown; and Hudson Motors—reduced hours as an alternative to layoffs.

The AFL's continued resistance to government hours regulation made corporate self-regulation appear to be the most realistic hope for limiting the workday. As late as 1931, the AFL Executive Council recommended opposition to a proposed constitutional amendment that would permit Congress to reduce legally the hours of service per day. "The American Federation of Labor," wrote the Council, "always opposed the fixing of hours or wages by law."[92]

WAGES

The regulation of working hours fell off the public agenda by the end of the Progressive Era. The regulation of wages, however, hardly appeared on that agenda at all. Florence Kelley and the NCL promoted the idea of minimum wage laws soon after the U.S. Supreme Court upheld the states' right to regulate working hours for women. Victoria, Australia, had established boards to set minimum wages in "sweated" industries in 1896. Great Britain established such boards in 1909. Inspired by the British effort, Kelley prepared a similar campaign in America. The NCL published a model bill based on the British act.

American minimum wage reformers, however, had adapted their bill "to the peculiar American conditions."[93] Those conditions included competitive American federalism, which mandated a uniform law strategy. "American conditions" also required that the bill limit minimum wage laws protection to women and children, the workers whose hours government constitutionally could protect under the *Muller* decision. The NCL allied with the Women's Trade Union League, the AALL, some progressive employers, and socialists to lobby for state minimum wage laws. State and local unions joined the effort in many places. The AFL, however, provided little support.[94] In Kelley's view, AFL opposition was understandable; the minimum wage boards proposed in many states would not include labor members, and so could "become sources of injury to workers."[95]

The campaign for minimum wage protection suffered as opposition to progressivism mounted. Massachusetts textile manufacturers and other employers protested that a mandatory minimum wage would disadvantage them in competition with businesses in other states. The Massachusetts legislature took the employers' opposition into account when it adopted the nation's first minimum wage law in 1912. That law established a commission to publish legal minimum wage rates. The commission could publicize, but not punish, employers whose wages fell below these rates. The Massachusetts law, then, allowed effected employers much more freedom than did the British, Australian, or New Zealand acts.[96]

Between February and August, 1913, eight more states—California, Colorado, Minnesota, Nebraska, Oregon, Utah, Washington, and Wisconsin—passed minimum wage legislation.[97] The minimum wage movement, though, faltered badly in the most industrialized states. The NCF had expressed interest in the issue in 1913 but turned against the minimum wage after the Oregon, Washington, and California laws raised wages for less efficient workers.[98] Mounting employer opposition to progressive reforms halted the minimum wage where their stakes were highest.

Of the sixteen states that had passed minimum wage laws by 1923, Texas and Nebraska had already repealed their laws by 1923, and Colorado never implemented the law. Arizona, South Dakota, and Utah set low flat rates that were below existing wage rates and had no practical impact. Less than 20 percent of all production workers in manufacturing were located in the other ten minimum wage states in 1919. Massachusetts alone accounted for about 8 percent of these workers.[99] In most of these states real or anticipated constitutional challenges delayed implementation.[100] California's unions supported the measure and the state implemented its law. In 1922, however, California trade unions reacted in outrage when the agency that administered the law, reacting to manufacturer's concerns about interstate competition, cut the minimum wage.[101]

When the U.S. Supreme Court struck down the minimum wage law for the District of Columbia in 1923,[102] the blow struck an already enfeebled movement. After the 1923 decision, state courts began to strike down their state laws.[103] Only Wisconsin attempted to resurrect state regulation of wages. Wisconsin's 1924 minimum wage law was not subjected to a constitutional test, however, because the Industrial Commission "avoided court cases applying to adult women."[104]

By the 1920s, employers set wage level unconstrained by government or, for the most part, by unions. When the cost of living dropped after the depression of the early 1920s, employers did not cut wages commensurably. Wages in the 1920s seemed to confirm the wisdom of the union shop strategy for the AFL's crafts leaders, but differences in wage patterns also confirmed that the union shop strategy provided very narrow wage protection for American workers. In 1926, crafts workers enjoyed higher wages than those in industries dominated by large companies, and wages in the latter were higher than those in competitive industries. The building trades made particularly appreciable gains.[105]

It was the narrowness of union wage protections, more than the lack of statutory minimum wages, that was becoming the distinctive characteristic of American wage policy in the 1920s. Abroad, only Great Britain, Australia and New Zealand provided a legislated minimum wage. The British law itself never reached more than 18 percent of industrial employment. Continental European laws typically attacked minimum wages only in the case of home work.[106] What differentiated the United States by the 1920s was that collective bargaining set wages for so few American workers. The craft unions largely had abandoned wage setting to employers, and public law could not reach them.

Ironically, the craft unions were the first to demand government protection when employers began to undermine their labor market leverage. In the late 1920s, when some contractors found nonunion labor to work on federal contract work, the building trades unions successfully lobbied for a law guaranteeing union wage rates on such projects. The Davis–Bacon Act of 1931 required that building contractors working on federal buildings pay the "prevailing rate of wages" (that is, the local union rate) to employees.[107]

Davis–Bacon, like the hours law for federal contracts, constituted protective legislation targeted to a specific, and relatively privileged, worker constituency.

THE DEPRESSION AND NATIONAL
LABOR MARKET REGULATION

By the late 1920s, the AFL seemed to have recovered some of its influence on the labor market policy agenda. Thirty years after the issue of convict labor first reached Congress, that body passed the Hawes–Cooper Convict Labor bill at the end of 1928. This law permitted states to regulate the flow of convict-made goods into their borders, permitting them to label the goods or license their distribution. Unlike the child labor bill, the convict labor law attracted a formidable coalition of support that included the AFL, the General Federation of Women's Clubs, and a number of individual manufacturers and employers' associations concerned about the competition from convict-made goods. Unlike the child labor amendment, the opposition remained small, limited to prison contractors and states with a stake in subsidizing their penal system with exported goods.[108]

The rising joblessness of the early 1930s temporarily drowned the AFL's obstinate aversion to broader labor regulation. Sinking membership and labor market leverage caused the AFL delegates in late 1932 to instruct leaders to prepare compulsory federal legislation shortening the workday for all workers.[109] Even John P. Frey, the AFL leader who vehemently had opposed the general eight-hour laws in 1914, now conceded that collective bargaining alone could not achieve the eight-hour day.[110]

The AFL's shorter hours bill sought to alter the balance of labor supply and demand by making a thirty-hour week the legal standard for American industry. Senator Hugo Black (D, Alabama) introduced the AFL's bill in Congress in December, 1932.[111] Opponents questioned southern Democrat Black about the bill's apparent disregard for state's rights. Black answered by pointing out "the utter impossibility and futility of attempting to obtain regulation of hours of labor by State activities or by agreements of manufacturers."[112]

By challenging the right to set operating hours, the Black bill challenged employer prerogatives directly. Employers scrambled after the U.S. Senate passed the bill early in the New Deal's "Hundred Days."[113] The Senate vote in its early weeks in office also galvanized the administration to search for an alternative. The AFL's position on hours legislation had changed so radically that almost any proposal seemed reasonable in comparison to the Black bill.

Business leaders, notably the U.S. Chamber of Commerce and James Emery of the NAM, persuaded President Franklin D. Roosevelt to embrace their proposal for industrial "self-government" as an alternative to the Black bill. This business approach, reflecting the natural employer impulse to limit competition, permitted businesses in a given industry to administer prices, production, and labor standards in an effort to stabilize each industry. Government would enforce the employers' standards as if they were statute laws. In response to the AFL's effort to limit employers' power to set working hours, employers proposed legal sanction for American manufacturers to enforce cartel arrangements. Their plan involved little compromise of their labor market sovereignty.

Roosevelt's National Industrial Recovery Act (NIRA) incorporated the employers' proposal for rule-governed employer cooperation. Title I of the NIRA permitted industries to establish codes of "fair competition" without violating the anti-trust laws.[114] The devastated cotton textile industry established the first such code. The textile code permitted employers to reduce production substantially. It also required them to pay minimum wages, set maximum hours, and bargain collectively with employees. It also banned child labor.[115]

After an encouraging start, though, the NIRA approach ran into increasing difficulty and hostility. The Supreme Court ruled the NIRA unconstitutional in 1935, and it quickly became apparent that the states were helpless to implement industrial labor standards on their own. When Wisconsin tried to maintain NIRA standards, interstate economic competition undermined its efforts. Cleaning and dying operators from Illinois seized the opportunity created by Wisconsin's industrial standards to establish drop-off points in southeastern Wisconsin cities. The Illinois firms collected the garments, transported them to Illinois for service by cheaper labor working under worse working conditions, and brought them back to Wisconsin.[116]

Reformers in the U.S. Department of Labor developed a Fair Labor Standards bill in 1937 to reestablish limitations on cutthroat wage and hour competition. Initially modeled on the British approach, the labor standards bill proposed labor standards boards for setting minimum wages, maximum hours, and child labor restrictions. Though most employers opposed the bill, some northern businesses supported it because it promised to reduce the cost advantage of southern competitors. Southern Democrats and low-wage businesses, seeking to protect their competitive advantage, opposed the proposal and invoked states' rights in their defense. The AFL continued to oppose the minimum wage for men as a scheme that would undermine unions' material benefits. The AFL, still instinctively opposed to permitting public officials to exercise discretion in governing labor markets, successfully lobbied federal officials to drop the idea of administrative boards with discretion to set the minimum wage. Instead, the bill included a fixed, national legal minimum above which unions could bargain for higher wages. The bill, then, did not affect most of the industries organized by the unions. Instead, it set a flat rate as a floor under unorganized industrial workers.[117]

Congress enacted the Fair Labor Standards Act (FLSA) of 1938 only after dramatic tactical maneuvers and divisive votes that split the Democratic Party. By excluding domestic and farm workers, the bill effectively excluded large numbers of female and African American workers from protection and delegated their welfare to the states.[118]

EMPLOYERS' PREROGATIVES AND WORKPLACE REGULATION

American employers had largely fended off legislative and union interference with their power to set wages and hours during the Progressive Era. Progressive reformers could not establish national standards even for child labor. Federalism, the union shop strategy, and politically mobilized employers constituted insurmountable obstacles to coherent, universal protections for vulnerable workers.

The FLSA provided the foundation for eventual incremental inclusion of most of the workforce in substantive wage and hour protection. Today the minimum wage law covers most American workers, in contrast to comparable countries where minimum wages cover only a fraction of the workforce in traditionally "sweated" industries.[119] The breadth of the Fair Labor Standards Act, however, belies unions' inability to establish wage, hour, and benefits standards for most of the American workforce. The FLSA establishes minimum terms of economic competition for employers. American employers, not unions, set most of the levels of worker protection above the wage and hour minimums in the act. Employers provide most of the insurance, pension, and leave benefits that lie beyond its scope. American employers' success in preserving their power over the terms of employment owed a great deal to their success in limiting trade union power, as the next chapter demonstrates.

NOTES

1. Florence Kelley, "The Federal Government and the Working Children," *Annals* 27 (February 1906): 289–92 (originally presented at the National Child Labor Committee in December 1905).

2. American Federation of Labor, *Proceedings* of the Thirty-fourth Annual Convention, 1914: 442; hereafter, cited as *AFL Proceedings*, [date].

3. Robert H. Wiebe, *The Search for Order, 1877–1920* (New York: Hill and Wang, 1967), 169.

4. Stephen B. Wood, *Constitutional Politics in the Progressive Era: Child Labor and the Law* (Chicago: University of Chicago Press, 1968), 3–8.

5. U.S. Commissioner of Labor, *Report on the Condition of Woman and Child Wage Earners in the United States*, U.S. Senate Document 61-645 (Washington, D.C.: Government Printing Office, 1910), 1: 187–97, 357–96; 6: 45, 134–35. See also Elizabeth Davidson, *Child Labor Legislation in the Southern Textile States* (Chapel Hill: University of North Carolina Press, 1939), 7–17.

6. F. B. Gordon, "Georgia's Tempting Invitation to Mill-man and Immigrant," *American Industries* 3, no. 2 (September 1, 1904): 13. Gordon was the president of the Georgia Industrial Association.

7. Davidson, *Child Labor Legislation in the Southern Textile States*, 55; U.S. Industrial Commission, *Final Report*, vol. 19 (Washington, D.C.: GPO, 1902), 922.

8. Walter Trattner, *Crusade for the Children: A History of the National Child Labor Committee and Child Labor Reform in America* (Chicago: Quadrangle Books, 1970), 45–67. On Irene Ashby's investigation of child labor for Samuel Gompers, see Davidson, *Child Labor Legislation in the Southern Textile States*, 25–26; *New York Times*, June 5, 1901: 2.

9. U. S. Industrial Commission, *Final Report,* 947; Kelley, "The Federal Government and the Working Children," 289–92; Theodore Roosevelt, Fourth Annual Message, December 6, 1904, in *A Compilation of the Messages and Papers of the Presidents* (Washington, D.C: Bureau of National Literature, 1914), 16: 7028.

10. Hayes Robbins, "The Necessity for Factory Legislation in the South," *Annals* 20 (July 1902): 181–88. In Holland, Belgium, France, and Sweden the minimum age for employment was twelve.

11. National Child Labor Committee, *Proceedings of the Second Annual Meeting*, in *Annals* 27 (February 1906): 371–99 (Hunter quote 380); Trattner, *Crusade for the Children*, 70.

12. *Congressional Record*, January 28, 1907: 1807–8, 1812; John Braeman, "Albert J. Beveridge and the First National Child Labor Bill," *Indiana Magazine of History* 40 (March 1964): 18–21.

13. *AFL Proceedings*, 1906: 164; 1907: 28. Letters, Theodore Roosevelt to Representative Richard Bartholdt, January 19, 1907; and Theodore Roosevelt to Albert J. Beveridge, November 12, 1907, in *The Letters of Theodore Roosevelt*, ed. Elting E. Morison (Cambridge: Harvard University Press, 1952), 5: 557, 844. On the AFL's sincerity, see Samuel Gompers, "Organized Labor's Attitude toward Child Labor," *Annals* 27 (February 1906): 79–83.

14. Letter, Louis Brandeis to John A. Sullivan, in *Letters of Louis D. Brandeis*, ed. Melvin I. Urofsky and David Levy (Albany: State University of New York, 1971), 1: 520–21; Woodrow Wilson quoted in Trattner, *Crusade for the Children*, 122.

15. Braeman, "Albert J. Beveridge and the First National Child Labor Bill," 20, 28–30; Trattner, *Crusade for the Children*, 88.

16. "No Control over Child Labor; No Control over Hours; Functions of the Federal Government," *American Industries* 5 (February 15, 1907): 1–3; *The Iron Age*, February 14, 1907: 502–3.

17. Trattner, *Crusade for the Children*, 105–7, 115; William F. Ogburn, *Progress and Uniformity in Child-Labor Legislation: A Study in Statistical Measurement* (New York: Columbia University, 1912), 203–5. It was understood that the federal investigation of woman and child labor would result in "legislation if possible by the National Congress; if not, then by the State legislatures in consequence of the publication of the facts produced by the Bureau of Labor. . . ." Theodore Roosevelt to Oscar S. Straus, letter, February 20, 1907, in Oscar S. Straus Papers, U.S. Library of Congress, Box 6.

18. Trattner, *Crusade for the Children*, 120–24.

19. House Committee on Labor, *Child-Labor Bill*, Report No. 1400, 63rd Cong., 3rd sess. (February 13, 1915), 7–8.

20. House Committee on Labor, *Child-Labor Bill*, 7, 17. Kelley, normally an especially shrewd observer of the American policymaking process, did not acknowledge the possibility that federal district courts could be very responsive to local economic interests, a fact which the southern textile industry exploited fully in legal challenges to Progressive Era federal child labor laws.

21. The House voted 233 to 45 in favor of the bill; *Congressional Record*, February 15, 1915: 3836. See Trattner, *Crusade for the Children*, 126–27; Wood, *Constitutional Politics in the Progressive Era*, 41–42.

22. Wood, *Constitutional Politics in the Progressive Era*, 42–45; U.S. Senate, Committee on Interstate Commerce, Hearings on *Interstate Commerce in Products of Child Labor* (Washington, D.C.: GPO, 1916), 241–81.

23. *Congressional Record*, January 26, 1916: 1569, 1581.

24. *Congressional Record*, January 26, 1916: 1577, 1589. Supporters who conceded the bill's questionable constitutionality included Senators Kenyon and Atlee Pomerene (D, Ohio); *Congressional Record*, August 5, 1916: 12214, 12220.

25. Senator Thomas Hardwick (D, Georgia), in *Congressional Record*, August 4, 1916: 12066.

26. *Congressional Record*, August 7, 1916: 12208. Similar arguments about unfair competition were made in the *Congressional Record* by Socialist Representative Meyer London of New York (January 26, 1916: 1591) and Senators William Kenyon (R, Iowa; February 24, 1916: 3026), Joseph Robinson (D, Arkansas: August 4, 1916: 12064), William Borah (R, Indiana; August 4, 1916: 12090), and Henry Lippitt (R, Rhode Island; August 8, 1916: 12308).

27. *Congressional Record*, January 26, 1916: 1584.

28. Arthur S. Link, *Wilson: Campaigns for Progressivism and Peace, 1916–1917* (Princeton: Princeton University Press, 1965), 58–59; *Congressional Record*, August 8, 1916: 12313; Trattner, *Crusade for the Children*, 130–31; *AFL Proceedings*, 1916: 85, 90–92.

29. Wood, *Constitutional Politics in the Progressive Era*, 83. A considerable number of southern textile mills disagreed with the tactic of a court challenge (82–83).

30. Wood, *Constitutional Politics in the Progressive Era*, 87–93.

31. *Hammer v. Dagenhart*, 247 U.S. 251 (1918).

32. Wood, *Constitutional Politics in the Progressive Era*, 198, 203.

33. Wood, *Constitutional Politics in the Progressive Era*, 206–9, 220–21. The new Owen bill was S. 4671; *Congressional Record*, June 6, 1918: 7432–33.

34. Wood, *Constitutional Politics in the Progressive Era*, 260–63.

35. Wood, *Constitutional Politics in the Progressive Era*, 267–74.

36. *Bailey v. Drexel Furniture Company,* 259 U.S. 20 (1922).

37. *Congressional Record*, April 26, 1924: 7295 (House vote); June 2, 1924: 10129, 10140, 10142 (Senate votes). See also Trattner, *Crusade for the Children*, 163–67.

38. Trattner, *Crusade for the Children*, 166–67; House Judiciary Committee, *Child-Labor Amendment to the Constitution of the United States*, Minority Report, No. 395, part 2, 68th Cong., 1 sess., March 29, 1924, 8.

39. *Congressional Record*, April 25, 1924: 7168; June 2, 1924: 10084–85, 10119; Trattner, *Crusade for the Children*, 172. Senator Nathaniel Dial (D, South Carolina) warned that "this is the first step to unemployment compensation. . . ." *Congressional Record*, June 2, 1924: 10129.

40. *Congressional Record*, January 8, 1925: 1438–47; January 28, 1925: 2571–73. Elizabeth Sands Johnson, "Child Labor Legislation," in *History of Labor Legislation in the United States,* ed. John R. Commons et al., 4 vols. (New York: Macmillan, 1935), 3: 445; Trattner, *Crusade for the Children*, 174–76; Wood, *Constitutional Politics in the Progressive Era,* 221; Jeremy P. Felt, *Hostages of Fortune: Child Labor Reform in New York State* (Syracuse: Syracuse University Press, 1965), 195–216.

41. Johnson, "Child Labor Legislation," 449.

42. Johnson, "Child Labor Legislation," 450–56.

43. A House committee later claimed that "It is a matter of common knowledge that Mr. Gompers . . . took a most keen interest in this legislation, as great, if not greater, than in any other matter which has arisen." U.S. Congress, House of Representatives, Lobby Investigation Select Committee, *Charges against Members of the House and Lobbying Activities*, Report 113, 63rd Cong., 2nd sess., December 9, 1913, 29.

44. U.S. Senate, Committee on Education and Labor, Hearings on *Eight Hours for Laborers on Government Work*, Senate Document 141 (Washington, D.C.: GPO, 1903), 11.

45. John Mitchell, in U.S. Industrial Commission, vol. 12, *Capital and Labor in the Mining Industries* (Washington, D.C.: GPO, 1901), 47.

46. *Congressional Record*, May 17, 1898: 4984–89.

47. The House vote to suspend the rules for a vote on the bill was 151–24; in the Senate, a motion to discharge the eight-hour bill from committee lost on a vote of 33–28 (31 of the "no" votes came from Republicans). *Congressional Record*, May 21, 1900: 5804–5; June 6, 1900: 6800.

48. *Congressional Record*, May 19, 1902: 5656; *New York Times*, May 20, 1902: 3; David M. Parry, "Will an Arbitrary Eight-Hour Workday Do?" *American Industries* 1 (September 1, 1902): 1. *Iron Age* congratulated the NAM on its vigorous and successful campaign in an article reprinted in *American Industries* 1 (March 15, 1903): 12 (see also 8).

49. U.S. Senate, Committee on Education and Labor, Hearings on *Eight Hours for Laborers on Government Work*, Senate Document 141 (Washington, D.C.: GPO, 1903), 18.

50. National Association of Manufacturers, *Proceedings* of the Eighth Annual Convention, 1903: 14–16; Lobby Investigation Select Committee, *Charges against Members of the House,* 8–9.

51. In the 59th Congress (1905–7), the House Labor Committee reported the bill only when minority Democrats seized a momentary majority; *New York Times*, May 21, 1906.

52. Elizabeth Brandeis, "Labor Legislation," in *History of Labor Legislation in the United States,* 3: 544–45.

53. *Atkin v. Kansas*, 191 U.S. 207 (November 30, 1903); Lindley D. Clark, "State Regulation of Employment on Public Work," *Monthly Review of the Bureau of Labor Statistics*, 4 (March 1917): 455–67; Brandeis, "Labor Legislation," 543–47. Twenty-eight states had enacted such laws by the New Deal. Elizabeth Brandeis speculates that the failure of such laws in the states "testifies either to the weakness of organized labor or their apathy on this question" at the state level (547). However, three of the largest industrial states with relatively strong labor movements considered or passed an eight-hour bill after 1903. Pennsylvania voters rejected a proposal to regulate hours on public works in November 1913. Ohio enacted an eight-hour law in 1913. New York amended its constitution to permit it to enact such a law, and it passed one again in 1906. Illinois employers helped defeat such a law in 1889 and 1891, and it enacted a law forty years later in the Depression; U.S. Bureau of Labor Statistics, *Labor Law of the United States*, Bulletin 148 (Washington, D.C.: GPO, 1914), 1:147; Earl R. Beckner, *A History of Labor Legislation in Illinois* (Chicago: University of Chicago Press, 1929), 181. One state that extended the eight-hour day, but that was not credited for doing so by Elizabeth Brandeis, was Connecticut. Its law reflected the strongest labor voices for protection and extended only to painters, carpenters, masons, electricians, machinists, engineers, firemen, and plumbers. See *American Labor Legislation Review* 1 (October 1911): 115–16.

54. *Congressional Record*, June 4, 1910: 7417; William Howard Taft, Second Annual Message, December 6, 1910, *Messages and Papers of the Presidents*, 17: 7921-22; "Federal Limitation of Hours on Public Works," *Monthly Review of the Bureau of Labor Statistics*, 3 (October 1916): 526–43.

55. *Congressional Record*, December 14, 1911: 382–85, 389.

56. *Congressional Record*, December 14, 1911: 394–96; May 22, 1912: 6941; May 31, 1912: 7453–55.

57. *AFL Proceedings*, 1915: 90, 103–4; 1917: 107–10. James Emery, "A Digest of the Eight-Hour Law," in Minutes of the National Industrial Conference Board, April 19, 1917, 9–11, NICB Records, Accession 1057, Series III, Book 1, Hagley Museum and Library; *American Labor Unions and Politics*, 98; Marion Cahill, *Shorter Hours: A Study of the Movement since the Civil War* (New York: Columbia University Press, 1932), 79–81.

58. Fourth Annual Message, December 6, 1904, in *Messages and Papers of the Presidents*, 16: 7027–28. The brotherhoods' 1904 resolution urged Congress "to enact a national law prohibiting the excessive hours that engineers on many roads are now held on duty." See *Congressional Record*, February 18, 1907: 3238.

59. *Congressional Record*, June 26, 1906: 9265; Letter, Theodore Roosevelt to James E. Watson, August 18, 1906, in *The Letters of Theodore Roosevelt*, 5: 373. The Senate vote, 36–32, is in *Congressional Record*, January 10, 1907: 891; the House vote, on February 18, 1907, is on 3252–53. On Roosevelt's intervention in the House, see letters, Roosevelt to

Cannon, January 16, 1907, and February 6, 1907, in *The Letters of Theodore Roosevelt*, 5: 555, 581. See also Belle Case La Follette and Fola La Follette, *Robert M. La Follette* (New York: Macmillan, 1953), 1: 208–9, 218–20.

60. Cahill, *Shorter Hours*, 85–86. In 1916, La Follette drew attention to the lax enforcement of the law. He noted that there had been half a million violations of the law because penalties were insignificant. Many courts had assessed the railroads only one cent for violating the law; *Congressional Record*, September 2, 1916: 13652.

61. Hyman Weintraub, *Andrew Furuseth: Emancipator of the Seamen* (Berkeley: University of California Press, 1959), 108–32. *AFL Proceedings*, 1915: 349–55; 1919: 107.

62. Link, *Wilson: Campaigns for Progressivism and Peace, 1916–1917*, 85–91. *Congressional Record*, August 29, 1916: 13336; September 1, 1916: 13581–82; September 2, 1916: 13655. See also *AFL Proceedings*, 1916: 5–6, 285–92.

63. *Congressional Record*, September 1, 1916: 13576–77.

64. *Lochner v. New York*, 198 U.S. 45 (April 17, 1905). See Paul Kens, *Judicial Power and Reform Politics: The Anatomy of* Lochner v. New York (Lawrence: University Press of Kansas, 1990); Howard Gillman, *The Constitution Besieged: The Rise and Demise of Lochner Era Police Powers Jurisprudence* (Durham, N.C.: Duke University Press, 1993), 214, fn. 41, 251–52, fn. 54. Wood, *Constitutional Politics in the Progressive Era:*, 121. The NAM reaction is in *American Industries* 3 (May 1, 1905): 8.

65. *AFL Proceedings*, 1905: 32.

66. Cahill, *Shorter Hours*, 112.

67. *Muller v. Oregon*, 208 U.S. 412 (1908). I am indebted to Eileen McDonagh for pointing out this critical element of the Muller decision. See also Julie Novkov, "Liberty, Protection, and Women's Work: Investigating the Boundaries between Public and Private," *Law and Social Inquiry* 21 (1996): 857–99.

68. U.S. Bureau of Labor Statistics, *Labor Law of the United States*, Bulletin 148, 1: 6; Elizabeth Brandeis, "Labor Legislation," 474–83.

69. Theda Skocpol, *Protecting Soldiers and Mothers: The Political Origins of Social Policy in the United States* (Cambridge: Belknap, 1992), 373–401. Clara Beyer, analyzing these developments in the early 1930s, described organized labor as the "largest single factor making for the passage of labor legislation for women" (*History of Labor Legislation in Three States*, 2–4)

70. *Congressional Record*, 62nd Cong., 3rd sess., 1914, Appendix, 179.

71. *Congressional Record*, February 12, 1914: 3403.

72. Thomas R. Pegram, *Partisans and Progressives: Private Interest and Public Policy in Illinois, 1870–1922* (Urbana: University of Illinois Press, 1992), 80–82; Beckner, *A History of Labor Legislation in Illinois*, 209–22.

73. John R. Commons and John B. Andrews, *Principles of Labor Legislation*, rev. ed. (New York: Harper and Brothers, 1927), 249–52.

74. Brandeis, "Labor Legislation," 458–59.

75. *Congressional Record*, February 12, 1914: 3413–15.

76. Vernon H. Jensen, *Lumber and Labor* (New York: Farrar and Rinehart, 1945), 121–22; "Washington's First Experiment in Direct Legislation," *Political Science Quarterly*

30 (June 1915): 235–53; Robert Edward Lee Knight, *Industrial Relations in the San Francisco Bay Area, 1900–1918* (Berkeley: University of California Press, 1960), 243; *AFL Proceedings*, 1914: 422, 425; Cahill, *Shorter Hours*, 24; Commons and Andrews, *Principles of Labor Legislation*, 229; *Bulletin of the Public Affairs Information Service* (White Plains, N.Y.: H. W. Wilson, 1915), 1:114–15.

77. The AFL tended to equate the public works law with the realization of the eight-hour day; see, for example, the article on "The Eight-Hour Day in Government Work" in *The American Federationist* 17, no. 12 (December 1910): 1057–58.

78. *AFL Proceedings*, 1914: 422, 433.

79. *Congressional Record*, February 12, 1914: 3406.

80. *Congressional Record*, December 14, 1911: 382–85, 389.

81. *AFL Proceedings*, 1914: 425, 436–37, 442.

82. *AFL Proceedings*, 1914: 421–44; 1915: 484–503. See also Mark Karson, *American Labor Unions and Politics, 1900–1918* (Carbondale: Southern Illinois University Press, 1958), 128–30.

83. *AFL Proceedings*, 1915: 484–504; see also Elizabeth Brandeis, "Labor Legislation," 557.

84. Cahill, *Shorter Hours*, 22.

85. Brandeis, "Labor Legislation," 558.

86. Robert Whaples, "Winning the Eight-Hour Day, 1909–1919," *Journal of Economic History* 50 (June 1990): 393–406.

87. John R. Commons, "Eight-Hour Shifts by Federal Legislation," *American Labor Legislation Review* 7 (March 1917): 139–54.

88. *AFL Proceedings*, 1912: 28–29.

89. Robert H. Zieger, *Republicans and Labor, 1919–1929* (Lexington: University of Kentucky Press, 1969), 97–98.

90. Zieger, *Republicans and Labor, 1919–1929*, 99–107; David Brody, *Steelworkers in America: The Non-Union Era* (New York: Harper and Row, 1969), 274.

91. David R. Roediger and Philip S. Foner, *Our Own Time: A History of American Labor and the Working Day* (New York: Greenwood, 1989), 238.

92. *AFL Proceedings*, 1931: 113.

93. The words are those of Harvard political economy professor Arthur Holcombe. Vivian Hart concludes that this phrase meant that the legislation would be gendered, that is, apply to women only. However, it is equally plausible that the phrase referred to the conditions that obstructed more comprehensive legislation—the limited powers authorized for the federal government and the adaptation of male craft unions to those conditions. See Vivien Hart, *Bound by Our Constitution: Women, Workers, and the Minimum Wage* (Princeton: Princeton University Press, 1994), 72–75, 100.

94. As Theda Skocpol points out, "it is testimony to the efficacy of women's politics that minimum wage laws made as much headway as they did" (p. 404). On California, see Jaclyn Greenberg, "The Limits of Legislation: Katherine Philips Edson, Practical Politics, and the Minimum-Wage Law in California, 1913–1922," *Journal of Policy History* 5 (1993): 207–30.

95. Kathryn Kish Sklar, "Two Political Cultures in the Progressive Era: The National Consumers' League and the American Association for Labor Legislation," in *U.S. History as Women's History: New Feminist Essays*, ed. Linda A. Kerber, Alice Kessler-Harris, and Kathryn Kish Sklar (Chapel Hill: University of North Carolina Press), 362–63, note 8751, 59.

96. Brandeis, "Labor Legislation," 508–10.

97. U.S. Bureau of Labor Statistics, *Minimum-Wage Legislation in the United States and Foreign Countries*, Bulletin 167 (Washington, D.C.: GPO, 1915).

98. James Weinstein, *The Corporate Ideal in the Liberal State: 1900–1918* (Boston: Beacon, 1968), 33; Hart, *Bound by Our Constitution*, 79–80.

99. Calculated from U.S. Department of Commerce, Bureau of the Census, *1972 Census of Manufactures*, vol. 3: Area Statistics (Washington, D.C.: GPO, 1976), 47–56.

100. Eventually, state courts in Minnesota, Arkansas, Washington, and Massachusetts upheld minimum wage laws when they were challenged, and the U.S. Supreme Court upheld the Oregon law in the 1917 case of *Stettler v. O'Hara* (243 U.S. 629); Melvin I. Urofsky, "State Courts and Protective Legislation during the Progressive Era: A Reevaluation," *Journal of American History* 72 (June 1985): 83. See also Brandeis, "Labor Legislation," 502–4, 516, 520–22.

101. Greenberg, "The Limits of Legislation."

102. On the District of Columbia's minimum wage law, see Vivien Hart, "Feminism and Bureaucracy: The Minimum Wage Experiment in the District of Columbia," *Journal of American Studies* 36 (April 1992): 1–22. .

103. *Adkins v. Children's Hospital*, 261 U.S. 525 (1923); Zieger, *Republicans and Labor*, 259; Kens, *Judicial Power and Reform Politics*, 156. See also Gillman, *The Constitution Besieged*, 186.

104. Brandeis, "Labor Legislation," 513.

105. Paul Douglas, *Real Wages in the United States, 1890–1926* (Boston: Houghton Mifflin, 1930), 562–63; Don D. Lescohier, "Working Conditions," in *History of Labor Legislation in the United States* 3: 69, 82–86.

106. Massimo Rocella, "Minimum Wage-Fixing: An Historical and Comparative Perspective," *Comparative Labor Law* 6 (Winter 1984): 82–93.

107. U.S. House of Representatives, Committee on Labor, Hearings on *Hours of Labor and Wages on Public Works* (Washington, D.C.: GPO, 1927); *Congressional Record*, February 28, 1931: 6504–21; Philip Taft, *Organized Labor in American History* (New York: Harper and Row, 1964), 415.

108. On the Hawes–Cooper Act, see *Congressional Record*, May 14, 1928: 8648–59, December 15, 1928: 654–67, and December 19, 1928: 864-876. See also Stephen P. Garvey, "Freeing Prisoners' Labor," *Stanford Law Review* 50 (January 1998): 339–70. The law was signed in 1929. It survived a constitutional challenge in *Whitfield v. Ohio*, 279 U.S. 431 (1936). The Ashurst–Summers Act of 1935 required labeling of convict-made goods.

109. *AFL Proceedings*, 1932: 296.

110. Quoted in *Congressional Record*, February 17, 1933: 4310.

111. *Congressional Record*, December 21, 1932: 820.

112. *Congressional Record,* February 17, 1933: 4312.

113. The Senate had defeated a Roosevelt administration substitute bill and approved the thirty-hour bill by a 53–30 vote; *Congressional Record*, April 6, 1933: 1350. See also Dubofsky, *The State and Labor in Modern America*, 107–10; Irving Bernstein, *The New Deal Collective Bargaining Policy* (Berkeley: University of California Press, 1950), 29–30.

114. Colin Gordon, *New Deals: Business, Labor, and Politics in America, 1920–1935* (New York: Cambridge University Press, 1994), 124, 171; Robert F. Himmelberg, *The Origins of the National Recovery Administration: Business, Government, and the Trade Association Issue, 1921–1933* (New York: Fordham University Press, 1976), 183–89; 204–5.

115. Arthur M. Schlesinger Jr., *The Coming of the New Deal* (Boston: Houghton Mifflin, 1958), 111–12; Charles Albert Pearce, *NRA Trade Practice Programs* (New York: Columbia University Press, 1939), 104–9, 152.

116. Testimony of Fred M. Wylie, Wisconsin Trade Practice Commission, in Senate Committee on Education and Labor and House Committee on Labor, Joint Hearings on *Fair Labor Standards Act of 1937* (Washington, D.C.: GPO, 1937), 411.

117. Joint Hearings on *Fair Labor Standards Act of 1937*; Paul H. Douglas and Joseph Hackman, "The Fair Labor Standards Act of 1938, I," *Political Science Quarterly* 53 (1938): 491–515.

118. Hart, *Bound by Our Constitution*, 153–69; Suzanne Mettler, *Dividing Citizens: Gender and Federalism in New Deal Public Policy* (Ithaca, N.Y.: Cornell University Press, 1998).

119. U.S. Senate, Committee on Education and Labor, *Fair Labor Standards Act*, Senate Report 75-884, July 6, 1937 (Washington, D.C.: GPO, 1937); Richard Franklin Bensel, *Sectionalism and American Political Development, 1880–1980* (Madison: University of Wisconsin Press, 1984), 160–63; James T. Patterson, *Congressional Conservatism and the New Deal: The Growth of the Conservative Coalition in Congress, 1933–1939* (Lexington: University of Kentucky Press, 1967), 149–54, 182–83, 193–98.

7

CONFINING TRADE
UNION POWERS

We have always looked upon the injunction as a beneficent
instrument and by far preferable to calling in troops. . . .

—Walter Gordon Merritt, representing the American
Anti-Boycott Association, 1928[1]

The success of the AFL's union shop strategy depended on unions' freedom
to use strikes, pickets, and boycotts to force employers to bargain with
them. American labor leaders, then, sought policy changes that would drive the
courts from the labor market and free unions to use all their economic weapons.
Such union policy demands, however, energized and focused the open shop
employers' policy counterattack. Employers defended the courts' legal power to
inhibit union organizing, asked their congressional allies to bottle up unfavorable changes in anti-trust and injunction law, and persuaded judges to use anti-
trust statutes and injunctions to abridge unions' economic power. Courts,
empowered by constitutional prerogatives and by ambiguous laws, became the
legal agents of the employers' counterattack.[2]

The employers' policy offensive largely succeeded. American public policy confined unions' economic power and the spread of the union shop in the
early 1900s. Reformers and politicians came to support some procedural protections for union in the 1910s, but refused to grant labor's demand for unlimited freedom to expand the scope of economic conflicts. Labor's hard-won
"Magna Carta," the Clayton Act of 1914, failed to free unions from the limitations of anti-trust and the reach of court injunctions. Courts limited union
actions even more in the 1920s than they had before 1914. "Company" unions
protected employer autonomy by precluding the independent unionization of
workers in some key firms. By the time unions won unprecedented legal protections in the 1930s, their victories occurred in a labor market that employers

183

had come to dominate over the preceding three decades. The Norris–La Guardia Anti-Injunction Act of 1932, the National Industrial Recovery Act of 1933 (NIRA), and the Wagner Act of 1935 provided protections for union organizing procedures and a mechanism for enforcing this protection. These laws, though, also reinforced geographically and industrially narrow collective bargaining and created potent barriers to a broad and effective union challenge to employer prerogatives.

COURTS AND INJUNCTIONS

At the turn of the century, labor leaders viewed the legal constraints on union activities as an increasingly urgent threat. If unions could not freely strike, picket, boycott, and conduct sympathy strikes (to bring other employers' pressure to bear on a targeted employer), it would be much more difficult to extend the union shop. If courts ordered unions to pay damages for economic harm suffered by employers, civil suits could destroy strike funds and insurance reserves. These union strike and insurance benefits constituted two incentives essential for attracting workers to join unions.

American courts were unusually well equipped to limit unions' freedom of action. The separation of powers gave American judges independent authority to intervene in labor disputes when asked to do so. Ambiguous labor laws enabled judges to define the limits on labor power much differently than did a bill's sponsors or labor administrators. American judges had relatively long experience in defining the precise legal limits of union power.

It is little wonder, then, that when invited to do so, American courts invented legal tools to limit unions' freedom of action earlier and elaborated them more extensively than jurists abroad did. American judges effectively used the common law doctrine of conspiracy to limit unions. This doctrine held that individuals could not collude to injure someone's property. By the late 1880s, American legal doctrine largely accepted that an individual's business constituted a form of property. Judges, then, could interpret a strike or a boycott as an illegal conspiracy that aimed to injure property, that is, an employer's business.[3]

America's anti-trust statutes strengthened the courts' hand in limiting unions. The Sherman Anti-Trust Act of 1890 and other anti-trust laws turned the unwritten common law of conspiracy into written, statute law. The Sherman Act declared a national policy against economic combinations that restrained interstate trade. The framers of the act evaded the question of whether unions constituted such an economic combination. Soon after it took effect, though, federal courts had ruled that strikes could constitute an illegal restraint of interstate trade under the anti-trust act.[4]

American judges used injunctions to implement the restrictions on union activity that they found in the conspiracy and anti-trust laws. By issuing an injunction that ordered a strike or picketing to cease, courts could undercut a union's ability to force employers to bargain collectively. Temporary injunctions allowed courts to stop a strike for a protracted period. A court could issue a temporary injunction and schedule a hearing weeks later. Such a delay in starting a strike could destroy a union's economic leverage by allowing an employer to weather a period of economic vulnerability. Many injunctions were not subject to jury review (when they were, juries often reversed the injunction, as in the Chicago teamsters strike of 1905).[5]

Many injunctions overtly aimed to destroy union expansion. Federal district judge J. J. Jackson of West Virginia explained one such injunction when the United Mine Workers (UMWA) launched a turn of the century organizing drive in that state.

> I do not recognize the right of laborers to conspire together to compel employees who are not dissatisfied to lay down their picks merely to gratify a professional set of agitators, organizers, and walking delegates, who roam all over the country as agents for some combination; who are vampires, that live and fatten on the honest labor of coal miners, and who are busybodies, creating dissatisfaction among a class of people who are quiet and do not want to be disturbed. . . . The strong arm of the court of equity is invoked in this case, not to suppress the right of free speech, but to restrain and inhibit these defendants, whose only purpose is to bring about strikes. . . . [6]

Federal district judges such as Jackson often reflected local economic leaders' prevailing attitude toward trade unions.

Injunctions multiplied as employers came to understand their effectiveness and used them to defeat unions. Before courts enjoined railroad strikes in the 1890s, few had considered the possibility of using injunctions against the unions.[7] By the early 1900s, the National Association of Manufacturers (NAM) championed the labor injunction. Proposals to limit the injunction, argued NAM spokesmen, constituted "class legislation" to benefit labor and to "legalize mob violence." The courts were wise and patriotic, argued employers, and their independence should remain inviolable.[8] Open shop employers especially wanted courts to enjoin boycotts and sympathy strikes. These union weapons particularly incensed small manufacturers because they expanded the scope of economic conflict.[9] When the open shop employers characterized labor as a trust, that characterization was as much a legal tactic as it was rhetorical vilification.

The number of labor injunctions nearly quadrupled from an estimated 105 in the 1880s to 410 in the 1890s, according to legal historian William Forbath. The number doubled again to 850 in the first decade of the twentieth century, when the open shop counterattack flourished. The number of labor injunctions held constant at 835 in the 1910s. When the open shop movement revived in the turbulent 1920s, the number of injunctions more than doubled to 2,130.[10]

Courts did not enjoin most strikes, but they increasingly enjoined sympathy strikes: 15 percent of sympathy strikes were enjoined in the 1890s, 25 percent in the 1900s, and 46 percent in the 1920s. These injunctions especially hampered the railroad and industrial unions, which employed large numbers of machinists.[11] The courts' frequent refusal to enjoin employer boycotts (such as blacklists of union sympathizers) made unions resentful of the courts' double standard.[12]

THE AFL DEMANDS EXEMPTION

AFL leaders responded to the employers' use of the courts by demanding that unions be exempted from the injunction and from anti-trust law. Andrew Furuseth, the AFL's chief lobbyist and analyst of the issue, argued that this use of judicial power interfered with individual rights. A seaman, Furuseth had battled to secure merchant sailors' right to be paid and to have shore leave. He likened the conditions on merchant ships to involuntary servitude, and he compared the judicial assault on labor to those shipboard conditions. The courts' interference with union freedoms harkened back to the "absolutist" rule of feudal lords over subservient vassals. He bitterly contested the claim that employers had a property right in labor and held that the legal abrogation of this claim offered the key to worker protection. Remove the legal limitations on workers' freedom of collective economic action, he argued, and workers would provide adequately for their own protection. Unions could win a fair fight in the labor market if government allowed them to use all the tools at their disposal. Legislation, then, should remove legal limitations on labor's use of its economic power, such as the labor injunction and the application of anti-trust laws to unions.[13]

The AFL leaders, then, sought to prevent government from interfering with its freedom of action. Eventually, AFL leaders would use the metaphor of serfdom to frame their demand as a magna carta.[14] This feudal metaphor reflected the libertarian approach of AFL leaders such as Furuseth and their perception that a "belated feudalism" haunted American labor relations.[15]

This cry for legal exemption, however, placed the AFL in the position of demanding legislation to protect the union shop and eliminate the employers' defenses against it. In other words, after opposing "class legislation" favorable to business, the AFL seemed to be demanding class legislation for itself, in the form of a special exemption from a general law. Countries that tolerated business collusion did not place unions in a similar logical dilemma. When workers asked to act collectively to assert their power in other nations, such exemptions were consistent with powers that employers already enjoyed. But uniquely in the United States, statute law condemned collusion. The logical problem for labor was that it had to claim that it should be exempted from these laws while employers should not.

In the absence of employer collusion, the battle over union power in the United States, then, became a zero-sum game. Either side could only gain at the others' expense. Collaboration for mutual benefit was impossible, given American political institutions, American anti-trust law, and the strategies of economic self-interest that both had set in motion.

Given this stark all-or-nothing choice by embittered economic adversaries, influential policymakers sought a middle ground. The political system gravitated toward a compromise position between the poles of full union freedom and full employer freedom. Policymakers in 1914 and in 1932 tried to give unions additional freedom without giving them substantial power to expand the scope of economic conflict.

American union leaders explicitly rejected an alternative middle ground when they flatly rejected arbitration early in the twentieth century. In 1900, union strength was peaking and unchallenged by the open shop proponents. The Murray Hill agreement hinted that business–labor collaboration might expand in the United States. Under these circumstances, some American labor leaders entertained the idea of a system of compulsory arbitration modeled on that in New Zealand.[16]

But the reversal of the Murray Hill agreement in 1901, the accelerating open shop drive, and the persistent unreliability of American government soured labor leaders on government-brokered collective bargaining. The rejection of arbitration helped to preclude government-led corporatism. The rejection of arbitration also strengthened labor's resolve to free the union shop drive from government interference, an ambition that was doomed from the start.

THE OPEN SHOP COUNTERATTACK
STYMIES EXEMPTION

AFL leaders initially experienced only frustration when they approached Congress with their plan to exempt unions from injunctions, conspiracy law, and anti-trust statutes. By 1900, the AFL's lawyers had drafted bills aimed to exempt unions from the legal definition of "conspiracy" and eliminate the use of injunctions in labor disputes.[17] A House subcommittee chaired by Charles Littlefield, however, altered the bill so that it restricted unions even further. The Littlefield revision eliminated any protection from conspiracy prosecution. For the first time in the history of U.S. federal law, the courts were explicitly permitted to enjoin labor, a provision that strengthened the courts' injunctive power by codifying it. The House Judiciary Committee favorably reported what the AFL now viewed as an anti-labor bill.[18]

Samuel Gompers and other labor leaders asked representatives to vote against the anti-injunction bill they had originally drafted. The House defeated the bill 54-to-145, a margin that indicates substantial political support for labor prior to the full force of the open shop counterattack.[19] In the spring of 1902, before the election of David Parry as NAM president, House and Senate committees reported the bill without amending it. The House passed it on a voice vote in May.[20]

Like the eight-hour bill, the AFL's anti-conspiracy and anti-injunction bill sank as open shop lobbying gained momentum after Parry's election. The NAM's new publication *American Industries* attacked the anti-injunction bill and featured many instructive examples of employers who successfully sought injunctions against strikes, picketing, and boycotts.[21] The bill, passed without dissent in the House, did not emerge on the Senate agenda.

By 1904, Gompers made the anti-injunction measure the top AFL priority.[22] Representatives of contractors, coal operators, printers, the Citizens' Industrial Association, and the American Anti-Boycott Association (AABA) testified against the bill at the 1904 hearings. The rhetorical war escalated. The open shop employers linked labor leaders to murder, the anti-injunction bill to socialism, and the strike to extortion. Daniel Davenport of the AABA characterized the boycott against D. E. Loewe's hat firm as "the crime of assassinating a man's business." Unlike the previous Congress, the House Judiciary Committee did not even report the AFL bill to the House.[23]

President Theodore Roosevelt abetted the open shop employers in his first term. Roosevelt's Anthracite Strike Commission of 1902 awarded striking Pennsylvania coal miners their short-term objectives of higher wages and shorter hours. However, the commission did not require employers to recognize the union or maintain the union shop. "The union must not undertake to assume, or to interfere with, the management of the business of the employer," the commission concluded.[24] When the typographical union demanded that the Government Printing Office fire a nonunion printer in 1903, Roosevelt refused to fire the worker. Righteously upholding the principle of the open shop, Roosevelt declared for hiring on the basis of merit independent of union affiliation.[25] Roosevelt's actions rallied business and embittered labor.[26]

Progressive reformers generally agreed with Roosevelt that "responsible" unions were desirable, but unlimited union freedom of action was not. Unions should serve public purposes and should enjoy a large, but limited, amount of freedom in return.[27] Louis Brandeis explained to Gompers that he opposed the AFL bill as "special class legislation" that improperly limited the powers of the federal courts. Workmen who have objected to such legislation in the past, Brandeis wrote, "ought not to set a bad example themselves of seeking class legislation."[28] In 1907, Woodrow Wilson, then president of Princeton University, also deplored the AFL's efforts to secure "exemption from the law" for the working class.[29]

The AFL's entry into politics in 1906 revived nominal support for the AFL measure. The opening of the 60th Congress in 1907 saw an unprecedented number of anti-injunction proposals.[30] Furuseth and the AFL lawyers had redesigned their bill in early 1906. Commonly cited as the Pearre bill for its sponsor, Representative George A. Pearre (R, Maryland), this new AFL approach aimed to expand union power by limiting employers' property rights. The bill prohibited federal judges from enjoining union actions in labor disputes unless these actions would cause irreparable damage to property. The bill limited the meaning of the word property to exclude business: "no right . . . to carry on business of any particular kind, or at any particular place, or at all, shall be construed, held, considered, or treated as property or as constituting a property Right." The bill also stated that the relation of an employer and an employee did not constitute a property right.[31]

Although Gompers compared the Pearre bill to the landmark British Trades Disputes Act of 1906,[32] politically revealing differences distinguished the British statute from the American proposal. The British law restored the status quo ante before the Taff Vale decision. British law in the 1870s had already exempted unions from prosecution as criminal conspiracies. The 1906 Trades Disputes Act reversed the Taff Vale decision by exempting unions from civil penalties as well. The American proposal, though, had to protect unions from both criminal and civil penalties. The Massachusetts Supreme Judicial Court, however, advised the state senate that a law similar to the British act would violate American constitutional protections of due process and equal protection.

There were many more differences between the British Trades Disputes Act and the Pearre bill. British liberals agreed to labor's demands. In contrast, few American progressives followed Columbia University's economist Henry Seager in praising the British Trade Disputes Act of 1906.[33] The British law did not address injunctions because they were not a serious issue in Great Britain.

Protection from injunctions was an essential feature of the AFL proposals. Many British employers could afford to put less effort into resisting unions than their American counterparts because they could collude to offset the higher costs imposed by an organized workforce. American employers, unable to collude, had much stronger motives to resist the union shop.

Although few American liberal reformers agreed with the AFL's demand for exemption from the courts, many were becoming convinced by the winter of 1907–8 that American courts were unfairly biased against the unions. Sweeping decisions eviscerated union activity. In October 1907, the Hitchman Coal and Coke Company of West Virginia initiated a suit to enjoin the UMWA and operators in other states from conspiring to set coal prices. A week before Christmas, a judge enjoined the AFL from promoting its boycott of Buck's Stove and Range Company, owned by NAM president James Van Cleave. The U.S. Supreme Court struck down the anti-yellow-dog contract provision of the Erdman Act on January 27, 1908. On February 3, the court decisively applied the Sherman Act to labor in *Loewe v. Lawlor*.[34] An Ohio court ruled that the Amalgamated Window Glass Workers of America, a union that had helped enforce an industrywide cartel agreement in the window glass industry, had violated the common law by limiting employer rights. The Ohio judge ordered the glass workers' union disbanded.[35]

These decisions increased sympathy for unions and softened the opposition to labor law reform. The Democratic Party's 1908 platform supported AFL anti-injunction legislation. Roosevelt had warned of injunction abuses in 1905. In 1908 Roosevelt and the Republican presidential nominee, William Howard Taft (depicted by the AFL as the "injunction judge"), hoped to blunt labor's criticisms of the Republican Congress by trying to include moderate injunction reforms in the Republican platform.[36] Republican conservatives such as Speaker of the House Joseph Cannon and Littlefield opposed any change in the Republican opposition to injunctions, however. Cannon removed Pearre from the Judiciary Committee in the 60th Congress (1907–8). The new Judiciary Committee "smothered" the anti-injunction bill.[37] The 1908 party platform committee, which included Cannon, refused to moderate the party position on the issue.[38]

After the 1908 election, President Taft tried but failed to locate a middle ground on injunctions. The NAM cooled toward Taft when he suggested even modest reforms of the injunction process.[39] The AFL vilified Taft's proposal to reform injunction procedures as an effort to legalize the labor injunction fully.[40] The proposal, attacked by both business and labor, died quietly.

"MAGNA CARTA": THE CLAYTON ACT

As Democrats and insurgent Republicans gained power in Congress in 1910, the AFL's battle against injunctions gathered political momentum. The Hughes amendment symbolized the change. Representative William Hughes (D, New Jersey) proposed an amendment to a federal appropriations bill that prohibited the Justice Department from using new funds to prosecute labor organizations. Soon after the revolt against Speaker Cannon in the spring of 1910, labor's supporters won House approval of the Hughes amendment. When the Senate approved the appropriations bill without the Hughes rider, the House voted 154–105 to insist on its inclusion in the final bill. After heavy lobbying managed by the NAM and helped by President Taft's personal intervention, the House rescinded its instructions with a narrow 138-to-130 vote in June 1910.[41] The more Democratic Congress elected the following November passed the Hughes amendment, but Taft vetoed the bill, damning the Hughes rider as "class legislation of the most vicious sort."[42]

Though President Woodrow Wilson showed no more enthusiasm for the Hughes amendment than Taft did, Gompers made the measure a test of the new Democratic administration's sincerity. When the NAM, the U.S. Chamber of Commerce, and a wide range of newspaper editorialists protested the bill, Wilson hedged. Wilson ultimately signed the bill, but he professed that he would have vetoed the Hughes amendment had it come to him as a separate measure. Wilson and his Republican successors routinely signed subsequent bills that included the amendment.[43]

The skirmish over the Hughes proposal foreshadowed the larger battle over the AFL anti-injunction bill. Representative William B. Wilson (D, Pennsylvania), the former UMWA official, current House Labor Committee chair, and future secretary of labor, introduced the AFL bill in the Democratic House elected in 1910. The House Judiciary Committee reported the bill in early 1912, but weakened it. The committee bill enumerated union actions that injunctions could not reach: strikes, peaceful picketing, and direct boycotts. The substitute bill, however, did not alter the meaning of conspiracy or permit secondary boycotts. It did not alter the legal definition of "property," so it did not eliminate employers' claim that business constituted a property right.[44] Unappeased, open shop employers condemned the Democratic injunction bill as dangerous and unconstitutional "class legislation" that would strip owners of the right to protect their businesses. The bill passed the House by a large margin (243–31), but the Senate failed to act.[45]

When the Wilson administration took office in 1913, it made anti-trust reform, but not labor law, a top legislative priority. Wilson sought stronger federal restrictions on anti-competitive business practices in the proposal that became the Clayton Act of 1914. Labor leaders insisted that anti-trust reform exempt unions and include injunction reform. Wilson agreed to moderate changes in injunction procedures and to a statement that labor unions did not constitute conspiracies per se. Labor leaders indicated that they would oppose the Clayton Act and Democratic candidates for Congress in the November 1914 elections unless Wilson and the Democrats met their demands more fully. President Wilson then agreed to incorporate most of the provisions of the House substitute bill from the previous Congress. Despite its dissatisfaction with Wilson's grudging concession, the AFL reluctantly agreed to his position.[46]

The House and Senate approved the Clayton Act by large margins in mid-1914.[47] Section 6 of the Clayton Act seemed to protect unions from the anti-trust laws:

> the labor of a human being is not a commodity or article of commerce. Nothing contained in the anti-trust laws shall be construed to forbid the existence and operation of labor, agricultural, and horticultural organizations . . . or to forbid or restrain individual members of such organizations, from lawfully carrying out the legitimate objects thereof; nor shall such organizations, or the members thereof, be held or construed to be illegal combinations or conspiracies in restraint of trade, under the anti-trust laws.[48]

Section 20 of the Clayton Act seemed to tighten the rules for granting injunctions. The section specified that no federal court could issue an injunction in any case arising from a dispute between an employer and an employee "unless necessary to prevent irreparable injury to property, or to a property right, for which injury there is no adequate remedy at law, and such property . . . must be described with particularity. . . ." Courts could not restrain employees who were peacefully engaged in meeting, picketing, striking, boycotting, or paying strike benefits.

Gompers declared that the Clayton Act constituted labor's magna carta,[49] but many contemporaries believed that it added little substantive protection for union powers. The clause concerning "irreparable injury" and the many adverbs used to qualify union behavior (such as "lawfully" and "peacefully") gave judges considerable discretion to interpret these terms and limit union action. The chair of the House Judiciary Committee, like President Wilson, asserted that the bill merely prevented the dissolution of trade unions and did not exempt unions from prosecution under the Sherman Act. Furuseth himself argued that the Clayton Act would not protect labor from injunctions.[50] The Clayton Act provides an outstanding example of a statute produced by the tortuous American policy process. In the Clayton Act, ambiguous language, rather than policy substance, marked the resolution of fundamental conflict between labor and employers. This ambiguity effectively delegated policy implementation to the courts.

Taft, the future chief justice, agreed that the Clayton Act added little legal protection for unions. Taft characterized section 6 as "a declaratory statement of existing law," and as "far less drastic and revolutionary than we had been led to expect. . . ." Congress, by removing any statement (as in the Pearre bill) that excluded business from the definition of property, left it to "the court to decide whether injury to a man's business of an irreparable character was not an injury to a property right." Concluded Taft: "This will be an additional reason for blaming and attacking the courts. It is really a shifting of responsibility from Congress to the judicial branch of the Government that has had to bear so many of the burdens conceived in political timidity of legislators."[51]

The Clayton Act, then, unexpectedly enhanced judges' power to interpret the legal constraints on American unions' freedom of action. Woodrow Wilson, many in Congress, and employer groups opposed a clear legal statement about union powers. In effect, these policymakers agreed to a law that invited the courts to exercise even more discretion in applying the anti-trust laws to labor. Edwin Witte later claimed that the purpose of the law's architects was to "please labor and yet make no change in the law."[52]

The AFL urged state federations to lobby for similar laws at the state level,[53] but predictably the unions had even less success in the state legislatures. Before Congress passed the Clayton Act, few states had responded to this campaign, and state courts usually nullified those laws enacted. Emery claimed that politically mobilized employers successfully turned back efforts to enact state-level versions of the Pearre bill in Missouri and Indiana and battled another version in New Jersey.[54] The Clayton Act modestly encouraged additional state action. Massachusetts enacted an anti-injunction law in 1914 that the AFL considered a model. The state's supreme court struck down the Massachusetts law in 1916, however, on the grounds that it annihilated the right to conduct a business and violated the guarantee of equal protection of the laws.[55] Between 1913 and 1932, when the federal government enacted the Norris–LaGuardia Anti-Injunction Act, nine states enacted laws largely the same as section 20 of the Clayton Act.[56] Arizona's supreme court upheld the constitutionality of that state's 1913 anti-injunction law, but the U.S. Supreme Court struck down the law in a widely noted 1921 decision.[57]

During World War I, federal war labor administrators such as Felix Frankfurter tried to ensure that workers enjoyed the freedom to join trade unions without employer interference. While these reformers rejected the AFL's call for extensive limitations on employers' property rights, they supported employees' right to join independent unions. The National War Labor Board required employers to bargain collectively; helped police workers' elections of union representatives; and helped organizers advance union growth in the meatpacking, steel, and other industries.[58] These wartime advances, however, did not establish permanent legal changes. American unions' freedom of action evaporated again with the postwar return to "normalcy."

THE ECLIPSE OF THE CLAYTON ACT
AND THE RISE OF THE COMPANY UNION

By 1917, it was becoming clear that the Clayton Act was not a very formidable magna carta for labor. Several major Supreme Court decisions drove home the impotence of labor's supposed "charter of freedom." The U.S. Supreme Court's decision in the *Hitchman Coal* case in December 1917 dashed hopes that the Clayton Act would help unions organize and stabilize competitive industries. The *Hitchman* case turned on the UMWA organizing drive in West Virginia. The Hitchman mine required its miners to sign a yellow-dog contract, promising not to join the union. When the union tried to organize the Hitchman workers secretly, the employer sought a federal injunction against the union. The Supreme Court recognized that the UMWA was trying to extend the collective bargaining agreement with the midwestern coal operators into the nonunion mines of West Virginia. The miners, concluded the Court, were trying to compel the owners of the West Virginia mines "to change their method of operation" rather than "to enlarge the union membership." This effort to alter an employer's behavior, even to benefit all competitors, could not be sustained under American law.

> [The d]efendants . . . are not competitors of [the Hitchman firm]; and if they were their conduct exceeds the bounds of fair trade. Certainly, if a competing trader should endeavor to draw customers from his rival, not by offering better or cheaper goods, employing more competent salesmen, or displaying more attractive advertisements, but by persuading the rival's clerks to desert him under circumstances rendering it difficult or embarrassing for him to fill their places, any court of equity would grant an injunction to restrain this as unfair competition.[59]

The Court concluded that courts could enjoin even peaceful union activity. Unions could not act as the agents of industry cartelization. Even worse for labor, the *Hitchman* decision also permitted the courts to enforce yellow-dog contracts. Now, with the blessing of the government, employers could compel their employees to sign contracts refusing to join unions. The *Hitchman* case dealt a severe blow to union efforts to organize whole industries and destroyed the AFL's faith in the Clayton Act.

In *Duplex v. Deering* (1921) the Supreme Court further disabled union-enforced employer agreements. Open shop lawyers Walter Gordon Merritt and Daniel Davenport represented the Duplex Company, an AABA member that manufactured a newspaper printing press in a nonunion plant in open shop Battle Creek, Michigan. There existed four manufacturers of such presses. By 1913, IAM had negotiated for a minimum wage, an eight-hour day, and other conditions with three of the manufacturers. The Duplex Company refused to join the agreement. Two of the other manufacturers instructed union leaders that they would terminate their contracts unless the machinists could unionize Duplex and apply uniform labor standards to all the industry's firms. After failing to organize the Duplex workforce, the IAM organized a secondary boycott against Duplex in New York, a nerve center of newspaper printing.[60]

A Supreme Court majority ruled in 1921 that the IAM's action violated the Sherman Anti-Trust Act. The justices explicitly referred to Congress's refusal to legalize the secondary boycott in the Clayton Act. The court used no "rule of reason" to soften the application of the Sherman Act's restraint of trade rule to unions, even though it had softened the application of the law in cases dealing with large corporations. In effect, it was instituting a double standard, holding unions to a more stringent test of restraining interstate commerce than the test it applied to such businesses as U.S. Steel.[61] The Supreme Court also read the Clayton Act as permitting employers legitimately to request injunctions against labor.[62]

Fueled by the renewed open shop drive and encouraged by the courts, employers obtained anti-strike injunctions in unprecedented numbers during the 1920s. The *Bedford Cut Stone* ruling upheld even the most inhibiting of these injunctions. Before 1921, the Bedford and Bloomington, Indiana, quarry operators contracted with the Journeymen Stone Cutters Association of North America. In 1921, however, the quarry owners broke with the union and set up "company" unions. The union then refused to handle the Bedford nonunion stone. On behalf of the employers' association, Walter Gordon Merritt sought injunctions against the union for violating the Sherman Act by restraining interstate commerce. District and appellate courts refused to enjoin the stone-cutters, but the Supreme Court granted the injunction. The court determined that the stonecutters had conspired to injure the Bedford employers. The unions and their members could be held financially liable for damages incurred by the employers. The Bedford decision now threatened all unions with the possibility that courts would penalize individual union members severely when they acted collectively against employers.[63]

While the courts limited union freedom, large companies were inventing the company union to fortify employer prerogatives. In 1918, Jersey Standard (now Exxon) initiated a plan that provided for representation for its employees. This company union worked well enough to inspire interest among other corporations. Once the Supreme Court upheld the enforceability of yellow-dog contracts in the *Hitchman* case in 1917, other employers became interested in these management-sponsored company unions. In 1919, top executives of ten large American corporations (Jersey Standard, Bethlehem Steel, Du Pont, General Electric, General Motors, Goodyear, International Harvester, Irving National Bank, U.S. Rubber, and Westinghouse) established a secret Special Conference Committee to coordinate and develop labor relations and personnel policies.[64] These firms, though fundamentally anti-union, rejected the smaller manufacturers' obstinate commitment to the open shop. Instead, they developed a plan for employee representation modeled on Jersey Standard's company union. The plan aimed to reduce the area of management–employee conflict and to preclude the development of independent unions.[65]

In the 1920s, many corporations established the company union as an alternative to the polar extremes of the union shop and the open shop. Company unions became especially popular as anti-union sentiment crested early in the decade. Four hundred and ninety firms created company unions between 1919 and 1924, while only seventy-three firms created these unions between 1924 and 1928, as labor turbulence ebbed.[66] A number of firms eliminated company unions during the early years of the Depression, when weakened trade unions posed little threat to these firms. One in five of the plans in existence in 1929 was eliminated by 1932.[67]

Company unions affected the development of trade union policy in three ways. First, by 1932 company unions dominated the steel industry; General Electric; Standard Oil; the Pennsylvania Railroad; and unorganized coal fields in Ohio, Pennsylvania, and West Virginia.[68] Many of these industries included the industrial workers that constituted a fundamental building block of industrial unionism and restrictions on employers' unlimited labor market power. Second, company unions were confined to a single enterprise rather than an entire industry. This precedent contributed to the decentralized pattern of collective bargaining that has characterized American labor relations ever since.[69] Third, company unions constituted an important impediment to the unionization of unorganized workers. As company unions became more important, proponents of trade union policy reform increasingly emphasized procedural reforms to ensure that workers, rather than companies, would select their collective bargaining representatives.

PROCEDURAL PROTECTIONS FOR TRADE UNIONS:
THE NORRIS–LA GUARDIA ANTI-INJUNCTION ACT

In the early 1930s, the AFL retreated from its insistence that unions have full freedom to expand the scope of economic conflict. Unions conceded substantial labor market power to employers. The American collective bargaining policy that began to emerge in the early 1930s protected workers' right to organize and bargain collectively but constricted the scope of bargaining in a way that precluded fundamental challenges to employer prerogatives.

The most conservative unionists—the railroad brotherhoods—were the first to concede full employer control of the labor market in exchange for legal protection of their right to represent employees. The Transportation Act of 1920 had created a Railway Labor Board with the power to settle labor disputes. When it became clear that railroads refused to comply with the board's decisions even when the brotherhoods acceded to wage cuts, the railroad unions turned against the board. The Railway Labor Act of 1926, drafted by brotherhoods' lawyer Donald Richberg, removed the compulsory features of the Transportation Act that the brotherhoods found objectionable. It recognized collective bargaining with the brotherhoods, though it permitted the railroad companies to continue to construct company unions for nonoperating employees outside the brotherhoods. President Calvin Coolidge signed the bill despite the opposition of the NAM, some of the railroads, and farm organizations.[70]

In 1930, the Supreme Court agreed with the unions that the Railroad Labor Act had given employees a legal right to choose their bargaining agent free from company interference.[71] The recognition that employees could choose their own unions seemed to be a major blow to the unlimited dominance of employers in the labor market. New Deal labor law placed a high priority on the public protection of workers' free selection of representatives chosen to bargain collectively on their behalf.

UMWA president John L. Lewis sought government help in organizing the miners working in the geographically scattered bituminous coal industry. Lewis now supported government's help "to enforce strict controls on coal competition until the full power of collective bargaining could be brought to bear."[72] To this end, Lewis supported a bill that Senator James Watson (R, Indiana) introduced after the major coal strike of 1927. Watson's bill proposed a bituminous coal commission that would set aside the Sherman Act's anti-trust provisions in the coal industry. Operators would be free of anti-trust if they obtained a federal license. To receive the license, operators would have to accept

collective bargaining with the UMWA. They also would have to accept industrywide labor standards. Though the bill failed, it anticipated the approach of
the NIRA.[73]

By the late 1920s, the AFL renewed its efforts to limit injunctions and anti-
trust law. Furuseth's new tactic was to limit equity courts' jurisdiction to "tan-
gible and transferable property," thus eliminating the possibility that courts
could use the protection of one's "business" as an excuse for enjoining union
action. Again, this approach simply removed the courts from industrial disputes.
Senator Henrik Shipstead (Farmer–Labor, Minnesota) introduced the new AFL
bill in December 1927.[74] Progressive reformers who supported injunction
reform viewed the Shipstead bill as both excessive and ineffectual. Such critics
of the injunction as Felix Frankfurter described the bill as "probably the most
sweeping proposal affecting injunctions that has ever come before Congress"
and "as an attempt to throw out the baby with the bath."[75]

Frankfurter and other reformers drafted an alternative to the Shipstead bill,
and their proposal was introduced by Senator George Norris (R, Nebraska) in
1928. The reformers' bill, as modified in a 1930 version, aimed to protect union
freedom in three ways. First, it undermined company unions by guaranteeing
that workers enjoy "full freedom of association, self-organization, and designa-
tion of representatives of his own choosing. . . ." Federal courts could no longer
enforce the yellow-dog contract, and (as provided in the Railway Labor Act)
workers could challenge company unions. Second, the Norris bill subtly
endorsed the kind of industrywide bargaining sought by the UMWA in the
Watson Coal bill. The bill provided protection against injunctions in "cases
involving . . . *labor disputes*" (italics added), a term broad enough to include
industrywide organizing drives. Third, the Norris bill limited federal courts'
powers to issue injunctions in labor disputes. It specified the conditions under
which courts could issue injunctions. It did not, however, prohibit courts from
enjoining sympathy strikes (as in *Duplex*) or boycotts (as in *Buck's Stove*).[76]

The AFL at first resisted the reformers' compromise and held out for the
full freedom of action they had sought since the turn of the century. They
insisted on protection of the boycott and the sympathy strike. Norris refused to
change the bill. The AFL finally capitulated in December 1931, accepting the
limited protections offered in Norris's proposal.[77] By surrendering on this issue,
the AFL in effect compromised away the aspiration of a union shop economy
in return for a measure of protection for union freedom in dealing directly with
individual employers.

The Depression and Democratic gains in the 1930 elections made it possible to enact the Norris anti-injunction bill. When it reached the floors of Congress in January 1932, the rising tide of reform and the eroding legitimacy of
business unleashed support for labor legislation that had not existed for nearly a

generation. Wisconsin had already enacted a state-level Norris bill in 1931. Pennsylvania and Ohio also limited injunctions in that year. The Norris–La Guardia bill passed 362-to-14 in the House, and 75-to-5 in the Senate. In 1933, nine more states enacted similar legislation.[78]

THE ROAD TO THE WAGNER ACT

The New Deal's NIRA made the conditional relaxation of anti-trust laws the centerpiece of the nation's recovery effort. Much like the Watson coal proposal, industries could write codes of fair competition that government would enforce.

As in the case of the Clayton Act, the AFL insisted that these anti-trust changes include labor protections for trade unions. In response, Richberg and Senator Robert Wagner (D, New York), drawing on the Railway Labor Act and the Norris–LaGuardia Act, added to Title I of the NIRA a section 7(a). This section required that each industry's "code of fair competition" include guarantees that "employees have the right to organize and bargain collectively through representatives of their own choosing" and that "employers shall comply with the maximum hours of labor, minimum rates of pay, and other working conditions approved or presented by the President." The section also protected the union shop and seemingly undercut company unions. By establishing that employees could bargain collectively "through representatives of their own choosing," the law carried forward the idea of free elections (already established by the War Labor Board and the Railway Labor Act) to determine the union that would represent workers and bargain on their behalf.[79]

Though the AFL influenced the wording of the NIRA, labor leaders had little role in shaping or implementing the hundreds of NIRA codes written for various industries. Employers routinely ignored rulings by the national labor officials. Many employers responded to section 7(a) by creating company unions that allowed them to meet the letter of the law while retaining control over their labor force. The National Labor Board (chaired by Senator Wagner), established to oversee section 7(a), attempted to enforce the law, but NIRA administrators refused to move against companies that established only company unions. Though company unions lost the majority of representation elections conducted by the labor board, by 1935 membership in these company unions swelled to more than two million workers, including those in the auto and steel industries.[80]

In 1934 Senator Wagner proposed a new legislation to strengthen the NIRA's labor provisions and to establish a stronger National Labor Relations Board (NLRB) to enforce them. The new NLRB would serve as a three-member "supreme court" for labor relations that would administer elections, investigate charges of unfair labor practices, and mediate labor disputes. Wagner emphasized that the bill mainly established procedural protections and included no new substantive protections that had not already been enacted in the Clayton Act, the Railway Labor Act, and the Norris–LaGuardia Act. After the Supreme Court ruled the NIRA unconstitutional in 1935, Wagner's labor relations bill gathered political momentum and won Roosevelt's belated endorsement. The National Labor Relations Act (NLRA) passed the House and Senate by large margins in 1935. Utah, Wisconsin, New York, Pennsylvania, Massachusetts, and Rhode Island enacted "little" (state-level) Wagner Acts.[81]

The NLRA constituted the most substantial policy challenge to employer labor market prerogatives up to that time. Independent union membership swelled. By the end of 1934, three and a half million workers were union members, a number not equaled since 1923. Between 1936 and 1939, another five million workers joined unions. In early 1937, the NAM reversed its antipathy to unions and recommended that its members adopt employment reforms to prevent labor difficulties. Unionized firms established seniority systems to protect employees, and many nonunion firms borrowed some of these measures.[82]

But while the Wagner Act guaranteed workers' right to unionize, it also confined their use of union powers and gave employers long-term advantages in protecting their control of the labor market. The NLRA reinforced the litigious spirit of American labor relations, creating a new quasi-judicial forum for labor disputes and a set of procedural rules about union recognition and bargaining aimed at containing labor market combat. These collective bargaining procedures advantaged employers in at least three ways. First, at the behest of the AFL (in a fierce rivalry with the Congress of Industrial Organizations when the NLRA was debated), the law limited collective bargaining to the plant, craft, or employer rather than the industry as a whole. This fragmented collective bargaining jurisdiction had the effect of limiting the scope of collective bargaining to "bread and butter" issues rather than pricing, production, and investment decisions. It also segregated collective bargaining into relatively small units determined by employers and vulnerable to an employer's "divide and conquer" strategy. Finally, it created a long and complex process of union recognition that gave employers opportunity to delay recognition.[83]

POLITICAL INSTITUTIONS AND
LABOR LEADERS' STRATEGY

By 1932, American labor leaders had surrendered their vision of a union shop economy that could establish protections for most workers by virtue of their union membership. Instead, these leaders acceded to a more modest vision of trade union power that limited the scope of not only collective bargaining but also of worker protection. The courts played a large role as the agent of this change. As William Forbath argues, "[v]oluntarism's victory resulted from many highly constrained and divisive collective choices that were imposed upon the American labor movement, largely by the nation's obdurate state of courts and parties."[84]

Though the courts were important agents of this change, they were not its architects. Without the challenge from obstinate hatmakers, printing press companies, coal operators, and open shop employers' associations, courts could not have intervened against unions. Without ambiguous statutes like the Sherman Act and the Clayton Act that invited courts to take charge of the implementation of American policy toward unions, the courts would have exercised considerably more restraint. As James Van Cleave put it in his posthumous report to the NAM in 1910: "We must bear in mind . . . that litigation, however successful, becomes ineffective if legislation modifies or repeals statutory rights or remedies. Moreover, legislation—National or State—which does this offers a powerful example for imitation by the rest of the States and thus lessens the vigorous administration and enforcement of all laws along these lines."[85]

It was the more complex interplay of separated powers, geographically divided government, and the strategic reaction of employers and unions to these factors that spun American trade union policy in a unique direction. The same factors prevented government from taking a more active role in labor market management.

NOTES

1. U.S. Senate, Subcommittee of the Committee on the Judiciary, Hearings on *Limiting the Scope of Injunctions in Labor Disputes* (Washington, D.C.: Government Printing Office, 1928), Part 5, 740.

2. William N. Eskridge Jr., *Dynamic Statutory Interpretation* (Cambridge: Harvard University Press, 1994), 81–105, esp. 105.

3. William E. Forbath, *Law and the Shaping of the American Labor Movement* (Cambridge: Harvard University Press, 1991), 86–87.

4. *United States v. Workingmen's Amalgamated Council* 54 Fed. 994 (1893); *United States v. Alger*, 62 Fed. 24 (1897); Benjamin J. Taylor and Fred Whitney, *Labor Relations Law*, 5th ed. (Englewood Cliffs, N.J.: Prentice Hall, 1987), 41–44.

5. Forbath, *Law and the Shaping of the American Labor Movement*, 100.

6. U.S. House, Committee on the Judiciary, Hearings on *Anti-Injunction Bill* (Washington, D.C.: GPO, 1904), 578. Other examples of injunctions are reproduced at pages 26–64.

7. Daniel R. Ernst, *Lawyers against Labor: From Individual Rights to Corporate Liberalism* (Urbana: University of Illinois Press, 1995), 55.

8. "The Day and the Hour," *American Industries* 1 (August 15, 1902): 6; John Kirby Jr., "Mob Rule in the Anti-Injunction Bill," *American Industries* 1 (January 15, 1903): 1; Senator Joseph B. Foraker (R, Ohio), "Wise, Patriotic, and Inviolable: the Courts," *American Industries* 2 (October 1, 1903): 9.

9. Walter Gordon Merritt, "The Boycott, the Neglected Side of Trade Unionism," *American Industries* 1 (October 15, 1902): 1–2.

10. Forbath, *Law and the Shaping of the American Labor Movement*, Appendix B, 192–98.

11. Forbath, *Law and the Shaping of the American Labor Movement*, 62.

12. Hearings on *Anti-Injunction Bill*, 503–4.

13. Hearings on *Anti-Injunction Bill*, 614–15; Hyman Weintraub, *Andrew Furuseth: Emancipator of the Seamen* (Berkeley: University of California Press, 1959), 88–89, 95; Forbath, *Law and the Shaping of the American Labor Movement*, 128–41.

14. See, for example, the Committee on the President's Report, American Federation of Labor, *Proceedings* of the Thirtieth Annual Convention, 1910: 309; hereafter, *AFL Proceedings* [date].

15. Karen Orren, *Belated Feudalism: Labor, the Law, and Liberal Development in the United States* (Cambridge: Cambridge University Press, 1992).

16. *New York Times*, September 18, 1900: 1; September 30, 1900: 24.

17. U.S. House of Representatives, Committee on the Judiciary, Hearings on *The Bill 'To Limit the Meaning of the Word Conspiracy . . .,'* 56th Cong., 2nd sess., Senate Doc. 58 (Washington, D.C.: GPO, 1900), 43. The bill, H.R. 8917, was introduced by Populist Representative Edwin R. Ridgely of Kansas. See Stuart B. Kaufman, Peter J. Albert, and Grace Palladino, *The Samuel Gompers Papers, Vol. 5: An Expanding Movement at the Turn of the Century, 1898–1902* (Urbana: University of Illinois Press, 1995), 244.

18. U.S. House of Representatives, Committee on the Judiciary, "Meaning of the Word 'Conspiracy,' etc." House Report 1987 (June 5, 1900), 56th Cong. 1st sess.; and "Meaning of the Word 'Conspiracy,' etc." House Report 2007 (December 3, 1900), 56th Cong., 2nd sess.

19. *Congressional Record*, February 18, 1901: 2589–98.

20. See House Judiciary Committee, "Limiting the Meaning of the Word Conspiracy," House Report 1522, 57th Cong., 1st sess. (April 10, 1902). On House passage, see *Congressional Record*, May 2, 1902: 4995.

21. "The Day and the Hour," 6; Kirby, "Mob Rule in the Anti-Injunction Bill."

22. *AFL Proceedings*, 1904: 28; the AFL bill was H.R. 89, introduced in the House by Representative Charles H. Grosvenor (R, Ohio).

23. Hearings on *Anti-Injunction Bill*, 93, 101–2, 196; *AFL Proceedings*, 1905: 193.

24. Quoted in Robert Wiebe, *Businessmen and Reform: A Study of the Progressive Movement* (Cambridge: Harvard University Press, 1962), 161. See also Melvyn Dubovsky, *The State and Labor in Modern America* (Chapel Hill: University of North Carolina Press, 1994), 40–42.

25. Letter, Theodore Roosevelt to the Executive Committee of the AFL, September 29, 1903, reprinted in U.S. Senate, Committee on the Judiciary, Hearings on *Limiting Federal Injunctions*, (Washington, D.C.: GPO, 1912), 260.

26. National Cash Register president John H. Patterson in *American Industries* 4 (October 16, 1905): 1; Helen Marot, *American Labor Unions* (New York: Henry Holt, 1914), 164; Dubofsky, *The State and Labor in Modern America*, 42–44.

27. Ruth O'Brien, "'Business Unionism' versus 'Responsible Unionism': Common Law, Confusion, the American State, and the Formation of Pre-New Deal Labor Policy," *Law and Social Inquiry* 18, no. 2 (Spring 1993): 255–96.

28. Louis Brandeis to Samuel Gompers, letter, February 13, 1905, in *Letters of Louis D. Brandeis*, ed. Melvin I. Urofsky and David Levy (Albany: State University of New York, 1971), 1: 283–84.

29. Ernst, *Lawyers against Labor*, 176.

30. In the first session of the 60th Congress alone, members introduced more than thirty bills on the subject of injunctions, exemption of unions from the Sherman Act and conspiracy doctrines, and exemption from liability for strike costs (see Index to the *Congressional Record*, 60th Cong., 1st sess.). No other type of labor market measure enjoyed such legislative activity. See also *AFL Proceedings,* 1909: 25.

31. U.S. Senate, *Argument of T. C. Spelling on Pearre Anti-Injunction Bill*, Senate Document 525, 60th Cong., 1st sess. (May 27, 1908); *AFL Proceedings*, 1906: 21–23, and 1908: 23; Forbath, *Law and the Shaping of the American Labor Movement*, 154–55; Felix Frankfurter and Nathan Greene, *The Labor Injunction* (New York: Macmillan, 1930), 155–56.

32. Gompers, in Hearings on *Limiting Federal Injunctions*, 1913, appendix, 54.

33. Commentary on the British Trades Union Act of 1906 was furnished in Report of the Fraternal Delegates to the British Trades Union Congress, *AFL Proceedings*, 1906: 97–99; Frankfurter and Greene, *The Labor Injunction*, 136–37; Ernst, *Lawyers against Labor*, 178–79; Henry Pelling, *A History of British Trade Unionism* (London: Penguin, 1963), 124–27.

34. *Adder v. U.S.*, 208 U.S. 161(1908); *Loewe v. Lawler*, 208 U.S. 274 (1908).

35. *Kelley v. Faulkner*, 18 Ohio Dec. 498 (1908), cited in Ernst, *Lawyers against Labor*, 168–69.

36. Donald Bruce Johnson, ed., *National Party Platforms,* rev. ed. (Champaign: University of Illinois Press, 1978), 2: 147–48. Theodore Roosevelt, Sixth Annual Message, December 5, 1905; and Special Message, April 27, 1908, in *A Compilation of the Messages and Papers of the Presidents* (Washington, D.C.: Bureau of National Literature, 1914), 16: 7363, 17: 7570.

37. *AFL Proceedings*, 1907: 33; 1908: 23.

38. Donald F. Anderson, *William Howard Taft: A Conservative's Conception of the Presidency* (Ithaca, N.Y.: Cornell University Press, 1968), 52–53; *The Letters of Theodore Roosevelt*, ed. Elting Morison (Cambridge: Harvard University Press, 1952), 6: 1077 (footnote).

39. John Kirby Jr., "Where Does President Taft Stand?" *American Industries* 10, no. 3 (October 1, 1909): 10. On Taft's recommendation, see William Howard Taft, First Annual Message, December 7, 1909, *Messages and Papers of the Presidents*, 17: 7811–12. Emery lobbied against Taft's bill to regularize injunctions; see James A. Emery, "A Critical Situation," *Square Deal* 6 (May 1910): 305–6.

40. *AFL Proceedings*, 1910: 27; 1911: 45–49.

41. *Congressional Record*, June 2, 1910: 7325–27; June 10, 1910: 7654; June 21, 1910: 8655–56; and June 23, 1910: 8847–53. *AFL Proceedings*, 1910: 32. On the NAM's participation, see James Emery to John Kirby, June 24, 1910, in *Congressional Record*, May 26, 1914: 9247–48. See also Frankfurter and Greene, *The Labor Injunction,* 141.

42. *Congressional Record*, March 4, 1913: 4838. The Supreme Court issued new, stricter guidelines (Rule 73) for issuing injunctions in 1913; *Congressional Record*, June 1, 1914: 9610.

43. Arthur S. Link, *Wilson: The New Freedom* (Princeton: Princeton University Press, 1956), 264–69; Frankfurter and Greene, *The Labor Injunction*, 141. The Hughes amendment was crucial in advancing the AFL's larger agenda; see Ernst, *Lawyers against Labor*, 175.

44. *Congressional Record*, May 14, 1912: 6415 (the committee bill); and 6422 (the Wilson bill). See also 6440.

45. Hearings on *Limiting Federal Injunctions*, 1912: 253. *Congressional Record*, May 14, 1912: 6407–71; February 7, 1913: 2685–86.

46. Link, *Wilson: The New Freedom,* 427–33; Dallas L. Jones, "The Enigma of the Clayton Act," *Industrial and Labor Relations Review* 10 (January 1957): 201–21.

47. The House approved the Clayton Act 277 to 54 (*Congressional Record*, June 5, 1914: 9911); the Senate approved it 46 to 16 (*Congressional Record*, September 2, 1914: 14610).

48. *Public Law 63-212*, October 15, 1914.

49. Samuel Gompers, "The Charter of Industrial Freedom—Labor Provisions of the Clayton Antitrust Law," *American Federationist* 21 (November 1914): 968–72.

50. Link, *Wilson: The New Freedom,* 427–33; Jones, "The Enigma of the Clayton Act," 187; Ernst, *Lawyers against Labor*, 187.

51. William Howard Taft, *Recent Antitrust and Labor Injunction Legislation*, U.S. Senate Document 614, 63rd Cong., 2nd sess. (Washington, D.C.: GPO, 1914), 10, 14, 17.

52. Ernst, *Lawyers against Labor*, 165–90 (quote 189); Jones, "The Enigma of the Clayton Act."

53. *AFL Proceedings*, 1910: 296; and 1916: 273. Samuel Gompers, "Labor's State Legislative Demand," *American Federationist* 23 (July 1916): 542–58.

54. *American Industries* 9 (May 1, 1909): 9; 13 (April 1913): 9–11.

55. Massachusetts State Federation of Labor, *History of the Massachusetts State Federation of Labor, 1887–1935* (Worcester, Mass.: Labor News Printers, 1935), 50; Frankfurter and Greene, *The Labor Injunction*, 163.

56. The states enacting laws similar to section 20 of the Clayton Act included Kansas, 1913; Minnesota and Utah, 1917; North Dakota, Oregon, Washington, and Wisconsin, 1919; Illinois, 1925; New Jersey, 1926; Frankfurter and Greene, *The Labor Injunction*, 181–82.

57. *Truax v. Corrigan* 257 U.S. 312 (1921); Frankfurter and Greene, *The Labor Injunction*, 153–54.

58. Dubofsky, *The State and Labor in Modern America*, 69–76. On employee representation and industrial democracy, see Joseph A. McCartin, *Labor's Great War: The Struggle*

for Industrial Democracy and the Origins of Modern American Labor Relations, 1912–1921 (Chapel Hill: University of North Carolina Press, 1998); Jeffrey Haydu, *Making American Industry Safe for Democracy: Comparative Perspectives on the State and Employee Representation in the Era of World War I* (Urbana: University of Illinois Press, 1997).

59. *Hitchman Coal and Coke Co. v. Mitchell*, 245 U.S. 229 (1917), 256, 259. In 1915, the Supreme Court struck down state anti–yellow-dog contract laws; *Coppage v. Kansas*, 236 U.S. 1 (1915). See Joel I. Siedman, *The Yellow Dog Contract* (Baltimore: Johns Hopkins University Press, 1932).

60. Ernst, *Lawyers against Labor*, 210; Louis Brandeis, dissenting opinion in *Duplex Printing Press Company v. Deering*, 254 U.S. 443 (1921).

61. See Brandeis dissent in *Duplex Printing Press Company v. Deering*, 479–80; Ernst, *Lawyers against Labor*, 190; Taylor and Whitney, *Labor Relations Law*, 54–55.

62. Jones, "The Enigma of the Clayton Act."

63. *Bedford Cut Stone Company v. Journeymen Stone Cutters' Association*, 247 U.S. 37 (1927); Frankfurter and Greene, *The Labor Injunction*, 175–76; O'Brien, "'Business Unionism' versus 'Responsible Unionism.'"

64. Sanford M. Jacoby, *Employing Bureaucracy: Managers, Unions, and the Transformation of Work in American Industry* (New York: Columbia University Press, 1985), 280–82; Daniel Nelson, "The Company Union Movement, 1900–1937: A Reexamination," *Business History Review* 56, no. 3 (Autumn 1982), 335–57.

65. Nelson, "The Company Union Movement."

66. Irving Bernstein, *The Lean Years* (Boston: Houghton Mifflin, 1966), 157.

67. Jacoby, *Employing Bureaucracy*, 221.

68. Frankfurter and Greene, *The Labor Injunction*, 149.

69. Alfred L. Bernheim and Dorothy Van Doren, eds., *Labor and the Government: An Investigation of the Role of the Government in Labor Relations* (New York: McGraw-Hill, 1935), 65–113; Nelson, "The Company Union Movement."

70. Robert H. Zeiger, *Republicans and Labor, 1919–1929* (Lexington: University Press of Kentucky, 1969), 119, 198–210; Orren, *Belated Feudalism*, 206–7; O'Brien, "'Business Unionism' versus 'Responsible Unionism.'"

71. *Texas & New Orleans Railroad v. Brotherhood of Railroad Clerks,* 281 U.S. 548 (1930).

72. David Brody, "Market Unionism in America: The Case of Coal," in *In Labor's Cause: Main Themes on the History of the American Worker*, ed. David Brody (New York: Oxford University Press, 1993), 153.

73. Zeiger, *Republicans and Labor*, 255–58.

74. Weintraub, *Andrew Furuseth*, 187–88; Forbath, *Law and the Shaping of the American Labor Movement*, 160; Bernstein, *The Lean Years*, 397–403.

75. Ernst, *Lawyers against Labor*, 210.

76. U.S. Senate, Subcommittee of the Committee on the Judiciary, Hearings on *Defining and Limiting the Jurisdiction of Courts Sitting in Equity* (Washington, D.C: GPO, 1930), 1–4; Bernstein, *The Lean Years*, 397–99; O'Brien, "'Business Unionism' versus 'Responsible Unionism'"; Taylor and Whitney, *Labor Relations Law*, 78–97. Barry Cushman, in *Rethinking the New Deal Court* (New York: Oxford University Press, 1998),

109–30, views the reformers' strategy as a "symmetrical protection" of workers' and employers' freedom of union choice.

77. Bernstein, *The Lean Years*, 401–11.

78. Maine, Indiana, Minnesota, Colorado, Utah, Wyoming, Idaho, Washington, and Oregon; John R. Commons and John B. Andrews, *Principles of Labor Legislation,* 4th rev. ed. (New York: Harper and Brothers, 1936), 415.

79. J. Joseph Huthmacher, *Senator Robert F. Wagner and the Rise of Urban Liberalism* (New York: Atheneum, 1971), 137–51; Irving Bernstein, *The New Deal Collective Bargaining Policy* (Berkeley: University of California Press, 1950), 32–38; Dubofsky, *The State and Labor in Modern America*, 111–12.

80. Jacoby, *Employing Bureaucracy*, 225–28; Joel Rogers, "Divide and Conquer: Further 'Reflections on the Distinctive Character of American Labor Laws,'" *Wisconsin Law Review* 1990: 1 (January/February): 80, fn. 217; Robert F. Himmelberg, *The Origins of the National Recovery Administration: Business, Government, and the Trade Association Issue, 1921–1933* (New York: Fordham University Press, 1976), 211; Don D. Lescohier, "Working Conditions," in *History of Labor Legislation in the United States*, 3: 352–53; Nelson, "The Company Union Movement, 1900–1937," 335–57.

81. James A. Gross, *The Making of the National Labor Relations Board* (Albany: State University of New York Press, 1974); Bernstein, *The New Deal Collective Bargaining Policy*; Dubofsky, *The State and Labor in Modern America,* 124–28; Christopher L. Tomlins, *The State and the Unions: Labor Relations, Law, and the Organized Labor Movement in America, 1880–1960* (New York: Cambridge University Press, 1986), 132–47; Taylor and Whitney, *Labor Relations Law*, 203. See also Michael Goldfield, *The Decline of Organized Labor in the United States* (Chicago: University of Chicago Press, 1987); and the controversy between Michael Goldfield and Theda Skocpol and Kenneth Finegold, "Explaining New Deal Labor Policy," *American Political Science Review* 84 (December 1990): 1297–315.

82. Jacoby, *Employing Bureaucracy*, 224, 242–46.

83. Gross, *The Making of the National Labor Relations Board*, 130–48; Colin Gordon, *New Deals: Business, Labor, and Politics in America, 1920–1935* (New York: Cambridge University Press, 1994), 303; Rogers, "Divide and Conquer," 117–23.

84. Forbath, *Law and the Shaping of the American Labor Movement*, 168–69.

85. National Association of Manufacturers, in *Proceedings* of the Fifteenth Annual Convention, 1910: 289.

8

MARGINALIZING LABOR MARKET MANAGEMENT

[The American Association for Labor Legislation] has, evidently, gone on the theory that the workers of America are still in the condition where they must be led by some "intellectual," that the workers have neither the judgment nor the will to protect and promote their own rights and interests, and that, therefore, this self-assumed guardianship must be exercised by would-be "uplifters."

—Samuel Gompers, 1916[1]

Policy experts and reformers, rather than trade unions, led the battle to establish a public role in labor market management. Public employment offices, they argued, could reduce unemployment and make the economy more productive. Vocational education could increase the skills of American workers and improve the nation's commercial competitiveness. Industrial commissions could turn the wasteful distrust between employers and workers into harmonious labor market cooperation for the common good.

These reformers, however, could not persuade employers or unions to surrender substantial labor market power to the new public agencies they helped create. Corporations could govern their own labor forces adequately without help from public agencies, and open shop employers instinctively shunned public programs that threatened to undermine their labor market position. Employers instead preferred private trade schools, fee-charging employment agencies, and corporate personnel departments. Labor leaders opposed efforts to undercut their control of material benefits such as apprenticeship and hiring halls. Employer and union disinterest, along with the nation's inherent constitutional obstacles, marginalized efforts to establish public labor market management. State and local governments created a patchwork of employment and training

207

programs that had relatively little impact on labor markets, and federal grants-in-aid institutionalized this decentralized patchwork of programs. Only in the area of immigration did federal authority and popular support permit effective public labor market management.

UNEMPLOYMENT AND PUBLIC EMPLOYMENT OFFICES

At the century's turn, the popular understanding of workers' problems was undergoing a dramatic change. Idle workers previously had been viewed as pitiable charity problems or suspected as indolent tramps. Rapidly changing job skills, young persons' poor preparation for jobs, and the disastrous levels of joblessness that followed panics and recessions exposed the fallacy that every individual determined his or her economic fate.

Reformers in Great Britain as well as the United States concluded that poor management, not indolence, caused joblessness. Employment was too unorganized and irregular. Training was too haphazard. Employers and workers clashed needlessly.[2] These reformers believed that carefully engineered public programs could dramatically overcome this labor market chaos. If well-administered employment offices organized labor markets, joblessness would ebb and productivity grow. In Great Britain, William Beveridge and Sidney and Beatrice Webb prescribed public employment offices as a key remedy for the problem of unemployment.[3]

In the first decades of the 1900s, John R. Commons and his students disseminated Beveridge's diagnosis and cure in the United States.[4] The American Association for Labor Legislation (AALL's) "Practical Program for The Prevention of Unemployment" provided the most comprehensive statement of the American reformers' strategy for alleviating joblessness. The program made a system of public employment offices its top priority.

> An essential step toward a solution of the problem of unemployment is the organization of the labor market through a connected network of public employment exchanges. This is vitally important as a matter of business organization and not of philanthropy. It is of as much importance for the employer to find help rapidly and efficiently as it is for the worker to find work without delay. The necessity of organized markets is recognized in every other field of economic activity, but we have thus far taken only timid and halting steps in the organization of the labor market. The peddling method is still, even in our "efficient" industrial system, the prevalent method of selling labor. Thus a purely business transaction is carried on in a most unbusiness-like, not to say medieval, manner.[5]

The AALL's "practical program" insisted that government establish public employment offices as the administrative foundation of active labor market management. The AALL urged the federal government to weave the offices together into a national job-finding network. Professional, nonpartisan experts would manage the offices, and they would maintain strict neutrality in labor disputes. The AALL's program also included industrial training, public job creation, unemployment insurance, restrictions on hours and child labor, and a "constructive" immigration policy.

The reformers' "practical program" invited employers and workers to set aside their animosities for the common good. It counseled employers to work with the public offices, establish personnel departments, reduce turnover and employment fluctuations, regulate production, and cooperate with other employers to reduce joblessness within industries. It pressed labor leaders to embrace the public employment offices and unemployment insurance and to break down the "strong demarcations" between the trades.[6]

The AALL's program, then, implicitly acknowledged the battle for the labor market raging over the issues of workplace regulation and union freedom. It proposed to interject reformers themselves—the kinds of trained experts who would manage public employment offices—as the brokers of labor market remedies that would benefit both workers and employers with "positive-sum" solutions.

Neither employers nor unions, however, had much reason to surrender such economic power to reformers in the early twentieth century. The AALL's support for government labor market management challenged the union shop and open shop strategies as these positions were hardening. Employers had little reason to cooperate with other employers to reduce unemployment because lower joblessness increased unions' leverage in the labor market. Only large corporations, with the power to resist unions unilaterally, had the economic luxury of responding positively to the reformers' remedies. Labor leaders, committed to the crafts-based union shop, naturally viewed the breakdown of crafts demarcations as a threat to union power.

Moreover, employers and trade unions alike had good reason to distrust the public employment offices, the centerpiece of the reformers' labor market program.[7] Few employers had reason to embrace these offices because private agencies provided more reliable workers for job openings. Where trade unionists staffed the public offices, they refused to provide strikebreakers and information on the union sympathies of job applicants. Even where more neutral civil servants staffed the offices, employers treated them with indifference or contempt. Larger employers could simply rely on queues at the factory gates to recruit low-skilled workers.[8]

Open shop employers often created local labor bureaus to maintain black-lists and provide strikebreakers. The National Metal Trades Association (NMTA), for example, required its local branches to establish and support such offices. In Cincinnati, Philadelphia, and other important industrial cities, NMTA labor bureaus were a key weapon for defeating the International Association of Machinists (IAM). The labor bureau established by the Employers' Association of Detroit accumulated referrals on more than half a million workers between 1902 and 1925. The free hiring hall created by the Los Angeles Merchants and Manufacturers' Association in 1921 helped to ensure the victory of the open shop in that city.[9]

Labor leaders had as much reason to distrust public employment offices as did the employers. Like their British and German counterparts, American trade unionists instinctively suspected that the offices would undermine unions.[10] Preoccupied with maintaining their collective bargaining leverage, the core craft unions of the AFL had little to gain by supporting the creation of the public offices unless the offices helped to protect the union shop. Unions could exercise more control over the placement of workers in construction and similar skilled trades through business agents or hiring halls. Union control over access to jobs constituted a key material benefit that strengthened crafts workers' incentive to join the union. Thus craft unions had no reason to surrender to public officials their control over hiring and placement in their industry. Asked in 1916 about his support for a network of public employment agencies, Gompers told a House committee that "I should prefer exchanges established by trades union agencies rather than government agencies."[11]

Labor leaders supported public employment offices when unionists ran them and when they refused employers' called for scabs. Reformers, though, insisted on strict neutrality and competence for employment office personnel. Unionists grew wary of the offices as reformers succeeded in staffing the offices with nonunion experts. Courts removed much of the power of the offices to aid union organizing. Illinois judges in 1903 ruled unconstitutional a law that prohibited the offices from referring job applicants to employers whose workers were out on strike.[12] Unions lost interest in the offices as the offices lost the ability to limit the supply of scabs.

Their experience with the federal labor bureaucracy in the early 1900s only reinforced labor leaders' suspicions about reformers' purposes. Unions opposed the creation of the Department of Commerce and Labor in 1903 because it threatened to subordinate the Bureau of Labor Statistics—labor's "voice in government"—to commercial interests. Speaker of the House Joseph Cannon, Representative Charles Littlefield, and other congressional conservatives helped fend off efforts to create a federal labor department at the same time.[13] After the Immigration Act of 1907 created a Division of Information in the Department of Commerce and Labor, Gompers attacked it as a strike-breaking agency. The division had been intended to help immigrants locate jobs in the United States. Gompers drew the conclusion that the division helped employers hire immigrants as scabs. He concluded that

> State and national labor exchanges and distribution bureaus in this country . . . are inevitably linked up with the schemes of the steamship combine to bring immigrants to, and distribute them over, the United States. . . . It is a serious question how State labor exchanges may be established, immigration being as it is, without their becoming simply one more advantage and benefit to the corporate or private capitalists whose business is to carry labor to markets for it which in many cases are already vastly oversupplied or which may readily be supplied by our own migratory laborers elsewhere idle.[14]

Public employment offices hurt rather than helped organized labor, Gompers implied. Secretary of Labor William B. Wilson objected to a proposal for a National Bureau of Labor Exchanges because it specified a bureau commissioner with "technical and scientific" knowledge of public labor office administration. Such provisions, Wilson feared, reflected "the prejudice that might exist against a bureau of this character in the Department of Labor."[15] (British unions also had viewed public labor exchanges suspiciously because they considered the offices a potential supplier of "blackleg," or scab, workers).[16]

The AFL shifted its position on public employment offices only after the Supreme Court made it impossible for states to ban private, fee-for-service employment agencies in 1917. Even when the federation agreed to study the issue of public employment offices at its convention following this decision, it treated the subject as one primarily relevant to establishing "the most effective manner of either abolishing entirely private employment offices or regulating them in such a manner as to eliminate their evil features."[17] Brief hopes of sustaining the nationalized wartime public employment office system were "swept away by a tide of reaction," as John Andrews put it to AALL members in 1920.[18] During recessions and depressions, labor leaders did not demand public employment offices, but instead demanded public works projects to employ skilled workers and increase the demand for labor. Some reformers joined this call for public works by supporting planning that would establish reserve funds that states could use for public works during recessions. In the wake of the 1903–4 recession, Massachusetts entertained a proposal to establish reserve funds for public works. Pennsylvania, California, and Wisconsin enacted laws providing for advance planning of public works. These laws had little effect, however, given the short-term focus of state budgets.[19] As unemployment rose before the outbreak of World War I, the AFL endorsed "a series of bills to be presented to Congress, which shall have as their purpose the employment by the government . . . of the unemployed."[20]

Neither business nor labor, then, had much reason to accede to the reformers' proposals for increased public administration of labor markets. Even though state and local labor leaders had supported the establishment of the offices in many places, the offices affected labor markets only marginally. Labor and employers preferred their own recruitment and job placement mechanisms under their own control. The free public offices gained a reputation as a dumping ground for unemployable workers with few skills. Employers turned to the offices only as a last resort.[21]

VOCATIONAL EDUCATION

In contrast to public employment offices, both the open shop employers and the AFL came to support public vocational education by 1910. Their mutual suspicion, though, ensured a program that could not affect the labor market enough to benefit their adversary.

Farm state interests already were advancing proposals for training teachers for vocational agricultural education as the open shop movement began.[22] Open shop employers viewed state-aided vocational education as a needed subsidy and, initially, as a potential weapon against unions. The smaller employers found it difficult to afford adequate skills training. The mobility of American workers made it difficult for an employer to count on a trained worker remaining in his firm. Competitors could and did lure skilled workers from employers who had invested in training them. Though smaller employers supported the creation of private trade schools in local communities, it cost much more money to establish such schools than to establish employer-controlled labor bureaus. Graduates of local schools could move to other areas, benefiting employers who had not invested in those institutions.[23] Large companies, unlike the smaller manufacturers, could afford to tailor training to their individual needs. General Electric, Westinghouse, American Telegraph & Telephone, and U.S. Steel created "corporation schools" for this purpose.[24]

Open shop employers blamed the "labor trust" for limiting apprenticeship and causing the skills deficiencies of the workforce.[25] Publicly provided industrial training, if controlled by employers, could create a workforce finely tuned to employer needs and willing to work in the open shops.[26] Business supporters hoped that business-dominated industrial training boards would oversee the training. The National Association of Manufacturers (NAM) enthusiastically supported the government provision of training by 1905.[27] For the NAM, cost was no object. "The people of the United States did not stop to count the cost when confronted by the . . . Civil War or the war with Spain. Patriotism demanded sacrifice."[28] International competitiveness required that the United States emulate its chief competitors: "In the world's race for commercial supremacy we must copy and improve upon the German method of education."[29]

Progressive educators committed to scientific labor market management also began to press for public vocational education around the same time. Coalitions of employers and progressive educators advanced plans for public vocational education in the states. Organized employers influenced the creation of a Massachusetts state commission to study the issue. When the Massachusetts commission in 1906 recommended separate, public industrial schools,[30] the movement spread to other states. Between 1906 and 1913, Massachusetts, Wisconsin, New York, Connecticut, New Jersey, Indiana, Pennsylvania, and Rhode Island established state-run or state-funded industrial education.[31]

New York educators organized a national group of educational leaders, businessmen, public officials, and social reformers into the National Society for the Promotion of Industrial Education (NSPIE) in 1906, the same year that the AALL was founded. The NSPIE immediately became the primary lobby for national aid to vocational education. Its leaders approached the American Federation of Labor for its support.[32]

The AFL had been suspicious of the vocational education movement. Craft unions sought to limit and control the number of workers entering a given trade to increase their bargaining power. The NAM's support for vocational education, in the midst of the open shop employers' judicial successes of 1907–8, put unions on the defensive. Massachusetts unions feared that the state's industrial education commission would result in "scab hatcheries" that would provide the open shop employers with manpower.[33]

The AFL's initial report on vocational education, in 1909, emphasized the importance of preventing employer control of industrial training. The report urged that manual training schools hire teachers with actual trade experience. The International Typographical Union's school for continuing printer education constituted a model, according to the committee, because "printer-tutors" administered it. The curriculum should include "the drawing, mathematics, mechanics, physical and biological sciences applicable to the trade, the history of that trade, and a sound system of economics, including and emphasizing the philosophy of collective bargaining."[34] In 1910, the federation's expert on the issue reported that "Enormous sums of money are being left by interested persons by will for the establishment and maintenance of schools to promote industrial education. . . . [A] watchful eye and guiding hand would do much that would be helpful to our movement in shaping the policy of these institutions."[35]

In the 1910s, the AFL endorsed vocational education if controlled by school boards rather than special, business-dominated boards of vocational education. Organized labor helped defeat a proposal of the latter type in a prominent legislative struggle in Illinois in the mid-1910s.[36] AFL treasurer John Lennon included the federation's perspective in the final report of the U.S. Commission on Industrial Relations: "The public schools, whether academic or vocational, should be entirely neutral as to unions and their control, and exactly the same should be true as to the exercise of any control for class interests by employers' or employers' organizations."[37] When the NSPIE also embraced the principle that vocational education should be neutral in the battle between employers and organized labor, business also acceded to the demand for economic neutrality.[38]

This business–labor consensus provided a powerful coalition for national aid to vocational education.[39] The NSPIE endorsed a 1912 proposal sponsored by Senator Carroll Page (R, Vermont) to provide sixteen million dollars in federal grants to the states for industrial training. The NAM, the AFL, and vocational reformers all supported the Page bill. In its first resolution on legislation at its first annual meeting, the Chamber of Commerce of the United States endorsed the Page bill in principle; the chair of the Chamber's vocational education committee, H. E. Miles, had advanced the cause as a key participant in NAM policy formulation.[40]

Rival state interests delayed the progress of this federal grant-in-aid program. Senator Hoke Smith (D, Georgia) and other supporters of agricultural education strongly opposed any effort to expand vocational education to the industrial cities.[41] This regional impasse led to the creation of the National Commission on National Aid to Vocational Education to broker the dispute. Chaired by Senator Smith and staffed by leaders of the NSPIE, the Commission in 1914 argued that the program could help democratize the workforce, respond to the economic challenge of Germany, and answer the need for investment in human resources. The states were not up to the task because they were "reluctant to tax themselves for the entire support of expensive forms of practical instruction when they see trained men and women drifting away to other States and carrying to them rich assets in citizenship and workmanship. . . ." [42] In 1916, Senator Page reiterated this concern. "[I]t is unlikely that the States will, on their own initiative, take up this work within a reasonable time," said Page. If the states eventually enacted such laws, "the movement will go forward at altogether too sluggardly a pace and with an accomplishment much too dilatory to meet the imperative, crying social and economic needs of this day and hour."[43]

Despite former House Speaker Cannon's continued concerns about federal intrusion on states' rights, both the House and Senate passed the Smith–Hughes Vocational Education Act by voice vote. It became law in February 1917, a few weeks before the United States declared war on Germany. It provided for one and a half million dollars in grants to the states for teachers' salaries and training in the first year, with the amount increasing each year thereafter until reaching seven million dollars in 1924.[44] The number of workers fourteen to eighteen years of age receiving part-time academic schooling under the act had increased from 18,000 in 1918 to more than 300,000 by 1929. By the 1930s, however, seventeen states provided no vocational instruction and seemed "not conscious of the 'vocational education' problem."[45]

Though the concept of vocational education reflected an interest in an active labor market policy, the southern legislators crucial to its design ensured that the Smith–Hughes Act in practice disproportionately benefited the economic interests of their region. State boards of vocational education enjoyed broad authority to distribute funds under the law, and in the South, these boards seized on federal funding for agricultural training. These boards, appointed by state political elites, heavily channeled subsidies to white districts. The policy, in short, "made it possible to train a racially segregated labor force without interference from the federal government." Over time, the AFL became increasingly disenchanted by the vocational education program, particularly when federal subsidies were directed to employers to train low wage workers in the south.[46]

THE LIMITS OF ACTIVE PUBLIC MANAGEMENT OF AMERICAN LABOR MARKETS

The establishment of a new Department of Labor in 1913 created an administrative beachhead for the extension of active labor market policy beyond vocational education. President Woodrow Wilson appointed William B. Wilson, the UMWA leader and U.S. representative, as the Labor Department's first secretary. William B. Wilson had pressed for the extension of federal worker protection while in Congress.

The creation of a new labor department headed by a former union leader encouraged women and other groups to expand the labor agenda. The Women's Trade Union League, the NCL and the Women's Clubs lobbied for the creation of a new bureau to publicize problems of women in the workforce. These groups insisted that a woman head the bureau and that she be answerable only to the labor secretary. William B. Wilson and the Bureau of Labor Statistics resisted this aspect of the proposal prior to the war, but the Woman's Bureau finally was created in 1920.[47]

Support for a national system of employment offices—an administrative prerequisite for active government direction of labor markets—seemed ascendant. Secretary Wilson enlarged the Division of Information and turned it into an embryonic "Bureau of Employment." In mid-1917 this bureau had ninety-three offices, chiefly engaged in directing farmhands to crops in agricultural states. Twenty-eight states had made some provision for public employment offices by the end of 1917.

After the 1912 election, Representative Victor Murdock (Progressive, Kansas) introduced legislation to create a permanent and national employment office system. The House Labor Committee reported a modest federal employment office bill in mid-1914, but did not act on it before Congress adjourned. Proponents of public employment offices now anticipated the report of the U.S. Commission on Industrial Relations the following year. They expected the commission to set the agenda for public labor market management much as the federal vocational education commission was setting the agenda for that issue.[48]

The U.S. Industrial Commission certainly had the opportunity to shape the national labor market policy agenda. The commission's nine members included labor lawyer Frank Walsh and three top labor leaders (machinist and AFL vice president James O'Connell; AFL treasurer Lennon; and Austin Garretson, president of the Railway Conductors). John R. Commons, another member, helped provide the commission's staff. It held extensive hearings and conducted far-reaching investigations of every aspect of labor market policy.

Instead of setting a consensus agenda, however, the commission bitterly divided labor leaders and reformers. It issued a majority report representing much of the AFL's perspective on labor market policy and a minority report representing the views of Commons and labor reformers. Signed by Walsh and the commission's union members, the majority report catalogued AFL grievances against American government and especially against the NAM. "[T]he mass of workers are convinced that laws necessary for their protection against the most grievous wrongs can not be passed except after long and exhausting struggles," the final report charged. Government could not be trusted, for courts nullified many labor protections while administrators ignored others. The majority charged that "the whole machinery of the Government has frequently been placed at the disposal of the employers for the oppression of the workers; that the Constitution itself has been ignored in the interests of the employers; and that constitutional guaranties erected primarily for the protection of the workers have been denied them and used as a cloak for the misdeeds of corporations." This rhetorical attack on past government practice overshadowed the majority's call for a more active public labor market policy through the creation of a national employment system with a well-paid, qualified staff.[49]

Commissioner John R. Commons's minority report offered a different vision of active labor market management. His report also emphasized that American government had proved itself an untrustworthy vehicle for worker protection, but argued that labor market governance could be made more trustworthy if delegated to industrial commissions. A national industrial commission would make labor market rules, administer laws, and adjudicate disputes. It would manage employment services, vocational education, workplace regulation, child labor, work insurance, immigration, and statistics. Thus "removed from the heat of political controversy," the state and national industrial commissions would have the confidence of labor and employers and could ensure the objective framing of proposals and the impartial administration of the laws. The Department of Labor, the AFL's long-sought voice in government, would be reduced to playing an advocacy and educational function.[50]

The labor reformers' industrial commission plan, then, aimed to eliminate much of organized labor's newly won administrative power just as it peaked. Small wonder, then, that the AFL reacted so negatively to the central tenet of Commons's plan, that Gompers quit the AALL over the industrial commission issue in New York (see chapter 3), and Gompers's action inspired organized labor to turn back proposals for industrial commissions in such states as Illinois.[51] The following year, the AFL reiterated the importance of securing "the election and appointment of men to the different official positions within the state to enforce labor laws that will give labor a square deal, that they be members, paid up and in good standing in their organization, participating in its activities. . . ."[52]

World War I forced the federal government to manage labor markets much more actively than any reformer had proposed. A War Labor Administration, directed by Secretary of Labor Wilson, bore responsibility for managing the supply and demand for needed labor. To supply workers for key industries, Secretary Wilson created a U.S. Employment Service in January 1918. This new federal agency nationalized existing state public employment offices and opened new ones. By February 1919, the U.S. Employment Service staffed about five hundred offices nationwide. It placed over two and a half million workers in jobs in 1918. The U.S. Employment Service had support from the U.S. Chamber of Commerce, and it won increasing support from the AFL as it used union members to staff offices and refused to send workers to firms being struck.[53]

National management of labor markets could not survive demobilization and a resurgent open shop drive. At the war's end, reformers and now the AFL supported the creation of a permanent peacetime U.S. Employment Service. Inspired by the precedent set by vocational education, public employment office officials and the AFL recommended federal grants-in-aid for state employment services. Senator William Kenyon (R, Iowa) and Representative John Nolan (R, California), both AFL allies, introduced a bill developed by the participants at a Labor Department conference.[54] The anti-labor backlash of 1919, however, swept away the employment office proposal. The NAM, fully aware that a permanent system of employment offices could aid their labor foes, challenged its constitutionality and its premises as a plan to "bribe" and "coerce" the states.[55] Representative Thomas Blanton (D, Texas), who lead the opposition in the House, complained that "we have virtually turned our government over to Mr. Gompers and unions."[56] In progressive Wisconsin, manufacturers lobbied against federal funding of the employment offices.[57]

Instead of enlarging the employment service, Congress cut its funding from a requested four and a half million dollars for the fiscal year beginning in June 1919 to four hundred thousand dollars. The federal agency's field services evaporated.[58] A skeletal U.S. Employment Service, funded with a mere two hundred thousand dollars per year, limped along through the 1920s and was totally unprepared to face the massive unemployment of the early 1930s.[59]

EMPLOYERS' ACTIVE LABOR MARKET MANAGEMENT

Employers filled the gap in labor market management as government withdrew. Labor shortages and federal encouragement prompted many businesses to initiate personnel management techniques from 1916 to 1920. Some large companies developed, in effect, internal labor markets with higher-level positions staffed by promotion and training of lower echelon employees. Federal policy had encouraged these developments. The War Industries Board trained personnel managers for the employers. The Federal Board for Vocational Education had arranged for training for workers for specific corporations and also offered training for foremen.[60]

The large corporations that participated in the Special Conference Committee of 1919 encouraged firms to coordinate and develop private employment management at the plant level.[61] Employee relations, for these corporate employers, included personnel management, corporate welfare work, and often employee representation through company unions. The American Management Association, founded in 1923, spread this model of employer-controlled personnel management to a broader range of firms.[62] John R. Commons's students Donald

Lescohier, John Andrews, and William Leiserson urged businesses to become more self-stabilizing through the creation of personnel departments, reduction of labor turnover, and leveling of output through inventory management.

The corporate labor management examples convinced influential American reformers that it was possible and desirable to maximize business leadership of labor market management. Commons observed that

> From 10 per cent to 25 per cent of American employers may be said to be so far ahead of the game that trade unions cannot reach them. Conditions are better, security is better, than unions can actually deliver to their members. The other 75 per cent to 90 per cent are backward, either on account of inefficiency, competition, or greed, and only the big stick of unionism or legislation can bring them up to the level of the 10 per cent or 25 per cent.[63]

"The best employment agencies in the United States are not the public employment offices," Commons told a Senate committee in early 1929. "They are the employers themselves." Commons criticized William B. Wilson's wartime U.S. Employment Service for staffing the service with "labor politicians" rather than the neutral administrative experts. Only with employers as equal partners in employment office management could a system of national offices enjoy a "monopoly as complete as that of the post office."[64]

During the depression of 1920–22, progressive employers and labor market reformers promoted plans for stabilizing the economy that depended on business self-governance and sovereignty. Two leaders of the American Management Association, Sam Lewisohn and Ernest G. Draper, coauthored the book *Can Business Prevent Unemployment?* with Commons and Lescohier. [65] The book, which concluded that business could and must prevent joblessness, emphasized long-range forecasting and planning of sales, production, and inventory. Companies such as Eastman Kodak, Hills Brothers, Dennison Manufacturing, and Procter and Gamble were held up as models of business self-stabilization. Commons extolled these plans for their demonstration that capitalism could manage itself. Efficient public employment offices would deal with residual unemployment.[66]

As in the case of company unions, however, these firms' personnel efforts remained exceptional. Only a minority of American firms made such self-conscious efforts to engineer their employment policies. The NAM membership largely ignored personnel management, welfare work, and employee representation.[67] Manufacturers opposed even modest government efforts to stabilize labor markets. When Commerce Secretary Herbert Hoover arranged a federal Unemployment Conference in 1921, manufacturers prevented serious discussion of active government remedies for joblessness. As the economy recovered, Hoover recommended that the federal government hold back nonessential public construction until the economy slowed down. Employers protested the announcement as government paternalism and insisted that "economic laws" be left to work out market problems. Though the federal government slowed its construction timetable, the state governments offset federal efforts with extensive highway and other construction projects.[68]

IMMIGRATION

Immigration constituted a notable exception to the trend of diminishing support for public labor market management in the 1920s. Immigration restriction enjoyed a broad range of support that split the usual coalition that opposed labor law.

Both the NAM and the AFL realized that immigration restriction could strengthen labor's bargaining position. "Cheap labor, ignorant labor, takes our jobs and cuts our wages," Gompers told a U.S. senator in 1902. Immigration in general and Chinese exclusion in particular constituted major concerns of the AFL in the 1906 "bill of grievances" laid before Congress. The AFL quarreled with the Roosevelt and Taft administrations over their enforcement of the immigration laws.[69] House Speaker Cannon and the NAM implicitly agreed that immigration limits helped unions when they strongly opposed immigration restriction while industries were "languishing for men." In 1907, the NAM briefly celebrated apparent federal support for South Carolina's policy of state funding for the immigration of contract laborers. Theodore Roosevelt, observing that "a great deal of feeling has arisen over the decision" and that it would mean "further damage to laborers in the Northern States," overruled his own Department of Commerce and Labor and rejected South Carolina's immigration initiative.[70]

By the early 1910s, support for immigration restriction had expanded beyond the AFL and such nativists as Senator Henry Cabot Lodge (R, Massachusetts), who championed the literacy test in the 1890s. Many Americans, including progressive reformers, feared that immigration from southern and eastern Europe undermined the Anglo-Saxon ethnic foundation of the United States.[71]

In 1911, a U.S. Immigration Commission proposed restrictions against both racially inferior and politically radical immigrants.[72] Congress revived the idea of a literacy test to limit immigration. In 1912, it sent President William Howard Taft legislation that required immigrants to pass the literacy test. Like Grover Cleveland in 1897, Taft vetoed the bill. An unusually broad Senate coalition of Democrats, conservative Republicans, and Republican insurgents voted to override the veto on a vote of 72-to-18. The House sustained Taft's veto by merely three votes.[73] The Democratic Congress sent President Woodrow Wilson an immigration measure with the literacy test in early 1915. Farm organizations, patriotic groups, and some social scientists joined the AFL in asking Wilson to sign the bill. Railroad managers, employers in mass industries that relied on unskilled labor, and Jewish and Catholic leaders lobbied against it. Wilson had promised foreign-born voters that he would not support such legislation, and he vetoed the bill.[74] Wilson vetoed the bill again in 1917, but this time bipartisan majorities voted to override the veto.[75]

The nationalism aroused by the war and the conservatism sparked by the armistice ending World War I propelled further immigration restriction. Republican officials assumed the leadership of the drive to restrict immigration despite opposition from the open shop manufacturers who supported the labor surplus that open immigration implied. After the 1920 election, President Wilson vetoed a proposal to limit immigration to about 350,000. President Warren Harding signed the bill in 1921 and in 1924 approved a permanent quota law that reduced the 1921 limit by half. The only opposition to these bills among Republicans came from those representing manufacturers and those, like Fiorello La Guardia (R, New York), who represented large urban immigrant constituencies.[76] It is notable that one of employers' most visible labor market policy defeats before the New Deal occurred in a conservative decade and on a rather conservative issue.

THE DEPRESSION AND PUBLIC LABOR MARKET MANAGEMENT

Unemployment was creeping up to the federal government's agenda well before the stock market collapsed in the fall of 1929. In his first Senate speech in April 1928, Senator Robert Wagner (D, New York) recommended legislation to expand the U.S. Employment Service, improve labor statistics, and establish a Federal Employment Stabilization Board to advise the president on public works planning.[77] After the 1928 election and at the urging of President-elect Herbert Hoover, Governor Ralph Brewster (R, Maine) suggested a three-billion-dollar federal reserve fund for public works. The AFL, still advocating public works as the primary government response to joblessness, supported this reserve fund idea.[78]

After the stock market crash, Congress moved on these unemployment measures. It enacted the Wagner public works planning bill and President Hoover signed the bill after the 1930 election. The Hoover administration, however, treated the Federal Employment Stabilization Board as an inconsequential statistical unit. It had accomplished little when the administration of President Franklin D. Roosevelt dissolved it in June 1933.[79]

Wagner's proposal for reviving the U.S. Employment Service also revived the postwar battle over the issue. The AALL and the AFL strongly lobbied for Wagner's bill.[80] When the Senate passed it by half a dozen votes in May 1930, the NAM launched an aggressive counterattack.[81] The Democratic gains in the 1930 election increased support for a revitalized U.S. Employment Service. The House approved the Wagner bill on voice votes as the final congressional session ended in early 1931.[82] Hoover pocket vetoed Wagner's employment office bill and ordered the expansion of the existing U.S. Employment Service instead. Its appropriations quadrupled to $883,780 in 1932.[83] As the Hoover employment service expanded, its administrators made it clear that the employment offices would serve employers: "That the employer must be satisfied with the applicant is of importance second to no other consideration, because there could be no satisfactory permanence to the employment if, for any reason, the applicant proved unsatisfactory to the employers. . . ."[84]

The quality of state and local labor market management remained uneven as the Depression deepened. Illinois provided substantial funding for its employment offices, and Wisconsin, Ohio, and New York provided high quality service. Offices in several of the smaller New England states, however, were barely more than "mail order" operations. Half the states had no law authorizing public employment offices at all. Patronage appointments plagued most of the offices that existed.[85] Nearly two hundred cities experimented with work relief, and a few state governments made major commitments to help them. New York's Temporary Emergency Relief Administration (TERA), initiated in the fall of 1931 and directed by Harry Hopkins, funded work relief. Over the next six months, New Jersey, Pennsylvania, Rhode Island, Wisconsin, and Ohio began similar programs. For the most part these state programs emphasized direct relief rather than the creation of jobs for the unemployed.[86]

Under the political pressure of mounting joblessness, President Hoover's reluctance to involve government in labor markets began to crumble. Before taking office, Hoover had planned to ask for a long-term, three-billion-dollar public works fund for "stabilizing prosperity," but he backed away from the plan as the Depression eroded federal revenues. Now Hoover reluctantly requested and Congress approved the creation of a Reconstruction Finance Corporation (RFC). The RFC aimed to alleviate distress by providing support for banks, insurance companies, and other financial institutions.[87] By the summer of 1932, Congress compelled Hoover to accept a much larger federal role in bankrolling anti-Depression measures. Senators Robert La Follette Jr. (R, Wisconsin) and Edward Costigan (D, Colorado), consulting with social work leaders in late 1931, worked out a 375-million–dollar, two-year program for federal jobless relief. The AFL supported the proposal while the NAM, conservative groups, and conservative Republicans opposed it.[88] In June 1932, leading industrialists in urban areas appealed to the president for federal help. The Emergency Relief and Construction Act of 1932 established a fund of $300 million for loans to the states for work and work relief. The law also allowed for another $322 million in direct federal public works, and the RFC could use $1.5 billion of lending power to underwrite corporate or state loans for "self-liquidating" relief projects.[89]

This law constituted the first federal job creation program, but its impact was very limited. Established to induce banks to address unemployment, the RFC used banker's criteria for administering relief. Though the law authorized the RFC to loan as much as $1.5 billion to the states, less than $16 million had been spent by January 1933. By the time Hoover left office in March 1933, the federal government had spent only $6 million of the $322 million authorized by the Emergency Relief and Construction Act for public works (another $3.7 million was obligated).[90]

The New Deal inherited the decentralized and underdeveloped labor market management programs of the previous thirty years. Bound by this legacy, his tenuous coalition of support, and his experience as a state governor, Franklin D. Roosevelt institutionalized three principles of public labor market management. First, national labor market management would be temporary. The New Deal's public jobs programs were emergency measures; it left no permanent counter-cyclical public works program to address future economic downturns. Second, public efforts would supplement, and not displace, private enterprise. Administrators refused to permit government subsidized employment from competing with private employers.[91] Third, permanent labor market management would be decentralized. The New Deal created a permanent national framework for labor market management, but it abandoned effective control of this framework to the states. The federal government initially nationalized the public employment system to deliver work relief and later turned the offices over to the states.[92] The federal government also withdrew its supervision of vocational education, despite labor's protests that states in some cases had used the system as an anti-union tool. The administration removed the powers of the Federal Board for Vocational Education in 1933 and abolished it in 1946.[93]

PUBLIC MANAGEMENT AT THE MARGINS

As the vigor of the populist critique of bigness faded away, the corporate ideal of labor market management grew more attractive in the 1920s. The AFL reinforced that view by arguing that unions could enhance, rather than reduce, corporate productivity. American government had asserted control during World War I and did so again in the first years of the New Deal and during World War II and the Korean War. Each time, though, the national government retreated from active labor market management. The United States never overcame the structural obstacles that prevented it from placing national labor market management on a permanent foundation. From the National Resources Planning Board during World War II to the Employment Act of 1946, the Manpower Development and Training Act of 1962, and the Full Employment and Balanced Growth (Humphrey Hawkins) Act of 1978, reformers have proposed alternative visions of an active national labor market policy. The rhetoric of these initiatives, though, far exceeded their ultimate labor market impact because the national government failed to lay permanent institutional foundations for public labor market management early in the twentieth century.

NOTES

1. Samuel Gompers, "Labor vs. Its Barnacles," in *American Federationist* 13 (May 1916): 271.

2. Paul T. Ringenbach, *Tramps and Reformers* (Westport, Conn.: Greenwood, 1973), 1–108; John A. Garraty, *Unemployment in History* (New York: Harper and Row, 1978).

3. William H. Beveridge, *Unemployment: A Problem of Industry* (London: Longmans, Green, 1909 and 1903); Sidney and Beatrice Webb, *The Minority Report of the Poor Law Commission* (1909), part 2: *The Public Organisation of the Labor Market* (London: Longmans, Green, 1909).

4. William Leiserson, "The Theory of Public Employment Offices and the Principles of the Practical Administration," *Political Science Quarterly* 29 (March 1914): 28–46 and "The Movement for Public Labor Exchanges," *Journal of Political Economy* 23 (July 1915): 707-16. Commons's student Donald D. Lescohier's book, *The Labor Market* (New York: Macmillan, 1919), was a functional American equivalent of the Beveridge book.

5. "The Prevention of Unemployment," *American Labor Legislation Review* 5 (June 1915): 176–92; quote, 176.

6. "The Prevention of Unemployment."

7. U.S. Commission on Industrial Relations, Final Report, Senate Doc. 415, 64th Cong., 1 sess., 11 vols. (Washington, D.C.: Government Printing Office, 1916), 11: 113.

8. Donald D. Lescohier, "Working Conditions," in *History of Labor in the United States* 4 vols., ed. John R. Commons et al. (New York: Macmillan, 1918 and 1935), 3: 189–90.

9. Udo Sautter, *Three Cheers for the Unemployed: Government and Unemployment before the New Deal* (New York: Cambridge University Press, 1991), 61–62; Stephen

Amberg, *The Union Inspiration in American Politics: The Autoworkers and the Making of a Liberal Industrial Order* (Philadelphia: Temple University Press, 1994), 45–46; Howell John Harris, "Getting It Together: The Metal Manufactures' Association of Philadelphia, c. 1900–1930," in *Masters to Managers: Historical and Comparative Perspectives on American Employers*, ed. Sanford M. Jacoby (New York: Columbia University Press, 1991), 123–27; Irving Bernstein, *The Lean Years* (Boston: Houghton Mifflin, 1966), 154–55. IAM president William Johnston "strenuously" objected to these employment bureaus in a letter to Secretary of Labor William B. Wilson, but noted that union members had gotten around the card index system to some extent by "changing their names as often as they change employment, so that these records contain names of men who cannot be found in the flesh"; letter, O'Connell to Wilson, May 13, 1914, in File 20/158, General Records, 1907–1942 (Chief Clerk's Files), General Records of the Department of Labor, RG-174, U.S. National Archives, College Park, Maryland.

10. David P. Smelser, *Unemployment and American Trade Unions* (Baltimore: Johns Hopkins University Press, 1919), 70.

11. Samuel Gompers, "Voluntary Social Insurance or Compulsory," *American Federationist* 23 (August 1916): 669.

12. *Mathews v. People*, 202 Ill. 389, 67 N.E. 28 (1903). See John R. Commons and John B. Andrews, *The Principles of Labor Legislation*, (New York: Harper and Brothers, 1916), 273–74; Earl R. Beckner, *A History of Labor Legislation in Illinois* (Chicago: University of Chicago Press, 1929), 392–93.

13. *Congressional Record,* January 22, 1902: 863. Efforts to keep the Department of Labor separate from the Commerce Department were defeated in the Senate by a 38-to-19 vote (*Congressional Record,* January 28, 1902: 1050–51). A motion to recommit and require a separate cabinet-level Department of Labor proposal was defeated in the House by a vote of 116–86 (*Congressional Record*, January 17, 1903: 928–29).

14. American Federation of Labor, *Proceedings* of the Thirty-first Annual Convention, 1911: 70; hereafter, cited as *AFL Proceedings*, [date]. See also Samuel Gompers, *Seventy Years of Life and Labour*, 2 vols. (New York: Dutton, 1925), 2: 168.

15. Letter, Secretary of Labor William B. Wilson to Senator Henry F. Ashurst, February 17, 1915, in File 20/39, National Employment Bureau, General Records, 1907–1942 (Chief Clerk's Files), General Records of the Department of Labor, RG 174, U.S. National Archives, College Park, Maryland.

16. Eric Hopkins, *Working-Class Self-Help in Nineteenth-Century England: Responses to Industrialization* (New York: St. Martin's, 1995), 164–65.

17. *Adams v. Tanner*, 244 U.S. 590 (1917); *AFL Proceedings,* 1917: 263.

18. Letter, John B. Andrews to "Our Members and Friends," November 23, 1920, in File 20/156, General Records, 1907–1942 (Chief Clerk's Files), General Records of the Department of Labor, RG-174, U.S. National Archives, College Park, Maryland.

19. Sautter, *Three Cheers for the Unemployed*, 109, 193–94; Pennsylvania's law, considered a model, was repealed in 1923.

20. *AFL Proceedings*, 1913: 350.

21. Sautter, *Three Cheers for the Unemployed*, 88–94.

22. Elizabeth Sanders, *Roots of Reform: Farmers, Workers, and the American State, 1877–1917* (Chicago: University of Chicago Press, 1999), 314–19.

23. National Association of Manufacturers, in *Proceedings* of the Eleventh Annual Convention, 1906: 54; hereafter, cited as *NAM Proceedings*, [date]. Amberg, *The Union Inspiration in American Politics*, 46–49.

24. Harvey Kantor, "Vocationalism in American Education: The Economic and Political Context, 1880–1930," in *Work, Youth, and Schooling: Historical Perspectives on Vocationalism in American Education*, ed. Harvey Kantor and David B. Tyack (Stanford, Calif.: Stanford University Press, 1982), 14–44; Bernard Elbaum, "Why Apprenticeship Persisted in Britain but Not in the United States," *Journal of Economic History* 49 (June 1989): 348–49. On the General Electric model's impact on the NAM, see, for example, "Apprenticeship Systems an Industrial Need," *American Industries* 6 (October 1, 1907): 10.

25. *NAM Proceedings*, 1905: 142.

26. William E. Wall, "Trade Schools as a Practical Proposition Discussed by Practical People," *American Industries* 5 (October 15, 1906): 11.

27. James W. Van Cleave, "Industrial Education a Vital Need," *American Industries* 7 (March 1, 1908): 24–25.

28. A. C. Marshall, secretary of the Dayton Employers' Association, in "Trade or Vocational Schools," *American Industries* 9 (August 1, 1909): 11–12.

29. *NAM Proceedings*, 1905: 145.

30. Report of the Massachusetts Commission on Industrial and Technical Education, 1906, in *American Education and Vocationalism: A Documentary History, 1870–1970*, ed. Marvin Lazerson and W. Norton Grubb (New York: Teachers College Press, Columbia University, 1974), 69–75; Roy W. Roberts, *Vocational and Practical Arts Education: History, Development, and Principles*, 3rd ed. (New York: Harper and Row, 1971), 96–97.

31. Roberts, *Vocational and Practical Arts Education*, 96–103.

32. Lawrence A. Cremin, *The Transformation of the School: Progressivism in American Education, 1876–1957* (New York: Knopf, 1962), 38–39; Larry Cuban, "Enduring Resiliency: Enacting and Implementing Federal Vocational Education Legislation," in *Work, Youth, and Schooling: Historical Perspectives on Vocationalism in American Education*, 45–78; Roberts, *Vocational and Practical Arts Education*, 92–93.

33. *NAM Proceedings*, 1907: 116.

34. *AFL Proceedings*, 1909: 137–39.

35. Minutes of the Executive Council of the AFL, in *American Federation of Labor Records: The Samuel Gompers Era* (Microfilm Corporation of America, 1979), Reel 3, January 15, 1910.

36. *AFL Proceedings*, 1909: 137–39; 1912: 270–74. Ira Katznelson and Margaret Weir, *Schooling for All: Class, Race, and the Decline of the Democratic Ideal* (Berkeley: University of California Press, 1985), 151–60.

37. U.S. Commission on Industrial Relations, *Final Report*, 258–60.

38. State industrial education programs generally anticipated and deflected AFL concerns. But when the Massachusetts commission tried to allay union fears by promising to provide general vocational training and not specific craft skills, open shop employers expressed disappointment with this "lame conclusion and lamentable result"; *NAM Proceedings*, 1907: 116.

39. Senator Page cited the unusual comity of the NAM and AFL on the proposal (*Congressional Record*, June 5, 1912: 7677), but noted that representatives of the two organizations refused to meet together with him on the bill; see Roberts, *Vocational and Practical Arts Education*, 103–6.

40. *American Industries* 13 (March 1913): 18; Minutes of the First Annual Meeting of the Chamber of Commerce of the United States, February 11–13, 1914, 124–25, in U.S. Chamber of Commerce Records, Accession 1960, Series I, Box 2, Hagley Museum and Library.

41. *Congressional Record*, March 2, 1907: 4501–2.

42. Commission on National Aid to Vocational Education, Report on *Vocational Education*, House Doc. 1004, 63rd Cong., 2nd sess. (June 1, 1914), 32–34.

43. *Congressional Record*, July 24, 1916: 11470.

44. *Congressional Record*, July 31, 1916: 11873–78; January 2, 1917: 778; Smith–Hughes Act, Public Law 64-347, February 23, 1917.

45. Lescohier, "Working Conditions," 281–83.

46. Regina Werum, "Sectionalism and Racial Politics: Federal Vocational Policies and Programs in the Predesegregation South," *Social Science History* 21 (Fall 1997): 399–453. Elizabeth Sanders emphasizes the agricultural priority of vocational education in *Roots of Reform*, 314–39.

47. File 120/1-A, Women's Bureau, Box 131, in General Records of the Department of Labor, RG 174, General Records, 1907–1942 (Chief Clerk's Files), U.S. National Archives, College Park, Maryland. See also Robyn Muncy, *Creating a Female Dominion in American Reform, 1890–1935* (New York: Oxford University Press, 1991).

48. Paul Douglas and Aaron Director, *The Problem of Unemployment* (New York: Macmillan, 1931); Shelby Harrison et al., *Public Employment Offices: Their Purpose, Structure, and Methods* (New York: Russell Sage Foundation, 1924); Ruth Kellogg, *The United States Employment Service* (Chicago: University of Chicago Press, 1933), 16–17; Sautter, *Three Cheers for the Unemployed*, 81–83.

49. U.S. Commission on Industrial Relations, *Final Report*, 38–39, 113–14.

50. U.S. Commission on Industrial Relations, *Final Report*, 172, 186. On the commission, see Clarence E. Wunderlin Jr., *Visions of a New Industrial Order: Social Science and Labor Theory in America's Progressive Era* (New York: Columbia University Press, 1992), 113–29; James Weinstein, *The Corporate Ideal in the Liberal State, 1900–1918* (Boston: Beacon, 1968); Leon Fink, "Expert Advice: Progressive Intellectuals and the Unraveling of Labor Reform, 1912–1915," in *Intellectuals and Public Life: Between Radicalism and Reform*, ed. Leon Fink, Stephen T. Leonard, and Donald M. Reid (Ithaca, N.Y.: Cornell University Press, 1996), 182–213. Despite Commons's mid-1910s optimism about the power of the industrial commissions' independence, conservatives' attacks on the Wis-

consin Industrial Commission helped to defeat the progressive movement in Wisconsin. National business associations attacked commission government as "paternalistic or socialistic." Herbert F. Margulies, *The Decline of the Progressive Movement in Wisconsin, 1890–1920* (Madison: State Historical Society of Wisconsin, 1968); Robert H. Wiebe, *Businessmen and Reform: A Study of the Progressive Movement* (Cambridge: Harvard University Press, 1962), 201.

51. See chapter 5. For Illinois, see Beckner, *A History of Illinois Labor Legislation*, 501. The subsequent behavior of the Colorado Industrial Commission suggested that AFL fears were not illusory. The Colorado commission forced striking packinghouse employees to return to work and authorized a wage cut for them. William Green, U.S. Senate Subcommittee of the Committee on the Judiciary, Hearings on *Limiting the Scope of Injunctions in Labor Disputes* (Washington, D.C.: GPO, 1928), part 1, 63.

52. *AFL Proceedings*, 1917: 266.

53. William J. Breen, *Labor Market Politics and the Great War* (Kent, Ohio: Kent State University Press, 1997), 89–103; Jonathan Grossman, *The Department of Labor* (New York: Praeger, 1967), 20–23; Sautter, *Three Cheers for the Unemployed*, 121–26; Lescohier, "Working Conditions," 206.

54. "Conference on National Employment Service, Washington, D.C., April 23 to 25, 1919," *Monthly Labor Review* 8 (May 1919): 1404–6; Sautter, *Three Cheers for the Unemployed*, 160–66; U.S. Congress, Joint Committee on Unemployment, *Hearings on National Employment System* (Washington, D.C.: GPO, 1919), 412.

55. Harrison et al., *Public Employment Offices*, 89; Douglas and Director, *The Problem of Unemployment*, 335–36; Sautter, *Three Cheers for the Unemployed*, 167–68.

56. *Congressional Record*, July 28, 1919: 8944; on the backlash against the wartime U.S. Employment Service, see Breen, *Labor Market Politics and the Great War*, 133–59.

57. Letters, Webster Manufacturing Company to Representative Augustus Nelson, May 29, 1919, June 5, 1919, August 30, 1919, in Adolphus Nelson papers, Wisconsin State Historical Society. See also the report by Senator William King (D, Utah) of the large volume of mail indicating the opposition of Utah Associated Industries to the bill; *Congressional Record*, June 18, 1919.

58. *Congressional Record*, July 1, 1919: 2161; *AFL Proceedings*, 1919: 122–24.

59. "The Public Employment Service System, 1933–1953," *Employment Security Review* 20 (June 1953): 7.

60. Sanford M. Jacoby, *Employing Bureaucracy: Managers, Unions, and the Transformation of Work in American Industry, 1900–1945* (New York: Columbia University Press, 1985), 163, 280.

61. Jacoby, *Employing Bureaucracy*, 280–82.

62. Jacoby, *Employing Bureaucracy*, 184–85, 189, 191, 281.

63. John R. Commons, "The Opportunity of Management," in *Industrial Government*, ed. John R. Commons (New York: Macmillan, 1921), 263.

64. John R. Commons, *Industrial Goodwill* (New York: McGraw-Hill, 1919), 76–81.

65. Sam A. Lewisohn, Ernest G. Draper, John R. Commons, and Don D. Lescohier, *Can Business Prevent Unemployment?* (New York: Knopf, 1925).

66. U.S. Senate Committee on Education and Labor, *Hearings on Unemployment in the United States* (Washington, D.C.: GPO, 1929), 218–20.

67. Jacoby, *Employing Bureaucracy*, 189, 191, 200–201.

68. Sautter, *Three Cheers for the Unemployed*, 142–145; Robert H. Zieger, *Republicans and Labor, 1919–1929* (Lexington: University Press of Kentucky, 1969), 90–97; Lescohier, "Working Conditions," 175–76.

69. Gompers quoted in Lescohier, "Working Conditions," 26; *AFL Proceedings,* 1906: 76–77; Gompers, *Seventy Years of Life and Labour,* 2: 164–66, 169.

70. Theodore Roosevelt to Oscar Straus, letter, January 18, 1907, in Oscar Straus Papers, U.S. Library of Congress, Box 5; *American Industries* 5 (February 15, 1907): 8, and (March 15, 1907): 1, 8; Gompers, *Seventy Years of Life and Labour,* 2: 171.

71. George Mowry, *The Era of Theodore Roosevelt, 1900–1912* (New York: Harper and Row, 1958), 92–94; Mark Karson, *American Labor Unions and Politics, 1900–1918* (Carbondale: Southern Illinois University Press, 1958), 43, 71.

72. Keith Fitzgerald, *The Face of the Nation: Immigration, the State, and the National Identity* (Stanford, Calif.: Stanford University Press, 1996), 127–28.

73. The House narrowly failed to override Taft's veto with a 213-to-114 vote (a two-thirds vote was required to override). *Congressional Record,* February 18, 1913: 3318; and February 19, 1913: 3429.

74. Arthur S. Link, *Wilson: The New Freedom* (Princeton: Princeton University Press, 1956), 274–76.

75. The override votes were 287–106 in the House and 62–19 in the Senate. *Congressional Record,* February 1, 1917: 2456–57; February 5, 1917: 2629. See also Link, *Wilson: The New Freedom,* 327–28.

76. *AFL Proceedings,* 1919: 76; Zieger, *Republicans and Labor,* 80–83.

77. *Congressional Record,* April 20, 1928: 6842; J. Joseph Huthmacher, *Senator Robert F. Wagner and the Rise of Urban Liberalism* (New York: Atheneum, 1968), 58–86.

78. Sautter, *Three Cheers for the Unemployed,* 271–72.

79. Sautter, *Three Cheers for the Unemployed,* 274–78; Leiserson, "Working Conditions," 178; Bernstein, *The Lean Years,* 270–73.

80. John B. Andrews to Robert F. Wagner, telegram, February 3, 1931; and Andrews to Wagner, letter, February 24, 1931, in Robert F. Wagner papers, Georgetown University, Legislative Files, Box 188, Folder 418. See also Sautter, *Three Cheers for the Unemployed,* 254–59; Desmond King, *Actively Seeking Work? The Politics of Unemployment and Welfare Policy in the United States and Great Britain* (Chicago: University of Chicago Press, 1995), 26–28.

81. Wagner accused Emery of single-handedly mobilizing the opposition to the bill; *Congressional Record,* April 28, 1930: 7798. See "Critics of Wagner Veto Dissect Federal Employment Service," *Business Week,* March 18, 1931: 28.

82. *Congressional Record,* February 23, 1931: 5774–77.

83. U.S. House Committee on Appropriations, *Hearings on State, Justice, Commerce, and Labor Appropriations* (Washington, D.C.: GPO, 1933–37).

84. U.S. Department of Labor, Employment Service Order #6, October 1, 1931, page 2, in Robert F. Wagner Papers, Georgetown University, Folder 416 ("Doak Substitute").

85. Douglas and Director, *The Problem of Unemployment*, 336–42; Sautter, *Three Cheers for the Unemployed*, 261–66.

86. Joanna C. Colcord, with William C. Koplovitz and Russell H. Kurtz, *Emergency Work Relief as Carried Out in Twenty-six American Communities, 1930–1931, with Suggestions for Setting Up a Program* (New York: Russell Sage Foundation, 1932); Sautter, Three Cheers for the Unemployed, 283–91.

87. Joan Hoff Wilson, *Herbert Hoover: Forgotten Progressive* (Boston: Little, Brown, 1975), 144–45, 238–41; Bernstein, *The Lean Years*, 460–62; Robert F. Himmelberg, *The Origins of the National Recovery Administration: Business, Government, and the Trade Association Issue, 1921–1933* (New York: Fordham University Press, 1976); James Stuart Olson, *Herbert Hoover and the Reconstruction Finance Corporation, 1931–1933* (Ames: Iowa State University Press, 1977).

88. Sautter, *Three Cheers for the Unemployed*, 295–301; Bernstein, *The Lean Years*, 462–66.

89. Sautter, *Three Cheers for the Unemployed*, 314; Bernstein, *The Lean Years*, 469–70.

90. Bernstein, *The Lean Years*, 470–71; Sautter, *Three Cheers for the Unemployed*, 314–17.

91. Arthur Burns and Edward Williams, *Federal Work, Security, and Relief Programs, WPA Research Monograph 24* (Washington, D.C.: GPO, 1941); Jonathan R. Kesselman, "Work Relief Programs in the Great Depression," in *Creating Jobs: Public Employment Programs and Wage Subsidies*, ed. John L. Palmer (Washington, D.C.: Brookings, 1978), 153–240; Robert Jerret III and Thomas A. Barocci, *Pubic Works, Government Spending, and Job Creation: The Job Opportunities Program* (New York: Praeger, 1979), 1–13; Alden F. Briscoe, "Public Service Employment in the 1930's: The WPA," in *The Political Economy of Public Service Employment*, ed. Harold L. Sheppard et al. (Lexington, Mass.: Heath, 1972), 95–115; Bonnie Fox Schwartz, *The Civil Works Administration, 1933–1934: The Business of Emergency Employment in the New Deal* (Princeton: Princeton University Press, 1984).

92. Raymond C. Atkinson, Louise Odencrantz, and Ben Deming, *Public Employment Service in the United States* (Chicago: Public Administration Service, 1938), 29; *Employment Security Review* (June 1953): 9–11.

93. Joseph F. Kett, "The Adolescence of Vocational Education," in *Work, Youth, and Schooling: Historical Perspectives on Vocationalism in American Education*, 106–8; Larry Cuban, "Enduring Resiliency."

9

CIRCUMSCRIBING
WORK INSURANCE

[N]o realistic plan [for unemployment insurance] can ignore the
individual employer's active and strategic position under our present economic system. . . . Obviously if Wisconsin is to pioneer in
this field it must do so on a modest scale. The contributions
required of employers must not be so great as to handicap them
unduly in interstate competition.

—Wisconsin Legislative Interim Committee on
Unemployment, 1931[1]

In most nations, public insurance against work accidents and unemployment
marked a necessary step away from the unfettered employer prerogatives of
the nineteenth century and toward the substantive, universal worker protections
of the twentieth-century welfare state. American work insurance, however, did
not displace employers' labor market prerogatives. Instead, American work
insurance evaded a challenge to employer control of the workplace and, in
doing so, modernized the protection of employer prerogatives.

Workers' compensation laws spread widely in the 1910s, usually on terms
beneficial to employers. In most states, workers' compensation expanded
employers' choices by providing a less expensive alternative to the risk of civil
suits. Progressive reformers pressed for health insurance as the next priority after
workers' compensation, but health insurance proposals brought together a fatal
coalition of opponents that included the American Federation of Labor (AFL),
insurance companies, the National Association of Manufacturers (NAM), and
doctors. By the 1920s, employers were proving that they could provide insurance and benefit plans unilaterally, inspiring reformers to redraw work insurance
proposals so that employers would assume proprietorship of them. Reformers

231

developed an "American" plan for public unemployment compensation that relied on employer reserves against joblessness. This plan was well suited to employers' emerging labor market dominance and interstate economic competition. Wisconsin's pioneering unemployment insurance program assuaged state business and politicians' concerns about competitiveness by guaranteeing a large measure of employer control over the plan's implementation. The Social Security Act's unemployment insurance program in effect encouraged the states to emulate this example.

WORKERS' COMPENSATION

Workplace hazards jeopardized employees in nearly every industry in the early twentieth century. Death, paralysis, blindness, and disability plagued workers in the nation's mines, mills, railroad yards, and factories. Insurance companies estimated that twenty-five thousand to thirty-five thousand industrial deaths and more than two million serious injuries occurred annually in the years after 1900.[2]

Bereaved families and mutilated workers usually had to sue employers to obtain some financial compensation for their losses. Though American courts had tended to treat workers more favorably than did British courts before 1880,[3] the law in both countries gave employers powerful legal defenses against liability lawsuits filed by injured workers or their survivors. If the employee had not exercised "reasonable" care, he was presumed responsible for his injury. Courts could absolve employers from responsibility if the worker contributed to his injury through his own negligence. Under the "fellow servant" doctrine, courts also could excuse an employer if a coworker's negligence caused the injury. In hazardous industries, courts presumed that workers had voluntarily accepted the risks that their work normally entailed.[4]

Unions sought policy changes that would attenuate employers' legal defenses and make it easier for injured workers to recover damages in court. Since workers often constituted a large proportion of jurors, such rollbacks in employers' legal defenses could turn courts into vehicles for worker protection. Large damage awards granted by juries occurred infrequently, but when they did occur they reinforced workers' determination to reform the employer liability system in their favor. Massachusetts (1887), Colorado (1893), New York (1902), Pennsylvania (1907), California (1907), and Ohio (1910) enacted laws that substantially limited employers' liability defenses. State courts generally upheld these changes as constitutional.[5] In 1906, Congress tightened a liability law for railroads. Two years later, Congress tightened liability law for railroads further and, at the urging of President Theodore Roosevelt, established a compensation program for some injured federal employees. Senator Robert La Follette, however, conceded that at this point the federal government had reached its constitutional limits with respect to employers' liability reform.[6]

Many American labor leaders at the turn of the century preferred cutbacks in employers' liability defenses to worker's compensation. When Great Britain enacted a workers' compensation law in 1897, the New York Social Reform Club drafted a bill based on the British law. In 1898, the bill became the first social insurance bill introduced in an American state legislature. Though the AFL supported the New York workers' compensation bill, the New York State Workingmen's Federation refused to support it. Labeled "too radical to pass" even by its Senate sponsor, the bill died in committee.[7] The New York City Central Labor Union instead drafted and lobbied for a bill reducing employers' liability defenses. In 1902, the state enacted the labor unions' proposal.[8] Similarly, Illinois appointed an Industrial Insurance Commission to study compensation issues. Though the Illinois commission recommended a voluntary, comprehensive system of workers' compensation in 1907, unions successfully killed the proposal.[9]

Where unions did not defeat workers' compensation, constitutional limits and interstate competition derailed it. In 1902 Maryland passed a workers' compensation law limited to mining, street railways, and a few other occupations. The bill eliminated all workers' rights under liability laws. It provided for meager compensation only in the case of death. When the bill was declared unconstitutional, no one appealed the decision.[10] A Massachusetts commission in 1904 recommended a workers' compensation plan inspired by the British law of 1897. Opponents objected that the law would handicap Massachusetts industry in interstate commerce. These arguments helped persuade Massachusetts legislators to reject the law (Connecticut legislators followed suit in 1909).[11]

Meanwhile, employers were becoming more supportive of workers' compensation laws. Though employers stoutly defended the judicial system's power to enjoin unions, they were growing increasingly dissatisfied with its management of employer liability. Juries awarded generous damages to defendants more frequently, and the amounts of awards were increasing. Yet the higher awards often failed to produce adequate compensation for the worker or his family. Costly and time-consuming litigation absorbed money and delayed settlements. In a sample of fifty-one cases investigated by a New York commission, the lawyer received more compensation than his client in fourteen cases. Cases dragged on from six months to six years in New York. In Ohio, it took two years on average to litigate fatal injury cases. Premiums for private employer liability insurance cost $22 million in 1908. Only a quarter of those premiums reached injured workers.[12]

The largest corporations could and did alleviate some of these problems unilaterally. The U.S. Steel Corporation introduced a corporate plan based on the German accident insurance system in 1910.[13] The steel company established a committee on safety that created an internal factory inspection system. Only a corporation with unusual size and capital could institute such a private plan. U.S. Steel had 143 manufacturing plants in 1908, and it also held mines and railroads. Other companies, such as International Harvester and the Chicago and Northwestern Railroad, also instituted extensive safety campaigns.[14]

Both the National Civic Federation (NCF) and progressive reformers sought to spread such corporate plans much more broadly. The costs of the liability system concerned even the large employers. The NCF warned that continued reliance on employer liability laws would "lead to social destruction."[15] John R. Commons, recalling his research in Pittsburgh early in the century, credited U.S. Steel with "my first lesson in accident prevention." Company experts maintained that, with company support, they could reduce industrial accidents by two-thirds. Workers' compensation could induce similar behavior among all employers. "Obviously," Commons concluded, "I wanted all employers to be forced by law to follow the lead of the Steel Corporation, and to make a profit by doing good, instead of defending themselves as alleged criminals for neglecting the safety of their employees."[16]

The American Association for Labor Legislation (AALL) began to spearhead the workers' compensation movement in 1909. Commons and the AALL drew on the U.S. Steel example to design a model workers' compensation law tailored to American circumstances. The AALL plan proposed that an individual employer's compulsory insurance premium would be adjusted upward if an unusual number of injuries occurred in his plant. Premiums would decline if the employer showed an exceptionally good safety record. This approach would induce employers to reduce accidents out of self-interest, while it left them substantially free to manage their plants as they saw fit.[17] The Commons group led the battle for workers' compensation in Wisconsin, while Henry Seager and other AALL members played a central role in the battle in New York.[18]

The smaller firms represented by the NAM cautiously moved toward support for workers' compensation. Ninety percent of NAM members surveyed in 1910 expressed dissatisfaction with employers' liability laws and liability insurance.[19] States such as Ohio were tightening the defenses against employer liability, encroaching "still further upon the employers' rights." A NAM spokesman observed that the average manufacturer lacked the time, the inclination, the capital, and the workforce "to establish his own insurance company [like U.S. Steel]. . . . He would much prefer to have some one do this for him."[20]

This mounting frustration impelled the NAM toward support for workers' compensation laws.[21] NAM strategists pursued beneficial government protection with the same zeal with which they attacked work regulation and union protections. F. C. Schwedtman, chair of the NAM Committee on Industrial Indemnity Insurance said that

> Every student of the history of relief schemes for work accidents in foreign countries knows that *compulsory* action through state or federal laws is necessary to make satisfactory progress. The progressive employers do more than the law demands and do it voluntarily and in co-operation with their employes. It is only just that the reactionary employers and employes should be compelled by legislation to do their share. A system providing for minimum relief by legal compulsion, and maximum relief by voluntary co-operative action is most desirable from every viewpoint.[22]

NAM leaders had little difficulty supporting government compulsion for some employers when "free rider" problems affected them directly and they could secure government action on favorable terms.

Labor leaders joined the emerging consensus favoring workers' compensation out of self-defense and frustration with the slow pace of liability law reform. Open shop employers by 1910 had too often defeated unions' efforts to reduce employers' legal defenses against work injury suits. As the open shop employers' interest in workers' compensation increased, so did that of the AFL. Though some union organizations, such as the Chicago Federation of Labor, continued to back employers' liability reform, the AFL endorsed workers' compensation. Unions, of course, supported workers' compensation plans that provided workers with more generous benefits and permitted less employer discretion than the NAM preferred. The AFL also emphasized the importance of preempting private insurance companies by requiring state government to monopolize workers' compensation insurance.[23]

Support for workers' compensation laws spanned the gulf between employers and unions by 1911. Forty state commissions studied employers' liability between 1909 and 1913. All of these commissions recommended the abolition of employers' liability.[24] All parties agreed that states, not the federal government, would have to provide accident insurance for most of the workforce because the latter lacked the authority to do so.[25] The NAM appreciated and welcomed the conservative effects of federalism on workers' compensation laws. Schwedtman observed in 1911 that "[s]tate action will probably solve the problem quicker than federal action under our form of government, because state action will be more or less competitive and the state which solves the problem in a manner equitably to all concerned will have such an advantage over other states that its successful system will be copied sooner or later by all the states of the Union."[26]

When New York enacted a workers' compensation law in 1910, the pressure of interstate economic competition narrowed its coverage substantially. Employers valued the additional choice of workers' compensation or electing to remain subject to the employers' liability system. New York limited the law to a few hazardous employments, those "in which there is little or no interstate competition," according to the AALL.[27] Judges found even this law unconstitutional. The New York Court of Appeals ruled that "In its final and simple analysis [compulsory workmen's compensation insurance] is taking the property of A and giving it to B, and that cannot be done under our constitutions."[28]

This judicial setback did not slow the progress of workers' compensation laws, though it did result in the adoption of more conservative programs. In the legislative sessions following the 1910 election, thirteen states enacted compensation legislation. Wisconsin's law became the first to survive a court challenge in 1911. In the sessions following the 1912 election, ten more states enacted workers' compensation laws; eleven more enacted laws in the sessions after the 1914 elections, and six more after 1916. By 1919 all the states outside the old Confederacy (except for Missouri) and half of the former Confederate states had enacted such laws.[29] Not until 1928, however, after virtually all the states had enacted workers' compensation laws, did Congress provide workers' compensation to wage earners in the District of Columbia.[30] Mississippi became the last state to adopt a worker's compensation law in 1948.[31]

A few states invested remarkable responsibility for managing workers' compensation in state government, given the nation's experience with patronage politics. Ohio notably established a compulsory workers' compensation fund fully monopolized by the state. State Senator William Green, a United Mine Workers of America leader and future AFL president, sponsored the Ohio plan.[32] Social insurance expert Isaac Rubinow observed in 1913, "there is already more straight state insurance against industrial accidents than in the whole of Europe, where the predominating type is the compulsory employers' association, and not the bureaucratic state insurance fund."[33]

The AFL endorsed the Ohio state-funded plan for all states.[34] By 1919, six states compelled employers to contribute to the state insurance fund. Seventeen additional states had elective state workers' compensation plans (three additional states established state mutual associations). These elective state plans covered an increasing share of small and medium-size employers[35] and accumulated large financial reserves. In 1919, New York and California employers each paid over three million dollars into their state funds.[36] By 1922, the Census Bureau reported that state governments together collected a total of $77 million annually in premiums for all insurance trust funds (excluding public employee retirement). These state trust fund revenues exceeded state revenues from individual income taxes ($43 million) and corporate income taxes ($58 million) at the time.[37]

Competitive federalism and employer opposition ensured that most states, however, would implement more conservative programs than Ohio's. Even though the Supreme Court upheld all the major types of plans in 1917,[38] by 1932 only three states other than Ohio (North Dakota, Washington, and Wyoming) had established the compulsory state monopoly over workers' compensation that the AFL supported. Only thirteen of the state workers' compensation laws were compulsory for employers in 1932.[39]

Many of the state laws plainly were inadequate. Over one quarter of the nation's workers in 1932 still depended on the courts to provide redress for work accidents. Some states did not require employers to maintain adequate insurance coverage. Some provided for no enforcement of the laws other than courts. Some states with elective systems allowed employers to require employees to "elect themselves" out of the workers' compensation system as a condition of employment.[40] Workers' compensation benefits and coverage on average were "miserably low measured by any standard" by the 1930s because of interstate competition. Many of the laws covered work injury in the narrowest sense. Only Massachusetts, Connecticut, California, Wisconsin, and North Dakota covered all occupational diseases, while four other states (including New York and Ohio) covered lists of specific occupational diseases. The workers' compensation programs helped employers in high-wage industries limit benefits and helped employers in dangerous industries secure relatively lower costs. Employers were less successful in using workers' compensation to limit costs in states with relatively high unionization rates, active reform movements, and public agencies dedicated to managing workers' compensation.[41] After a generation, concluded a workers' compensation expert at the beginning of the New Deal, "but a small fraction of the burden of industrial accidents had been shifted from injured workers and their dependents."[42]

HEALTH INSURANCE

While leaders of the AALL pressured legislatures to adopt workers' compensation programs, they were expanding the work insurance agenda to include industrial diseases.[43] Compulsory health insurance laws aimed at industrial disease constituted "the biggest next step in labor legislation" for the AALL.[44] The association published a model compulsory state health insurance bill in 1916.[45] The bill resembled the German and British plans in funding and coverage. As in Great Britain, employers' contributions would rise proportionately for exceptionally low-paid workers.[46]

The AALL's model bill combined elements of foreign programs with features tailored to "American conditions." Since the federal government had almost virtually no authority to deal with industrial diseases, the reformers designed a bill that state legislatures could adopt despite interstate economic competition. Compared to the British plan, government would provide a smaller share of funding for the program. Employers and employees would each contribute 40 percent of the funds. Like workers' compensation, the health insurance plan recommended "experience rating," that is, rate reductions for employers with low rates of sickness, in the hope that such a provision would link sickness prevention to business self-interest. Workmen's compensation acts, the AALL argued, demonstrated that if workers and employers bore a high share of the costs, they would have strong incentives to prevent disease.[47] Reformers explicitly refuted the claim that patronage politics would corrupt state health insurance programs. The worker's compensation experience proved that such programs could be managed in an effective and nonpartisan way.[48]

Optimistic about health insurance in the wake of the rapid spread of workers' compensation, the AALL circulated thirteen thousand copies of the "model" state law. Reformers were enthusiastic about expanding the agenda to health insurance.[49] The American Medical Association endorsed public health insurance, and in early 1916 some of its leaders worked closely with the AALL in drafting the model legislation. The NAM endorsed public health insurance in principle in May 1916, and Congress held hearings on social insurance in the same year. Potential opponents believed that public health insurance was inevitable, with a growing tide of support cresting as legislatures met in early 1917.[50]

Sympathetic legislators had introduced the model law in fifteen of the state legislatures by 1917. Ten states funded commissions to investigate health insurance. These states included the largest industrial states in the East and California in the West. Of these ten commissions, California, New Jersey, Ohio, and New York reported in favor of compulsory health insurance. A pair of Massachusetts commissions came to opposite conclusions in 1917 and 1918.[51]

The AFL leadership, noncommittal about social insurance as recently as 1914, now weighed in as an opponent of health insurance.[52] By 1916, Samuel Gompers had broken with reformers over the industrial commission issue and the U.S. Commission on Industrial Relations. Gompers turned against health insurance as the reformers pressed the issue and the NAM announced its tentative support. Gompers criticized the fundamental premise of the AALL bill, arguing that, "if employers are to have financial interests at stake in the sickness or disease or death that may come upon their employes," then they would become intimately interested in manipulating workers' private lives. "The visits of the company's doctor to the homes of the employe would mean, therefore, that the employer would not only have jurisdiction over the employe in the factories, shops, and work places, but would extend that jurisdiction to the homes." Moreover, the laws would build up independent bureaucracies such as industrial commissions that could control and coerce trade unions. Given Gompers's lifelong frustrations with the implementation of labor market programs and the NAM's recent advocacy of periodic physical examinations, his opposition to this extension of government power seems, from the AFL's perspective, more prudent than paranoid.[53]

Gompers defined union shop strategy as the appropriate alternative to work insurance. Workers' organized economic power constituted "the most potent and the most direct social insurance of the workers."[54] "[T]he trade union movement," he argued, "has secured a reduction in the hours of daily labor and better standards of wages and conditions of employment which have improved the physical and mental health of the workers."[55] In 1907, eighty-four of the approximately 125 American national unions in existence had benefit funds. Nineteen of the unions offered disability benefits. These nineteen included the powerful railroad brotherhoods, as well as core AFL craft unions such as the carpenters, painters, iron molders, and glass workers.[56]

Gompers proposed a commission to study, among other things, "to what extent the government of the United States may aid in the establishment of a federal insurance system of which the wage earners of the United States may avail themselves." This commission would be constituted of two representatives of employers and two trade unionists, but would be chaired by the secretary of labor (the incumbent, William B. Wilson, a reliable friend of the AFL).[57] He also expressed support for voluntary health insurance subsidized by the government and run by trade unions. Government should help unions to the fullest extent possible to create "mutual insurance under the authority of the government, mutual insurance based upon the voluntary action of the men and women of the labor world."[58]

Twenty-nine state labor federations, predictably including New York, Massachusetts, and the other most industrialized states, broke with the national AFL and endorsed public health insurance by 1919. The New York State Federation of Labor worked closely with the AALL in drafting and lobbying on behalf of the state's proposal. The New York bill won Senate approval in a 30-to-20 vote in 1919. This bill included several concessions to opponents, including more autonomy for doctors and more limited coverage to mollify employers.[59] This was the only favorable legislative vote for public health insurance in Progressive Era America.

Devastating opposition to health insurance emerged from both large and small employers, as well as doctors. Although they had supported workers' compensation, the NCF opposed health insurance immediately. The NAM became an opponent by early 1917.[60] Workers' compensation promised lower costs and more predictability for employers. Health insurance, however, promised more costs and fewer benefits than workers' compensation. Many companies already had established medical departments.[61] Employees had a much more difficult time in court establishing employer liability for disease than for an on-the-job injury.[62] State liability laws did not facilitate such lawsuits for diseases, so employers had little reason to support a health insurance law to trump the tort system.

No segment of business more vigorously battled compulsory public health insurance than the private insurance industry. The AALL plan directly threatened these insurers' profitability and market share.[63] Reformers thought that funeral benefits would enhance the bill's support among wage earners.[64] However, public funeral benefits threatened one of the most lucrative products of the insurance companies. The Prudential and Metropolitan Life Insurance companies, which issued about two-thirds of the private funeral benefits policies in the United States, provided vigorous lobbyists for the opposition.[65] Skilled in lobbying in the states, the insurance companies created the Insurance Society of America to discredit the AALL effort. In California, insurance companies funded the anti–health insurance campaign directly (and indirectly, through support for Christian Science opposition). The Insurance Society widely circulated anti–health insurance literature that linked the proposal with Kaiser Wilhelm's Germany. In November 1918, California voters crushed the proposal in a referendum by a two-and-a-half-to-one margin.[66]

American doctors joined with business to defeat the Progressive Era state health insurance initiatives because the plan threatened their income and independence. Like some of the craft unions, doctors had secured state laws that licensed the practice of medicine in the state. Nominally part of state government, medical licensing panels consisted of doctors, who determined the requirements for practicing medicine in the state. By tightening these requirements, doctors restricted the number of practicing physicians competing with others. By limiting supply, doctors gained control over their profession and their fees (much like a cartel). From 1916 to 1920, doctors benefited from an especially dramatic drop in the number of practicing physicians because of stiffer licensing requirements.[67]

As licensing raised doctors' income, their view of public health insurance changed from apathy to hostility. British doctors supported national health insurance because the law raised and stabilized their incomes. State licensing laws had the same result for American doctors. Because licensing laws provided adequate market control for physicians, they had every reason to oppose any scheme that would reduce their professional autonomy. What the British doctors won through national health insurance, the American doctors had already won through self-regulation under state auspices.[68]

Doctors' opposition to the AALL's health insurance bill burst angrily from county medical societies because the bill threatened their autonomy. The doctors' opposition offset the support of state union federation in New York. Supported by the doctors, the manufacturers could defeat the health insurance proposal in the lower house of the New York legislature. The Speaker of the state assembly, Thaddeus C. Sweet, blocked the 1919 bill that the state senate had approved. Sweet was a New York manufacturer allied with the Associated Manufacturers and Merchants of New York.[69] The health insurance defeats in New York and California left John B. Andrews "shell-shocked." He and the AALL retreated to more mundane reforms and more conservative policy designs as the nation retreated to normalcy in the 1920s.[70]

CORPORATE WELFARE: EMPLOYER-CONTROLLED WORK INSURANCE

As the progressive spirit dissolved, reformers looked to private enterprise as a source of worker security. "Welfare capitalists" became more important to reformers because these business leaders provided working models for the kinds of work insurance that was practical under "American" conditions.[71]

John R. Commons became an especially strong proponent of private assumption of work insurance. He predicted in 1919 that "group insurance and welfare systems are coming, because, like accident compensation, they fill the next largest gap in the struggle of capital and labor." Government should require employers to provide these benefits: "If all employers are required by law to insure all their workers against death, old age, and premature old age, then not only is this form of welfare made universal but it cannot be practiced at the cost of liberty."[72]

The fact that private business could manage welfare without political corruption made the corporate alternative particularly attractive to Commons and his allies. Even in corrupt cities, businessmen could force essential services to be provided effectively. "When business men want factory inspectors to be made exempt from politics, because they want them to help keep down the accident-tax on business, then the factory inspector becomes a new man," Commons observed.[73] Firms that had established work insurance proved that private companies could promote social welfare without sacrificing competitiveness or employer control of the enterprise.

By 1911, the NCF was encouraging such welfare work. The NCF's committee on welfare work included over five hundred employers and public officials. In a 1926 survey of the nation's 1,500 largest companies, 80 percent reported that they made some form of welfare provision and half had established comprehensive programs including accident, sickness, and pension plans. Group insurance covered six million workers in 1928.[74]

Company "welfare work" provided several advantages for employers who could afford to provide it. Such programs increased worker loyalty to the firm and discouraged challenges to managerial authority. They also increased workers' dependence on individual employers, because employer-provided insurance plans were not portable. An employee who left an employer sacrificed his claim to the employers' benefits.[75]

UNEMPLOYMENT INSURANCE

European involvement in unemployment insurance originated when municipalities, following the example of Ghent, Belgium, subsidized the unemployment insurance funds of trade unions. France began national funding of union jobless insurance funds in 1905, and several other continental European nations followed suit. From the start, then, many European plans substantially strengthened trade unions by giving them a central place in insurance administration.[76] In effect, publicly funded unemployment insurance became a powerful material inducement to join unions. But in the United States, unemployment insurance ultimately strengthened employers more than unions. It did so because "American conditions" induced reformers to develop unemployment insurance proposals that minimized the programs' potential cost to employers.

When the AALL took up the issue of unemployment in the 1910s, it viewed unemployment compensation as the "final link" in its Practical Program for the Prevention of Unemployment:

> Just as workmen's compensation has already resulted in the nation-wide movement for "safety-first," and just as health insurance will furnish the working basis for a similar movement for the conservation of national health, so the "co-operative pressure" exerted by unemployment insurance can and should be utilized for the prevention of unemployment. For although much regularization of industry can be accomplished through the voluntary efforts of enlightened employers, there is also needed that powerful element of social

compulsion which can be exerted through the constant financial pressure of a carefully adjusted system of insurance. . . . To be regarded as secondary to this function of regularization is the important provision of unemployment insurance for the maintenance, through out-of-work benefits, of those reserves of labor which may still be necessary to meet the unprevented fluctuations of industry.[77]

Early on, then, the primary architects of an American unemployment insurance system justified it in part on grounds of employer efficiency. The AALL plan addressed the same "free rider" problem that prompted the NAM leaders to endorse compulsory workers' compensation for all employers. Income maintenance was a secondary concern.

Neither employers nor the AFL leaders had any more incentive to support Progressive Era unemployment insurance proposals than to support health insurance. Work injuries posed much more uncertainty and cost for employers than did unemployment. Unlike victims of work accidents (but like disease-stricken employees), jobless workers could not sue employers for damages resulting from a layoff. Unemployment insurance was not as popular or as well understood as workers' compensation or health insurance.[78]

AFL leaders continued to emphasize shorter hours and public works as remedies for unemployment. These leaders opposed all compulsory social insurance beyond workers' compensation, even though only a few unions had unemployment insurance funds in the early twentieth century. Unemployment and other insurance schemes in Great Britain had "taken much of the virility out of the British trade unions," concluded Gompers.[79] Though some state and local unions endorsed unemployment insurance despite AFL opposition to it, Progressive Era unionists who favored social insurance placed a higher priority on health insurance and old-age pensions.[80]

Opposed by the AFL leadership and by manufacturers, and viewed as secondary even by its supporters, unemployment insurance received little serious consideration in the Progressive Era. In 1918, the U.S. House of Representatives considered a proposal to establish a federal commission to study social insurance. The House voted to strike out the enacting clause, thus rendering the bill moot. The vote divided labor stalwarts. Pro-union representative Frank Buchanan (D, Illinois) joined open shop champion Thomas Blanton (D, Texas) in voting to strike out the clause.[81]

Unemployment insurance made no more headway in the states. The first such bill, drafted by the Massachusetts branch of the AALL and endorsed by the state labor federation, was introduced in the state legislature in 1915. A nine-member Special Commission on Social Insurance in 1916 endorsed the Massachusetts bill in principle but declared that the time was not yet "ripe" for

state action. It recommended instead that businessmen set up their own independent reserves.[82] Pressure from the AFL hierarchy helped defeat unemployment insurance legislation in Illinois and New York in the mid-1920s.[83]
Andrews, Commons, and their allies kept an unemployment insurance bill alive
in Wisconsin, but they could not persuade the legislature to enact it despite several efforts in the 1920s.

Discouraged AALL reformers found some employers more willing than
government to experiment with unemployment insurance. Henry Dennison,
the Massachusetts tag manufacturer, first discussed the possibility of an
employer unemployment reserve fund with Andrews in early 1915, when
Massachusetts reformers were developing plans for state unemployment insurance legislation. Dennison, both an AALL member and president of the Taylor Society (a group dedicated to spreading the principles of scientific management), initiated the first employer-funded plan for jobless insurance in the
United States in 1916. His company contributed nearly $150,000 to the fund
by 1920. When his employment stabilization plan and insurance reserves
seemed to work magnificently during the 1920–22 depression, Dennison
took it as a validation of his technique and the potential for employer self-
stabilization.[84]

Other employers followed Dennison's lead. The first employer to copy the
Dennison plan was Morris Leeds, head of Leeds and Northrup Company (and
president of the open shop Philadelphia Metal Manufacturers' Association from
1923 to 1930). General Electric, the largest firm to establish unemployment
insurance before 1932, managed the most comprehensive private plan. Fourteen
employers in Rochester, New York, lead by Eastman Kodak, also established a
notable plan. Between 1916 and 1934, about two dozen company unemployment insurance plans were in effect. These plans covered about sixty thousand
workers.[85] Leeds, Ernest Draper of Hills Brothers, and Sam Lewisohn, president
of the American Management Association, became key national advocates for
employer reserve funds for unemployment.[86]

Commons, Andrews, and their allies reinvented unemployment insurance
for an American economy in which employers largely had won the battle for
labor market control. The Wisconsin group originally sought a bill modeled on
the British plan, including contributions by workers. Trade unions persuaded
Commons and his allies to remove the employee contributions. The bill introduced in the Wisconsin legislature in 1921 depended fully on employer financing, much like workers' compensation. During the 1920s, the Wisconsin
reformers decisively rejected the British social insurance models they once
embraced. Like Commons, British unemployment insurance expert William
Beveridge believed that employers' tax burdens should vary with their "experi-

ence" in creating joblessness. Beveridge, though, meant that an *industry* should bear collective responsibility for its performance. This burden was easier to bear abroad, where employers encountered fewer obstacles to collusion. Beveridge believed that social insurance should be funded by business, labor, and the state, so that each had a stake in protecting the integrity of the program.[87] Commons believed that each large enterprise should bear the cost of the unemployment it generated and that each individual company above a certain size should be required to hold reserve funds to compensate its unemployed. Unemployment insurance could only succeed by forcing financiers, boards of directors, and managers to take the costs of joblessness into account, by forcing "a larger productivity of industry" (that is, individual large firms).[88]

The performance of the European programs in the 1920s strengthened reformers' resolve to take a different approach. Great Britain modified its system and extended benefits indefinitely. Contributions now had little relation to benefits. Both the German and British systems encountered severe financial crises in the 1920s. AALL reformers, business leaders, and the AFL agreed that the British system resulted in an undesirable dole. The *American Labor Legislation Review* approved of Great Britain's ability to provide for the jobless, but criticized the British system because it provided no inducement for business to prevent unemployment.[89]

The Depression put unemployment insurance, along with other unemployment remedies, back on the American policy agenda. By 1930, the AALL produced an alternative "American Plan for Unemployment Reserve Funds" suited to "the conditions prevailing in this country" (the NAM protested to Andrews that the AALL had twisted the meaning of its open shop "American Plan" slogan from the early 1920s). Employers would contribute to fully fund this reserve scheme, which the AALL explicitly did *not* term "unemployment insurance." The plan would strictly limit the amount and duration of benefit payments, and beneficiaries would be given a work test. Full employer financing relieved state governments of the need to devote general revenues to social insurance.[90]

In Wisconsin, a younger group of Commons's students designed a plan that ensured even more business control of unemployment compensation. Drawing lessons from the politically successful workers' compensation campaigns, General Electric, and a successful private plan in the Chicago garment industry, the students developed a bill that made each *individual employer* responsible for joblessness. The Wisconsin plan simply required employers to maintain reserve funds to tide over their workers during periods of involuntary idleness. Employers would contribute until the fund reached a certain level, and then they could stop contributing. If they prevented joblessness, employers would benefit. If instead they failed to prevent joblessness, their unemployment reserve funds would be depleted, penalizing them, in effect, for creating unemployment.[91]

For Commons, the Wisconsin experience-rating proposal constituted "extraordinarily an individualistic and capitalistic scheme" that offered "the employer a profit to the extent that he succeeds in preventing unemployment." The Wisconsin proposal, a logical extension of workers' compensation principles to unemployment insurance, clearly was superior to the "socialistic and paternalistic" schemes of Europe.[92] The Senate Committee on Education and Labor held extensive hearings in 1928 and 1929 on the unemployment problem. This Senate committee rejected the British approach and endorsed individual employer reserves. Commons testified before this committee at length, and the committee's findings cited Commons's comments and philosophy extensively.[93]

Though opposed by employers and only grudgingly approved by the state federation of labor, Wisconsin legislators considered the bill more seriously as the Depression deepened. The Wisconsin Legislative Interim Committee on Unemployment, set up in 1931 to consider the bill for a special legislative session, endorsed the bill. The committee acknowledged that the state could hardly subject its industries to a more far-reaching plan (see the quote at the beginning of this chapter). To weaken employer opposition further, supporters amended the bill so that the program would not go into effect unless Wisconsin employers failed to cover two hundred thousand workers with voluntary plans by mid-1933. The legislature enacted a somewhat weaker version in 1932. Some Wisconsin employers expressed gratitude that they had escaped the more ambitious plans being considered in other states.[94]

The enactment of the Wisconsin law fueled interest in unemployment insurance elsewhere, but no state enacted a similar law until 1935. New York governor Franklin D. Roosevelt called an Interstate Conference of Governors in the northeast to study the unemployment relief measures in light of the interstate competition problem. The interstate conference endorsed the principle of the Commons approach to unemployment reserves. Roosevelt endorsed an unemployment insurance bill based on individual employer reserves in 1932. Three years later, New York, Massachusetts, and Ohio enacted unemployment insurance programs. Employers in Pennsylvania, Illinois, and New Jersey held similar proposals in check in those states until after the approval of the federal Social Security Act of 1935.[95]

The Depression, meanwhile, was shattering both the employer reserve model and the AFL's resistance to unemployment compensation. Henry Dennison had guaranteed employment to his workers in 1928. By 1932, however, Dennison had permanently laid off hundreds of workers and canceled the unemployment insurance program. The General Electric and Rochester plans, though surviving the Depression, reduced guarantees and raised employee premiums.[96] Organized labor's opposition to public unemployment insurance cracked under the pressure of mounting unemployment. The Machinists endorsed unemployment insurance as early as 1927. State labor federations in New York, Pennsylvania, Minnesota, Montana, Utah, Rhode Island (in 1930), Massachusetts (1931), and Ohio (1932) also endorsed it. The AFL leadership held fast against this turning tide. Even Gerald Swope of General Electric lobbied the AFL leaders to alter their opposition to the program. When the UMWA endorsed the idea in 1932, AFL endorsement became virtually inevitable. Old school AFL strategists such as John Frey still warned that unemployment insurance would dilute incentives for workers to join unions. At its 1932 convention, though, the AFL endorsed unemployment insurance as it had endorsed federal legislation establishing the thirty-hour week.[97]

By the time Franklin D. Roosevelt was inaugurated, even conservative business groups were conceding the inevitability of unemployment insurance. Now reformers' disagreements about program details became more apparent. Senator Robert Wagner, Ohio reformers, and their allies explicitly rejected the conservatism of the Wisconsin approach in favor of higher benefits and pooled funds that would spread the risks of unemployment. They pressed for unemployment insurance rather than unemployment reserves. In early 1934, Wagner had introduced a bill that proposed a new federal tax on employers, a tax that would be offset if their states created acceptable unemployment compensation laws. The plan's authors designed this approach to maximize the likelihood that the Supreme Court would rule the plan within the constitutional authority of the federal government.

Roosevelt, opposed to any British-style dole, turned over the issue to the Committee on Economic Security (CES). These pragmatic architects of the Social Security Act of 1935 developed a plan that they thought could survive the shoals of interstate competition, the limitations of national authority, and reformer disagreements. Roosevelt insisted on a state-based plan that left decisions about coverage, tax rates, and benefit levels in the hands of the states. Responding to Roosevelt's preferences, the committee produced a plan for a federal–state unemployment insurance system, with the Wagner tax offset plan included as an incentive for the states to enact unemployment compensation laws. Both Edwin Witte (the executive director of the CES) and Secretary of Labor Frances Perkins (the chair of the CES) viewed the Commons prevention approach through "experience rating" as politically and constitutionally expedient. The prevention approach would elicit less opposition and had "become so entrenched that anything remotely resembling the original British or German Act was almost out of the question." To help ensure its constitutionality, the federal government would permit states full freedom to implement the employer reserves plan or the unemployment insurance plan. There would be no national benefit standards. Congress approved unemployment insurance along these lines in 1935.[98]

The unemployment insurance title of the Social Security Act permitted the states to exercise virtually unlimited discretion over eligibility, benefit levels and the duration of benefits, waiting periods, and financing. The Senate made certain that the states could impose a zero tax rate on individual employers but prohibited state experiments with other forms of experience rating, for example, by industry. Given the possibility of complete exemption from state unemployment insurance taxes, employers lobbied states for experience rating. Fear of interstate economic competition shaped the states' implementation of unemployment insurance from the start. Had the Social Security Act not withstood the Supreme Court test, state legislators had provided that the unemployment insurance laws of California, New Hampshire, and Massachusetts would be discontinued automatically.[99] All the states adopted unemployment insurance by the end of 1937. Most included a provision for experience rating, and eventually all did.[100] The states and their Congressional representatives have effectively resisted proposals to nationalize unemployment benefit standards and rules ever since.[101]

WORK INSURANCE AND EMPLOYER PREROGATIVES

The United States provides work insurance, in effect, by requiring employers to compensate workers for injuries and joblessness. This unique approach has given American employers exceptional influence over the funding of work insurance and the validity of claims for benefits. The battle between the union shop and the open shop, and the limits of American political institutions, doomed more ambitious plans for work insurance. The AFL's union shop strategy evolved into fatal opposition to health and unemployment insurance. By the time the AFL decisively came around to support unemployment insurance, the work insurance agenda was dominated by plans that were deferential to employers and hypersensitive to interstate competition. This agenda became institutionalized in state law, and state law then became national law. As economist Paul Douglas observed during the New Deal, interstate economic competition "restrained the more progressive states from pioneering [in social insurance] as they would have liked and kept the country as a whole closer to the legal conditions in the less progressive states."[102]

Its unusual approach to work insurance constituted the final element of a uniquely American approach to governing labor markets. Instead of decisively supplanting employers' labor market prerogatives, the United States adapted policy to protect these prerogatives. Put another way, the United States modernized, rather than broke with, the nineteenth-century approach to governing labor markets. This set the United States on a unique labor market policy path from which it has not deviated since.

NOTES

1. Wisconsin Legislative Interim Committee on Unemployment, *Report* (Madison: Wisconsin Industrial Commission, 1931), 41–42.

2. Crystal Eastman, *Work Accidents and the Law* (New York: Charities Publication Committee, 1910); Ross M. Robertson and Gary M. Walton, *History of the American Economy* (New York: Harcourt Brace Jovanovich, 1979), 326.

3. U.S. Industrial Commission, *Final Report*, vol. 19 (Washington, D.C.: Government Printing Office, 1902), 932–39; Lindley D. Clark, *The Legal Liability of Employers for Injuries to Their Employees in the United States*, U.S. Bureau of Labor Statistics Bulletin 74 (January 1908): 95. Earl R. Beckner pointed out that Illinois courts limited the reach of the fellow servant rule beginning about 1880; Beckner, *A History of Labor Legislation in Illinois* (Chicago: University of Chicago Press, 1929), 431.

4. John R. Commons and John B. Andrews, *Principles of Labor Legislation*, (New York: Harper and Brothers, 1916), 358–62.

5. Robert Asher, "Failure and Fulfillment: Agitation for Employers' Liability Legislation and the Origins of Workmen's Compensation in New York State, 1876–1910," *Labor History* 24 (Spring 1983): 198–222. See also Harry Weiss, "Employers' Liability and Workmen's Compensation," in *History of Labor in the United States*, 4 vols., ed. John R. Commons et al. (New York: Macmillan, 1935), 3: 564–69; James Weinstein, *The Corporate Ideal in the Liberal State: 1900–1918* (Boston: Beacon, 1968), 43–44; Irving Yellowitz, *Labor and the Progressive Movement in New York State, 1897–1916* (Ithaca, N.Y.: Cornell University Press, 1965), 107–9; I. M. Rubinow, *Social Insurance, with Special Reference to American Conditions* (New York: Henry Holt, 1913), 156; Melvin I. Urofsky, "State Courts and Protective Legislation during the Progressive Era: A Reevaluation," *Journal of American History* 72 (June 1985): 85. Asher provides the list of states that substantially limited employers' defenses against tort action by injured workers. Montana (in 1903 and 1905) limited employers' defenses in the mining industry, and Nevada (1907) limited employers' defenses in mining and mills.

6. "An Act Granting to Certain Employees of the United States the Right to Receive from It Compensation for Injuries Sustained in the Course of Their Employment," May 30, 1908; see *Statutory History of the United States: Income Security*, ed. Robert B. Stevens (New York: Chelsea House, 1970), 38–43; *Congressional Record*, May 29, 1908:

7191. Though Congress strengthened the compensation law for federal employees in 1916, it did not act on a 1912 recommendation from an Employers' Liability and Workmen's Compensation Commission to establish a workers' compensation program for common carriers and the District of Columbia.

7. U.S. Commissioner of Labor, *Compulsory Insurance in Germany*, 4th Special Report (Washington, D.C.: GPO, 1893); Testimony of P. H. Logan, Chicago Trades Assembly, and W. H. Foster, Cincinnati Trades Assembly, in U.S. Congress, Senate Committee on Education and Labor, *Report of the Committee of the Senate on the Relations between Labor and Capital*, 47th Cong., 2nd sess., 4 vols. (Washington, D.C.: GPO, 1885), 1: 406–7, 584; Robert W. Ozanne, *The Labor Movement in Wisconsin: A History* (Madison: State Historical Society of Wisconsin, 1984), 123; Asher, "Failure and Fulfillment"; Yellowitz, *Labor and the Progressive Movement in New York State*, 107–8.

8. Asher, "Failure and Fulfillment," 203.

9. Joseph L. Castrovinci, "Prelude to Welfare Capitalism: The Role of Business in the Enactment of Workmen's Compensation in Illinois, 1905–1912," *Social Service Review* 50 (March 1976): 80–102; Beckner, *A History of Labor Legislation in Illinois*, 433–39. On the Wisconsin State Federation of Labor, which passed a resolution supporting workers compensation in 1894, see Ozanne, *The Labor Movement in Wisconsin: A History*, 123.

10. Rubinow, *Social Insurance*, 157.

11. Thomas I. Parkinson, "Problems and Progress of Workmen's Compensation Legislation," *American Labor Legislation Review* 1 (January 1911): 55–71; Hace Sorel Tishler, *Self-Reliance and Social Security, 1870–1917* (Port Washington, N.Y.: Kennikat Press, 1971), 108–9. Massachusetts passed a commission-endorsed law in 1908 enabling employers and employees to enter into contracts with fixed rates for industries, but the commission rejected a compulsory insurance law.

12. Castrovinci, "Prelude to Welfare Capitalism," 272; Tishler, *Self-Reliance and Social Security*, 117; F. S. Baldwin, "Advantages and Disadvantages of State Funds in Workmen's Compensation," *American Labor Legislation Review* 6 (1916): 3–10; Weiss, "Employers' Liability and Workmen's Compensation," 574.

13. Weinstein, *The Corporate Ideal in the Liberal State*, 45–46.

14. Don D. Lescohier, "Working Conditions," in *History of Labor Legislation in the United States*, 3: 367–68.

15. Weinstein, *The Corporate Ideal in the Liberal State*, 45–56.

16. John R. Commons, *Myself: The Autobiography of John R. Commons* (Madison: University of Wisconsin Press, 1963), 141–43.

17. Daniel Nelson, *Unemployment Insurance: The American Experience, 1915–1935* (Madison: University of Wisconsin Press, 1969), 105–6.

18. David A. Moss, *Socializing Security: Progressive-Era Economists and the Origins of American Social Policy* (Cambridge: Harvard University Press, 1996), 121–22; Tishler, *Self-Reliance and Social Security*, 115.

19. National Association of Manufacturers, in *Proceedings* of the Fifteenth Annual Convention, 1910: 207; hereafter cited as *NAM Proceedings*, [date].

20. Henry Rosenfeld, in *NAM Proceedings*, 1910, 174–75. See also John Kirby, "A Year's Work of the Association, *American Industries* 11, no. 1 (June 1911), 12; Weinstein, *The Corporate Ideal in the Liberal State*, 47.

21. "[T]he waste, delay, and harmful bitterness engendered by litigating claims for personal injury in a legal system based upon fault as the sole ground of recovery justify and require that the state in the public interest make other equitable provision for the speedy adjustment of such controversies." Ferdinand C. Schwedtman and James A. Emery, *Accident Prevention and Relief* (New York: National Association of Manufacturers, 1911), 259–60. Manufacturers assumed the leadership of the drive for worker's compensation in Illinois, for example; see Castrovinci, "Prelude to Welfare Capitalism."

22. "Relief Tendencies in the United States," *American Industries* 12 (August 1911): 19–21. See also Schwedtman and Emery, *Accident Prevention and Relief*, 263–66; "Accident Prevention and Relief," *American Industries* 11 (February 1911): 11.

23. Yellowitz, *Labor and the Progressive Movement in New York State*, 110–11.

24. Weiss, "Employers' Liability and Workmen's Compensation," 572–73. On the link between the defeat of employer liability reform and labor's interest in workers' compensation, see Beckner, *A History of Labor Legislation in Illinois*, 434–35; Castrovinci, "Prelude to Welfare Capitalism"; Yellowitz, *Labor and the Progressive Movement in New York State*, 109–10.

25. William B. Wilson in American Federation of Labor, *Proceedings* of the Twenty-ninth Annual Convention, 1909: 315; hereafter, cited as *AFL Proceedings*, [date].

26. "Relief Tendencies in the United States."

27. Thomas I. Parkinson, "Problems and Progress of Workmen's Compensation Legislation," *American Labor Legislation Review* 1 (January 1911): 60.

28. *Ives v. South Buffalo Railway Co.*, 201 N.Y. 271 (March 24, 1911); Lindley D. Clark and Martin C. Frinke, Jr., *Workmen's Compensation Legislation of the United States and Canada*, BLS Bulletin 272 (Washington, D.C.: GPO, 1921), 75.

29. Clark and Frinke, *Workmen's Compensation Legislation of the United States and Canada*; Weiss, "Employers' Liability and Workmen's Compensation," 575–77; *Borgnis v. Falk Co.*, 147 Wis. 327, 133 N.W. 209 (1911).

30. Clark and Frinke, *Workmen's Compensation Legislation of the United States and Canada*; John B. Andrews, "Congress at Last Enacts Compensation Law for Wage-Earners in the District of Columbia!" *American Labor Legislation Review* 18 (June 1928): 139–43.

31. Weiss, "Employers' Liability and Workmen's Compensation," 571–75; Robert Eyestone, *From Social Issues to Social Policy* (New York: Wiley, 1978), 129–33.

32. Patrick D. Reagan, "The Ideology of Social Harmony and Efficiency: Workmen's Compensation in Ohio, 1904–1919," *Ohio History* 90 (Autumn 1981): 317–31.

33. I. M. Rubinow, *Social Insurance, with Special Reference to American Conditions* (New York: Henry Holt and Company, 1913), 184.

34. *AFL Proceedings*, 1920: 424.

35. U.S. Bureau of Labor Statistics, *Workmen's Compensation Legislation of the United States and Canada*, BLS Bulletin 272 (Washington: GPO, 1921), 17–19.

36. *Monthly Labor Review* 12 (January 1921): 179; (April, 1921): 113.

37. U.S. Census Bureau, *Historical Statistics on State and Local Government Finances, 1902–1953, State and Local Government Special Studies,* No. 38 (Washington, D.C.: GPO, 1955), 19. While most of these insurance trust funds reflected workmen's compensation programs, not all did. Some plains states, for example, had instituted public hail insurance programs. Although Ann Shola Orloff and Theda Skocpol argue that state workmen's compensation programs involved "little or no public spending" and in most places "merely required businesses to insure their employees against injuries" through private insurers or self-insurance," these figures belie that assertion; see Ann Shola Orloff and Theda Skocpol, "Why Not Equal Protection? Explaining the Politics of Public Social Spending in Britain, 1900–1911, and the United States, 1880s–1920," *American Sociological Review* 49 (December 1984): 736.

38. *New York Central Rail Company v. White,* 243 U.S. 188 (1917); *Mountain Timber Co. v. State of Washington,* 243 U.S. 219 (1917); *Hawkins v. Bleakly,* 243 U.S. 210 (1917).

39. Weiss, "Employers' Liability and Workmen's Compensation," 579, 584, 589, 597.

40. Weiss, "Employers' Liability and Workmen's Compensation," 593–94.

41. Price V. Fishback and Shawn Everett Kantor, "The Political Economy of Workers' Compensation Benefit Levels, 1910–1930," *Explorations in Economic History* 35 (1998): 109–39.

42. Weiss, "Employers' Liability and Workmen's Compensation," 579, 584, 589, 594, 599–600; quote 610.

43. The AALL won an early legislative victory when Congress in 1912 placed a high tax on white phosphorus matches and forbade their importation after mid-1914. This measure aimed to eliminate "phossy" jaw, a "loathsome" industrial disease that resulted from producing phosphorus matches. Commons and Andrews, *Principles of Labor Legislation,* 297; Lescohier, "Working Conditions," 360–67; Moss, *Socializing Security,* 79–96.

44. John B. Andrews, quoted by Moss in *Socializing Security,* 132.

45. Henry R. Seager, "Plan for a Health Insurance Act," *American Labor Legislation Review* 6 (March 1916): 21–25.

46. "Tendencies in Health Insurance Legislation," *American Labor Legislation Review* 6 (June 1916): 140–41.

47. Henry R. Seager, "Plan for a Health Insurance Act," "Tendencies in Health Insurance Legislation" [chart], and "Health Insurance: Tentative Draft of an Act," in *American Labor Legislation Review* 6 (1916): 22–25, 140–41, 238–68.

48. F. Spenser Baldwin, "Advantages and Disadvantages of State Funds in Workmen's Compensation," *American Labor Legislation Review* 6 (March 1916): 3–10.

49. *Report of the Social Insurance Commission of the State of California* (Sacramento, Calif.: State Printing Office, 1917), 280–83.

50. Tishler, *Self-Reliance and Social Security,* 169–73; Moss, *Socializing Security,* 141.

51. "Second National Conference of Health Insurance Commissioners," *American Labor Legislation Review* 8 (1918): 133–35.

52. *AFL Proceedings,* 1914: 66–68.

53. Eugene Lyman Fisk, M.D., "Periodic Physical Examination of Employes, Its Economic and Social Value," *American Industries* 15 (June 1915): 22–23; Magnus W.

Alexander, "The Physician in Industry," *American Industries* 16 (April 1916): 15–17. Note that the Alexander article appeared in the month before Gompers's attack on compulsory health insurance.

54. Samuel Gompers, December 8, 1916, in U.S. Bureau of Labor Statistics, *Proceedings of the Conference on Social Insurance,* Bulletin 212 (Washington, D.C.: GPO, 1917), 846.

55. Samuel Gompers, "Labor vs. Its Barnacles," in *American Federationist* 13 (May 1916): 270–74. See also "Voluntary Social Insurance vs. Compulsory," *American Federationist* 23 (August 1916): 680.

56. U.S. Commissioner of Labor, *Workmen's Insurance and Benefit Funds in the United States,* Twenty-third Annual Report (Washington, D.C.: GPO, 1909), 23, 31.

57. Gompers, "Voluntary Social Insurance vs. Compulsory," 335–36.

58. Gompers, "Voluntary Social Insurance vs. Compulsory," 350.

59. Odin W. Anderson, *The Uneasy Equilibrium: Public and Private Financing of Health Services in the United States, 1875–1965* (New Haven, Conn.: College and University Press, 1968), 76; Roy Lubove, *The Struggle for Social Security, 1900–1935* (Cambridge: Harvard University Press, 1968), 84–86; Moss, *Socializing Security,* 153.

60. Compare Edson S. Lott, "Fallacies of Compulsory Social Insurance," *American Industries* 17 (January 1917): 18–19, 45; A. Parker Nevin, "Un-American Tendencies of Compulsory Health Insurance," *American Industries* 17 (February 1917): 13–14. On the NCF, see Moss, *Socializing Security,* 145.

61. U.S. Bureau of Labor Statistics, *Welfare Work for Employees in Industrial Establishments in the United States,* Bulletin 250 (Washington, D.C.: GPO, 1919), 14–36.

62. Tishler, *Self-Reliance and Social Security,* 181–83.

63. Massachusetts Special Commission on Social Insurance, *Report,* January 15, 1918 (Boston: Wright and Potter Co., State Printers, 1918), 29–32.

64. Massachusetts Special Commission on Social Insurance, *Report,* 22.

65. Ronald Numbers, *Almost Persuaded: American Physicians and Compulsory Health Insurance, 1912–1920* (Baltimore: Johns Hopkins University Press, 1978), 78; Paul Starr, *The Social Transformation of American Medicine* (New York: Basic, 1982), 252.

66. Lubove, *The Struggle for Social Security,* 26, 82–84.

67. Starr, *The Social Transformation of American Medicine,* 102–16.

68. Ronald Numbers, *Compulsory Health Insurance: The Continuing American Debate* (Westport, Conn.: Greenwood, 1982), 6; Numbers, *Almost Persuaded;* Starr, *The Social Transformation of American Medicine,* 252–57.

69. Moss, *Socializing Security,* 153–54.

70. Paul Douglas, *In the Fullness of Time* (New York: Harcourt Brace Jovanovich, 1971), 68.

71. Elizabeth Lewis Otey, *Employers' Welfare Work,* U.S. Bureau of Labor Statistics, Bulletin 123 (Washington, D.C.: GPO, 1913); Edward Berkowitz and Kim McQuaid, *Creating the Welfare State: The Political Economy of Twentieth-Century Reform* (New York: Praeger, 1980).

72. John R. Commons, *Industrial Goodwill* (McGraw-Hill, 1919), 89–90.

73. John R. Commons, "A Reconstruction Health Program," in *The Survey* 42 (September 6, 1919): 799.

74. Stuart D. Brandes, *American Welfare Capitalism, 1880–1940* (Chicago: University of Chicago, 1976), 23–28; David Brody, *Workers in Industrial America: Essays on the Twentieth Century Struggle*, 2nd ed. (New York: Oxford University Press, 1993), 48–66; Neil J. Mitchell, *The Generous Corporation* (New Haven: Yale University Press, 1989).

75. Lizabeth Cohen, *Making a New Deal: Industrial Workers in Chicago, 1919–1939* (New York: Cambridge University Press, 1990), 159–211.

76. "The Prevention of Unemployment," 190; Nelson, *Unemployment Insurance*, 6–10. On the role of unemployment insurance in strengthening European trade unions, see Selig Perlman, *A Theory of the Labor Movement* (New York: Macmillan, 1928), 90–91; Bo Rothstein, "Labor-Market Institutions and Working-Class Strength," in *Structuring Politics: Historical Institutionalism in Comparative Analysis*, ed. Sven Steinmo, Kathleen Thelen, and Frank Longstreth (New York: Cambridge University Press, 1992), 33–56; Bruce Western, *Between Class and Market: Postwar Unionism in the Capitalist Democracies* (Princeton: Princeton University Press, 1997).

77. "The Prevention of Unemployment," 189–90.

78. Nelson, *Unemployment Insurance*, 17.

79. Gompers, "Voluntary Social Insurance vs. Compulsory," 677; Nelson, *Unemployment Insurance*, 65–67, 77. By 1928, less than a dozen international unions had adopted unemployment relief plans; all but four abandoned those plans by the start of the Depression. Bryce M. Stewart and his associates explained the American unions' lag in adopting unemployment funds partially in terms of the "fact that the American labor movement has not yet entirely emerged from its militant stage" and that battles for wage and hour concessions absorbed resources that could have been used for "less immediate benefits"; Stewart, *Unemployment Benefits in the United States: Their Plans and Their Setting* (New York: Industrial Relations Counselors, 1930), 84–85.

80. Nelson, *Unemployment Insurance*, 71, 107; Alexander Keyssar, *Out of Work: The First Century of Unemployment in Massachusetts* (New York: Cambridge University Press, 1986), 214–15.

81. *Congressional Record*, January 16, 1918: 903–7.

82. Nelson, *Unemployment Insurance*, 17–18; Keyssar, *Out of Work*, 276–80.

83. Nelson, *Unemployment Insurance*, 76.

84. Nelson, *Unemployment Insurance*, 41–42, 50–52.

85. Nelson, *Unemployment Insurance*, 47–63.

86. Sam A. Lewisohn, Ernest G. Draper, John R. Commons, and Don D. Lescohier, *Can Business Prevent Unemployment?* (New York: Knopf, 1925); Irving Bernstein, *The Lean Years* (Baltimore: Penguin, 1966), 489–90; Nelson, *Unemployment Insurance*, 29–46.

87. Harris, *William Beveridge*, 356–57, 391–92.

88. John R. Commons, "The True Scope of Unemployment Insurance," *American Labor Legislation Review* 16 (March 1926): 33–44.

89. Nelson, *Unemployment Insurance*, 23, 155; Leo Wolman, "Unemployment Insurance for the United States," *American Labor Legislation Review* 21 (March 1931): 17–25; Herbert Feldman, "New Methods in the Stabilization of Unemployment," *American Labor Legislation Review* 16 (March 1926). See also Jerrold Waltman, *Copying Other Nations' Policies: Two American Case Studies* (Cambridge: Schenkman, 1980), 31.

90. "An American Plan for Unemployment Reserve Funds," *American Labor Legislation Review* 20 (September 1930): 349–56; Bernstein, *The Lean Years*, 491.

91. Nelson, *Unemployment Insurance*, 118–21; Sanford M. Jacoby, "Employers and the Welfare State: The Role of Marion B. Folsom," *Journal of American History* (September 1993): 525–56.

92. John R. Commons, "The Groves Unemployment Insurance Law," *American Labor Legislation Review* 22 (March 1932): 9; U.S. Senate Committee on Education and Labor, Hearings on *Unemployment in the United States* (Washington, D.C.: GPO, 1929), xiii.

93. Senate Hearings on *Unemployment in the United States*, iii–xv, 212–44.

94. Nelson, *Unemployment Insurance*, 122–28.

95. Nelson, *Unemployment Insurance*, 162–91.

96. Nelson, *Unemployment Insurance*, 52–53, 61–62.

97. Bernstein, *The Lean Years*, 347–55; *AFL Proceedings*, 1932: 325–60; Nelson, *Unemployment Insurance*, 155–59, 183, 189–90; Kenneth Casebeer, "The Workers' Unemployment Insurance Bill: American Social Wage, Labor Organization, and Legal Ideology," in *Labor Law in America: Historical and Critical Essays*, ed. Christopher J. Tomlins and Andrew J. King (Baltimore: Johns Hopkins University Press, 1992), 231–59.

98. Nelson, *Unemployment Insurance*, 197–220, quote 219.

99. Paul H. Douglas, *Social Security in the United States: An Analysis and Appraisal of the Federal Social Security Act* (New York: Whittlesey House, 1936), 252; Raymond Munts, "Unemployment Compensation in Wisconsin: Origins and Performance," in *Unemployment Insurance: The Second Half Century*, ed. W. Lee Hansen and James F. Byers (Madison: University of Wisconsin Press, 1990), 395–410.

100. Edwin E. Witte, *The Development of the Social Security Act* (Madison: University of Wisconsin Press, 1962), 115–53.

101. For early examples of the debate over nationalizing unemployment insurance, see Wilbur J. Cohen, "Need for a Uniform National System of Unemployment Compensation," *American Labor Legislation Review* 32 (March 1942): 36–40; Edwin Witte, "'Federalization' of Unemployment Compensation?" *American Labor Legislation Review* 32 (March 1942): 41–48.

102. Paul H. Douglas, *Social Security in the United States*, 5.

10

THE AMERICAN MODEL OF
LABOR MARKET POLICY

In the industrializing nations in the 1890s, employers could hire, fire, and set the terms of employment with little government interference. Governments abroad began to limit employers' prerogatives substantially in the early twentieth century. These governments began to weave labor regulations, trade union protections, public labor market management, and work insurance into a fabric of worker protections. Though the United States also implemented new initiatives in each of these areas, in none of them did its public policy decisively break with the principle of employer sovereignty inherited from the nineteenth century. On the eve of the Great Depression, American employers exercised more control over labor markets than did their counterparts elsewhere, and American government was more disengaged from the labor market than governments abroad.

This policy has endured despite important challenges to employer prerogatives in the New Deal. By the 1980s and 1990s, American labor market policy had become noted for the exceptional freedom it afforded employers. For some, the American style of labor market governance became a model worth emulating. The success of American labor market policy at the end of the twentieth century, however, was considerably more ambiguous than these enthusiasts allow.

SUMMARY OF THE ARGUMENT

The systematic study detailed in this book shows how American labor market policy became exceptional. By the early 1920s, American labor regulation remained a patchwork of limited protections, uneven laws, and poor enforcement, lacking basic national standards even for child labor. American employers had considerable legal room to evade unions, while unions had very narrow power to challenge employers. Government administered labor markets

257

only at their margins and failed to establish the institutions that served as the foundation for a more active labor market policy abroad. The United States lagged behind other nations in instituting work insurance, and when it did so its program provided for an extraordinary degree of employer control.

American employers lost many individual policy skirmishes. Reform movements, workplace tragedies, or widespread joblessness sometimes created unstoppable momentum for legal protections for workers. Employers could not always block government from enacting programs they opposed, especially in the most industrialized states. Employers themselves advocated that the government step in to inhibit competition or offer subsidies. American employers, though, largely won the war for the control of labor markets by the early 1920s, and they enjoyed unrivaled freedom in labor markets as the Depression overwhelmed the world economy. Labor market programs since 1932 have sometimes challenged employer prerogatives and the institutions that supported them. With few exceptions, however, American worker protections since 1932 have either posed a more limited challenge to employer freedom than programs abroad or failed to withstand erosion during periods of retrenchment.

American labor market policy developed so distinctly because America's singular policymaking institutions forced labor leaders, employers, reformers, and politicians to invent distinct strategies for labor market control. These institutions made it much more difficult for American business, labor, and government to cooperate for mutual gain as extensively as did their counterparts abroad. Competitive American federalism and the fragmentation of power made it difficult for trade unions to count on public policy to advance their power in the workplace, protect workers who were difficult to organize, build an inclusive trade union movement, or establish a political party that could advance labor's policy agenda. Federal officials lacked the authority and the opportunity to manage these fundamental conflicts and to broker more harmonious labor relations. By 1900 the American Federation of Labor (AFL) had defined labor's goal as the direct control of the terms of American employment and labor's means as the union shop.

As unions pursued their goals more inflexibly, employer resistance to unions stiffened. Employers defined their goal as the defense of their prerogatives. The vacuum of political authority and the economic rivalry of the states encouraged the creation of large corporations that could unilaterally dictate the terms of employment. Smaller firms, caught in an economic vice between the large corporations and militant labor, vehemently turned against organized labor and its policy agenda. After 1900, leaders of the AFL and expert policy reformers gradually ceded ground to employers. Employer strength solidified. Corporations developed forms of private labor market governance that became influential in public policy design. Politicians gradually adjusted their electoral strategies to the reality of employer dominance in American labor markets. When labor and government again challenged employers' prerogatives in the New Deal, employers had the strength and institutional base to limit or outlast serious challenges to their prerogatives.

America's political institutions permitted no public official to work with reformers and exercise the leadership in labor market policy that Prime Minister David Lloyd George had exercised in Great Britain. Congress and the federal system frustrated Theodore Roosevelt's ambitions for a national corporate policy, very possibly a necessary prelude to the more comprehensive labor market policy laid out in the Progressive Party platform of 1912. Roosevelt and other reformers acknowledged explicitly that federal power could address only a fraction of the labor market reform agenda. Senator Robert La Follette and Labor Secretary William B. Wilson could not dictate labor market policy to Congress. The nation's foremost labor policy expert, John R. Commons, could not create a labor market policy subgovernment—with legislative, executive, and judicial powers—in the form of industrial commissions with sweeping powers to bring coherence to public labor market management. The structure of Congress gave legislators substantial power to resist or support proposals on the basis of their expected impact on the economic advantages of the region they represented.

Political institutions did not *determine* that the United States would be so protective of employer freedom; they simply made it much more difficult for American government to limit employer prerogatives than did governments abroad. Racism, ethnic rivalry, gender roles, and a tradition of cultural liberalism also contributed powerfully to the unique development of American labor market policy. If some circumstances had been different, American labor market policy might have resembled developments abroad more closely. The AFL might have turned to government more readily if tenement house cigar manufacture had been effectively regulated in the 1880s. Different court decisions, particularly those decided by a single-vote majority, could have tempered distrust of the political system. Different mine worker or machinist union leaders might have posed a more effective socialist challenge to Samuel Gompers's AFL leadership in the 1890s or early 1900s. A more moderate Speaker of the House than Joseph Cannon would have acquiesced to Theodore Roosevelt's effort to meet labor halfway between 1904 and 1909.

HOW DID AMERICAN LABOR MARKET
POLICY REMAIN EXCEPTIONAL?

During the Depression, mounting unemployment and an increasing sense of national urgency made fundamental changes in labor market policy politically feasible. Franklin D. Roosevelt's administration took steps to govern American labor markets that were without precedent in peacetime. The New Deal mounted the most formidable challenge to employers' labor market prerogatives in the nation's history, and it produced lasting national labor standards and protections for unions. If ever American labor market policy were to be redirected in a way similar to that of comparable nations, it was in the 1930s.

But the New Deal inherited a legacy of existing institutions, interests, and strategic commitments forged over half a century of policy development. By the early 1950s, long after the New Deal had passed its apogee and after reaction against it had altered its policy legacy, American employers remained exceptionally free to manage labor as they saw fit. They remain so today.

Most New Deal policymakers drew lessons from their personal experiences of the formative years of American labor market policy. Franklin D. Roosevelt, National Recovery Director Hugh Johnson, and Felix Frankfurter had helped manage World War I industrial mobilization. Senator Robert Wagner, AFL president William Green, railroad union lobbyist Donald Richberg, and NAM lobbyist James Emery had played a major role in constructing Progressive Era labor market policy. These leaders sought labor market policy solutions from among a set of alternatives that had been considered for a generation or more and that had been tried in one or more states. The U.S. Employment Service, the Fair Labor Standards Act, and the unemployment provision of the Social Security Act were the descendants of policy ideas that had been gestating for many years.

The National Industrial Recovery Act (NIRA), the most notable anti-Depression measure of the New Deal's first hundred days, revived the possibility of coupling employer cooperation with worker protection. In early 1933, business leaders, particularly the U.S. Chamber of Commerce and Emery of the NAM, persuaded Roosevelt to embrace their proposal for industrial "self-government" as an alternative to the Black bill (proposing a maximum thirty-hour workweek in private employment). This approach, reflecting a natural business impulse to limit competition, permitted businesses in a given industry to administer prices, production, and labor standards in an effort to stabilize each industry. Government would give the employers' standards the force of law. This employers' plan had all the advantages of industrial cartels while involving little or no surrender of employers' labor market sovereignty. The

NIRA essentially imported this idea into its Title I, permitted industries to establish codes of "fair competition" without violating the anti-trust laws.[1]

After proposing legalized employer collusion and firming up business support, the Roosevelt administration next tried to win labor support by adding restrictions on employers to the NIRA. Drawing on the Railway Labor Act and the Norris–La Guardia Act, the administration added a requirement that each industry's code guarantee that "employees have the right to organize and bargain collectively through representatives of their own choosing" and that "employers shall comply with the maximum hours of labor, minimum rates of pay, and other working conditions approved or presented by the President." The AFL and Wagner added the latter's large public works program as Title II of the bill.[2] The NIRA, then, provided for a substantial extension of three types of labor market policy: regulation, trade union law, and active labor market management (a new, federalized U.S. Employment Service already had been approved by Congress).

The NIRA became law, but was not successful. The Supreme Court struck down the NIRA as an unconstitutional interference in intrastate commerce in 1935, though the program already was weakened by disharmony, rivalry, and administrative failures. The NIRA's aspirations for federal labor market governance, however, survived it. The National Labor Relations Act of 1935 and the Fair Labor Standards Act of 1938 were the policy descendants of the NIRA.

The National Labor Relations Act (NLRA) made permanent much of the trade union law incorporated in the NIRA, notably reducing the courts' ability to restrict unions and regularize the process of union organization. As chapter 7 discussed, the NLRA contributed to a dramatic growth in union membership; while the Nazi and Fascist governments were destroying free trade unions, the United States was encouraging them. By 1947, one-third of the nonagricultural labor force was unionized. Two out of five manufacturing workers, more than three out of four miners, and more than seven out of eight construction workers were unionized.[3] But the NLRA designed a labor relations system that was very decentralized and litigious; both of these features made it more difficult to build labor influence at the level of entire industries and the economy as a whole. The Taft–Hartley Act of 1947 amended these and other features of the NLRA in ways that expanded employers' power to battle against unions. Taft–Hartley limited the population of workers who would be permitted to unionize (eliminating, for example, foremen from the potential labor union population). It provided for public supervision of union internal affairs and limitations on strikes in national emergencies. It gave power to the states to prohibit the union shop (section 14b). The National Labor Relations Board, which often had encouraged large bargaining units, now accepted relatively small bargaining units (such as individual stores) that further fragmented worker collective action and protected employer leverage. Most important, section 14b effectively utilized the natural competitiveness of the American states to blunt the expansion of trade unions in the Sunbelt, which would become the nation's fastest growing labor market in the second half of the century. Twelve states had enacted laws banning the union shop by the end of 1947, and eventually all the former Confederate States, along with Arizona, enacted right-to-work laws as authorized by Taft–Hartley. In the large states of Texas and Florida, union density, already well below the national average, declined faster than the national average between the 1950s and the 1980s. The percentage of nonagricultural employees organized in unions peaked in 1953–54 and shrank steadily to less than 14 percent by the end of the century.[4] Since World War II, most continental European laws regulating collective bargaining have been more supportive of unions than has American law.[5]

The Fair Labor Standards Act (FLSA) laid a foundation for the eventual incremental expansion of the workforce covered by federal wage and hour regulations (though it excluded domestic and farm employees, and therefore many female and African American workers). Today the minimum wage law covers most American workers, in contrast to Great Britain and other countries where minimum wages cover only a fraction of the workforce in traditionally "sweated" industries.[6]

Beyond the NLRA and the FLSA, New Deal labor market policy was shaped by the impediments of competitive American federalism and the separation of powers. The New Deal's public works programs were a succession of temporary programs that were designed to minimize interference with the private labor market. These programs disappeared as private employment recovered.[7] In the late 1930s, the federal government evacuated the field of active labor market management by abandoning effective control of employment offices and vocational education. Decentralization of responsibility for unemployment insurance to the states had the effect of heightening the public employment offices' subservience to employers and of reinforcing their narrow and local role in the labor market.[8] Congress dismantled the federal capacity to manage labor markets after the war ended.

In some nations abroad, public employment offices and unemployment insurance systems established by the 1950s had created an institutional framework for active labor market policy and trade union growth. American programs, however, reinforced managerial prerogatives and marginalized government's role in labor markets. By the 1950s, the interest groups representing the employment security offices and the vocational educators (respectively, the Interstate Conference of Employment Security Agencies and the American

Vocational Association) dominated policymaking in their areas of expertise, and they resisted pressures to broaden their established, narrow labor market roles. Responsibility for unemployment insurance made the public employment offices (now often described as employment security offices) more dependent on employers because of the unusual design of the American program. Unemployment insurance also reinforced the offices' narrow role in local labor markets.[9] This focus on limiting the cost of jobless insurance for employers gave states additional tools for gaining advantages over their neighbors in interstate economic competition. State control also meant that southern states could use federal funding to maintain segregation. Public employment offices in the United States played virtually no role in postwar active labor market management, as they did in Sweden and Germany.[10] The United States adopted a fiscal policy characterized by Margaret Weir as "commercial" Keynesianism. This policy aimed at the indirect stimulation of demand without interfering with management rights and was epitomized by the tax cuts promoted by the administration of John F. Kennedy in the early 1960s.[11]

After World War II, corporations reasserted their role as the premier managers of American labor markets. Though Ford, General Motors, and other large employers came to accept a unionized workforce, they also sought to guarantee their position in labor markets by maintaining a decentralized collective bargaining system and limiting its scope. More than two hundred thousand United Auto Workers (UAW) members struck against General Motors, seeking not only wage increases but also a peacetime role in determining the price of the company's products. A determined management defeated the union. Not only did the UAW withdraw its demands for powersharing in the workplace, but General Motors limited collective bargaining to a narrow range of pure and simple issues: wages, hours, and conditions of employment. By 1950, the UAW, the nation's largest militant union, had withdrawn its claim to share in directing General Motors's decisions about investment, pricing, and production. The UAW settled instead for the union shop, high wages, and benefits[12]—a strategic compromise reminiscent of the AFL's strategy of half a century earlier.

The General Motors victory set a pattern for postwar labor relations. Employers refused to engage in industrywide bargaining. Welfare capitalism became accepted in the large manufacturing industries. Trade unions profited from the high wages and generous benefits that companies provided through the union shop. Employers with strong market positions gained a stable and relatively quiescent workforce and a government that generally left them alone to manage their labor forces as they saw fit.[13]

AMERICAN LABOR MARKET POLICY TODAY

Most of the industrialized democracies have transformed the labor market policy established by the Depression into a fabric of extensive protections for workers and limitations on employers' prerogatives.[14] The United States remains exceptional in the limited labor protections its workers possess and the broad scope of employment prerogatives its employers command.

Trade Union Law

American trade union law helps to fragment and decentralize union power, limiting unions ability to contest employers' autonomy on a broad scale. Under the amended NLRA, union representation is decentralized to the workplace level to an unusual degree. This process makes it difficult to expand union gains won in a single plant to workers across an entire industry, and it excludes most American workers from the protections won in union contract negotiations. At the beginning of the 1990s, collective bargaining agreements covered fewer than one in five American workers. This percentage constituted less than half that of any other major OECD (Organization for Economic Cooperation and Development) nation except for Japan. The American legal framework for union representation and collective bargaining has limited the reach of collective bargaining.[15]

Continental European collective bargaining tends to be more centralized and therefore tends to provide security to a large majority of workers. European officials often play a more active role in brokering conflicts between employer associations and unions and in extending agreements industrywide.[16] "Right to work" laws, now in effect in twenty-one states, ban unions from requiring employees to join a union in order to retain employment.[17] Permitted legally to resist and to evade unions, many American employers have redoubled their efforts to evade unionization in recent decades.[18] American employers use complex legal procedures to postpone unionization or grievance settlement indefinitely.[19] While the federal government supervises the process of union organization and requires financial and other reports from unions, American employers, in contrast, need not file reports on the use of consultants hired to help them indirectly resist or break unions. European governments tend to ignore internal union affairs.[20]

Abroad, collective bargaining terms are extended to most of the workforce; unions are the chief determinants of worker security. Indeed, union agreements may substitute entirely for certain kinds of worker protections, such as legal minimum wages.[21] Moreover, trade unions are the most politically important advocates for the adoption, extension, and retention of other labor market policies. Unions also can play a major role in policing policy implementation. Swedish unions, for example, monitor job health and safety regulations, manage unemployment benefits, and contribute to active labor market policy.[22] Labor courts, works councils, and codetermination laws, which institutionalize worker rights and collective bargaining, are common abroad but absent in the United States.[23]

Regulations

The employer's right to hire and fire a worker is most indispensable to his authority. Most industrialized nations limit employers' right to hire and fire workers and provide workers with a basic property right in their jobs. American law, in contrast, still rests on the doctrine of "employment at will." The United States clearly provides less protection against arbitrary dismissal than any other industrialized nation.[24] By the end of the 1970s Canada, France, Sweden, West Germany, the United Kingdom, and Japan had enacted laws that required private employers to notify their employees before a large layoff. The United States did not enact a similar law until 1988. The law required employers to provide much shorter notice than foreign laws, it exempted more employers from the law, and it did not (as other nations) require employers to compensate dismissed employees.[25]

The FLSA established a legal, nationwide minimum wage that covers virtually all workers. The FLSA, however, offers very limited protection for wage earners' purchasing power. In the 1960s, American minimum wage represented 54 percent of the average private sector wage, but this percentage had fallen to 35 percent of average earnings by 1990 (it was restored to about 40 percent of the average private sector wage in the mid-1990s). Belgium, Greece, France, and the Netherlands maintain a minimum wage that is about one-half of the average wage,[26] while in other countries union wage bargains are extended to cover unorganized workers. Other labor market regulations, such as equal opportunity laws, do not interfere with the employers' control of wages above the legal minimum.[27]

The FLSA limit for a normal workweek is much the same in the United States as in other industrialized nations, but other regulations for working hours, vacations, and leaves are largely absent.[28] The United States enacted its Family and Maternal Leave Act in 1993, several years after every other OECD nation, and the U.S. law permitted fewer weeks of leave than did other nations, provided for no income replacement, and permitted employers to deny leave to their highest salaried workers.[29] Some American regulations of the 1960s and 1970s were very strict and even adversarial. Other nations drew on American law in developing employment discrimination and occupational health laws.[30] Insufficient long-term enforcement of all labor market regulations, however, has permitted American employers more latitude than such statutes imply.[31]

Labor Market Management

The United States puts less effort into managing its labor markets than do comparable nations. American workers depend heavily on their own initiative, their employers' efforts, and private labor market institutions to improve their job prospects. The United States provides little direct training for the labor market, despite its tradition of free public schooling and postsecondary education for higher status occupations. There is less coordination between formal secondary education in the United States than in nations such as Germany, Japan, and Sweden. U.S. public support for apprenticeship is minuscule.[32]

Public employment offices play a relatively small part in American labor markets. Some nations (notably Germany, Sweden, and Austria) have largely forbidden, private, fee-charging employment agencies; these private offices play a remarkably large role in labor markets in the United States. Most OECD nations provide for labor participation in office policy through tripartite supervisory or advisory boards, but the United States does not.[33] Of the major industrial democracies, the United States had the least coordination of active labor market programs.[34] In 1995, the federal government funded 163 job training programs, located in ten cabinet departments and several smaller independent agencies.[35]

American policymakers in the 1960s and 1970s claimed that new employment and training programs constituted a more active government approach to labor market management. Despite the bold rhetoric, though, these programs reinforced employer autonomy in American labor markets. U.S. expenditures on these programs never approached the 1 percent of GDP spent on such programs by Sweden and Germany in the 1960s and 1970s and by Great Britain in the late 1980s. While other nations developed additional jobs programs and protections for workers in the late 1970s and early 1980s, the United States cut labor market policy significantly in the same period. By the late 1980s, then, the United States spent substantially less than other comparable nations on labor market management.[36] In the mid-1990s, U.S. spending on active labor market measures was about half that of any of the other wealthiest two-thirds of OECD nations, except for Japan.[37]

Moreover, those public management programs that do exist in the United States carefully protect employer predominance in labor markets. First, most of the employment and training initiatives have aimed to adapt workers to business needs without interfering in managerial prerogatives.[38] Second, American employment and training programs are primarily part of the U.S. welfare system for poor adults, rather than part of a broader strategy for managing labor markets and increasing worker security. Employment programs under the Economic Opportunity Act of 1964, the Comprehensive Employment and Training Act of 1973 and 1978, and the Job Training Partnership Act of 1982 all aimed primarily at the poverty population and sought to remove this population from the relief system. Welfare reforms enacted in the late 1980s and 1990s echo the federal Work Incentive program of the late 1960s by requiring welfare recipients to register for employment and training services as a condition of remaining eligible for income support.[39]

Work Insurance

American work insurance is less generous and equitable than work insurance in comparable nations. State governments bear most of the responsibility for workers' compensation and unemployment insurance, and state laws, tax rates, and benefits vary enormously, with every state feeling competitive pressure to minimize the burden of its taxes on employers. In 1978, state workers' compensation programs replaced anywhere from 43 to 67 percent of the average disabled workers' income in the United States. In Great Britain the Industrial Injury benefit replaced 107 percent of the income for the average worker.[40]

American unemployment insurance differs from most Western European schemes in ways that strengthen employers' policy influence. First, employers provide all the funds for the program (among the large OECD nations, only Italy also relies on employer funding). Full employer funding maximizes employers' policy influence in the program. Second, most states still use "experience rating" to set employer tax rates. Experience rating sets higher rates for employers with more unstable employment records. Because of experience rating and interstate competition, states tightened eligibility requirements during the fiscal stresses of the 1970s and 1980s, thus making jobless insurance inaccessible to a large number of citizens as unemployment worsened. American unemployment compensation consequently offers workers less protection against income loss. Benefits vary widely, though even the most generous are limited in comparison to similar nations. In many European states in the 1990s, replacement rates varied from 50 to 70 percent of lost income.[41] In the United States, average weekly jobless benefits in 1997 constituted 34 percent of weekly wages. This figure varied from 51 percent of average weekly wages in Hawaii and 45 percent in Arkansas to 24 percent in California and less than 30 percent in Alabama, Alaska, Arizona, Connecticut, the District of Columbia, Georgia, Louisiana, Missouri, New Hampshire, and New York.[42]

American unemployment insurance theoretically covers the entire work-force, but in practice states have increasingly limited coverage by restricting eligibility and the duration of benefits. While 75 percent of unemployed American workers qualified for unemployment insurance in the recession of 1974–75, only 38 percent qualified in the recession of the early 1990s.[43] The percentage of unemployed receiving jobless benefits also dropped in Germany, the United Kingdom, and the Netherlands, but these nations provided alternative sources of support for the jobless that are unavailable in the United States. The United States is the only wealthy OECD nation without a regular income safety net for the jobless who no longer qualify for unemployment insurance. American collective bargaining agreements provide better coverage for employees, but as in the case of protective regulations such agreements cover a small and shrinking fraction of the workforce.[44]

In sum, American labor market policy permits employers to exercise much more latitude in labor markets than do their counterparts abroad. This policy has made it more difficult for workers to organize into unions to counterbalance employer market power. Thus, unions offer benefits and protections to only a fraction of American workers. For the rest, according to Benjamin Aaron, a leading expert on comparative labor law, "unorganised workers have less constitutional and statutory protection against economic risks and unfair treatment than do workers in most industrialized nations of the world.[45]

AMERICAN LABOR MARKET POLICY AS AN INTERNATIONAL MODEL

U.S. leaders actively promoted the notion that the American labor market had become a prolific job creation machine in the 1980s.[46] Over the next decade, many foreign observers embraced this view.[47] Government did not meddle as much in American labor markets, it was said. As a result, American labor markets could adapt much more quickly and efficiently to global competition and rapid technological change. Most European nations, in contrast, had hung onto hopelessly inflexible worker protections. These countries consequently suffered high unemployment. If only European nations were more like the United States, some suggested, they, too, could turn into "job machines." Employers must control hiring, firing, and wages to adjust to changing markets as quickly as possible, according to this view. Government or trade union interference with the going rate of wages or with dismissals causes the economy to perform less efficiently.[48] From this perspective, then, excessive regulation of job security, wages, and excessively generous unemployment benefits have strangled employer prerogatives in European nations. These countries were said to suffer from "Eurosclerosis," a sort of hardening of labor market arteries that makes labor markets too inflexible to allow for dynamic job creation.[49]

In the 1980s, American policymakers urged foreign policymakers to copy the American model. Great Britain's Thatcher government explicitly sought to import such American ideas about governing labor markets. These British officials aimed to "price workers into jobs" by systematically (if incrementally) reducing trade union protections, encouraging wider wage disparities, and fostering wage earners' compliance with employers' decisions.[50] In the early 1990s, the OECD diagnosed the problem of high European unemployment in fundamentally similar, though much gentler, terms. The OECD conceded that U.S. labor markets had a number of problems, but American labor market change was occurring, in the OECD's terms, "against a background of buoyant employment growth." The OECD jobs report of 1994 prescribed fewer public limitations on labor markets.[51] Even Swedish employers attacked their country's egalitarian policies.[52]

Its job creation record encouraged foreign observers to consider emulating American policy. From 1970 to 1990, total employment in the United States increased 40 percent, compared to 10 percent in Germany, 8 percent in France, and 3 percent in the United Kingdom. U.S. Bureau of Labor Statistics figures indicated that private employment (adjusted seasonally) rose from 89.5 million in early 1992 to about 110 million in early 2000.[53] Since 1982, American manufacturing productivity growth has been relatively robust, though productivity in the service sector did not grow as quickly in the United States as it did in Japan, France, and Germany in the 1980s.[54]

If foreign policymakers import U.S. labor market policy, will their labor markets also generate vast numbers of new jobs? Answering this question involves three distinct issues. First, is American labor market policy the cause of the recent U.S. success in job creation? Second, is it possible for other nations to import American labor market policy? Third, would it be desirable for other countries to borrow from the American model even if they are able to do so?

It is extraordinarily difficult to draw firm conclusions about whether any labor market policy has desirable effects. Unique circumstances rather than policy choices seem to account for a large portion of the American jobs that have been created. The sheer growth of the American labor force supported the growth of service sector jobs. Fueled by relatively high birthrates and immigration, the U.S. labor force grew on average 1.4 percent a year from 1984 to 1994, and high U.S. divorce rates strongly encouraged divorced spouses to enter the labor market. Central and western European labor forces grew at less than half that rate during this period.[55] Ostensibly lower American jobless rates, however, also conceal a significant segment of jobless male workers who are in prisons. The population of prisoners grew by 300 percent from 1980 to 1996, to over a million and a half, a population that is a much larger percentage of the workforce than is true in comparable nations. If these individuals were counted in the labor force, U.S. male unemployment rates would be virtually indistinguishable from those in western Europe.[56]

Can other countries replicate the U.S. job creation record by adopting the American model of labor market policy? The small literature on policy borrowing suggests that there are many obstacles to borrowing another nation's public policy successfully.[57] Contemporary American labor market policy has developed under unique economic, ideological, and political circumstances that do not exist in most other societies. The size of the nation, including its vast domestic market and its self-contained natural resources, made it possible to develop self-sufficient production of nearly every type of good by the beginning of this century. Its geographical and economic size encouraged the development of large mass production firms. These large corporations altered the path of the American political economy and, after mid-century, played an important role in providing labor market protections for workers in the primary labor market. American political culture emphasizes self-reliance and minimal government in a way that discourages more extensive worker protections and public labor market management.

Even more important, America's unique political institutions profoundly shaped the way strategies for governing labor markets evolved in the United States. Competitive American federalism continues to motivate state officials to limit jobless benefits, workers' compensation awards, labor regulations, employment services, and trade union laws to ease the burden on employers.[58] Because American labor market policy developed under decentralized conditions, substantial confusion, overlap, and inefficiency characterize American labor market governance. Further confusion results from the multitude of private community-based training organizations, fee-charging private employment offices, state and local welfare agencies, and for profit employment and training firms that are involved in American labor markets. The separation of powers has compounded the difficulties of making effective American labor market policy. American legislatures, executives, and judges sometimes have acted as rivals who undermine the policy initiatives of other institutions. The complex implementation structure of American labor market policy makes it costly and difficult to put initiatives into effect and hard to evaluate results. Litigation and contentiousness often flare up because these procedural safeguards introduce so much institutional rivalry into the implementation of public policy.

Even if policymakers abroad felt confident that they could borrow American labor market policy successfully, they may have good reason to hesitate to do so. It is far from clear that American labor market policy is successful even in terms of the economic criterion of efficiency. Even if the U.S. model were proven unarguably successful at promoting economic efficiency, however, it seems to be accompanied by social insecurity and inequality.

Research has revealed little conclusive evidence that employment protection laws, generous jobless benefits, or increased minimum wages actually increase unemployment as they are alleged to do.[59] It may be that the expansionary fiscal policy of the United States had more impact on American job creation in the 1980s than its labor market policy. In the 1980s, when U.S. unemployment rates began to deviate downward from those in Europe, the federal government's tax cuts and military procurement constituted a rate of fiscal expansion unmatched by other OECD nations.[60]

The nominal job creation success of American labor market policy masks some potentially serious economic shortcomings. Skill training often has positive externalities for society (for example, higher overall productivity) that does not have a direct payoff for the individual employer who provides the training. American and British employers tend to seek low-skilled workers. This approach permits individual employers to make short-term economic gains, though at a substantial cost to long-term national economic productivity. Without additional public support for employment and training, then, private employers may undersupply skills training and, in turn, contribute to the underperformance of the economy as a whole.[61] Poor information about job vacancies, job applicants, and training opportunities burdens the economy with higher than necessary transaction costs. Overlapping programs, the lack of relocation assistance, and the absence of centralized employment policy coordination may increase the cost and duration of unemployment. The result is a less efficient economy and unnecessarily prolonged involuntary joblessness. Such inefficiencies as "substitution" (in which an employer receiving a job subsidy hires someone the firm would have hired without the subsidy, in effect substituting public funds for those of the firm) or "creaming" (the practice of selecting the least disadvantaged, most employable people for public employment and training services) may be more pervasive under American circumstances, where employer autonomy is more pronounced.

American labor market policy, then, may not be especially efficient, when these broader and longer-term issues of economic efficiency are taken into account. Its consequences for other social values, such as security and fairness, raise more fundamental questions.

The perception of job insecurity has increased in nearly all industrialized nations since the 1980s. Despite the vaunted job creation record of the United States, American, British, French, and Japanese workers felt more insecure about employment than workers in other OECD nations (where surveys were available). In 1997, Federal Reserve Board chairman Alan Greenspan argued that the labor market insecurity of workers had tempered their wage demands and made it possible for the United States to experience economic growth with low inflation.[62] American workers' sense of insecurity follows from the real problem of obtaining income when one is jobless and the reality that a laid-off worker's new job tends to pay less than her or his previous job. The U.S. Council of Economic Advisors (1996) reported that, for several years after a job loss, an average displaced worker's earnings remain roughly 10 percent below what they could have otherwise expected to earn. Clearly a lower jobless rate helps alleviate workers' concerns about income security. The OECD found, however, that a more extensive safety net—particularly in the form of broader and more centralized collective bargaining and more generous unemployment insurance—promotes an increased sense of economic security among workers.[63]

Increased inequality in the American workforce suggests that the American job machine may be better understood as a job sharing machine for low-wage workers. A much larger fraction of full-time American workers than European workers earn less than half or two-thirds of the median wage. This data is consistent with the view that wages for low-paid workers have remained low as the number of low-paid jobs expanded, creating in effect a work-sharing scheme among full-time workers at the low end of the American labor market.[64] Average hourly earnings (in constant 1982 dollars) in the U.S. private sector dropped from $8.60 in early 1973 to $8.00 in late 1979 and $7.50 in 1990 and remained at that level until late 1997. In 1999, average hourly earnings were at $7.85.[65]

American workers receive widely unequal remuneration. A. B. Atkinson recently used data from the Luxembourg Income Study (LIS) to study trends in inequality in the United States and fourteen west European nations (including the relatively poorer nations of Ireland, Spain, Portugal, and Italy). The LIS is a comprehensive effort to develop comparable cross-national data on, among other things, disposable income. This measure includes cash transfer programs within nations (but does not take into account indirect taxes or public spending on health care, education, and other services). Atkinson found that American disposable income clearly became more unequal in the 1970s, and has continued to grow more unequal over time. The bottom 10 percent of income earners is much worse off in the United States than in any of the European nations, and this earnings disparity caused the United States to have a much more unequal distribution of income by several different measures. The average income of the least well compensated fifth of Americans (that is, the bottom 20 percent) was substantially lower than the average income of earners in any of the European nations. Even if Europe were considered a single labor market, the distribution of compensation would be more unequal within the United States than in a common European labor market of 325 million people.[66]

At the beginning of the twenty-first century, the American model of governing labor markets has reanimated the classic debate between employer prerogatives and worker protection. The American model is more powerful as a symbol than a policy template, for it evolved under circumstances unique to its economy, political institutions, and culture. American labor market policy, then, cannot easily be borrowed. Moreover, its consequences are far more complex and ambiguous than the label "American job machine" implies. The American model's appeal is better understood as an ideological tool that offers powerful lessons—not to mention political and rhetorical weapons—to those who currently are trying to understand how economic efficiency, security, and fairness can and should be balanced in the capitalist order of the twenty-first century.

NOTES

1. Colin Gordon, *New Deals: Business, Labor, and Politics in America, 1920–1935* (New York: Cambridge University Press, 1994), 124, 171; Robert F. Himmelberg, *The Origins of the National Recovery Administration: Business, Government, and the Trade Association Issue, 1921-1933* (New York: Fordham University Press, 1976), 183–89; 204–5.

2. J. Joseph Huthmacher, *Senator Robert F. Wagner and the Rise of Urban Liberalism* (New York: Atheneum, 1971), 137–51; Irving Bernstein, *The New Deal Collective Bargaining Policy* (Berkeley: University of California Press, 1950), 32–38; Melvyn Dubofsky, *The State and Labor in Modern America* (Chapel Hill: University of North Carolina Press, 1994), 111–12.

3. Leo Troy and Neil Sheflin, *U.S. Union Sourcebook: Membership, Finances, Structure, Directory* (West Orange, N.J.: Industrial Relations Data and Information Services, 1985), table 3.63.

4. Sanford Cohen, *State Labor Legislation, 1937–1947* (Columbus: Bureau of Business Research, Ohio State University, 1948); Benjamin J. Taylor and Fred Whitney, *Labor Relations Law*, 5th ed. (Englewood Cliffs, N.J.: Prentice-Hall, 1987) 203, 213–20, 383–85; Leo Troy, "The Rise and Fall of American Trade Unions: The Labor Movement from FDR to RR," in *Unions in Transition: Entering the Second Century*, ed. Seymour Martin Lipset (San Francisco: Institute for Contemporary Studies, 1986), 75–109; Janice A. Klein and E. David Wanger, "The Legal Setting for the Emergence of the Union Avoidance Strategy," in *Challenges and Choices Facing American Labor*, ed. Thomas A. Kochan, (Cambridge, Mass.: MIT Press, 1985), 75–88; James A. Gross, *Broken Promise: The Subversion of U.S. Labor Relations Policy, 1947–1994* (Philadelphia: Temple University Press, 1995).

5. Janice R. Bellace, "The State and Industrial Relations: A Strategic Choice Model," *Comparative Labor Law Journal* 14 (1993): 249–70; James A. Gross, *The Making of the National Labor Relations Board* (Albany: State University of New York Press, 1974),

130–48; Joel Rogers, "Divide and Conquer: Further 'Reflections on the Distinctive Character of American Labor Laws,'" *Wisconsin Law Review* (1990): 117–23.

6. Vivien Hart, *Bound by Our Constitution: Women, Workers, and the Minimum Wage* (Princeton: Princeton University Press, 1994), 153–69; Suzanne Mettler, *Dividing Citizens: Gender and Federalism in New Deal Public Policy* (Ithaca, N.Y.: Cornell University Press, 1998); U.S. Senate, Committee on Education and Labor, *Fair Labor Standards Act*, Senate Report 75-884, July 6, 1937 (Washington, D.C.: Government Printing Office, 1937); Richard Franklin Bensel, *Sectionalism and American Political Development, 1880–1980* (Madison: University of Wisconsin Press, 1984), 160–63; James T. Patterson, *Congressional Conservatism and the New Deal: The Growth of the Conservative Coalition in Congress, 1933–1939* (Lexington: University of Kentucky Press, 1967), 149–54, 182–83, 193–98.

7. Jonathan R. Kesselman, "Work Relief Programs in the Great Depression," in *Creating Jobs*, ed. John L. Palmer (Washington, D.C.: Brookings, 1978), 158.

8. Desmond King, *Actively Seeking Work? The Politics of Unemployment and Welfare Policy in the United States and Great Britain* (Chicago: University of Chicago Press, 1995); Oscar Weigert, *Administrative Problems of Employment Services in Eight States* (Chicago: Public Administration Service, 1940).

9. Weigert, *Administrative Problems of Employment Services in Eight States*; David Brian Robertson, "Planned Incapacity to Succeed? Policymaking Structure and Policy Failure," *Policy Studies Review* 8 (Winter 1989): 241–63; King, *Actively Seeking Work?*; James T. Patterson, *The New Deal and the States: Federalism in Transition* (Princeton: Princeton University Press, 1969); Edward J. Harpham, "Federalism, Keynesianism, and the Transformation of the Unemployment Insurance System in the United States," in *Nationalizing Social Security in Europe and America*, ed. Douglas E. Ashford and E. W. Kelley (Greenwich, Conn.: JAI Press, 1986), 155–80; David G. Williams, *Cooperative Federalism in Employment Security: The Interstate Conference* (Ann Arbor, Mich.: Institute of Labor and Industrial Relations, 1974).

10. Thomas Janoski, *The Political Economy of Unemployment: Active Labor Market Policy in West Germany and the United States* (Berkeley: University of California Press, 1990).

11. Margaret Weir, *Politics and Jobs: The Boundaries of Employment Policy in the United States* (Princeton: Princeton University Press, 1992), 27–61.

12. Howell John Harris, *The Right to Manage: Industrial Relations Policies of American Business in the 1940s* (Madison: University of Wisconsin Press, 1982), 139–44.

13. Joel Rogers, "Divide and Conquer," *Wisconsin Law Review* (1990): 103–6.

14. OECD, *Labour Market Policies for the 1990s* (Paris: OECD, 1991), 52–53.

15. Joseph B. Rose and Gary N. Chaison, "The State of the Unions in the United States and Canada," *Journal of Labor Research* 6 (Winter 1985): 97–112; Richard Freeman, "Lessons for the United States," in *Working under Different Rules*, ed. Richard B. Freeman (New York: Russell Sage Foundation, 1994), 223–39.

16. David G. Blanchflower and Richard B. Freeman, "Unionism in the United States and Other Advanced OECD Countries," *Industrial Relations* 31 (1992): 56–79; Franz Traxler, "Collective Bargaining and Industrial Change: A Case of Disorganization? A Comparative Analysis of Eighteen OECD Countries," *European Sociological Review* 12

(1996): 271–87; Hans Slomp, *Labor Relations in Europe: A History of Issues and Developments* (Westport, Conn.: Greenwood, 1990).

17. Noah M. Meltz, "Labor Movements in Canada and the United States," in *Challenges and Choices Facing American Labor*, 315–44; Robert W. Crandall, *Manufacturing on the Move* (Washington, D.C.: Brookings, 1993).

18. Cynthia L. Estlund, "Economic Rationality and Union Avoidance: Misunderstanding the National Labor Relations Act," *Texas Law Review* 71 (1993): 921–92; Thomas A. Kochan, Harry C. Katz, and Robert B. McKersie, *The Transformation of American Industrial Relations* (Ithaca: ILR Press, 1994).

19. Gross, *The Making of the National Labor Relations Board*; Clyde Summers, "Patterns of Dispute Resolution: Lessons from Four Countries," *Comparative Labor Law Journal* 12 (1991): 165–77.

20. Taylor and Whitney, *Labor Relations Law*, 603–6; Gian Primo Cella and Tiziano Treu, "National Trade Union Movements," *Comparative Labour Law and Industrial Relations*, 6th ed., ed. Roger Blanpain, (Deventer, Netherlands: Kluwer, 1998), 305–40.

21. Traxler, "Collective Bargaining and Industrial Change: A Case of Disorganization?"

22. Bo Rothstein, "Labor-Market Institutions and Working-Class Strength," in *Structuring Politics: Historical Institutionalism in Comparative Analysis*, ed. Sven Steinmo, Kathleen Thelen, and Frank Longstreth (New York: Cambridge University Press, 1992), 33–57; Bo Rothstein, *The Social Democratic State: The Swedish Model and the Bureaucratic Problem of Social Reforms* (Pittsburgh: University of Pittsburgh Press, 1996).

23. Benjamin Aaron, ed., *Labour Courts and Grievance Settlement in Western Europe* (Berkeley: University of California, 1971); U.S. Department of Labor, *Foreign Labor Trends: Germany* (Washington, D.C.: GPO, 1992); M. Donald Hancock, John Logue, and Bernt Schiller, eds. *Managing Modern Capitalism: Industrial Renewal and Workplace Democracy in the United States and Western Europe* (Westport, Conn.: Greenwood, 1991).

24. Derek C. Bok, "Reflections on the Distinctive Character of American Labor Laws," *Harvard Law Review* 84 (1971): 1394–463; Alan B. Krueger, "The Evolution of Unjust-Dismissal Legislation in the United States," *Industrial and Labor Relations Review* 44 (1991): 644–60; OECD, *The OECD Jobs Study: Evidence and Explanations*, 2 vols. (Paris: OECD, 1994), 2: 74.

25. U.S. Department of Labor, Secretary of Labor's Task Force on Economic Adjustment and Worker Dislocation, *Economic Adjustment and Worker Dislocation in a Competitive Society* (Washington, D.C.: GPO, 1986), 32; U.S. Bureau of Labor Statistics, data on National Employment, Hours, and Earnings, Total Private Average Hourly Earnings, 1982 dollars, 1964–1997, Series EES005000049, <http://stats.bls.gov:80/cgi-bin/survey-most> (accessed September 8, 1997); Katherine G. Abraham and Susan N. Houseman, *Job Security in America: Lessons from Germany* (Washington, D.C.: Brookings, 1993). France subsequently repealed its notification law.

26. OECD, *Employment Outlook, 1997* (Paris: OECD, 1997), 11–14.

27. Paul Weiler, "The Wages of Sex: The Uses and Limits of Comparable Worth," *Harvard Law Review* 99 (1986): 1728–807.

28. Lawrence Mishel, Jared Bernstein, and John Schmitt, *The State of Working America, 1996–1997* (Armonk, N.Y.: Sharpe, 1997), 413.

29. OECD, *OECD Observer*, 166 (October / November, 1990): Center Insert, 8.

30. Harish C. Jain, *Disadvantaged Groups in the Labour Market and Measures to Assist Them* (Paris: OECD, 1979); Ronnie Steinberg Rattner, "The Policy and the Problem: Overview of Seven Countries," in *Equal Employment Policy for Women: Strategies for Implementation in the United States, Canada, and Western Europe*, ed. Ronnie Steinberg Ratter (Philadelphia: Temple University Press, 1980), 28–40; Steven Kelman, *Regulating America, Regulating Sweden: A Comparative Study of Occupational Safety and Health Policy* (Cambridge, Mass.: MIT Press, 1981); Charles Noble, *Liberalism at Work: The Rise and Fall of OSHA* (Philadelphia: Temple University Press, 1986).

31. Kenneth J. Maier, *Regulation: Politics, Bureaucracy, and Economics* (New York: St. Martin's, 1985), 219–21; U.S. General Accounting Office, *"Sweatshops" in the United States: Opinions on Their Extent and Possible Enforcement Options*, GAO/HRD-88-130BR (Washington, D.C.: GPO, 1988).

32. OECD, *Labour Market Policies for the 1990s* (Paris: OECD, 1991), 41; U.S. General Accounting Office, *Transition from School to Work: Linking Education and Worksite Training*, Report GAO/HRD-91-1-5 (Washington, D.C.: Government Accounting Office, 1991), 10–11; Freeman, "Lessons for the United States."

33. OECD, *Labour Market Policies for the 1990s* (Paris: OECD, 1991), 26; OECD, *Employment Outlook, 1997* (Paris: OECD, 1997), 183–90; see Janoski, *The Political Economy of Unemployment* and King, *Actively Seeking Work?*

34. Harold L. Wilensky and Lowell Turner, *Democratic Corporatism and Policy Linkages: The Interdependence of Industrial, Labor-Market, Incomes, and Social Policies in Eight Countries* (Berkeley: Institute of International Studies, University of California, 1987), 25–28, 55–58; Bo Rothstein, "The Success of the Swedish Labour Market Policy: The Organizational Connection to Policy," *European Journal of Political Research* 13 (1985): 153–65.

35. U.S. General Accounting Office, *Multiple Employment and Training Programs: Information Crosswalk on 163 Employment Training Programs*, Report GAO/HEHs-95-85FS, (Washington, D.C.: GAO, 1995).

36. OECD, *Labour Market Policies for the 1990s*, 52–53; Wilensky and Turner, *Democratic Corporatism and Policy Linkages*, 55–64; Günther Schmid, Bernd Reissert, and Gert Bruche, *Unemployment Insurance and Active Labor Market Policy: An International Comparison of Financing Systems* (Detroit: Wayne State University Press, 1992).

37. OECD, *Employment Outlook, June 1999*, (Paris: OECD, 1999): 248–52.

38. David Brian Robertson and Jerold L. Waltman, "The Politics of Policy Borrowing," in *Something Borrowed, Something Learned? The Transatlantic Market in Education and Training Oxford Studies in Comparative Education*, ed. David Finegold, Laurel McFarland, and William Richardson (Washington, D.C.: Brookings, 1993), 21–44.

39. Wilensky and Turner, *Democratic Corporatism and Policy Linkages*, 56, 61; David Brian Robertson, "Labor Market Surgery, Labor Market Abandonment: The Thatcher and Reagan Unemployment Remedies," in *Political Economy: Public Policies in the United*

States and Britain, ed. Jerold L. Waltman and Donley T. Studlar (Jackson: University Press of Mississippi, 1987), 69–97.

40. Robert H. Haveman, Victor Halberstadt, and Richard V. Burkhauser, *Public Policies toward Disabled Workers: Cross-National Analyses of Economic Impacts* (Ithaca, N.Y.: Cornell University Press, 1984), 128–33.

41. Schmid, Reissert, and Bruche, *Unemployment Insurance and Active Labor Market Policy*; Bernd Reissert and Günther Schmid, "Unemployment Compensation and Active Labor Market Policy," in *Labor Market Institutions in Europe*, ed. Günther Schmid (Armonk, N.Y.: Sharpe, 1994), 83–119.

42. U.S. Department of Health and Human Services, *Social Security Bulletin, Annual Statistical Supplement, 1999* (Washington, D.C.: GPO, 1999), 336.

43. U.S. Department of Labor, Secretary of Labor's Task Force on Economic Adjustment and Worker Dislocation, *Economic Adjustment and Worker Dislocation in a Competitive Society* (Washington, D.C.: GPO, 1986), 4, 30; Economic Policy Institute, *Unprepared for Recession: The Erosion of State Unemployment Insurance Coverage Fostered by Public Policy in the 1980s* (Washington, D.C.: Economic Policy Institute, 1992).

44. Martin Rein, "Is America Exceptional? The Role of Occupational Welfare in the United States and the European Community," in *The Privatization of Social Policy? Occupational Welfare and the Welfare State in America, Scandinavia, and Japan*, ed. Michael Shalev (Armonk, N.Y.: Sharpe, 1996).

45. Benjamin Aaron, "Settlement of Disputes over Rights," in *Comparative Labour Law and Industrial Relations*, 4th ed., 2 vols., ed. Roger Blanpain (Deventer, Netherlands: Kluwer, 1990), 1: 256.

46. Richard B. McKenzie, *The American Job Machine* (New York: Universe Books, 1988); Melvin M. Brodsky, "Labor Market Flexibility: A Changing International Perspective," *Monthly Labor Review* 117 (1994): 53–60.

47. "Europe Hits a Brick Wall," *Economist*, April 5, 1997, 21–23; Arne Heise, "A Different Transatlantic View: The American Job Machine," *Challenge* 40 (1997): 50–56.

48. Government intervention in markets may promote economic efficiency if it can supply goods and service that markets underproduce, such as education and training (assuming that government is efficient in producing greater benefit than cost).

49. Edward Balls, "Europe's Jobs Crisis: A Labour Market 'Gripped' by Euro-sclerosis,'" *Financial Times*, June 21, 1993, 3; "Is the Model Broken?" *Economist*, May 4, 1996, 17. Conservatives warn that recent legislation and court decisions gradually have imposed the kinds of restrictions on employer prerogatives that portend creeping "Eurosclerosis" even in the United States; see David R. Henderson, "The Europeanization of the U.S. Labor Market," *Public Interest* 113 (1993): 66–81.

50. U.K. Department of Employment, *Employment: Challenge to the Nation*, Cmnd. 9474 (London: Her Majesty's Stationary Office, 1985), 1, 13, 19–20; Robertson, "Labor Market Surgery, Labor Market Abandonment."

51. OECD, *The OECD Jobs Study: Facts, Analysis, Strategies* (Paris: OECD, 1994); OECD, *The OECD Jobs Study: Evidence and Explanations* (Paris: OECD, 1994), 1: 55, 69; OECD, *The OECD Jobs Study: Implementing the Strategy* (Paris: OECD, 1995).

52. Jonas Pontusson and Peter Swenson, "Labor Markets, Production Strategies, and Wage Bargaining Institutions: The Swedish Employer Offensive in Comparative Perspective," *Comparative Political Studies* 29 (1996): 223–50; Balls, "Europe's Jobs Crisis."

53. Derek C. Bok, *The State of the Nation: Government and the Quest for a Better Society*, (Cambridge: Harvard University Press, 1996), 29; U.S. Bureau of Labor Statistics data on National Employment, Hours, and Earnings, Total Private Employment, seasonally adjusted, 1939–1997, Series EEU005000001, *<http://stats.bls.gov:80/cgi-bin/surveymost>* (accessed February 11, 2000).

54. Bok, *The State of the Nation*, 26–28; Robert Z. Lawrence, *Single World, Divided Nations? International Trade and OECD Labor Markets* (Washington, D.C.: Brookings, 1996), 31–34, 68–70.

55. Harold L. Wilensky, "The Great American Job Creation Machine in Comparative Perspective," *Industrial Relations* 31 (1992): 473–88; Brodsky, "Labor Market Flexibility: A Changing International Perspective"; OECD, *The OECD Jobs Study: Evidence and Explanations*, 1: 5; OECD, *Employment Outlook*, June 1999, 3.

56. Bruce Western and Katherine Beckett, "How Unregulated Is the U.S. Labor Market? The Penal System as a Labor Institution," *American Journal of Sociology* 104 (1999): 1030–60.

57. Richard Rose, *Lesson-Drawing in Public Policy: A Guide to Learning across Time and Space* (Chatham, N.J.: Chatham House, 1993); Robertson and Waltman, "The Politics of Policy Borrowing," 21–44.

58. See, for example, Albert R. Karr, "States Lure Industry by Touting Low Unemployment Insurance Taxes," *Wall Street Journal*, February 11, 1997: A1.

59. Brodsky, " Labor Market Flexibility: A Changing International Perspective"; OECD, *The OECD Jobs Study: Evidence and Explanations*, 1: 172; OECD, *Employment Outlook, June 1999*, 49–132; David Card and Alan B. Kruger, *Myth and Measurement: The New Economics of the Minimum Wage* (Princeton: Princeton University Press, 1995).

60. International Labour Organization, *World Labour Report, 1995* (Geneva: ILO, 1995), 142–43.

61. David Finegold, "The Changing International Economy and Its Impact on Education and Training," in *Something Borrowed, Something Learned?* 47–73.

62. Louis Uchitelle, "Job Insecurity of Workers Is a Big Factor in Fed Policy," *New York Times*, February 27, 1997: C6.

63. OECD, *Employment Outlook 1997*, 129–50.

64. OECD, *The OECD Jobs Study: Evidence and Explanations*, 1: 22.

65. Richard B. Freeman and Lawrence F. Katz, "Rising Wage Inequality: The United States versus Other Advanced Countries," in *Working under Different Rules*, ed. Richard B. Freeman (New York: Russell Sage Foundation, 1994), 29–62; Lawrence, *Single World, Divided Nations?* 18–24; U.S. Bureau of Labor Statistics, data on National Employment, Hours, and Earnings, Total Private Employment, not seasonally adjusted, 1964–1999,

Series EEU00500049, <*http://146.142.4.24/cgi-bin/dsrv*> (accessed February 11, 2000). Lawrence uses compensation rather than earning to measure changes in American workers' position over time because compensation includes health, retirement, and other benefits provided workers as a compensation package. Lawrence finds that, in contrast to earnings, American workers' compensation grew from 1979 to 1994 and grew about as much as output.

66. A. B. Atkinson, "Income Distribution in Europe and the United States," Luxembourg Income Study Working Paper number 133 (Walferdange, Luxembourg: Centre d'Etudes de Populations, de Pauvreté et des Politiques Socio-Economique/International Networks for Studies in Technology Environment, Alternatives, Development, 1995). See also Freeman, *Working under Different Rules.*

INDEX

281

Drexel Manufacturing Company, 159
Du Brul, E. F., 108
Duncan, James, 67–68, 167
Duplex Printing Press Company v. Deering,
  (1921), 195
Du Pont, 196

Easley, Ralph, 99, 109
Eastman Kodak Company, 219, 244
economic depressions: *1893,* 23; *1920–22,*
  133, 219; Great (*1929–36*), 171, 196,
  221–23, 246–47, 257–58, 260; report on,
  U.S. Bureau of Labor, 79
Economic Opportunity Act (1964), 267
economic stagnation, 1970s, xviii
education, compulsory, 39
eight-hour leagues, state and local, 42, 78
eight-hour workday, 5, 41–42, 46. *See also*
  hours of labor, regulation of; individual
  states
elections, United States: *1886,* 41; *1904,* 143;
  1906, 70, 143; *1908,* 70, 143–44, 190;
  1910, 144, 162, 191; *1911,* 24; *1912,* 24,
  144, 163, 216, 236; *1914,* 192, 236; *1916,*
  158, 163, 236; *1924,* 145; *1928,* 221; *1930,*
  198, 221–22; electoral rules, 25, 69–70
Elkins, Stephen B., 132
Ellis, George H., 107
Emergency Relief and Construction Act
  (1932), 7, 222
Emery, James, 111, 114, 157, 160
employee representation, 194, 196–98,
  199–200, 218–19, 260
employers, 68, 95, 98, 107n48, 114–15, 144,
  146, 200, 258–59; American, compared
  with European employers, 98, 115, 190;
  blacklists, 186; cooperation among, 23–24,
  95–102, 114–15, 122n68, 135, 172, 187,
  189–90, 245, 260; cooperation with
  unions, 51, 95–100, 131, 133, 135, 187,
  194–95, 197–98, 258; dismissal rights, 11,
  265; evasion of unions, 11, 200, 257, 264;
  hours of labor, 43, 52, 160, 166–68; and
  immigration, 83; intensity of opposition to
  labor, 2, 24, 95, 100, 108–9, 115, 200;
  interstate competition, use of against labor
  market policy, 52, 154–55, 157, 169; and
  labor scarcity, 68, 100, 105; litigation, 48,
  54, 110–12, 195, 201; lobbying, 110, 161,
  165, 188, 218, 240, 246; open shop drive,
  xvii–xviii, 23–24, 95–96, 104–13,131, 145,
  161, 183, 209–10, 212, 258–59; policy

strategy, xv, xvii, 15–16, 23, 34n71, 53,
  111–12, 115, 172, 183, 186, 207, 212;
  prerogatives in the labor market and
  managerial control, xv, xvii–xviii, 4, 8,
  10–13, 15–16, 18, 26, 43, 68, 75, 80, 85, 95,
  107, 125, 134, 138, 143, 154, 172, 190, 231,
  242, 248–49, 257–58, 260, 265–66;
  property rights, 20, 49, 184, 191–93, 198,
  236; shadow labor market policy, 13, 196,
  210, 218–20, 224n9, 231, 240–42; support
  for federal labor law, 51, 172, 214; tactics,
  labor market, 83, 98, 104, 108, 128, 134;
  trade schools, 108; vocational education,
  212; workers' compensation, 233–36. *See
  also* corporations; individual firms and
  leaders; manufacturers, small and medium
  sized; National Association of Manufacturers; state and city employer groups;
  trade associations; United States Chamber
  of Commerce
employers' associations, state, 111
employers' liability, 7, 12, 41, 232–35, 240
employers' reserve funds for unemployment,
  244, 246–47
Employment Act (1946), 224
employment agencies, private, 5, 40, 80–81,
  108
"employment at will," 265. *See also* employers,
  prerogatives in the labor market
employment offices, public, 6, 8, *9,* 12, *13,* 39,
  41, 66, 79–81, 146, 207–12, 217, 219, 262.
  See also United States Employment Service
enforcement of labor laws, 8, 11–12, 43, 45,
  47–48, 50, 53–54, 83–84, 132, 160–61,
  165, 178n60, 220, 237, 266. *See also* policy
  implementation
Engels, Friedrich, 38
equal employment opportunity, 265–66
Erdman Act (1898), *6,* 75–76, 137, 190
"Eurosclerosis," 269
executives, political, 16, 20, 22, 25, 48, 53–54,
  70
experience rating in work insurance, 12, 234,
  238, 245–48, 267

factory inspection, 3 *5,* 8, *9, 10,* 18, 39–41,
  46–48, 55, 79, 241; comparison of U.S. and
  Europe, 48
Fair Labor Standards Act (FLSA, 1938),
  172–73, 260–62, 265–66
Fairchild, Fred Rogers, 80
Fall River, Massachusetts, 46

ABOUT THE AUTHOR

David Brian Robertson, associate professor and chair of the Department of Political Science at the University of Missouri at St. Louis, is the author of *The Development of American Public Policy: The Structure of Policy Restraint* (with Dennis R. Judd) and many articles. His is the editor of *Loss of Confidence: Politics and Policy in the 1979's.* He is the associate editor of the *Journal of Policy History* and edits *Clio*, the newsletter of the Politics and History section of the American Political Science Association.